UNITED NATIONS CONFERENCE ON TRADE AND DEVELOPMENT
——— GENEVA ———

TRADE AND DEVELOPMENT
REPORT, 2006

Report by the secretariat of the
United Nations Conference on Trade and Development

UNITED NATIONS
New York and Geneva, 2006

Note

PER
UN1
TD
T62

- Symbols of United Nations documents are composed of capital letters combined with figures. Mention of such a symbol indicates a reference to a United Nations document.

- The designations employed and the presentation of the material in this publication do not imply the expression of any opinion whatsoever on the part of the Secretariat of the United Nations concerning the legal status of any country, territory, city or area, or of its authorities, or concerning the delimitation of its frontiers or boundaries.

- Material in this publication may be freely quoted or reprinted, but acknowledgement is requested, together with a reference to the document number. A copy of the publication containing the quotation or reprint should be sent to the UNCTAD secretariat.

UNCTAD/TDR/2006

UNITED NATIONS PUBLICATION
Sales No. E.06.II.D.6
ISBN 92-1-112698-3
ISSN 0255-4607

FOREWORD

According to this year's *Trade and Development Report*, if the current momentum in the world economy is sustained, we can expect decisive progress towards the Millennium Development Goals. Moreover, the *Report* shows that there has been growing demand around the world for developing-country exports – including those that are of crucial importance for their economic fortunes.

These positive trends add to a number of other factors that are supportive of development and poverty reduction. For example, the developed countries have taken some initial steps to honour the commitments made in the Monterrey Consensus adopted at the International Conference on Financing for Development in 2002. Considerable progress has been achieved in alleviating the debt burden of the poorest countries. Aid flows are on the rise.

These gains, and donor commitments for future support, represent major improvements in the external environment. Granting improved market access for their exports would further improve those conditions, and is absolutely essential. That is why the recent suspension of the Doha negotiations was so dismaying. Some participants have even contemplated settling for something less than a true development round, or for no round at all. That must not be allowed to happen. But if the negotiations are to succeed in generating the opportunities that are so sorely needed, negotiators must show greater determination and political courage than they have to date.

At the same time, let us also remember that the global partnership for development is based on the conviction that responsibility for development lies primarily with the developing countries themselves. It is therefore essential for them to find ways to translate improvements in the external environment into sustained growth and development at home.

This is not an easy task, to say the least. This *Report* offers new ideas for designing macroeconomic, sectoral and trade policies that can help developing countries to succeed in today's global economic environment. Particular attention is given to policies that support local ownership, the creative forces of markets and the entrepreneurial dimension of investment.

Finally, the *Report* argues that a global partnership for development will be incomplete without an effective system of global economic governance – one that takes into account the specific needs of developing countries, and ensures the right balance between sovereignty in national economic policy-making on the one hand, and multilateral disciplines and collective governance on the other.

This year's *Trade and Development Report* aims to contribute to the debate on how best to make the global partnership for development bring real opportunity and positive change into the lives of people everywhere. I recommend its analysis and suggestions to all stakeholders and to a wide global audience.

Kofi A. Annan
Secretary-General of the United Nations

Contents

Page

FOREWORD .... *iii*

Explanatory notes .... *xiii*

Abbreviations .... *xiv*

OVERVIEW .... *I-XXI*

Chapter I

GLOBAL IMBALANCES AS A SYSTEMIC PROBLEM *1*

A. Global growth *1*

B. Turbulences in financial markets *3*

C. The systemic character of the global imbalances *5*
   1. Alternative views on external imbalances *5*
   2. The main players *7*
   3. Benign or malign unwinding of global imbalances? *10*

D. Low real interest rates: global savings glut versus global monetary conditions *12*
   1. A savings glut? *12*
   2. Monetary policy and interest rates *13*

Notes *16*

References *16*

Annexes to chapter I

Annex 1 **Commodity Prices and Terms of Trade** *17*

Annex 2 **The Theoretical Background to the Saving/Investment Debate** *31*

Chapter II

**EVOLVING DEVELOPMENT STRATEGIES –
BEYOND THE MONTERREY CONSENSUS** *41*

A. **Introduction** *41*

B. **The emergence of the "Washington Consensus"** *42*

C. **The outcome of orthodox reforms** *45*

D. **Second-generation reforms and debt reduction** *50*

    1. A new focus on poverty and institutions *50*

    2. Debt relief and the proliferation of conditionality *53*

E. **The MDGs and the Monterrey Consensus** *55*

F. **Beyond the Monterrey Consensus** *58*

G. **Towards a fundamental policy reorientation** *60*

Notes *67*

References *69*

Chapter III

**CHANGES AND TRENDS IN THE EXTERNAL ENVIRONMENT
FOR DEVELOPMENT** *73*

A. **Introduction** *73*

B. **Export opportunities for developing countries** *75*

    1. Market access conditions *75*

    2. Non-tariff measures (NTMs) *80*

    3. Import demand growth in developing countries' trading partners *82*

C. **Debt relief and official development assistance** *89*

    1. The framework for official debt relief *89*

    2. Extent and impact of the HIPC Initiative *92*

    3. Additionality of debt relief and ODA *96*

    4. Debt problems of middle-income countries *98*

D. Migrants' remittances *100*

    1. Recent trends in migrants' remittances *100*

    2. The economic impact of migrants' remittances *102*

    3. National and international policies to enhance remittances' impact *104*

E. A strengthened role for FDI? *105*

    1. FDI in developing countries: trends and patterns *105*

    2. The role of international production systems and networks *110*

    3. The potential impact of FDI on development *111*

F. Conclusions *114*

Notes *116*

References *119*

Annex tables to chapter III *123*

Chapter IV

MACROECONOMIC POLICY UNDER GLOBALIZATION *127*

A. Introduction *127*

B. Coping with the macroeconomic implications of liberalization and globalization *128*

    1. Financial integration and capital inflows *128*

    2. Domestic financial liberalization *129*

    3. Changes in the fiscal structure *131*

    4. Exchange-rate and monetary policy *131*

C. Macroeconomic policies in support of a dynamic investment and growth process *134*

    1. Monetary policy and interest rates *134*

    2. The exchange rate *136*

    3. Confidence game or counter-cyclical policies? *138*

    4. Capital controls *140*

D. Towards a new assignment of policies *142*

Notes *146*

References *147*

Chapter V

NATIONAL POLICIES IN SUPPORT OF PRODUCTIVE DYNAMISM *149*

A. Introduction *149*

B. Stimulating the dynamic forces of markets *152*

    1. Maintaining productive dynamism *152*

    2. Principles and types of policies for stimulating the dynamic forces of markets *162*

C. Restrictions imposed by international agreements on policy autonomy: an inventory *166*

    1. The Agreement on Trade-related Investment Measures (TRIMs) *168*

    2. The Agreement on Subsidies and Countervailing Measures (SCM) *169*

    3. The Agreement on Trade-related Aspects of Intellectual Property Rights (TRIPS) *171*

    4. Industrial tariffs *174*

D. Industrial dynamism and national policies: recent experiences *180*

    1. Industrial dynamism: recent empirical evidence *180*

    2. National policies for industrial development: some recent experience *182*

E. Conclusions: options for policy innovation *193*

Notes *196*

References *201*

Chapter VI

INSTITUTIONAL AND GOVERNANCE ARRANGEMENTS SUPPORTIVE OF ECONOMIC DEVELOPMENT *205*

A. Introduction *205*

B. National institutional and governance structures in support of sustained economic growth *207*

    1. Institutions and governance *207*

    2. Institutions and market efficiency *209*

    3. Institutions and structural transformation *213*

    4. Conclusions *216*

C. Multilateral institutions and global economic governance *217*

    1. Introduction *217*

    2. International monetary and financial rules and disciplines *220*

    3. Rules and commitments in the multilateral trade regime *222*

Notes *225*

References *227*

List of tables

Table		*Page*
1.1	World output growth, 2001–2006	*2*
1.A1	World primary commodity prices, 2000–2005	*18*
1.A2	Growth in consumption of selected primary commodities: China and the rest of the world, 2002–2005	*21*
1.A3	Total exports and copper exports in major copper exporting countries, 2002–2005	*25*
1.A4	Impact of changes in terms of trade and net income payments on national disposable income in selected developing-country groups, average for 2003–2005	*27*
2.1	GDP growth in selected developing countries and regions, 1960–2004	*46*
2.2	Per capita GDP growth in selected developing countries and regions, 1960–2004	*47*
3.1	Effectively applied tariffs in developed and developing countries by selected product group, 1994 and 2005	*76*
3.2	Developing countries with the highest concentration of exports to a single destination, 2000–2004	*83*
3.3	Main markets for developing-country exports and number of developing countries for which they are the most important market	*84*
3.4	Ranking of developing economies with the largest and smallest increases in export opportunities from world import demand growth, 1990–2004	*85*
3.5	Increase in exports due to rising export opportunities from world import demand growth, 2000–2004	*87*
3.6	Dynamic products in developing-country exports by category, 1995–2003	*88*
3.7	Paris Club terms and reschedulings	*90*
3.8	Debt indicators of decision point HIPCs, 1995–2004	*94*
3.9	Major developing host economies of FDI in 2004	*108*
3.10	Major developing-economy recipients of FDI inflows in 2004	*108*
3.11	FDI in relation to gross fixed capital formation and GDP in selected regions and economies in 1990 and 2004	*109*
3.A1	Progress under the HIPC Initiative, 1997–2006	*123*
3.A2	Progress of the 29 decision point HIPCs towards various Millennium Development Goals	*124*
4.1	Central government interest payments and taxes on international trade in selected developing countries, 1971–2004	*132*
5.1	Tariffs on manufactured products and per capita income in selected developed countries, 1820–1980	*176*
5.2	Tariffs on manufactured products and per capita income in selected developing countries and country groups, 1985–2005	*178*
5.3	Share of selected developing economies and regional groups in world manufacturing value added and manufactured exports, 1980–2003	*181*
6.1	Governance indicators and per capita income growth, 1995–2005	*211*

List of figures

Figure   *Page*

1.1 Number of developing and transition economies with current-account deficit, selected regions, 1990–2005 ... *4*

1.2 Current-account balance as a percentage of GDP in China, Germany, Japan and the United States, 1980–2005 ... *6*

1.3 Interest rates, inflation and changes in unit labour cost in the G-7, 1970–2005 ... *14*

1.A1 Monthly commodity price indices by commodity group, 1995–2006 ... *19*

1.A2 Non-fuel primary commodity prices, nominal and real, by commodity group, 1960–2005 ... *20*

1.A3 Net barter terms of trade, selected developing countries, 2000–2005 ... *27*

2.1 Gross Fixed Capital Formation in selected developing regions and China, 1965–2004 ... *49*

3.1 TBT and SPS notifications to the WTO since 1995 ... *82*

3.2 Total external debt of HIPCs, 1970–2004 ... *92*

3.3 Decision point HIPCs: terms of new loan commitments, 1980–2004 ... *93*

3.4 Decision point HIPCs: debt service and poverty reducing expenditures as a percentage of government revenue, 1998–2008 ... *95*

3.5 Decision point HIPCs: per capita GDP growth and ratio of total debt to GNI, 1980–2004 ... *95*

3.6 Decision point HIPCs: ODA flows and debt relief, 1990–2004 ... *97*

3.7 ODA less debt relief by DAC members, 1990–2004 ... *98*

3.8 Migrants' remittances and financial flows to developing countries, 1990–2004 ... *101*

3.9 Major remittance-receiving developing countries, 1995, 2000 and 2004 ... *102*

3.10 FDI inflows to developing economies by region, 1980–2004 ... *106*

3.11 Shares in inward FDI stock of developing economies by region, 1980, 1990, 2000 and 2004 ... *107*

4.1 Capital flows and current-account balance in emerging-market economies, 1976–2004 ... *130*

4.2 Monetary conditions and GDP growth in China, 1980–2005 ... *145*

5.1 Stylized representation of support policies for different categories of manufactures ... *159*

5.2 Share in total manufacturing value added of major product categories in the Republic of Korea, Brazil and Mexico, 1980–2003 ... *182*

6.1 Correlation between institutional quality and per capita income, 2004 ... *210*

6.2 Governance and per capita income growth, selected groups of economies, 1995–2005 ... *212*

List of boxes

Box   *Page*

1.A1   The changing pattern of commodity speculation *22*

1.A2   Two models for choice *34*

2.1   The Monterrey Consensus on investment-friendly policies *56*

2.2   Economic Growth in the 1990s - Learning from a Decade of Reform:
quotations from the World Bank report.. *59*

2.3   Economic openness and national policy autonomy *62*

Explanatory notes

Classification by country or commodity group

The classification of countries in this *Report* has been adopted solely for the purposes of statistical or analytical convenience and does not necessarily imply any judgement concerning the stage of development of a particular country or area.

The major country groupings used in this *Report* follow the classification by the United Nations Statistical Office (UNSO). They are distinguished as:

» Developed or industrial(ized) countries: the countries members of the OECD (other than Mexico, the Republic of Korea and Turkey) plus the new EU member countries which are not OECD members (Cyprus, Estonia, Latvia, Lithuania, Malta and Slovenia) and Israel.

» The category South-East Europe and Commonwealth of Independent States (CIS) replaces what was formerly referred to as "transition economies".

» Developing countries: all countries, territories or areas not specified above.

The terms "country" / "economy" refer, as appropriate, also to territories or areas.

References to "Latin America" in the text or tables include the Caribbean countries unless otherwise indicated.

References to "sub-Saharan Africa" in the text or tables include South Africa unless otherwise indicated.

For statistical purposes, regional groupings and classifications by commodity group used in this *Report* follow generally those employed in the UNCTAD *Handbook of Statistics 2005* (United Nations publication, sales no. E/F.05.II.D.29) unless otherwise stated.

Other notes

References in the text to *TDR* are to the *Trade and Development Report* (of a particular year). For example, *TDR 2005* refers to *Trade and Development Report, 2005* (United Nations publication, sales no. E.05.II.D.13).

The term "dollar" ($) refers to United States dollars, unless otherwise stated.

The term "billion" signifies 1,000 million.

The term "tons" refers to metric tons.

Annual rates of growth and change refer to compound rates.

Exports are valued FOB and imports CIF, unless otherwise specified.

Use of a dash (–) between dates representing years, e.g. 1988–1990, signifies the full period involved, including the initial and final years.

An oblique stroke (/) between two years, e.g. 2000/01, signifies a fiscal or crop year.

A dot (.) indicates that the item is not applicable.

Two dots (..) indicate that the data are not available, or are not separately reported.

A dash (-) or a zero (0) indicates that the amount is nil or negligible.

A plus sign (+) before a figure indicates an increase; a minus sign (-) before a figure indicates a decrease.

Details and percentages do not necessarily add up to totals because of rounding.

Abbreviations

AGOA	African Growth and Opportunity Act (United States)
AMS	Aggregate Measures of Support
ATC	Agreement on Textiles and Clothing
BIS	Bank for International Settlements
CAC	collective action clause
CGE	computable general equilibrium
CIS	Commonwealth of Independent States
CPI	Consumer Price Index
DAC	Development Assistance Committee (OECD)
EBA	Everything But Arms (EU initiative)
ECA	Economic Commission for Africa
ECLAC	Economic Commission for Latin America and the Caribbean
EIU	Economist Intelligence Unit
ESAF	Enhanced Structural Adjustment Facility
EU	European Union
FAO	Food and Agriculture Organization of the United Nations
FDI	foreign direct investment
FFE	foreign-funded enterprise
FTA	free trade agreement
GATS	General Agreement on Trade in Services
GATT	General Agreement on Tariffs and Trade
GDP	gross domestic product
GFCF	gross fixed capital formation
GNI	gross national income
GNP	gross national product
GSP	Generalized System of Preferences
GTAP	Global Trade Analysis Project
HIPC	heavily indebted poor country
ICSG	International Copper Study Group
IDA	International Development Association
IEA	International Energy Agency
IEO	Independent Evaluation Office of the IMF
IMF	International Monetary Fund
IT	information technology
LDC	least developed country
M&A	merger and acquisition
MDG	Millennium Development Goal
MDG-BPRS	MDG-based poverty reduction strategies
MFN	most-favoured nation
MDRI	Multilateral Debt Relief Initiative
MVA	manufacturing value added
NAFTA	North American Free Trade Agreement
NAMA	non-agricultural market access

NIE	newly industrializing economy
NPV	net present value
NTB	non-tariff barrier
NTM	non-tariff measure
ODA	official development assistance
OECD	Organisation for Economic Co-operation and Development
OPEC	Organization of the Petroleum Exporting Countries
PRGF	Poverty Reduction and Growth Facility
PRSC	Poverty Reduction Support Credit
PRSP	Poverty Reduction Strategy Paper
R&D	research and development
REER	real effective exchange rate
RTA	regional trade agreement
SAF	Structural Adjustment Facility
SCM	subsidies and countervailing measures (also a WTO Agreement)
SDR	special drawing right
SDRM	sovereign debt restructuring mechanism
SDT	special and differential treatment (also a WTO Agreement)
SME	small- and medium-sized enterprise
SPLT	Substantive Patent Law Treaty
SOE	State-owned enterprise
SPS	sanitary and phytosanitary (also Uruguay Round SPS Agreement)
TBT	technical barrier to trade (also Uruguay Round TBT Agreement)
TDR	Trade and Development Report
TNC	transnational corporation
TRAINS	Trade Analysis and Information System (an UNCTAD database)
TRIMS	trade-related investment measures (also Uruguay Round TRIMS Agreement)
TRIPS	trade-related aspects of intellectual property rights (also Uruguay Round TRIPS Agreement)
UN COMTRADE	United Nations Commodity Trade Statistics Database
UN-DESA	United Nations, Department of Economic and Social Affairs
UNCDB	United Nations Common Database
UNCTAD	United Nations Conference on Trade and Development
UNDP	United Nations Development Programme
UNESCO	United Nations Educational, Scientific and Cultural Organization
UNIDO	United Nations Industrial Development Organization
UNSD	United Nations Statistics Division
UR	Uruguay Round
URAs	Uruguay Round Agreements
WDI	World Development Indicators
WIPO	World Intellectual Property Organization
WITS	World Integrated Trade Solution
WTO	World Trade Organization

OVERVIEW

Since 2002, world economic expansion has had a strong positive impact on growth and helped support progress towards the United Nations Millennium Development Goals (MDGs). Most developing countries have benefited from this growth momentum as a result of strong demand for their exports of primary commodities and, to an increasing extent, of manufactures. In addition, a number of other changes in the external environment for development over the past 10 to 15 years have benefited individual developing countries in different ways, depending on their economic structure and state of development. These changes include some improvements in market access, provision of debt relief and commitments by donors to substantial increases in ODA, as well as new opportunities to benefit from FDI and increasing migrants' remittances. In order for all developing countries to reach the MDGs and to reduce the large gap in living standards with the more advanced economies, the global partnership for development, stipulated in Goal 8 of the MDGs, needs to be strengthened further. Much depends on the ability of developing countries to adopt more proactive policies in support of capital formation, structural change and technological upgrading, and on the latitude available to them in light of international rules and disciplines.

Strong growth but increasing imbalances in the world economy

The expansion of world output continued unabated in 2005, and is expected to maintain its pace, with a projected GDP growth of 3.6 per cent in 2006. Output growth in developed countries is likely to continue, at 2.5–3 per cent, despite high prices for oil and industrial raw materials and a tendency towards more restrictive monetary policies. So far, turbulence in the financial markets has not adversely affected global growth to any appreciable extent, but the risks of a slowdown are clearly higher than a year ago. Developing countries, including many of the poorest, have benefited from continuing strong demand and rising prices for primary commodities, but for some of them this has also meant a higher import bill for oil and other raw materials. On the other hand, there are serious imbalances in the world economy, which suggests the need for caution in assessing prospects for the coming years, as their correction could have strong repercussions on developing countries.

The developing countries have contributed to the fast pace of global growth, with strong investment dynamics and an overall growth rate averaging about 6 per cent for the group as a whole. In particular, rapid growth in China and India has contributed to this outcome. It is also noteworthy that many African countries have maintained high growth rates. Growth in that region has accelerated every year since 2003, and projections of around 6 per cent growth for sub-Saharan Africa in 2006 signify an exceptional performance.

Strengthened position of emerging-market economies

Recently, there have been signs of increasing volatility in stock, commodity and currency markets, as well as in short-term capital outflows from some emerging markets – some of the ingredients of financial crises in the past. The dollar is highly vulnerable, and international investors appear to have become nervous in the face of continuing global imbalances and rising interest rates. A number of developing countries have experienced a sharp drop in their stock market prices and some emerging-market currencies have fallen markedly against the dollar, the euro, the yen and those currencies closely attached to them. However, the turbulence is limited to some areas and to a number of countries with fairly high current-account deficits. There is little evidence of a looming major financial crisis, comparable to the Asian or Latin American crises some 10 years ago.

Most emerging-market economies are much less vulnerable than at the time of the big shocks that occurred over the past two decades. In 2005, East and South Asian countries recorded a large surplus on their current accounts and Latin America as a whole was also in surplus. After the Asian and Latin American crises more and more developing countries have sought to follow similar paths of adjustment that have involved stabilizing their exchange rates at a rather low level, running sizeable current-account surpluses and accumulating large amounts of dollar reserves. While this practice is widely considered as being suboptimal, in many respects it represents the only feasible way in which developing countries can successfully adapt to the systemic deficiencies afflicting today's global economic order characterized by the absence of symmetric obligations of surplus and deficit countries.

It is no surprise that the undervaluation-*cum*-intervention strategy is especially prevalent among developing countries that have recently experienced currency crises following previous liberalization of their financial systems and capital accounts. Having learned that reliance on foreign savings rarely pays off as a sustainable development strategy, a growing number of developing countries have shifted to an alternative strategy that relies on trade surpluses as the engine for investment and growth. This strategy requires them to defend strategically favourable post-crisis competitiveness positions. But it can only function as long as there is at least one country in the global economy that accepts running the corresponding trade deficit.

Redressing the imbalances

At this juncture, it is mainly because of the flexibility and pragmatism of macroeconomic management by the United States that the systemic deficiencies in the global economic order have not yet led to global deflation, but "only" to these imbalances. There is, however, a risk, that the United States may become overburdened in playing the lead role as the global engine for growth for too long. So far, it has been able to neglect its external imbalance as this presented no serious conflict with efforts to sustain full employment and price stability, but there is growing potential for such a conflict. Moreover, there are rising concerns, including among financial market participants, that the imbalance is still growing. It is unlikely that the United States personal savings rate will decline by another 5 percentage points over the next decade, or that the public budget will be allowed to deteriorate by another 6 per cent of GDP. Thus the world economy might soon be without the growth stimuli that have driven it for the past 15 years. There is the prospect of a further dollar depreciation, which would help restore competitiveness and rebalance the external accounts. But the effect of a marked slowdown in United States imports would be spread and amplified across the world economy just as the positive impulses were for all these years. This could quite easily halt the momentum in development progress and poverty reduction achieved in developing countries in recent years, for no fault of theirs.

Notwithstanding the large surpluses of a number of developing countries, the main reason for the United States' perhaps increasingly unmanageable global burden is that some other key industrialized countries, rather than assuming a supportive role, have added to the global burden of the United States. Given the huge external surplus of Japan and Germany, and the significant improvements in their competitive positions in recent years, the required competitiveness gains of the United States should now come mainly at their expense, a process that would be greatly facilitated if the stagnant demand that has prevailed in these economies for all too long were to become more buoyant.

China's role in a benign redressing of global imbalances differs from that of Japan and Germany. Since the beginning of the 1990s, China's domestic demand, along with its imports, has grown very strongly, and the country has played a vital role in spreading and sustaining growth momentum throughout the developing world – a process that must not be derailed. Therefore, renminbi revaluation should continue gradually, rather than abruptly, taking due account of the regional ramifications. Similar to China, oil-producing countries have only recently begun to play a significant part in the imbalances. Should the high level of oil prices persist, they could contribute to a benign redressing of global imbalances through stronger domestic demand growth and greater social and physical investment with a view to diversifying their economies.

Crucially, what is needed for redressing global imbalances is a responsible multilateral effort, rather than pressure on parts of the developing world. A well-coordinated international macroeconomic approach would considerably improve the chances of the poorer countries to consolidate their recent gains in growth performance. In the absence of such an approach, developing countries should defend their strategically advantageous competitive positions and use the favourable overall environment for investing more and reducing their foreign indebtedness.

Failure of the standard reform agenda

The present phase of relatively fast growth in developing countries, driven by strong global demand originating mainly in the United States and amplified by the rapid expansion of the large Chinese economy, comes after two decades of unsatisfactory growth in most developing countries, especially in Africa and Latin America.

During the 1980s and 1990s, most developing countries undertook far-reaching market-oriented reforms with the expectation that improved factor allocation would be key to their integration into a globalizing world economy. The Bretton Woods institutions played a dominant role in this context, both as lenders, imposing their policy conditionality on borrowing countries, and as "think tanks" with a major impact on the international policy debate. As a result, the principles underlying the reform agenda not only shaped the economic policies of countries that borrowed from the international financial institutions; they also came to be widely accepted as the standard reform package for other countries that were reviewing their development strategies for achieving closer integration into the globalizing world economy.

The reform agenda focused almost exclusively on market forces for more efficient resource allocation through improvements in the incentive structure and on reduced discretionary State intervention. Efficiency enhancement in resource allocation was sought through liberalization and deregulation at the national level, and through opening up to competition at the global level. Over the years, the reform agenda has been extended to include additional elements such as capital-account liberalization and improvements in national governance on the one hand, and greater emphasis on poverty reduction and social aspects of development on the other.

The orthodox reform agenda was based on the belief that capital accumulation, a precondition both for output growth and for changes in economic structures, including diversification, industrialization and technological upgrading, would follow automatically from improved allocation of existing resources. This expectation was rarely met. Indeed, the orthodox reforms were frequently accompanied by low rates of investment and deindustrialization, often with negative social consequences. The fast pace of trade liberalization caused trade deficits associated with any given rate of growth to become larger, adding to payments difficulties and increasing dependence on capital inflows. And efforts to attract capital inflows involved raising interest rates – which hindered domestic investment and slowed growth – and currency appreciation, which compromised the international competitiveness of domestic producers and adversely affected trade performance. In most countries of Africa and Latin America, capital accumulation did not keep pace with the increased need for productivity enhancement and technological innovation, which are basic requirements for the success of export-oriented development strategies. Moreover, although liberalization and deregulation may have generated efficiency gains, these gains did not automatically translate into faster income growth. Instead, they often led to growing inequality. Policies promoted with a view to getting relative prices "right" at the micro level failed, because in too many cases they got prices "wrong" at the macro level.

At the same time, a number of East Asian countries succeeded in their catch-up efforts, based on a high level of capital accumulation combined with gradual and often strategic opening up to international markets. However, a dramatic downturn occurred in these countries in the late 1990s, when, distinct from earlier prudent and strategic management of trade liberalization, governments undertook premature capital-account liberalization, which made their economies vulnerable to the vagaries of international capital markets.

The crisis was a turning point in several respects. First, there was mounting criticism of the IMF's diagnoses before and after the crisis and of its policy prescriptions, leading the Fund to soften its stance with regard to capital-account management. Second, not all the countries affected by the crisis accepted the IMF's prescriptions for adjustment, resulting in a sharp decline in demand for IMF assistance as countries sought to avoid the conditionality attached to it. Moreover, some regional initiatives for closer monetary and financial cooperation were launched or strengthened with a view to reducing dependence on the IMF in crisis situations. Third, the belief that integration into international capital markets is generally beneficial because it allows access to foreign savings, and that domestic monetary policies have to be geared to generating confidence in international financial markets, was severely shaken. Experts and international institutions as well as governments began to view managed exchange-rate systems in a more favourable light, and many countries changed their policy objectives in favour of generating trade surpluses and accumulating reserves.

A new focus on poverty reduction

The meagre results of the traditional reform policies led to the growing perception in the course of the 1990s that the standard reform agenda would have to be complemented by measures for strengthening property rights – as the key institutional element for solving the problem of insufficient investment. It was also recognized that additional efforts were needed to mitigate the effects of poverty, in response to a universally perceived humanitarian need, and to make the reforms socially acceptable. Poverty reduction was to be achieved by redirecting public expenditure to address the symptoms of poverty. But such a policy is unlikely to have a lasting impact as long as structural change remains slow and capital accumulation is insufficient to boost growth, increase productive capacity and create employment for the poor. While increased efforts for poverty eradication are a global ethical imperative, it is equally imperative to finance such expenditure out of additional resources; shifting public finances away from investment that can have long-lasting effects on the causes of poverty to social spending that might temporarily cure the symptoms of poverty can be counterproductive in the long run.

The formulation of the MDGs in 2000 reflected the degree of dissatisfaction among global policymakers with progress in development and in the fight against poverty under the conditions that had prevailed over the previous two decades. Goal 8 of the MDGs – Develop a global partnership for development – therefore added an international dimension to the reform agenda. Furthermore, in 2002, the Monterrey Consensus recognized that the capacity of developing countries to realize the MDGs is heavily influenced by external factors, including, *inter alia*, the international macroeconomic and trading environment, aid flows and an international solution to the debt problem. The Consensus also recognized the challenge facing developing countries to create the necessary internal conditions for adequate levels of productive investment and ensure complementarity of public and private investment in the development of local capacities – aspects that were largely neglected in earlier reform programmes. There can be little doubt that an enabling environment for economic development is strongly influenced by the way markets operate, but it is also characterized by externalities of various kinds. Yet policy prescriptions focusing on "getting the prices right" through market liberalization limit the scope for proactive government policies to address such externalities, which in many cases can be decisive for investment decisions.

Improved export opportunities

The external environment for development is determined by the growth performance, cyclical and structural changes as well as economic policy decisions of developed countries. Fast and sustained growth in East and South Asia has added an additional dimension to this interdependence, but global demand conditions, and thus developing countries' export opportunities, continue to be shaped by the major industrialized countries. In addition to expanding global demand, improved market access conditions in developed countries are a key determinant of developing countries' export opportunities. These market access conditions have somewhat improved as a result of multilateral trade liberalization, regional trade agreements and non-reciprocal preferential trading agreements, but, overall, the conditions continue to be biased against developing countries. It is also noteworthy that the reduction in tariff barriers has been accompanied by an increase in the use of non-tariff measures, particularly anti-dumping measures, which have emerged over the past 25 years as the most widespread impediment to international trade, and to exports from developing countries in particular. Trade preferences often have not been fully utilized and have generated limited benefits, not only because of uncertainty surrounding the schemes, along with restrictive rules of origin and insufficient product coverage, but also because of supply-capacity constraints. High hopes are attached to the ongoing Doha Round of multilateral trade negotiations, but unless its development ambition is fully realized, the Round is unlikely to bring major improvements in the overall export opportunities of developing countries. Estimates of the aggregate gains that can be expected to result from a successful conclusion of the Round in terms of exports and income are relatively modest, and the rise in total developing-country exports will be distributed unequally across countries.

Progress with debt relief and new ODA commitments

Another important factor shaping the external environment of many developing countries, in particular the poorest ones, is official development assistance (ODA) and international support for solving external debt problems. In this regard, the launching of the Heavily Indebted Poor Countries (HIPC) Debt Initiative in 1996 was a landmark. However, after 10 years of implementation, this Initiative has not yet succeeded in meeting all its goals. So far, less than half of the eligible countries have benefited from the full amount of debt relief possible under the Initiative, and a number of countries continue to have unsustainable levels of debt, or are expected to again exceed the debt sustainability thresholds in the coming years. Moreover, so far there is no clear evidence that debt relief has been fully additional to ODA flows.

In an additional push to resolve the debt problem of the poorest countries, in July 2005 the G-8 announced the Multilateral Debt Relief Initiative, whereby multilateral financial institutions undertook to cancel the entire debt of countries that have fulfilled the requirements for full bilateral debt relief under the HIPC Initiative. While ample debt relief is a necessary condition for many countries to increase public and private investment, it does not constitute a universal solution to the broader structural problems that led to the accumulation of debt in the first place, and it certainly will not ensure against a recurrence of debt problems.

The challenge of solving these problems has also been recognized by the major ODA donors. Since the beginning of the new millennium many donors have committed to stepping up aid flows to support developing countries in their efforts to reach the MDGs. But even under the most optimistic scenario (i.e. that all donor countries will fully honour their commitments), many developing countries will continue to lack the necessary financial resources for achieving the MDGs. Certainly, most HIPCs will need additional financing in the form of grants, rather than loans, in order to avoid new debt servicing difficulties.

Increasing potential of migrants' remittances and FDI

It is noteworthy that even after a considerable rise in ODA since 2001 and expectations of further increases in the coming years, ODA flows are likely to remain considerably lower than migrants' remittances, which have become an important source of foreign exchange for many developing countries. Remittance inflows to developing countries have been more stable than export earnings and capital flows to these countries, and they are spread more evenly among developing countries than, for example, FDI flows. The effects on economic growth and long-term development of migrants' remittances, which supplement household incomes, are not very clear, but they are likely to have a direct positive impact on poverty alleviation. As migrants' remittances, which are private income, are expected to grow further for many years to come, consideration might be given to providing incentives for using such inflows for capital formation. This could strengthen their impact on long-term development and at the same time help solve the problems that have been causing emigration in the first place.

After strong and sustained expansion during the 1990s, FDI flows to developing countries have become less stable since the turn of the millennium. While China has emerged as the largest FDI recipient among all developing countries, there has recently been a resurgence of FDI flows to Africa and Latin America, driven by prospects for greater earnings in the extractive industries. The growth of FDI relative to domestic capital formation or GDP suggests that inward FDI has come to play a more significant role in developing economies than it did 20 years ago. But the amount of FDI alone is not an indicator of its contribution to development. Empirical evidence points to considerable variation in the benefits that host countries actually reap from FDI inflows, depending on how FDI policies are integrated into a broader development strategy and on the extent to which private business interests of foreign investors and national development objectives can be reconciled. Weak bargaining and regulatory capabilities on the part of host-country governments can result in an unequal distribution of benefits or an abuse of market power by transnational corporations by crowding out domestic investment.

FDI is increasingly intended to serve global and regional markets, often in the context of international production networks, and the spread of such networks offers, in principle, new possibilities for developing countries and economies in transition to benefit from FDI in the manufacturing sector. In Africa and Latin America and the Caribbean, FDI is still heavily concentrated in the extraction and exploitation of natural resources, with weak linkages to the domestic economy. Host-country regulations can influence the creation of linkages between domestic producers and foreign affiliates, and also induce FDI to contribute to technology transfer.

An evolving external environment

In sum, there have been improvements over the past decade in several elements shaping the external environment for development, partly as a result of a strengthened global partnership for development. However, not all initial promises or expectations have been fulfilled, and in some areas new challenges have emerged. The various factors that have shaped the external environment for development since the mid-1980s can contribute to faster growth and poverty alleviation by providing new opportunities for trade and sectoral development, or by alleviating financial constraints. Nevertheless, there remains considerable scope for rendering the global trading and financial environment more development friendly. Equally important is the need to strengthen the different elements of global economic governance and achieve greater coherence among these elements. The challenge for developing countries is to translate positive external developments into faster growth of domestic value added, employment and income. Meeting this challenge will require more than a mere reliance on market forces and strengthened social policies. In order to obtain long-term benefits for growth and poverty alleviation from existing and possible future improvements in the external environment developing countries should be able to develop additional support policies for domestic investment, productivity growth and technological change.

Towards a fundamental reorientation of policy

In order to reach the MDGs, developing countries will have to grow much faster than they have done over the past 25 years. But to meet the challenges facing open developing economies, the scope for policy-making will have to be widened beyond what has been acceptable under the standard reform agenda. More proactive policies in support of capital accumulation and productivity enhancement are needed for successful participation in international economic relations, and for sustained improvements in the welfare of all groups of the population. In the past, the potential impact of efficiency gains on growth has frequently been overestimated. The unsatisfactory outcomes of the market-oriented reforms pursued in a majority of developing countries since the early 1980s may largely be due to the reduced number of policy instruments available to policymakers under the development paradigm of the past 25 years.

As a result of integration into global production and financial markets, external influences over national policy targets have become stronger, and the trade-offs between internal and external objectives have intensified. The reduction in policy autonomy is often viewed in connection with commitments undertaken by countries in multilateral agreements, especially in the area of trade. But bilateral or regional trade agreements often involve even tighter constraints, and there are also many other channels outside the trade area through which policy autonomy can be constrained, with consequences that can be even more serious. One prominent example is the conditionalities attached to credit extended by international financial institutions. The proliferation of these conditionalities over the past 20 years has given rise to increasing criticism, especially as they have extended into structural and even non-economic areas without taking sufficient account of country-specific factors in their formulation.

But apart from such *de jure* constraints of national policy autonomy that are the result of commitments to obligations and acceptance of rules set by international economic governance systems and institutions, there are also a number of important constraints that result *de facto* from policy decisions relating to the form and degree of a country's integration into the international economy. Most notable among these is the loss of the ability to use the exchange rate as an effective instrument for external adjustment, or the interest rate as an instrument for influencing domestic demand and credit conditions, because of a reliance on private capital inflows to finance trade deficits following the opening up of the capital account.

The need for policy innovation

Even in a rather closed economy, formal command over policy instruments does not automatically translate into full control over national targets. It is therefore necessary to analyse the range and kind of policy instruments that individual developing countries have at their disposal to remedy the widespread weaknesses in private capital formation, productivity growth and technological upgrading, as well as the structural and institutional conditions under which these instruments can be effectively used. Moreover, in a highly interdependent and integrated world economy, policies at the national level need to be complemented by some policies operating and controlled at the international level. Indeed, the economic interdependence of countries provides the principal rationale for multilateral disciplines because it gives rise to externalities, spillovers and arbitrage opportunities.

With the liberalization of international trade, external demand conditions have become increasingly important determinants of national investment decisions: the smaller the domestic market and the greater the degree of openness of an economy, the greater is the need to rely on external demand for growth and employment creation. Therefore, policies pursued in other countries, and competition with producers in those countries, become co-determinants of domestic growth. This implies that appropriate multilateral rules and regulations in trade and finance can be of considerable benefit for launching and sustaining a dynamic growth process in developing countries.

On the other hand, widening the scope of national policy instruments beyond those that were deemed acceptable under the development paradigm of the past 25 years would not only allow the pursuit of additional goals, they would also increase the number of potential combinations of instruments, which in many cases will be decisive for the success or failure of a strategy. At the national level, additional policy instruments may need to be explored to ensure price stability and to support domestic producers in their efforts to achieve international competitiveness and maintain it in a dynamic process. As the options for such national instruments are circumscribed by international policies, the latter should be designed in a way that allows greater scope and flexibility for the application of domestic instruments to address the most serious obstacles to growth and development, which differ considerably across countries.

Strengthening the creative forces of markets

As a consequence of the failure of past economic policies that relied primarily on market forces, many developing countries have begun to reconsider the use of proactive trade and industrial policies in their development strategies, despite much controversy concerning their justification and the feasibility of adopting them. Some authors have questioned the efficacy of such policies, tending to associate them with failed inward-looking, import-substituting strategies with open-ended government interventions and a strong bias towards protectionism. The rationale for proactive trade and industrial policies has occasionally been questioned also because of their possible adverse effects on efficient resource allocation and because they could lead to protracted rent-seeking. But recent development research has produced evidence that an exclusive concentration on allocative efficiency implies a lack of sufficient attention to stimulating the dynamic forces of markets which underlie structural change and economic growth, and that industrial policies were an important supportive factor for East Asia's economic catch-up as well as for industrialization in today's mature economies.

Proactive trade and industrial policies should not be understood to mean inward-looking, protectionist defence mechanisms to support industries where production and employment are threatened by foreign competitors that have successfully upgraded their production. Rather, the role of national support policies should be to strengthen the creative forces of markets and related capital formation. The policies should help solve information and coordination problems arising in the process of capital formation and productivity enhancement. They should also ensure that cumulative production experience is translated into productivity gains. This industrial policy support should be complemented by a trade policy designed to achieve international competitiveness in increasingly more sophisticated products. But recognizing the potential benefits of trade for growth does not mean that across-the-board opening up to international markets is necessary. Rather, acquiring the ability to competitively produce goods that were previously imported is inherent in economic transformation and goes hand in hand with export development. Implementing some temporary protection does not imply adopting an "anti-trade" strategy, rather it should be considered a key element of a policy aimed at "strategic trade integration".

Flexible support policies

Which production should receive industrial and trade policy support and for how long will depend on many factors, which are likely to change in the course of economic development. Policy support for a specific product category may be introduced once the technological barriers to entry are no longer out of reach for domestic manufacturers. But it should be withdrawn when domestic manufacturers attain technological mastery, when domestic production becomes unprofitable at an internationally competitive level, or when benefits from economies of scale and learning by doing get exhausted. With such an approach, any specific product category is a candidate for public support policies only for a limited period of time. The aim is not to pick winners, but to identify and discipline under-performing firms.

Maintaining dynamic scale economies requires both successive innovative investments and learning processes. Temporary subsidies facilitate such investments, while temporary protection allows learning processes to unfold. However, as the potential for learning in a specific activity diminishes with growing experience, learning and innovative investment depend on each other: new, innovative investments open new possibilities for further learning, which in turn provides the basis for the productive use of a new round of innovative investments, and so on.

Any prescription for development policy must recognize the large differences among countries and respect their unique characteristics. Nevertheless, there are some common features that permit consideration of some general policy principles, which need to be translated into individualized, country-specific policies. Such general principles include policies supportive of innovative investment and of adapting imported technologies to local conditions. Support for domestic as well as foreign investment should be combined with an appropriate regulatory and fiscal framework to secure optimal gains for development. In this context, there is need for a pragmatic and strategic perspective to integrate FDI into a broader development strategy geared to structural and technological change. There is a greater likelihood of industrial policy measures succeeding if they are complemented by trade policies designed to achieve international competitiveness in increasingly sophisticated products. Policy support should be provided only on the basis of clearly established operational goals, observable criteria for monitoring them and within a specified time horizon.

Restrictions imposed by international trade agreements

There are widespread concerns that the international trade rules and regulations, which are emerging from multilateral trade negotiations and a rising number of regional and bilateral trade arrangements, could rule out the use of the very policy measures that were instrumental in the development of today's mature economies and late industrializers. This would imply a considerable reduction in the flexibility of national governments to pursue their development objectives. Another concern is that these rules and commitments, which in *legal* terms are equally binding for all countries, in *economic* terms might impose more binding constraints on developing than on developed countries, because of the differences in their respective structural features and levels of industrial development.

The imposition of performance requirements on foreign investors is a key regulatory measure that has been curtailed by the Agreement on Trade-Related Investment Measures (TRIMs). While developed countries extensively employed such requirements at earlier stages of their industrial development, developing countries have only recently started to use these policy tools to foster their industrialization and technological upgrading. In efforts to participate in international production networks, for example, domestic content requirements have been introduced with a view to increasing technology transfer and the use of domestically produced inputs. Empirical evidence suggests that such measures can help meet these objectives. However, developed countries have brought a number of cases against developing countries before the World Trade Organization (WTO) dispute settlement mechanism, especially in the automotive sector, invoking the rules and commitments of the TRIMs Agreement.

The Agreement on Subsidies and Countervailing Measures (SCM) applies to specific subsidies, and thus affects the selective function of policy. It is asymmetrical insofar as subsidies impose a cost on public budgets, which developed countries can afford more easily than developing countries. It prohibits making subsidies conditional on export performance. Yet this has been an important instrument in the reciprocal control mechanisms applied in some East Asian countries, which have often been identified as key to the greater success of industrial policy in that region compared to Latin America.

Many observers consider the Agreement on Trade-related Aspects of Intellectual Property Rights (TRIPS) to be the most controversial of the Uruguay Round Agreements (URAs) because of its potential to restrict access of developing countries to technology, knowledge and medicines. The limitations introduced by TRIPS imply an asymmetry that favours the owners of protected intellectual property – mainly in developed countries – at the expense of those trying to gain access to such intellectual content, mainly in developing countries. Moreover, the provisions in the Agreement are specific, binding and actionable with regard to the protection of intellectual property, and non-compliance can be challenged under the WTO's dispute settlement mechanism. By contrast, provisions regarding technology transfer and technical cooperation, which are of importance mainly for developing countries, are of a "best endeavour" nature and difficult to enforce, and non-compliance is not subject to a penalty. The TRIPS Agreement has, nonetheless, left room for variation across countries. For example, developing countries can impose stringent rules on patent disclosure and subsequently grant narrow patents, or they can have flexible discretionary use of compulsory licensing. However, in many cases regional and bilateral trade agreements foreclose part of the autonomy left open to developing countries by TRIPS.

Industrial tariffs in support of diversification

The use of industrial tariffs is in many respects not the best tool to promote diversification and technological upgrading. Nonetheless, developing-country policymakers may be hesitant to abandon such tariffs, for three main reasons. First, tariffs remain an important source of fiscal revenue for many developing countries. Second, since the Uruguay Round Agreements reduced the degrees of freedom for developing countries to use other policy instruments to support diversification and technological upgrading, the relative importance of industrial tariffs has increased. Third, and perhaps most importantly, the economic impact of changes in industrial tariffs is often assessed in terms of welfare gains or losses resulting from the reallocation of existing resources. From this perspective, a trade policy aimed at low and uniform tariffs across industrial sectors with full binding coverage will maximize a country's welfare benefits. But such an assessment pays little attention to the implications of tariff cuts and harmonization for capital accumulation, technological change and productivity growth, which underlie industrialization and economic development. To this end, it is important for developing countries to be able to modulate applied industrial tariffs levied on particular product categories in accordance with their path of technological upgrading as a key instrument of sectoral policy. To be sure, this kind of tariff policy does not imply either the imposition of high applied tariffs for all sectors at any one time or the imposition of high average applied tariffs. On the contrary, it is likely to result in lower average applied tariffs than would be the case if tariff policy were looked at from a tariff line-by-tariff line perspective.

This kind of flexible tariff policy would be best accommodated by a strategy of maintaining bound tariffs at a relatively higher level (or maintaining a large part of industrial tariffs unbound) and modulating applied tariffs on particular industrial sectors around a relatively lower average level. This would be possible if industrial tariff reduction obligations from international agreements extended only to average tariffs, and not to individual tariff lines as has been the case in all multilateral trade agreements concluded so far. A number of developing countries have maintained a tariff regime that allows them to modulate applied tariffs on manufactured goods. However, the current multilateral negotiations on non-agricultural market access are set to reduce this flexibility in tariff setting and binding that developing countries have so far been able to maintain.

The scope for proactive trade and industrial policies

Thus an assessment of the extent to which various international trade arrangements have restricted the degrees of freedom of developing countries to pursue proactive trade and industrial policies gives a mixed picture. On the one hand, WTO rules and commitments have made it far more difficult for developing countries to combine outward orientation with the kind of policy instruments that today's mature and late industrializers employed to promote economic diversification and technological upgrading. On the other hand, under the current set-up of multilateral trade rules, countries still have the possibility to pursue policies that will help them generate new productive capacity and new areas of comparative advantage. Such policies largely concern the provision of public funds in support of R&D and innovation activities. Countries in a position to use the WTO rules and commitments to this effect can continue to support their own industries, target national champions, and generally promote national efforts towards technological advancement.

Therefore there remain considerable degrees of freedom for national policy-making that have not been circumscribed by the URAs. However, the asymmetries in the URAs should not be underestimated. They result from the fact that while the negotiated agreements apply to all WTO members equally in terms of *legal* obligations, they are much more burdensome for developing countries in *economic* terms. It is therefore crucially important to look at the "level playing field" metaphor not only in terms of *legal* constraints, but also, and more importantly, in terms of *economic* constraints, considering countries' different structural features and levels of industrial development. Moreover, what is left of the degrees of freedom for developing-country policymakers after the URAs has been further reduced by a number of regional and bilateral free trade agreements with developed countries.

The Doha Work Programme has yet to deliver on the development promises of the Doha Declaration. The eventual outcome may well further reduce flexibility in policy-making by developing countries, particularly in the area of industrial tariffs. On the other hand, lack of progress in the multilateral negotiations may result in greater importance being given to regional or bilateral free trade arrangements as the legal mechanisms that define rules and disciplines in international trade. While these arrangements may improve developing countries' access to developed-country markets, they may entail further reduction in the degree of freedom in national policy-making than that emerging from a Doha Round Agreement. This could make it even more difficult for developing countries to create the supply capacity needed to take advantage of improved export opportunities.

Financial markets and the choice of the exchange-rate regime

The ongoing process of globalization has also changed the framework of national macroeconomic policy. For many developing countries and economies in transition, opening their borders to international trade and private capital flows has been associated with crises that were triggered by instability and turmoil in the international financial markets.

Deregulation of domestic financial markets, including the elimination of credit controls, deregulation of interest rates and the privatization of banks, was a key element in the reform agenda of the 1980s and 1990s. It was based on the belief that lifting "financial repression" and freeing prices on the capital and money markets would improve intertemporal resource allocation, enhance willingness to save and attract additional resources to the banking system. Combining this with a liberalized capital account, developing countries would attract financial savings originating in more prosperous and capital rich economies, and thus overcome a major barrier to growth.

At the same time, however, there was no clear concept of how the most important international price, the exchange rate, and, closely related to it, the interest rate, should be determined or regulated. The two options for national exchange-rate policy that eventually came to be considered viable were either to let the currency float freely or to adopt a completely fixed exchange rate ("hard peg"), options that came to be known as the "corner solutions".

For small open economies, and developing countries in particular, the exchange rate is the most important single price, as it has a strong impact on the domestic price level and on overall competitiveness. It must be flexible enough to prevent persistent misalignments that would harm the competitiveness of domestic producers and their trade performance. At the same time, excessive volatility of the exchange rate must be avoided, as this would heighten the risks for long-term investment, increase domestic inflation and encourage financial speculation.

The "corner solutions" are based on the assumptions that, in the case of free floating, international financial markets smoothly adjust exchange rates to their "equilibrium" level, while in the case of a hard peg, product, financial and labour markets would always smoothly and rapidly adjust to a new equilibrium at the predetermined exchange rate. In reality, however, exchange rates under a floating regime have proved to be highly unstable, leading to long spells of misalignment, with dire consequences for the real economic activity of the economies involved. The experience with hard pegs has not been satisfactory either: as the exchange rate could not be corrected in cases of external shocks or misalignment, adjustments were costly in terms of lost output, and the real sectors of the domestic economy bore the brunt.

Given this experience with both rigidly fixed and freely floating exchange rates, "intermediate" regimes have become the preferred option in most developing countries with open capital markets; they provide more room for manoeuvre when there is instability in international financial markets and enable adjustment of the real exchange rate to a level more in line with a country's development strategy. None of the "corner solutions" offer these possibilities. Combining a *completely* open capital account with *full* autonomy in monetary policy and *absolute* exchange-rate stability is impossible, but engaging in a *managed-floating* exchange-rate regime, combined with *selective* capital controls, (i.e. reclaiming *some* monetary policy autonomy) seems to be a viable second-best solution.

Towards a more effective assignment of macroeconomic policies

The perception that price stability is the most important condition for satisfactory growth performance has dominated the assignment of macroeconomic policy instruments in both developed and developing countries in the last two decades. The orthodox approach for "sound macroeconomic policies" has assigned to monetary policy the role of a guardrail for any combination of fiscal and structural policies, and against any kind of shock, regardless of whether it originated on the supply or the demand side. The role of fiscal policy in this assignment has been limited to assisting monetary policy in keeping budget deficits low.

Price stabilization has also been a key target in the most successful cases of economic catch-up, but here the assignment of policies to reach this target has been different. In the Asian newly industrializing economies (NIEs), stabilization was achieved mainly through heterodox, non-monetary instruments, such as an incomes policy or direct intervention in the goods and labour markets. At the same time, monetary and fiscal policies adopted instruments to achieve fast growth and high investment: low interest rates and, at least since the Asian financial crisis, a slightly undervalued exchange rate, combined with fiscal stimulus whenever that was required in light of cyclical developments.

The point of departure of such policies is the perception that in a world where higher planned savings do not automatically generate higher fixed investment, economic policy has to focus on the creation of savings through investment and the resulting income growth. This approach requires a monetary policy that will provide financing possibilities to enterprises that do not yet exist. Such a policy is potentially inflationary, but it does not lead to inflation if real investment and growth absorb the excess liquidity that is created. There is thus a narrow link between the process of catching up and structural change, on the one hand, and the development of a country's monetary system and stabilization instruments, on the other.

External financing remains necessary to the extent that greater imports of capital goods as a result of higher investment lead to a current-account deficit. But many successful cases of economic catch-up, and most recently China, have shown that such deficits do not necessarily occur, and that domestic financing of investment can substantially lift growth rates without net foreign savings. The decisive factor for catching up is domestic accumulation of capital in a process of rising real incomes for all groups of society.

In any case, price stabilization is crucial for sustaining a dynamic growth process: in countries that are prone to high inflation it is much more difficult to start and sustain a process of development and catching up because of the frequent need to tighten the creation of money and credit. Without a sufficient number of policy instruments that can be used effectively to dampen inflationary risks, the attempt to boost development through expansionary macroeconomic policies is likely to fail, as inflation will rapidly flare up. Conversely, countries that successfully use heterodox instruments to achieve price stability have more room to employ macroeconomic policy to spur an investment-led development process.

Exchange rates, interest rates and capital inflows

In the absence of effective multilateral arrangements for exchange-rate management, macro-economic policy in many developing countries has aimed increasingly at avoiding currency overvaluation. This has not only been a means to maintaining or improving international competitiveness, it has also been a necessary condition for keeping domestic interest rates low and an insurance against the risk of future financial crises.

Independence from international capital markets allows central banks to use the instruments at their disposal for actively pursuing development targets, provided that an acceleration of inflation is kept in check by non-monetary measures, such as an incomes policy, institution-building in support of creating a national consensus on reasonable wage claims, or direct government intervention in determining prices and, even more importantly, nominal wages. Examples of this approach are the policy mix in some Asian NIEs, and in China following its financial crisis in 1994, and, more recently, the experimentation with new price stabilization devices in Argentina. Many other developing countries that lacked the additional policy instruments to stabilize inflation had to choose between a policy of low interest rates that favour domestic investment and discourage capital inflows, but fuel inflation, and one of relatively high interest rates that keep inflation low, but discourage domestic investment and attract capital inflows, which required intervention and, often costly, sterilization.

The heterodox Asian policy mix has been complemented by various forms of capital-account regulation. While such regulation may help to contain, and to some extent also prevent, crises, the prime objective of economic policy should be to prevent the emergence of large interest rate differentials, arbitrage possibilities and incentives for speculation. However, as speculation on currency appreciation and the concomitant destabilizing inflows of hot money cannot completely be avoided, a pragmatic approach to managing such flows has proved helpful.

National institutions and governance arrangements

There is an increasing consensus among economists and policymakers that national institutions matter as a critical determinant of growth. There is much less agreement as to what exactly the role of institutions should be in the pursuit of development objectives, and what types of institutional arrangements are the most appropriate to achieve these objectives.

Conventional wisdom suggests that the main role of institutions should be to reduce transaction costs so as to create new markets and make existing markets function more efficiently. Economic policies should be supported by universally applicable types of institutions, particularly for granting and protecting property rights, in line with "global best practices", derived from the current institutional set-up in developed countries. Proponents of this approach point to empirical evidence from cross-country analyses, which typically find a positive correlation between the quality of institutions and the level of income. However, this does not imply that an improvement in market-enhancing institutional conditions (such as the protection of property rights, the rule of law and anti-corruption policies) is a precondition for growth and convergence with advanced countries. Rather, good institutions and good economic performance are interrelated.

A closer analysis of the relationship between institutional quality and income convergence of developing countries with developed countries reveals that diverging and converging developing economies alike score relatively low in terms of institutional quality. This suggests that large-scale institutional reform is seldom necessary at the initial stages to accelerate growth. It is only after developing countries have achieved sustained economic convergence that it may be necessary to create institutions similar to those existing in today's developed countries.

Institutions in support of proactive trade and industrial policies

An emphasis on industrialization and structural change leads to an additional role for institutions, which is to provide mechanisms for the effective implementation of policies designed to achieve high rates of investment and encourage the adoption of new technologies. Thus the guiding principle of institutional change should be to address the information and coordination problems that undermine entrepreneurial decision-making and improve checks and balances on the use of government discretion. While such institutional arrangements have to fulfil largely similar functions in different countries, their form may vary considerably from country to country, as well as within the same country over time.

A large number of developing countries pursued proactive trade and industrial policies until the beginning of the 1980s. However, at the time, it was not well recognized that the successful implementation of such strategies required a complementary set of institutional and administrative capabilities. It was only after the successful experiences of the late industrializers, particularly in East Asia, had been properly assessed that the importance of supportive institutional arrangements for making domestic policy instruments more effective came to be more widely acknowledged.

For initiating and supporting a process of sustained growth and structural change, it is particularly important to create institutional arrangements that manage economic rents associated with proactive trade and industrial policies. Once an economy is on a path of sustained catch-up growth, the government's capacity to support the creation of high-quality institutions through increasing public expenditure will also increase. These two processes are closely interrelated and create a virtuous circle of improved economic performance, enhanced institutional transformation and more effective public policies.

Linking support to performance requirements ensures that the initial rents are part of a nurturing exercise, and that they will eventually be withdrawn as the supported activity matures. In a sense, the enforcement of such performance requirements represents the "stick" that is a necessary complement to the "carrot" provided by the creation of temporary rents from subsidies or protection. The relationship between the State bureaucracy and the private sector should be one of "embedded autonomy". The effectiveness of proactive trade and industrial policies for achieving their objectives depends on the professionalism of the bureaucracy and the efficiency of information exchange between the public and private sectors. It also depends on the extent of the authority wielded by public policy-making entities and on their access to budgetary resources that can be directed to those goals, including through the creation and withdrawal of rents. Yet it should not be presumed that the institutional arrangements required to implement more orthodox policies (such as rapid liberalization and privatization) are less demanding than those needed to accompany proactive support policies.

Multilateral institutions and global governance

The considerable and still growing degree of global interdependence in contemporary world economic relations provides a strong rationale for a well-structured system of global economic governance. Self-centred national economic policies, if left unchecked, can generate adverse international spillover effects. Moreover, global economic interdependence provides an opportunity for policymakers in influential economies to deliberately adopt beggar-thy-neighbour types of policies. They may be tempted to employ commercial, macroeconomic, financial or exchange-rate policies in pursuit of certain national economic objectives – such as attaining mercantilist goals or postponing the adjustment of internal or external imbalances – which may harm the economic performance of other countries. In the absence of multilateral disciplines and cooperation, retaliatory action by adversely affected countries could lead to instability and disruptions in international economic relations that might leave all countries worse off.

But for such global collective action to be acceptable to all parties, it must result from a consultative process based on full, equal and voluntary participation of all the parties concerned. Any perception that multilateral disciplines extend too far and constrain the attainment of legitimate national development goals greatly depends on an individual economy's structural characteristics and its level of development. There is no single quantifiable balance between multilateral disciplines and national policy autonomy that would suit all countries or apply across all spheres of economic activity.

The multilateral trade regime overseen by the World Trade Organization contributes to certainty and predictability in international trade, as it provides a framework for an orderly, rules-based system of international trade, with appropriate checks and balances, arbitration of inter-State disputes and determination of the sanctions to be applied. This regime has been under increasing pressure to expand the number of areas regulated by multilateral disciplines and to move towards the establishment of a homogeneous regulatory framework. However, such changes are unlikely to take adequate account of the asymmetries existing between the different actors in the world economy. In order to avoid a deadlock in multilateral negotiations, which would have adverse effects on the substantial gains that multilateral disciplines in the area of international trade have achieved so far, the multilateral trade regime must be fully inclusive, and have a sufficient degree of flexibility to reflect the interests and needs of all its members.

How can the multilateral trade regime move forward?

Further discussions and negotiations will need to explore a range of options aimed at creating a new framework or new guidelines for special and differential treatment (SDT) in the WTO. This endeavour would probably need to start from the recognition that SDT for developing countries means redressing structural imbalances rather than giving concessions. From this perspective, and in the spirit of the global partnership for development, developed countries would need to agree to a new framework or new guidelines for SDT without receiving concessions in return.

Differences among countries in their structural characteristics or approaches to economic policy can be reflected in two ways. The first is to adopt a country-specific approach that would allow member countries to selectively opt out of certain rules and commitments, depending on their specific national priorities. This would provide flexibility to enable developing countries to seek some latitude in the application of multilateral disciplines consistent with the pursuit of national development goals. Its main drawback is that it would result in a multi-track trade regime, thus conflicting with the basic rule of non-discrimination and complicating adherence to the consensus-based norm of the existing regime. Moreover, it runs the risk of leading to a proliferation of specific agreements, with disciplines that may well go beyond the scope desired by developing countries for many years to come. Thus countries that opt out will not enjoy the benefits of existing multilateral disciplines, and might not be able to renegotiate them once they decide to sign on to a specific agreement.

The second option is to adopt an agreement-specific approach that would set specific criteria for individual agreements, which would form the basis for determining whether members could opt out of the application of negotiated disciplines for a limited period of time. As with the first option, following this second option would lead to differentiation between developing countries, but in this case differentiation would be based on objective criteria. The criteria used and the specific levels chosen would need to be the outcome of negotiations that strike a balance between a country's needs and the potential damage inflicted on other members by relaxing an agreed rule.

The options suggested here are intended simply to sketch out some possible ways forward. Multilateral discussions and negotiations may well lead to other solutions, but no matter which option is chosen, it should take account of the wide disparity in structural characteristics and approaches to economic policy among the many members of the WTO, and the consequent need for greater flexibility.

Asymmetries in global economic governance

An appropriate balance between national policy space and international disciplines and commitments requires not only strengthening the development dimension in the multilateral trading system but also an improvement in the global governance of international monetary and financial relations. At present, this balance is not warranted largely because of two asymmetries. First, contrary to the existing institutional structure in international trade, current international monetary and financial arrangements are not organized around a multilateral rules-based system that applies a specific set of core principles to all participants. This asymmetry has particularly strong adverse impacts on developing countries, because self-centred national monetary and financial policies can have much more damaging effects than those caused by trade and trade-related policies. Second, the multilateral rules and commitments governing international economic relations are, in legal terms, equally binding on all participants, but in economic terms they are biased towards an accommodation of the requirements of the developed countries.

Taken together, these two asymmetries result in international rules and practices that seek to deepen economic integration in a number of areas crucial to the interests and priorities of developed countries, and reduce the degrees of freedom for national economic policies in areas crucial for industrialization and economic catch-up in developing countries. Thus, in qualitative terms, and from the perspective of development, the scope of multilateral disciplines in the current pattern of global economic governance appears to be too narrow in the area of international monetary and financial relations, but may well be too broad in the area of international trade.

This is so because the rapid pace of globalization in monetary and financial relationships has not been accompanied by an equally rapid change in multilateral monetary and financial rules and disciplines. Above all, the existing system lacks institutional arrangements for the enforcement of multilateral discipline on exchange rates. Until the early 1970s, the Bretton Woods system obliged central banks to intervene in foreign-exchange markets in order to maintain exchange-rate stability within a narrow band and restrict short-term arbitrage flows which had proven so damaging in the inter-war period. By defining narrow exchange-rate bands, the Bretton Woods system limited the ability of governments to manipulate the exchange rates of their currencies. These institutional arrangements allowed the system to maintain a balance between national policy autonomy on the one hand and multilateral disciplines on the other. Sacrificing formal monetary autonomy was rewarded by stability in the financial markets and better foresight in international trade and in related decisions concerning investment in fixed capital.

The IMF Articles of Agreement provided for changes in par values in cases of fundamental disequilibria in foreign trade in order to allow the member countries to prevent or correct balance-of-payments disequilibria without having to resort to measures "destructive of national or international prosperity" (Article 1). In many cases such measures were supported by appropriate financing of foreign obligations to soften adjustment pressures. However, following the termination of the Bretton Woods exchange-rate system, the balance between financing and adjustment in crisis situations was gradually lost. The provision of liquidity to allow countries to weather payments difficulties was often inadequate, while the IMF started to impose extensive adjustment requirements in macroeconomic and even in structural policies.

Today, the IMF may intervene in a country's exchange-rate policy only if that country asks for financial support from the Fund and thus becomes subject to IMF conditionality. By contrast, negotiations on exchange rates among the most important currencies, when they occur, are held outside the IMF, mainly in the G-7 meetings or in bilateral talks among the major industrialized countries. Indeed, the institution that is in charge of promoting exchange-rate stability and preventing excessive and prolonged payments disequilibrium is unable to impose meaningful disciplines over the policies of those countries that run the most significant external imbalances and whose exchange-rate volatility has the greatest – negative – impact on the international economy. The Fund's policy oversight is confined primarily to its poorest members who need to draw on its resources because of their lack of access to private sources of finance and, occasionally, to emerging-market economies that experience disruptions in financial markets and financial crises. As a result, the bulk of adjustment in case of external imbalances is concentrated on a group of developing and transition economies, despite the fact that the source of such imbalances may occur in the developed world.

The lack of a functioning financial framework in a globalized economy requires a new and multilateral approach to the management of the most important international price – the exchange rate. A new or reformed institution that promotes a system of stable exchange rates to ensure a predictable trading environment would need to provide more symmetrical treatment to all member countries. The main objective of such an institution would be the prevention of systemic financial crises based on a close monitoring of trade imbalances and global exchange-rate misalignments in both surplus and deficit countries. Separating surveillance from lending decisions and assigning it to an independent authority could improve its quality, legitimacy and impact.

Supachai Panitchpakdi
Secretary-General of UNCTAD

Chapter I

GLOBAL IMBALANCES AS A SYSTEMIC PROBLEM

A. Global growth

Since 2002 the performance of the world economy has had a strong positive impact on growth and poverty reduction in the developing countries, thereby contributing to progress towards the Millennium Development Goals (MDGs). The expansion of world output continued unabated in 2005, with a growth rate of 3.6 per cent. Output is expected to expand in 2006 at a similar pace as in 2005. High prices for oil and industrial raw materials and a tendency towards more restrictive monetary policies as well as turbulence in the financial markets have not yet had a significant negative impact on global growth. Nevertheless, the risks of a slowdown are increasing.

The upswing of the world economy after 2002 has been shared by all regions, although expansion in the economies in transition has slowed down somewhat since 2004. Developing countries, including many of the poorest countries, have benefited from continuing strong demand for primary commodities but some of them have also had to carry a higher burden of rising costs for imported oil and other raw materials (see annex 1 to this chapter for an analysis of commodity prices and terms of trade). On the other hand, global eco-

nomic performance continues to be accompanied by serious imbalances in the world economy, and these should give rise to caution regarding prospects for the coming years as their correction could have serious repercussions for developing countries.

To some extent, developing countries have themselves contributed to setting the pace for global growth, with strong investment dynamics and an overall growth rate of about 6 per cent for the group as a whole. In particular, rapid growth in China and India has contributed to this outcome, not only because of their statistical weight as large economies but also because they serve as an engine for trade in manufactures within Asia. Moreover, their rapid growth, combined with their increasingly intense use of energy and metals,[1] has sustained international demand for a wide range of primary commodities. Inflation has remained subdued despite some countries reducing or even suppressing subsidies for energy prices. In this environment of moderate inflation, macroeconomic policies have remained accommodating and domestic demand in developing countries has been contributing increasingly to gross domestic product (GDP) growth.

Table 1.1

WORLD OUTPUT GROWTH, 2001–2006[a]

(Annual percentage change)

Region/country	1990–2000[b]	2001	2002	2003	2004	2005[c]	2006[d]
World	**2.9**	**1.5**	**1.8**	**2.7**	**4.1**	**3.6**	**3.6**
Developed countries	**2.5**	**1.2**	**1.2**	**2.0**	**3.1**	**2.7**	**2.7**
of which:							
Japan	1.1	0.4	0.1	1.8	2.3	2.7	2.8
United States	3.5	0.8	1.6	2.7	4.2	3.5	3.1
European Union	2.2	1.9	1.2	1.2	2.5	1.6	2.3
of which:							
European Union-15	2.2	1.9	1.1	1.1	2.3	1.4	2.2
Euro area	2.1	1.8	0.9	0.8	2.1	1.3	2.0
France	2.0	2.1	1.2	0.9	2.3	1.2	2.1
Germany	1.8	1.2	0.1	-0.2	1.6	0.9	1.8
Italy	1.6	1.8	0.4	0.3	1.2	0.0	1.0
United Kingdom	2.7	2.2	2.0	2.5	3.2	1.7	2.3
South-East Europe and CIS	**-4.3**	**5.9**	**5.2**	**7.2**	**7.9**	**6.3**	**6.0**
CIS	-5.0	6.2	5.3	7.8	8.2	6.8	6.3
South-East Europe	-1.0	4.8	4.8	4.5	6.6	4.6	4.8
Developing countries	**4.9**	**2.6**	**3.8**	**5.1**	**7.0**	**6.2**	**6.2**
Developing countries, excluding China	**4.0**	**1.4**	**2.6**	**3.9**	**6.2**	**5.3**	**5.3**
Latin America	3.2	0.3	-0.8	2.0	5.7	4.4	4.6
Africa	2.7	3.7	3.4	4.7	5.1	5.3	5.9
Asia	6.3	3.6	6.1	6.5	7.9	7.2	7.0
West Asia	3.9	-0.2	3.9	5.0	7.3	5.7	5.1
East and South Asia	7.0	4.5	6.5	6.8	8.0	7.4	7.3

Source: UNCTAD secretariat calculations, based on UNCTAD *Handbook of Statistics* online; United Nations, Department of Economic and Social Affairs (UN/DESA); and national sources. 2006 forecasts: UN/DESA, *World Economic Situation and Prospects as of mid-2006.*
a Calculations are based on GDP at constant 2000 dollars.
b Average.
c Preliminary.
d Forecasts updated in May 2006.

As a result economic growth in East and South Asia, which exceeded 7 per cent in 2005, is expected to continue at similar rates in 2006 (table 1.1). Other parts of the developing world will also continue to grow relatively quickly. For 2006, a growth rate of 4.6 per cent in Latin America, 6 per cent in Africa and in the Commonwealth of Independent States (CIS) should be possible; in West Asia, growth will probably remain at around 5 per cent even if the volume of oil production cannot keep growing at the same rate as in previous years. With monetary policy freed from the chains of un-

sustainable exchange-rate regimes, Latin America as a whole has succeeded in transmitting external stimulus into the domestic economy without reviving inflationary tendencies. Real per capita GDP in the region will grow significantly for the third consecutive year. The recovery was accompanied by a significant decline in unemployment; the unemployment rate fell from 11 per cent in 2002 to 9.1 per cent in 2005.

Another remarkable feature in the evolution of the world economy has been the ability of many

African countries to maintain high growth rates since 2003. Regional growth has accelerated in every year since 2003, and the 6.6 per cent growth expected for sub-Saharan Africa (excluding Nigeria and South Africa) in 2006 is the highest growth rate of a sub-region after East Asia. In several countries, higher government revenues following the hike in the prices of some export commodities seemed to spill over into the domestic economy and stimulate domestic spending without causing higher inflation.

Developed countries will maintain an economic expansion of between 2.5 and 3 per cent. In the United States a more neutral monetary policy, a likely slowdown of housing prices and the impact of high energy prices are expected to decelerate private consumption and investment in the second half of 2006. United States exports have recovered somewhat since 2003, but imports will continue outpacing exports. The opposite is true for Western Europe. There, despite a modest recovery of domestic demand, exports remain the driving force for output growth in the major economies. In Japan, the long deflationary phase appears to have come to an end; GDP growth will remain stable at 2.8 per cent and domestic demand is recovering, following a breakneck increase in exports during the last four years. However, the foreseeable end of a very expansionary monetary policy associated with measures aimed at fiscal consolidation might temper the rapid growth witnessed in the last quarter of 2005 and the first quarter of 2006.

B. Turbulences in financial markets

There have recently been signs of increasing volatility in stock, commodities and currency markets as well as in short-term capital outflows from some emerging markets, some of the ingredients that have made for financial crises in the past. The dollar is highly vulnerable and international investors appear to have become nervous in the face of continuing global imbalances and rising interest rates. After years of calm, with increasing private capital flows to the emerging markets, there is a new threat of hot money being withdrawn overnight. Indeed, a number of developing countries have experienced a sharp drop in their stock market prices and some emerging-market currencies have lost markedly against the dollar, the euro and the yen as well as against those currencies that are closely attached to them.

After years of calm, with increasing private capital flows to the emerging markets, there is a new threat of hot money being withdrawn overnight.

However, this turbulence is limited only to some areas and to a number of countries with rather high current-account deficits. There is hardly any evidence that a major financial crisis is looming, comparable to the Asian or Latin American crises some ten years ago. Taking the current account as an indicator of external vulnerability, most emerging-market economies appear to be less vulnerable than at the time of the big shocks during the past two decades. Overall, the situation of developing coun-

Figure 1.1

NUMBER OF DEVELOPING AND TRANSITION ECONOMIES WITH CURRENT-ACCOUNT DEFICIT, SELECTED REGIONS, 1990–2005

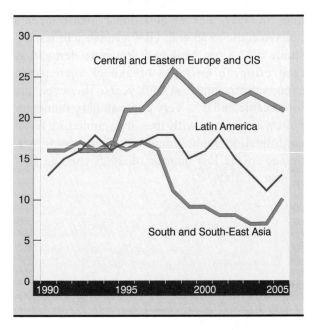

Source: UNCTAD secretariat calculations, based on IMF, *World Economic Outlook*, April 2006.

Note: For Central and Eastern Europe and CIS, the number of new reporting countries increased from 24 to 25 in 1995, and to 27 in 1998. South and South-East Asia correspond to the country grouping of East and South Asia, excluding Macao (China) and the Democratic People's Republic of Korea.

tries is much better today than it was before the big crises of the 1990s. In 1996, the current account of a group of 22 countries in South Asia and South-East Asia had turned slightly into deficit (-1.2 per cent of GDP) after a decade of consistent surpluses. Seventeen out of the 22 countries recorded deficits. Latin America in 1998, one year before its crisis, had increased its traditional deficit to 4.5 per cent, with all the 19 countries on the continent recording current-account deficits (fig. 1.1). This compares with a deficit of nearly 6 per cent at the beginning of the debt crisis in the early 1980s.

By contrast, in 2005 the group of South and East Asian countries recorded a large surplus on its current account (4.6 per cent of GDP), and only ten of the 22 countries were in deficit, after that

number had been down to seven in 2004. The Latin American region as a whole is also in surplus, on the order of 1.3 per cent of GDP, and only some smaller countries in Central America are presenting significant current-account deficits. The group of countries most vulnerable to capital flight and financial stress is located in Central and Eastern Europe and the CIS. In that region (excluding the major hydrocarbon exporters, the Russian Federation and Kazakhstan), 21 out of 25 countries recorded relatively high and stable current-account deficits of around 5 to 6 per cent of GDP during the last ten years.

During the second quarter of 2006, several East European countries and some other emerging economies were hit by financial turbulences, recording losses in their stock market values (among them Hungary, Latvia, Lithuania, Romania, South Africa, Turkey and Ukraine) or their currency values (as in Hungary, South Africa and Turkey), while the spreads on their international debt increased moderately. In some cases these episodes show similarities to the typical speculative cycle as experienced in the Asian as well as in the Latin American or Russian crises.[2] In the context of fighting inflation, relative high short-term interest rates attracted short-term capital inflows that triggered nominal and real appreciation of the currency, expanded domestic credit and fed price bubbles in financial markets; at some point, overvalued currencies widened the current-account balance and increased the nervousness of investors as well as the vulnerability of the economy to sudden capital outflows. So far these financial turbulences have been contained, but some observers warn that there is a significant risk of contagion because several countries share similar vulnerabilities and common creditors (Roubini and Menegatti, 2006).

Nevertheless, apart from the economies mentioned, which carry relatively high current-account deficits, the risk of a financial crisis on a global scale originating in the developing world is relatively small. Most of the countries affected by the former crises have been careful not to jeopardize the beneficial situation brought about by a certain currency undervaluation or high export prices, and have protected a current-account surplus that they had been able to achieve under the strains of devaluation and recession.

C. The systemic character of the global imbalances

1. Alternative views on external imbalances

Despite growing surpluses in the current account in the developing world, a conclusive explanation of the global imbalances cannot be found without looking carefully at the relationship between the United States on the one hand and a small number of big surplus countries including Japan, Germany, China and the major oil exporters on the other (fig. 1.2). At this moment, however, there is not even consensus among policymakers and experts on the very nature and the seriousness of the imbalances, let alone on the politics of a multilateral approach to correct them. Without a comprehensible approach identifying the potential risk involved in huge current-account deficits and surpluses shared by the major players, a solution is out of reach.

In general, conclusive explanations for current-account balances are not easy to find. But beyond the traditional approaches that have been tried out to explain trade flows in the past, in the current discussion it is not even clear whether the current-account imbalances are mainly caused from the trade side or from the capital side of the balance. One view places primary responsibility on trade flows, stressing the fact that, by definition, a current-account balance describes the difference between current receipts and expenditures for internationally traded goods and services and income payments. The other view, putting major emphasis on capital flows, focuses on the fact that from a national perspective, the current-account balance always exactly equals the gap between national saving and domestic investment. Although it should be clear from the outset that such *ex post* identities cannot by themselves provide an explanation or indicate a direction of causality, they are nonetheless taken as starting points for divergent tracks of analysis that lead to different policy recommendations.

The view that puts capital flows and national savings at centre stage concludes that the decision to save a high share of disposable income leads to a capital-account deficit (i.e. net capital outflows), as not all these savings can be used productively inside national boundaries. The opposite outcome, a current-account deficit, is the result of the domestic propensity to invest being in excess of the national propensity to save. Again, this view flirts with stating a tautology by using the identity of the current-account balance being always equal to the difference between national saving and domestic investment as a meaningful explanation. The advocates of this hypothesis assert that trade balances are basically the result of the decisions by national agents to consume either

> Unforeseen shocks can occur and macroeconomic prices can go fundamentally wrong, with entire economies losing competitiveness and suffering dire consequences for growth and jobs.

Figure 1.2

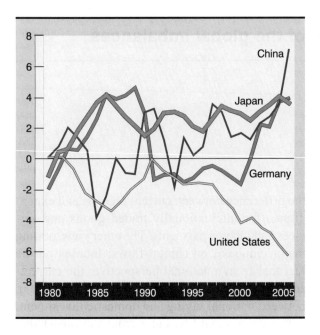

CURRENT-ACCOUNT BALANCE AS A
PERCENTAGE OF GDP IN CHINA, GERMANY,
JAPAN AND THE UNITED STATES,
1980–2005

Source: IMF, *World Economic Outlook*, April 2006.
  Note: Before 1992, data for Germany refer to West Germany.

now or at a later stage. Consequently, in this approach a balanced current account is not regarded as a meaningful economic policy target for individual countries. Rather, this view asserts that in a world of liberalized financial markets, global savings should always flow toward their best use. It is held that through the arbitrage of capital flowing from excess-saving countries toward countries with more plentiful profitable investment opportunities, the global economy achieves a more efficient allocation of resources than would ever be possible without free capital mobility.

The alternative explanation of imbalances is more substantive in its main message, as it does not simply rely on a description of import and export movements but considers swings in trade flows induced by large movements in the relative prices of tradable and non-tradable goods and services, and in the international competitiveness of countries to be the main forces of change. For

example, it stresses the role of commodity prices in the development of the current accounts of producers of important commodities like oil. According to this view, the decision of private households to save less does not by itself affect the trade balance if the additional demand can be satisfied by competitive domestic production. The decline in the private household savings rate could be compensated by other sources of national savings: business profits in the first place, but also by higher government saving or lower government de-saving due to higher tax receipts. Hence, in the approach that focuses on the causes of trade flows, the relationship between national saving and the trade balance is much more complex than in the other approach, as it involves all the relevant agents in one country and all the agents in all the other countries, including policymakers.

In such an environment unforeseen shocks can occur and macroeconomic prices like the nominal and the real exchange rates can go fundamentally wrong, with entire countries losing competitiveness and suffering dire consequences for growth and jobs. Hence, deficits or surpluses in the current account may not just be the result of voluntary decisions by well-informed agents or groups of agents; those imbalances may indicate overall policy errors or pathological developments in the broadest sense. Based on this view, under the Bretton Woods regime of fixed but adjustable exchange rates, long-lasting current-account deficits were considered as indicating "fundamental disequilibria" in international trade pointing to the need to depreciate the nominal exchange rate and thereby improve the international competitiveness of the country concerned.

A radical change in the perception of balance-of-payments imbalances occurred by the mid-1980s. Accordingly, the developing world's domestic financial liberalization was increasingly accompanied by capital-account liberalization so as to allow for maximum efficiency in the international allocation of resources through unfettered market forces. Obviously the free flow of capital, even if precipitating long-lasting net flows into one country associated with current-account deficits, would not indicate any pathological phenomenon according to this perspective. By the early 1990s, the view that put capital flows first and recommended a hands-off approach by governments concerning regulation of flows and of the exchange rate was far advanced, spanning the whole of the developed world and an increasing portion of the developing world as well.

Financial turmoil and crisis, however, became the almost natural concomitant of the liberalized system. Latin America, Eastern Europe and even the notoriously stable Asian emerging markets had to face tremendous financial problems after having had high and/or lasting current-account deficits (see fig. 1.1). The resulting outcome of crisis and the related policy actions to fight the outflow of capital was dramatic for the real economies of these countries, their populations and their politics.

Consequently, many developing countries moved away from the open-capital-account-*cum*-floating-rate approach and back to a position of strength that would reduce their exposure to external events, limiting their dependence on international capital flows. To achieve this, a significant number of countries in Asia and in Latin America tried to preserve the favourable competitive positions they had reached after their financial crises and devaluations by unilaterally pegging their currency vis-à-vis the dollar at a slightly undervalued level (see *TDR 2004*, chap. IV). With that move the key assumptions of the position that advocates fully liberalized capital flows, namely that net saving flows are harmless and that capital tends to flow from capital-rich industrial countries to capital-poor developing countries, have been contradicted. In fact, since the Asian crisis capital has been flowing in the opposite direction: many well-performing developing countries do not import net savings from the rich industrial countries, where profitable investment opportunities are supposedly becoming scarcer, but are exporting their own savings (see UNCTAD, 2006). The stark fact, which is closely related, is that many developing countries are accumulating huge amounts of foreign exchange reserves that are reinvested mainly in securities, such as government bonds, in the rich countries. Indeed, global savings flows head primarily in the direction of the largest and richest industrial country, the United States and their government bonds.

2. The main players

With a few exceptions, *Japan's* current account has been in surplus since the start of the 1980s. At the same time, the Japanese performance strongly challenges the approach to explaining current-account imbalances mainly by saving-investment imbalances. According to that explanation, a current-account surplus in the industrial economies outside the United States derives from "high desired savings" of an ageing population and "low prospective returns to domestic investment" (Bernanke, 2005). If this were the case, the household savings rate should have increased in Japan and business savings – arising from profits – should have decreased in parallel with the investment rate. However, exactly the opposite of that has happened: gross household saving in Japan declined steadily from 12 per cent of GDP in 1998 to 6 per cent in 2005, while business saving increased considerably.

Additionally, government saving plummeted from a surplus or a positive saving contribution of 2.1 per cent of GDP to a negative rate of 6 per cent in 2005, thus calling into question the widespread hypothesis that current-account deficits (national dis-saving) and budget deficits (government dis-saving) are intertwined. Therefore, Japan's current-account surplus can hardly be explained by an autonomous expansion of national savings. The more convincing explanation draws on Japan's export competitiveness, due to low inflation and low unit labour cost increases as well as Japan's policy to defend the value of its currency over extended periods through central bank intervention. Recently the effects of fast economic expansion in Asia, particularly in China, and rising net foreign investment income, which now even exceeds the positive trade balance, play a particularly important role.

> Many countries with open capital accounts moved from floating to policies that give them greater control over the exchange rate and reduce their dependence on capital inflows.

The other major industrialized country with a large current-account surplus, *Germany*, also has a long-standing tradition as a surplus country. This tradition was interrupted in the early 1990s in the wake of unification (fig. 1.2). Recently, the swing in the German current account to renewed surpluses is closely associated with the Government strategy of raising international competitiveness by limiting the rise of national unit labour costs. From the German perspective, wage disinflation has proved highly successful in boosting external competitiveness and net exports ever since attaining export surpluses became re-established as a key policy target in the mid-1990s. As a result, Germany's current-account balance has improved – from -1.7 per cent of GDP in 2000 to 4.1 per cent of 2005 – while its closest trading partners saw corresponding movements into deficit.

It is quite remarkable that Germany, the world's third largest economy after the United States and Japan and the world's biggest exporter, hardly features in today's intense international debate over global imbalances. Germany's huge surplus is hidden behind the euro area's overall fairly balanced current-account position.[3] Even more than Japan, Germany during the 1990s has relied on belt tightening policies and low unit labour cost increases to stimulate GDP growth through exports. The flip side of this policy has been low domestic income growth and low domestic demand, as employment growth did not compensate for anaemic income development. In this way, import growth was not only confined by limited competitiveness but by low domestic absorption as well.

Since 2002 *China's* current-account surplus has been on the rise and attained a globally significant level of $160 billion, or 7 per cent of its GDP, in 2005. This sharp rise in its external surplus position has emerged despite the fact that China is growing at a breakneck pace and, as a major oil importing country, has suffered a sharp increase in its oil bill. A number of factors are behind the recent explosion in China's external position, an explosion that is also remarkable given the fact that some of its direct regional competitors sharply devalued their real exchange rates in the context of the 1997–98 Asian crisis, whereas China did not.

This structural change concerning China seems to be closely related to foreign direct in-

vestment (FDI). FDI growth during the 1990s can be seen as a key factor explaining the rapid increase in Chinese competitiveness. Targeting world markets, foreign investors producing manufactures in China were able to combine state-of-the-art foreign technology with well-educated but low-paid Chinese labour, which secured them absolute cost advantages by a very large margin. Despite Chinese money wages in manufacturing growing strongly, between 12 and 16 per cent annually in recent years, unit labour costs in manufacturing are falling (*TDR 2005*, chap. I, section E). Labour productivity, with growth rates of close to 20 per cent in manufacturing, is virtually exploding. Moreover, with the Chinese renminbi's nominal exchange rate pegged to the dollar, falling unit labour costs in manufacturing have effectively delivered a massive but untypical "real devaluation in manufacturing".

Of course China is today under heavy criticism for allegedly preserving an "undervalued exchange rate". And, beginning in July 2005, China has undertaken steps to make its exchange-rate regime more flexible, albeit very gradually (since July 2005 the renminbi has appreciated from its previous dollar peg of 8.28 to around 8 by May 2006). However, when the role of FDI is taken into account the verdict on China's alleged undervalued exchange rate is anything but straightforward. It should be recalled that the renminbi appreciated in line with the dollar until 2001, withstanding the regional currency storms of 1997–98. In nominal effective terms the renminbi has depreciated by less than the dollar since 2002. Gains in external competitiveness arising from strong labour productivity growth in one sector, at the same time as overall money wages are growing in line with nominal GDP growth, are normally not considered to be the result of a "beggar-thy-neighbour" strategy.

As part of an orderly unwinding of global imbalances, and in view of China's very high investment rate, advocates of the saving approach urge China to reduce its saving and to consume more. But such an assertion is difficult to understand, given the fact that the private households saving rate, at 16 per cent (IMF, 2006), is not outside the normal range, while consumption in China has been growing at a rate of around 9 per cent annually since the beginning of the 1990s in real terms. Additionally, China's investment rate (fixed capital investment as per cent of GDP), at over 40 per cent, is extremely high. This undermines the argument based on "underinvestment" or "oversaving" that advocates of the saving approach to understanding the current account would have to use to explain the net export of capital from that country.

Commodity producers, particularly the big oil producers in OPEC and the Russian Federation, form another group of surplus countries that is gaining importance as a counterpart to the United States deficit. Oil producers provide the classic example of dramatically rising current-account surpluses in the wake of, from their point of view, big positive shocks triggered by soaring energy prices and improving terms of trade. Clearly, the oil price boom since 2004 has not turned oil producers into net capital exporters because they "decided" to save more or invest less as their export revenues increased. Rather, as the main beneficiaries of the global redistribution of income induced by a rapid increase in oil prices, they are simply unable to boost their spending for imports at the same speed as their incomes rise. Basically, the additional saving in these countries is induced by windfall profits, not by the decision of any agent in the country to save more out of a given income.

The economy of the *United States* is very often seen as the original and ultimate cause of these global imbalances and it is undeniable that this economy has played a key role in the emergence of the present global disequilibrium. The prevailing view, however, that the United States attracted more and more global savings out of a given global income or a given global savings pool is questionable. Rather, it is the United States' role as driver of the global income generation process that was the precondition for the creation of these savings, as embodied in rising current-account surpluses elsewhere. Its role as the key global growth engine has pushed the United States economy to become the main demander of global capital.

> The prevailing view that the United States attracted more and more global savings out of a given global income or a given global savings pool is questionable.

The Economic Report of the President recently described the external imbalance of the United States as a "capital account surplus", mainly caused by domestic saving and investment balances both in the United States and in the rest of the world. According to this Report, some major economies are net capital exporters because they "have supplies of domestic saving that exceed domestic investment opportunities": Japan and Germany due to falling investment rates; China and the Russian Federation owing to rising saving rates. In this view, capital inflows to the United States reflect the low rate of national savings on the one hand, and several factors of economic strength, namely high output and productivity growth and a favourable business climate favouring "global competitiveness" on the other. Consequently, "in principle, the United States can continue to receive net capital inflows (and run current account deficits) indefinitely, provided it uses these inflows in ways that promote its future growth and help the United States to remain an attractive destination for foreign investment" (*Economic Report of the President 2006*: 144, 146).

Again, the alternative view attaches more relevance to trade outcomes and puts a loss of competitiveness of United States industry on centre stage, with the noticeable exception of high-technology branches (Aglietta, 2005). The fact that industrial production grew by only 5 per cent between 2000 and 2005 in the United States, while the consumption of durable goods expanded during the same period by more than 30 per cent, indicates that the reason is not that American consumers are saving too little, but that they are consuming too many imported goods.

Again, the causal nexus between national saving and the trade balance is a rather complex phenomenon. The current-account balance is not just determined by "decisions" taken on the level of private or public agents in one country; rather, it is determined by all the influences that shape decisions to spend or save inside and outside the country under consideration. There is generally no easy way to attribute the results of this complex interaction to the "saving decisions" of any one particular group of actors in any one particular country. All-important interdependencies exist. As private households undertake efforts to save more, this may force public and corporate savings down. Likewise, with trade-offs between the saving behaviour of the different sectors in any one country, the external balance cannot simply be attributed to the autonomous decisions of any one of them.

3. Benign or malign unwinding of global imbalances?

Today's global imbalances are to an important extent a reflection and consequence of vital systemic deficiencies. The lack of a viable multilateral financial system is the most important of these. At this juncture it owes mainly to the flexibility and pragmatism of the United States macroeconomic policy management that the systemic deficiencies in the global economic order have not led to global deflation yet, but have "only" resulted in these imbalances. But even with the United States macroeconomic policy pragmatism, the global structure of production, trade and finance has become precarious. China, based on the long-lasting renminbi-dollar peg, has transformed itself into a kind of back boiler of the United States growth locomotive. After the Asian and Latin American crises, more and more developing countries have come to follow a similar path of adjustment by stabilizing their exchange rate at a relatively low level, running sizeable current-account surpluses and accumulating huge dollar reserves.

While this practice is widely suspected to be sub-optimal, in many respects it represents the only feasible way in which developing countries can successfully adapt to the systemic deficiencies afflicting today's global economic order, i.e., the absence of symmetric obligations of surplus and deficit countries. It is no surprise that the undervaluation-*cum*-intervention strategy is especially prevalent among developing countries that have gone through currency crises in their recent past, following previous liberalization of their respective financial systems and capital accounts. Having learned the hard way that reliance on supposedly benign capital inflows rarely pays off as a sustainable development strategy, a growing number of developing countries have shifted to an alternative approach that relies on trade surpluses as their engine for investment and growth. This strategy requires them to defend the competitiveness positions they achieved in the wake of financial crises. But this also presupposes that at least one country in the global economy accepts running the corresponding trade deficit.

The problem is that the United States may have become overburdened by having played the lead role as global growth engine for too long. It could largely ignore its external imbalance because no serious conflict between it and sustaining full employment and price stability has arisen up to this point. The potential for such a conflict is itself one key risk. Globally rising concerns, including among financial market participants, about the continuously growing external imbalance is another. It must be considered unlikely that the United States' personal saving rate will decline by another 5 percentage points over the next decade or that the public budget will be allowed to deteriorate by another 6 per cent of GDP. In this case the world economy will have to do without the growth stimuli it has become used to over the last fifteen years.

> The problem is that the United States may have become overburdened by having played the lead role as global growth engine for too long.

The possibility of a slowdown in the United States economy looks increasingly likely. There is the prospect that this would entail further dollar depreciation, which would tend to restore competitiveness and, together with the economic slowdown, would help re-balance the United States economy. Alas, given the existing structure and concentrated dependence of global growth on demand stimuli from the United States, it is indeed to be feared that a marked slowdown in United States growth would be spread and amplified in just the same way as the positive impulses have been all these years. This could quite easily unravel the momentum in development progress and poverty reduction seen in developing countries in recent times, and do so without there being any obvious fault on the part of these countries themselves.

The main reason for the increasingly unmanageable global burden of the United States is not *per se* to be seen in rising numbers of developing countries running current-account surpluses. Rather, the gravity and urgency of the matter relates primarily to the fact that other key industrial countries, such as Japan and Germany, could have done more to contribute to the reduction of the global imbalances. Their huge external surplus positions, based on improved competitive positions, suggest that the required competitiveness gains on the part of the United States should mainly come at their expense. This process would be greatly eased if this were to occur in the context of buoyant domestic demand rather than the stagnant demand that has prevailed in these economies for all too long.

China's part in a benign unwinding of global imbalances differs from these two countries' roles. Since the beginning of the 1990s, China's domestic demand and its imports have grown very strongly indeed, and the country has played a vi-

> Japan and Germany could have done more to contribute to the reduction of the global imbalances.

tal role in spreading and sustaining growth momentum throughout the developing world, a process that must not be derailed. Therefore, renminbi revaluation should continue gradually rather than abruptly, taking due account of regional implications. Similar to China, oil producing countries have only recently come to play a significant role in the global imbalances. Oil producers should generally use benevolent terms-of-trade developments in favour of investment and diversification of their production structure. Should elevated oil prices persist, their contribution to a benign unwinding of global imbalances consists of a stronger domestic demand growth in line with higher incomes, extra expenditure being oriented towards social and physical investment aimed at diversifying the economy.

Crucially, what is needed for a benign unwinding of global imbalances is a responsible multilateral effort rather than pressure on the developing world. A well-coordinated international macroeconomic approach would considerably enhance the chances of the poorer countries to consolidate recent improvements in their growth performance. Without such an approach, developing countries have to defend their strategically favourable competitiveness positions and use the still-favourable monetary conditions to invest more and reduce their foreign indebtedness.

D. Low real interest rates: global savings glut versus global monetary conditions

1. A savings glut?

In the economic model explaining current-account imbalances by autonomous decisions of private households, the solution to the global imbalance problem is closely related to the problem of "too high savings" in the surplus countries. In this view, the alleged surplus of saving over investment finds evidence also in the historically-low real interest rates. Indeed, both long-term market rates and short-term policy rates have been extraordinarily low in recent years in developed and developing countries. Those observers (Bernanke, 2005; IMF, 2005, for instance) attributing the phenomenon to a "global savings glut" argue that while the supply of saving has substantially increased, the demand for saving, or, in other words, investment, has not kept up pace with the rise in supply, or has even diminished. Hence, excess supply in the capital market led to the observed decline of global interest rates.

This hypothesis offers a rebuttal to the widespread charge against the United States of causing global imbalances by saving too little; bouncing the ball back into the surplus countries' court. Rising capital exports (negative foreign saving) of a number of saving surplus countries in the industrial and developing world – the argument goes – have been passively mirrored by increasing capital imports (positive foreign saving) by the United States, enabling the latter to import more goods and services than it exports and run a current-account deficit. Rising capital-account surpluses in the balance-of-payments statistics at low interest rates are seen as evidence of a global savings surplus.

Yet, at a global level and from an *ex post* perspective – which is implied by the balance-of-payments approach as it focuses on *ex post* variables as observed in statistics – saving cannot exceed investment. The visible excess in saving over investment in current-account surplus countries implies the corresponding excess of investment over saving in current-account deficit countries. A *global* saving glut is a contradiction in terms. By linking the visible current-account imbalances with globally low interest rates, the proponents of the global savings glut hypothesis identify *ex post* visible variables with the plans of investors and savers in models of perfect foresight of the future income.

Of course, balance between saving and investment at the global level does not preclude the possibility of regional imbalances, which is what the current debate on global imbalances is really all about. But rising current-account surpluses (or excess national saving) cannot occur without corresponding current-account deficits (or deficient

> If "excess saving" could explain lower interest rates in surplus economies, the symmetrical "saving shortage" in deficit countries should have the opposite effect.

national saving) arising concomitantly elsewhere. A rising current-account surplus in one country, be it due to a slump in investment or more general demand weakness, currency depreciation or otherwise improved competitiveness, or income gains owing to improved terms of trade, can only arise if demand is sufficiently strong elsewhere so as to generate the income out of which the saving of the current-account surplus country is made possible in the first place. And if "excess saving" could explain lower interest rates in surplus economies – within the orthodox framework where the interest rate is the price that equilibrates saving and investment –, the symmetrical "saving shortage" in deficit countries should have the opposite effect, which means, the "saving glut" hypothesis cannot explain low levels of interest rates in the main deficit country, the United States (see annex 2 to this chapter for the theoretical background of the saving-investment relationship).

But if the idea of excess saving depressing interest rates in global capital markets is not a sound one, then why have interest rates fallen to historically low levels? Would they start rising again once the unwinding of global imbalances were under way? What other risks are present that could drive up interest rates, taking earlier experiences into account? And how can developing countries best benefit from low interest rates and protect themselves against rising rates?

2. Monetary policy and interest rates

Interest rates, both long-term market rates and short-term policy rates, have been extraordinary low in recent years in developed and developing countries. This seems to be not so much the result of a "global savings glut" but of global monetary conditions.

Paradoxically, there is widespread agreement concerning the decisive role of monetary policy for short-term rates but great hesitation to ac-

knowledge any influence of monetary policy on long-term rates. In fact, monetary policy directly controls short-term interest rates at a given market demand for money, but monetary tightening or easing will also impact on financial conditions in general through arbitrage and expectations, thereby indirectly influencing long-term interest rates. Longer-term interest rates can move in response to monetary policy decisions or in anticipation of them. In any case, arbitrage linkages mean that the level of interest rates is ultimately determined by monetary policy: either by national monetary policy, if sufficient policy space exists, or by global monetary conditions.

Essentially, given the very low inflation environment of today, low levels of interest rates are mainly a reflection of low cost pressure and correspondingly easy monetary policies. The macroeconomic situation in Japan and the euro area, as well as in countries in East Asia and Latin America that have gone through financial crises, is highly relevant in this context. In particular, the steep real devaluation in East Asian countries after their crises and the expansion of the Chinese industrial supply introduced a deflationary bias in manufacture markets that have more than compensated up to now for the rising price pressures they have put on several commodity markets. Moreover, higher oil prices have not spoiled the benign inflation outlook as wage growth has remained moderate in the face of high unemployment rates in many important countries.

> Given the very low inflation environment of today, low levels of interest rates are mainly a reflection of low cost pressure and correspondingly easy monetary policies.

In a nutshell, then, historically-low interest rates have been due to very easy monetary policies in place since the beginning of the new century. The burst in global liquidity is owed to the monetary policy response to deficient demand in some developed countries and to low cost pressure in labour markets.

During the 1970s, nominal short-term interest rates set by the G-7 central banks soared to 10 per cent and even reached 13 per cent in the early 1980s; they subsequently declined to around 4 per cent by 1993 and were cut below 2 per cent

Figure 1.3

INTEREST RATES, INFLATION AND CHANGES IN UNIT LABOUR COST IN THE G-7, 1970–2005

(GDP weighted average)

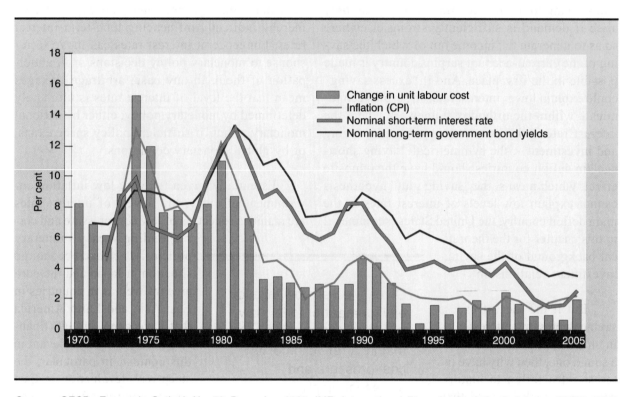

Source: OECD, *Economic Outlook No. 78*, December 2005; IMF, *International Financial Statistics* Database; OECD, *Main Economic Indicators* Database; and national sources for Germany.

Note: Unit labour cost is the ratio of labour compensation at current prices to value added at constant prices. It represents the current cost of labour to produce one unit of output and serves as an indicator of cost competitiveness.

ten years later. The picture for yields on G-7 government bonds with a maturity of 10 years is very similar: declining below 4 per cent in recent years compared with their peak of 13 per cent in the early 1980s (fig. 1.3). The tight monetary policy of the early 1980s, in response to the preceding inflationary experience of the 1970s, caused a severe recession in industrial countries. The adverse effects of tight money were even stronger in developing countries, especially in a number of middle-income countries that had accumulated large amounts of dollar-denominated debt at variable interest rates owed to commercial banks and were therefore particularly vulnerable to monetary decisions taken by the major industrial countries, especially the United States. Subsequently, interest rates in developed countries progressively

declined; even during the investment boom of the 1990s, interest rates remained relatively low. The Federal Reserve Funds rate peaked at only 6.5 per cent in May 2000, following a mild rise in inflation. As the investment boom turned into bust, interest rates were slashed aggressively. The United States Federal Reserve's aggressive monetary easing led the way to historically-low interest rates worldwide and global liquidity surged, spurred by the United States external deficit that led to a massive increase of liquidity elsewhere.

Monetary tendencies in developing countries followed conditions in industrial countries with a time lag. Short-term interest rates set by central banks in developing countries were quite high at the beginning of the 1980s, but ranged from 2 to

10 per cent in the majority of developing countries in 2005. Long-term government bond yields declined to low levels as well in recent years as yield spreads of emerging-market debts over G-7 debts shrank markedly and across the maturity spectrum. Global investors' search for yield raised the demand for high-yielding emerging-market instruments, especially as their issuers' trade positions and balance sheets started to look healthier. This was reinforced as emerging-market economies used the liquidity obtained through running current-account surpluses for repayment of debts, i.e. reductions in the supply of what global investors were keen to buy.

For other reasons as well, the historically-low interest rate cannot be explained by the mainstream theory. According to many observers, globalization has meant that capital has become relatively scarcer and labour relatively more abundant. This would seem to argue in favour of setting high real interest rates so as to induce sufficient saving, which is seen as the prerequisite for faster capital accumulation. In actual fact, however, real interest rates have fallen to historically-low levels. They have remained low despite global demand acceleration in 2004 and the gradual monetary tightening initiated by the United States Federal Reserve in June 2004.

> Workers and trade unions have learned that they cannot win the direct confrontation with employers and the indirect one with central banks, particularly in the case of an oil shock.

On the other hand, the increased relative abundance of labour due to globalization, or the threat of it at least, does seem to have contributed to keeping wages and unit-labour-cost increases in check. Cost-push inflation impulses from labour markets have been absent during the ongoing recovery in both developing and developed economies. Growth in unit labour costs, the main determinant of cost-push inflation, has remained subdued. Management threats to relocate production or outsource certain activities may be one factor in explaining this moderation. An alternative hypothesis is that workers and trade unions have learned the lesson that they cannot win both the direct confrontation with employers and the indirect one with central banks at the same time, particularly in the case of an oil shock.

Nevertheless, it is worth noting that despite supposedly uniform downward pressures on wages due to globalization, those industrial countries with a strong export performance but poor GDP and employment growth, like Germany and Japan, have had more pressure on wages than those faster-growing countries with better labour market performance like the United States and the United Kingdom that are poor export performers, and, respectively, have been subjected to greater pressure from globalized labour markets. ∎

Notes

1   For a detailed discussion of the determinants and implications of raw-material-intensity of production, especially in the fast-growing Asian economies, see *TDR 2005*, chap. II, section B.

2   For a general discussion of this phenomenon, see *TDR 2004*, chap. IV.

3   For instance, the IMF no longer mentions either Germany or the euro area in assessing rising global imbalances: "The U.S. current account deficit has continued to rise, matched by large surpluses in oil exporters, China and Japan, a number of small industrial countries, and other parts of emerging Asia" (IMF, 2006: 5).

References

Aglietta M (2005). L'hégémonie du dollar peut-elle être contestée? In CEPII, *L'économie Mondiale 2006*. Paris, Editions La Découverte, November.

Bernanke B (2005). The Global Saving Glut and the U.S. Current Account Deficit. Remarks at the Sandrige Lecture, Virginia Association of Economics, Richmond, Virginia, 14 April. Available at: www.federalreserve.gov/boarddocs/speeches/2005/200503102/default.htm.

Economic Report of the President (2006). Transmitted to the Congress in February 2006. United States Government Printing Office. Washington, DC.

IMF (2005). *World Economic Outlook*. Washington, DC, International Monetary Fund, September.

IMF (2006). *World Economic Outlook*. Washington, DC, International Monetary Fund, April.

Roubini N and Menegatti C (2006). Vulnerabilities in Central and Southern Europe, 1 June. Available at: www.rgemonitor.com.

UNCTAD (2006). *World Investment Report 2006*. United Nations publication, sales no. E.06.II.D.11, New York and Geneva.

UNCTAD (various issues). *Trade and Development Report*. United Nations publication, New York and Geneva.

COMMODITY PRICES AND TERMS OF TRADE

1. The commodity price boom since 2002

Since 2002, commodity producers in many developing countries have benefited from price increases for most of their products. The UNCTAD price index for non-fuel commodities rose by 44.8 per cent between 2002 and 2005 in current dollar terms (table 1.A1). While prices rose for all commodity groups, this upward movement was driven primarily by the minerals, ores and metals group, which increased by almost 100 per cent during this period. Prices of energy commodities also surged, particularly for crude petroleum, which increased by 114 per cent. At the beginning of 2006, nominal prices for metals and minerals, such as copper, nickel and zinc, as well as for crude petroleum reached historical record highs. Some soft commodities, such as coffee, rice, sugar and natural rubber have also experienced a significant upward push in prices in recent years.[1]

In 2005, commodity prices continued to increase, with the exception of vegetable oilseeds and oils, although they registered more moderate growth rates than in 2004. This reflects a certain correction at the beginning of the year on account of expectations that the commodity price boom was reaching its peak. However, prices rebounded in the second half of the year and continued rising into 2006 (fig. 1.A1). Commodity prices in real terms have therefore remained above their long-term trend, although they are still far below their levels of the 1970s and early 1980s. In 2005, the price index in real terms for all commodities was 56.6 per cent of the average of 1973–1981 and just 39 per cent of the peak of 1974. For soft commodity groups, even nominal prices thus far have not reached the levels of other previous peaks (fig. 1.A2).

The boom in commodity prices is the result of a combination of robust global demand and a slower than expected supply response, and, in recent months, a low level of inventories in a number of commodities. Moreover, there has been strong additional upward pressure from financial markets in the form of heavy investments in commodities as a financial asset. In 2005, a distinguishing feature in comparison with the previous two years was the effect of the dollar exchange rate on commodity prices. The increase in dollar-denominated commodity prices during 2002–2004 could also partly be explained by the depreciation of the dollar, as, typically, commodity prices move in the

Table 1.A1

WORLD PRIMARY COMMODITY PRICES, 2000–2005

(Percentage change over previous year)

Commodity group	2000	2001	2002	2003	2004	2005	2002–2005[a]
All commodities[b]	1.7	-3.6	0.8	8.1	19.4	12.1	44.8
All commodities (in SDRs)[b]	5.1	0.2	-0.8	-0.2	13.1	12.5	27.0
Food and tropical beverages	-0.1	0.4	0.4	2.3	13.2	8.8	26.0
Tropical beverages	-15.4	-20.6	11.7	6.2	6.4	25.5	41.8
Coffee	-25.1	-29.0	4.7	8.7	19.8	43.8	87.2
Cocoa	-22.1	22.7	63.3	-1.3	-11.8	-0.7	-13.5
Tea	6.8	-20.2	-9.5	8.4	2.1	9.1	20.8
Food	2.1	2.8	-0.5	1.9	13.9	7.2	24.4
Sugar	30.4	5.6	-20.3	2.9	1.1	37.9	43.6
Beef	5.6	10.0	-0.3	0.4	17.8	4.1	23.2
Maize	-2.8	1.1	10.4	6.5	5.0	-12.0	-1.6
Wheat	3.4	9.0	16.6	-0.7	6.8	-1.4	4.5
Rice	-18.2	-15.3	11.0	4.1	23.1	17.1	50.1
Bananas	-2.3	38.8	-9.6	-28.7	39.9	9.9	9.5
Vegetable oilseeds and oils	-20.3	-6.4	24.9	17.4	13.2	-9.5	20.3
Soybeans	5.0	-7.5	8.6	24.1	16.1	-10.4	29.2
Agricultural raw materials	3.1	-3.9	-2.4	19.8	9.9	7.1	41.0
Hides and skins	11.2	5.5	-2.9	-16.8	-1.7	-2.1	-19.9
Cotton	11.5	-19.0	-3.6	37.2	-3.3	-11.6	17.2
Tobacco	-3.7	0.0	-8.2	-3.5	3.6	1.5	1.4
Rubber	7.9	-14.1	33.1	41.7	20.3	15.2	96.3
Tropical logs	3.7	6.4	-10.5	20.1	19.2	0.3	43.6
Minerals, ores and metals	12.4	-10.8	-2.7	12.4	40.7	26.2	99.6
Aluminium	13.8	-6.8	-6.5	6.0	19.8	10.6	40.6
Phosphate rock	-0.4	-4.6	-3.3	-5.9	7.8	2.5	4.0
Iron ore	2.7	4.5	-1.1	8.5	17.4	71.5	118.5
Tin	0.6	-17.5	-9.4	20.6	73.8	-13.2	81.8
Copper	15.3	-13.0	-1.2	14.1	61.0	28.4	135.9
Nickel	43.7	-31.2	14.0	42.2	43.6	6.6	117.6
Tungsten ore	12.1	45.5	-41.8	18.0	22.9	120.7	220.1
Lead	-9.7	4.9	-4.9	13.8	72.0	10.2	115.7
Zinc	4.0	-21.0	-12.1	5.1	29.1	27.9	73.7
Gold	0.1	-2.9	14.4	17.3	12.6	8.7	43.5
Crude petroleum	55.6	-13.3	2.0	15.8	30.7	41.3	113.9
Memo item:							
Manufactures[c]	-4.8	-2.2	0.7	8.7	7.7	2.8	20.3

Source: UNCTAD, *Commodity Price Bulletin*, various issues; and United Nations Statistics Division (UNSD), *Monthly Bulletin of Statistics*, various issues.

Note: In current dollars unless otherwise specified.

   a   Percentage change between 2002 and 2005.
   b   Excluding crude petroleum.
   c   Export unit value of manufactured goods of developed countries.

opposite direction to that of the dollar exchange rate. A depreciating dollar meant that commodity prices rose much less, or fell, in terms of other major currencies. In the course of 2005, the dollar appreciated, although the average exchange-rate change for the year was quite similar to that of 2004. However, this was not associated with a weakening of dollar-denominated commodity prices; in terms of special drawing rights (SDRs), the commodity price index rose by 12.5 per cent in 2005, close to the increase in current dollars of 12.1 per cent (table 1.A1).

Typically, commodity prices exhibit cyclical behaviour, with alternating booms and busts. This is reflected in fig. 1.A1, which shows the evolution of monthly commodity prices since their last peak of 1996–1997. The subsequent commodity crisis was particularly dramatic, as the worldwide contraction of demand was reinforced by the financial crisis in Asia. The new turnaround was then stimulated by the dynamism and catch-up growth of the Chinese economy. For the industrial raw materials and energy sectors, this cyclical behaviour is strongly influenced by demand and correlates with global industrial and economic activity. For agricultural commodities, variations arise mostly from the supply side and in some cases (e.g. non-tree crops), where supply takes less time to react to the increasing prices, cycles may be shorter. Agricultural prices are often also influenced by external factors, such as meteorological conditions, plant diseases and pests. For instance, recent coffee prices have been favoured by smaller than expected crop output in major producing countries. Crops were affected by drought followed by heavy rains in Viet Nam, hurricanes in Central American countries, and drought and lower yields in Brazil.

At the present relatively high levels of commodity prices, there are diverging views among analysts as to which phase of the cycle commodity markets are going through, and even about the nature of the cycle itself. According to some analysts, the current cycle is no different from previous ones, and as expectations vis-à-vis prices change, prices should begin to fall in the course of the coming year. In the longer term, this trend will be reinforced by new production coming on-stream. Other analysts believe commodity prices will remain high for a long time, and will even continue

Figure 1.A1

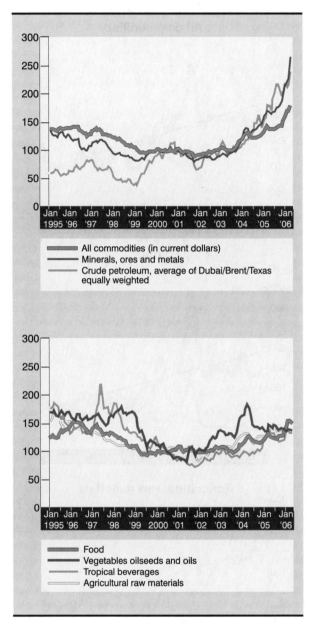

MONTHLY COMMODITY PRICE INDICES BY COMMODITY GROUP, 1995–2006

(Index numbers, 2000 = 100)

Source: UNCTAD, *Commodity Price Bulletin*, various issues.

to rise as a result of the constantly increasing raw material needs of China and other emerging economies. Another factor in support of this view is the long lead time for new investment in fuels and metals and minerals.

Figure 1.A2

NON-FUEL PRIMARY COMMODITY PRICES, NOMINAL AND REAL,[a]
BY COMMODITY GROUP, 1960–2005

(Index numbers, 2000 = 100)

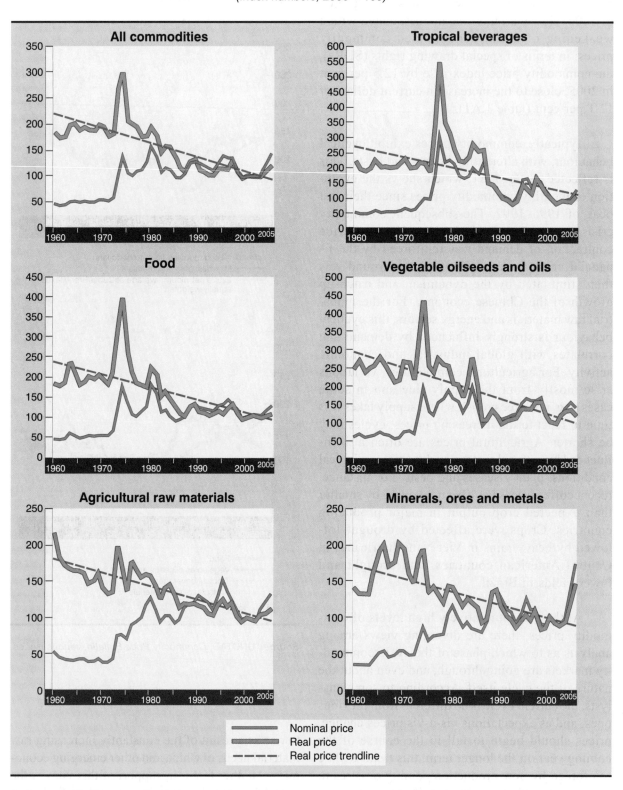

Source: UNCTAD, *Commodity Price Bulletin,* various issues; and UNSD, *Monthly Bulletin of Statistics,* various issues.
   a Real prices are deflated by the export unit value of manufactured goods of developing countries.

Table 1.A2

**GROWTH IN CONSUMPTION OF SELECTED PRIMARY COMMODITIES:
CHINA AND THE REST OF THE WORLD, 2002–2005**

(Per cent)

	Consumption growth			Contribution of China to global consumption growth	Share of China in global consumption	
	China	*Other countries*	*World*			
	2002–2005				*2002*	*2005*
Copper	31.6	3.4	8.6	67.3	18.3	22.2
Cotton	59.5	3.0	19.6	89.2	29.4	39.2
Natural rubber	46.6	11.9	18.0	45.2	17.4	21.6
Oil	32.0	5.8	7.5	27.6	6.4	7.9
Soybeans	49.9	5.2	10.9	58.7	12.8	17.3

Source: UNCTAD secretariat calculations, based on United States Department of Agriculture, *Oilseeds: World Markets and Trade*, May 2006; International Cotton Advisory Committee, *World Cotton Situation*, 9 May 2006; Economist Intelligence Unit (EIU), *World Commodity Forecasts*, January 2005 and April 2006; International Copper Study Group, *Copper Bulletin*, April 2006; and International Energy Agency, *Oil Market Report*, April 2006.

Current vigorous demand for commodities is supported by strong global economic growth, particularly in the emerging Asian economies, such as China and India, as well as in the United States. Their external demand has also stimulated output growth in many other developed and developing countries. In addition, there are signs of economic recovery in Japan and the euro area. China has seen consistently rapid growth, at an average annual rate of about 10 per cent in the past three years, and a similar rate is expected for 2006. The dynamism of Chinese growth is the result of its rapid industrialization and urbanization process, accompanied by high rates of investment and construction in housing and infrastructure. In 2005, industrial production grew by 11.4 per cent and the gross fixed investment rate was 44.4 per cent of GDP (National Bureau of Statistics of China, 2006). China, like several other developing countries that have been undergoing rapid industrialization, has strong demand for commodities, especially because it is in a phase of development in which the intensity of use of energy, metals and raw materials is on the rise. Equally, rising standards of living will increase demand for food imports, particularly because of the limited arable

land in China. Thus China has become a major player in many commodity markets, both as a consumer and producer, with a strong influence on prices (*TDR 2005*, chap. III). Table 1.A2 shows how the growth of consumption in China is influencing global markets. But although Chinese demand for commodities is expected to remain robust for some time, the outlook for commodity prices is still strongly determined by the evolution of the global economy. Therefore, it will be highly dependent on how the global imbalances are addressed. A recessionary correction could have devastating consequences for commodity markets, notably for metals.

On the supply side, the upward pressure on commodity prices has been the result of the sluggish response of production to rising demand, particularly for energy and metals and minerals. There are indications that producers have been more conservative in their investment plans than in previous commodity booms (IMF, 2006; Morrison, 2006a; and Banks, 2005a). This underinvestment is partly the result of their expectations of a price correction to more historical levels and their fears that the long period of low prices towards the end

Box 1.A1

THE CHANGING PATTERN OF COMMODITY SPECULATION

Speculative activities have always been an integral component of commodity markets. Commodity futures exchanges, which are usually natural reference points for physical trade, help the price discovery process and provide price risk protection from uncertain adverse price movements (hedging), would not function without speculation. Under normal conditions, speculation by a large variety of participants with differing views on market and price developments plays a significant role, as it tends to increase financial and market efficiency (e.g. arbitrage[1]) and brings liquidity to the market. However, during the last three years, changes in the pattern of commodity speculation may have distorted the yield curve (the relationship between near and future prices) and affected the functioning of commodity industries. Most importantly, while in the 1990s most participants were actually involved – or had an interest – in commodity production or trade, more recently speculators with no stake in the commodity sector, and using exotic financial vehicles, have become important players.

In the past, most of the speculative activities were related more to physical trades or sectors, and the objective of the speculators was either to take shares in commodity-related companies (with a longer perspective) or to place money directly in commodity futures. Although some squeezes and manipulations used to be observed in commodity markets, the correlation between spot and futures prices tended to be quite high as physical commodities could always be delivered as a last resort to the exchange itself. This particularity used to limit the scope, length and amplitude of speculation in this field, since the aim of investors was usually not to buy or sell a cargo of, say, cocoa or copper. However, in the recent past, when gloominess in markets for traditional financial products has spread, commodities have been considered an attractive asset class, based on the perception that they are different from stocks, bonds and other conventional equities and, therefore, useful for portfolio diversification. Thus investors seeking both a low correlation with traditional asset classes and above-average returns,[2] have suddenly re-routed massive financial flows to comparatively thin commodity markets. In the mining industry, returns on equity reached 25 per cent in 2005, compared with 19 per cent in 2004 and 6 per cent in 2002, which attracted investors to mining stocks.[3] In addition to increasing their purchase of stocks in commodity-related multinationals (mainly companies in mining and energy), speculators seem to have preferred indirect strategies to avoid the risk of being forced into the physical market. To do so, investors, and particularly hedge funds, put large amounts of money in commodity-based indices, which have the characteristics of traditional financial asset. About 200 billion euros are currently invested in commodities worldwide, half of them in commodity indices.[4] The driving forces behind this are less related to the fundamentals of commodity supply and demand per se than to macroeconomic and financial factors. The greater appetite for commodity-based financial instruments has been fuelled mainly by low interest rates and relatively robust economic growth worldwide. Furthermore, there has been a strong perception amongst speculators, supported by analytical studies, that commodity financial instruments are negatively correlated with other equities. Simple bullish strategies have been devised, based, for instance, on backwardation curves (when prices for delivery in the near future are above prices for delivery in the distant future). The principle of investing in a commodity index consists of entering into a forward contract and closing it when it reaches maturity. Not only do such actions exacerbate price volatility,[5] they also induce asymmetry in the price discovery mechanism.[6]

of the 1990s might recur. Additionally, under the tight market conditions, disruptions in supply caused, for example, by labour disputes in the mining sector, such as the strike at Codelco – the world's largest copper producer – in Chile in early 2006 (*Financial Times*, 2006),[2] had a significant impact on prices. Higher prices have also been due to rising production costs as a result of increased energy costs, particularly for aluminium, and the need to explore in more remote areas and exploit deeper deposits (Banks, 2005c and 2006). Mining exploration budgets continued to increase

Box 1.A1 (concluded)

Moreover, they introduce a systemic risk since the decisions of most of the influential players are synchronized.[7] The second quarter of 2006 provides a good illustration of this phenomenon, as a number of commodity markets have simultaneously shifted away from deep backwardation.[8]

The recent trend towards treating commodities as financial assets has had an impact on different stakeholders in a variety of ways. First, massive speculative flows have supported major mining and energy companies, providing them with resources to invest in exploration and increased production capacities while giving them a comparative advantage vis-à-vis smaller companies that are less interesting to investors (mainly because their stocks are seen as too speculative even for speculators and because their total capitalization is too small to allow significant investment). Second, greater price instability has been making it more difficult for agricultural and mining companies and producers to plan ahead, especially with commodities that take a few years to be produced and to reach the market place. Third, as the result of high basis risk, it is becoming increasingly difficult for producers to hedge, since the "normal" correlation between the physical and futures prices has been, at least temporarily, destroyed. Future developments will depend on the strength of the appetite for commodity-related speculation when central bank monetary policies become more restrictive and interest rates rise worldwide, particularly as commodities are currently showing an unusually positive correlation with conventional equities. In this situation, commodities may not be as attractive to speculators as they have been recently.

---

[1] Arbitrage can be defined as a "low-risk activity" centred on anomalies in pricing. There are several types of arbitrage: spatial arbitrage (between two markets) and arbitrage between spot and futures markets and between different futures maturities. There is also arbitrage between different instruments (i.e. between options with different strike prices as well as between futures, put and call options).

[2] In 2005, returns on commodity indices and commodity-related stocks were in the order of 48.10 per cent, and over the period 2003–2005 they were in the order of 103.82 per cent.

[3] PricewaterhouseCoopers, "Mine, let the good times roll: Review of global trends in the mining industry", June 2006.

[4] In France, speculative investment in commodity-related financial instruments accounted for 3.16 billion euros in the spring of 2006, a 676 per cent increase compared to 1998 (*Le Monde, Dossier économie,* Matières premières, pourquoi les marchés perdent leurs repères? 13 June 2006; and *Les Echos,* La correction sur les métaux suscite des questions sur sa profondeur, 13 June 2006).

[5] Finance industry sources commonly estimate that as much as a third of the price movement in some commodities has been caused by speculation (personal communication).

[6] According to Hansen (2006), the problem with the new generation of index products is that they are only taking advantage of upward price trends and ignoring the significant downside price risk that passive investors have when invested in commodity products.

[7] Institutional speculators often use the same types of technical analyses and computer programs, and tend to get in or out of markets simultaneously, as they have a propensity to trade in the same direction. This was the case when the Long Term Capital Management model led to problems in the markets in 1998.

[8] A case in point is copper (and to some extent zinc) in which the cash-to-three-month backwardation "spread" lessened from $250 in July–September 2005 to less than $20 in April–June 2006.

---

in 2005, to the tune of 34 per cent. Since 2002, when they were at the lowest level of the last decade, they have risen by 168 per cent (Metals Economics Group, 2006). As production resulting from these investment projects comes on-stream, it is likely that the tight situation in the metals market will ease. However, the expansion of production may in many cases take a long time and will vary for different metals.

The price of crude petroleum has made particularly strong gains, continuing to escalate in

2005 and 2006. The oil price rose from $24.9 per barrel in 2002 to $53.4 in 2005 and it reached $68.6 in May 2006.[3] Price developments in some other commodities have also been influenced by the rise in oil prices, through the impact of higher oil prices on production costs and through substitution effects. For example, sugar prices have risen in part as a result of increased demand for ethanol as an alternative source of energy, particularly in Brazil. The demand for natural rubber has also risen significantly owing to the higher price of substitute synthetic rubber.

Most recently, oil prices have reached record levels as a result of geopolitical uncertainty in West Asia, disruptions of supply in Nigeria due to internal conflicts and the nationalization of hydrocarbons in Bolivia. In spite of strong growth in the demand for oil in recent years, global oil markets are not in deficit. In 2005, world oil supply was 0.5 million barrels per day higher than global demand (IEA, 2006). However, there are concerns that spare supply capacity is limited and that any future disruption in supply may have dramatic effects on prices. Therefore oil prices are essentially affected by expectations of future supply constraints, and the fear that supply will not be able to cope with increasing demand. Speculators are playing a fundamental role in the mounting oil prices.

Beyond the physical commodity demand and supply context, commodity prices have attracted greater amounts of investment from participants in the financial markets, such as hedge funds, pension funds, investment funds and insurance companies. Interest in commodities as an asset has increased owing to expectations of a depreciating dollar, and because they provide a hedge against inflation, allow diversification of the investment portfolio and currently provide higher returns in comparison to equity. It is also the result of the existing high liquidity in international financial markets and relatively low interest rates globally. The increase in commodity investment activity in 2005 is reflected in the 8.1 per cent growth in the volume of global futures and options trading in agricultural commodities, energy products and non-precious metals (Burghardt, 2006).[4] According to Morrison (2006b), "funds under management that track commodity indices, such as the Goldman Sachs Commodity Index, have risen from about

$5 billion at the start of the decade to more than $80 billion today". Compared with this 16-fold increase, the increase in the value of world primary commodity exports was 33 per cent between 2001 and 2004 (UN COMTRADE). However, the problem with speculation, contrary to other longer-term investment, is that speculative hedge funds may suddenly decide to reap profits and withdraw from commodity markets, which increases their vulnerability.[5] For instance, in May and June 2006 episodes of commodities selling by financial investors occurred as a result of fears of higher inflation and further increases in the interest rate in the United States. Box 1.A1 describes the changing pattern of commodity speculation.

The increasing commodity prices have contributed to significant improvements in the external accounts of many developing countries, especially those that are still highly dependent on primary commodities. These improvements vary according to the weight of each commodity in the export earnings of the different countries and price developments for each commodity. For example, the 136 per cent surge in copper prices between 2002 and 2005 has led to a threefold increase in the export value of copper from Chile, the major copper producer in the world, accounting for a quarter of total mine production and about half of world exports of copper ores and concentrates, in volume terms (ICSG, 2006). This has meant that the total value of Chile's exports increased by 2.3 times over three years, with the share of copper in total exports growing from 37.1 per cent to 47.1 per cent, and the share of copper mining in GDP rising from 5.8 per cent, in current prices, in 2002 to 13.9 per cent in 2005. The latter increase is almost entirely due to the price increase, because in constant prices the share of copper mining in GDP has remained stable. Thus, high copper prices contributed significantly to Chile's economic growth of over 6 per cent in 2004 and 2005.[6] Similar arguments apply to two other major copper-exporting countries, Peru and Zambia, where GDP growth rates have averaged 5.2 per cent in the last three years. Table 1.A3 presents estimates of the contribution of copper to the total increase in export values of these three countries between 2002 and 2005.

Another example of the potentially strong impact of primary commodity prices on individual countries is coffee, which was the hardest hit by

Table 1.A3

TOTAL EXPORTS AND COPPER EXPORTS IN MAJOR COPPER EXPORTING COUNTRIES, 2002–2005

(Millions of dollars and per cent)

	Total exports		Copper exports		Share of copper in total exports		Contribution of copper to increase in total exports
	2002	*2005*	*2002*	*2005*	*2002*	*2005*	*2002–2005*
	($ million)				(Per cent)		
Chile	17 053.5	38 860.8	6 323.2	18 305.6	37.1	47.1	54.9
Peru	7 713.9	17 247.1	1 187.1	3 360.1	15.4	19.5	22.8
Zambia	916.0	2 095.0	521.4	1 449.3	56.9	69.2	78.7

Source: UNCTAD secretariat calculations, based on Banco Central de Chile, *Series de Indicadores* Database at: www.bcentral.cl/esp/infoeconomica/seriesindicadores/; Banco Central de Reserva del Peru, *Series Estadísticas* Database at: www1.bcrp.gob.pe/VariablesFame/csm_01.asp; Bank of Zambia, *Quartely Media Briefing*, 13 April 2006; and IMF, *Zambia: 2005 Article IV Consultation*, January 2006.

the commodity crisis of the late 1990s and early 2000s. The value of global coffee exports, a commodity produced mainly in the developing world, rose by 68 per cent between 2002 and 2005 (Dubois, 2006). Although recent price increases have enabled a slight recovery from the crisis for coffee-producing countries, in many of them the value of coffee exports still remains below the levels of the mid- and late 1990s.

Clearly, the extent to which commodity-exporting developing countries will continue to benefit from this bonanza depends on how global demand for, and supply of, the different commodities evolve. There is a downside risk on demand related to the possibility of a recessionary correction to the current global imbalances, which would negatively affect global economic growth. In any case, as supply should also increase in response to the tight market conditions, prices will show some correction. This means that while prices may

remain above their long-term declining trend for some time, it is improbable that they will remain at their present level. But in any case, it would be strategically imprudent for commodity-exporting countries to ignore the need for diversification of their exports and for structural change. One reason is that, to the extent that export earnings depend on non-renewable metals and hydrocarbons, the income and welfare gains from an accelerated exploitation of these natural resources will not be sustainable for long. Another reason is that the manufacturing sector offers greater opportunities for the creation of mass employment and the generation of value added than the primary sector. Therefore the benefits for developing countries will also depend on their ability to use their higher commodity export earnings for diversification and industrialization. By reducing their dependence on commodities, this will also make their export earnings less vulnerable to fluctuations in commodity prices.

2. Implications of commodity price developments for the terms of trade

The importance of translating gains from higher commodity export earnings into domestic capital formation in support of industrialization and structural change is also evident when looking at recent developments in international commodity markets from the terms-of-trade perspective. The evolution of the terms of trade has had a significant impact on the economic performance of several developing countries in recent years.

Since 2003, terms of trade have experienced sizeable changes: countries exporting oil and mining products saw substantial gains, while those exporting mainly manufactures and importing raw materials, especially oil, experienced losses (fig. 1.A3). Changes were less significant for countries that export mainly manufactures but also some primary commodities, such as Brazil, Malaysia, Mexico, South Africa and Viet Nam. The terms of trade have varied the most among exporters of agricultural commodities, reflecting large differences in the movements of prices for specific products and also differences in the share of oil in their imports: while there have been gains for some countries of this group, others have registered losses; for instance, in 2005, terms of trade improved for coffee exporters, but deteriorated for cotton exporters, such as Benin and Burkina Faso, and soybean exporters such as Argentina and Uruguay. As a result, the relatively smooth trend in the average terms of trade of this group hides considerably changes for individual countries.

Changes in the terms of trade have a direct effect on the domestic income of a country, which may lead to secondary effects on consumption or investment in that country. However, the gains in domestic income as a result of higher terms of trade may be partly offset by an increase in profit remittances from countries where transnational corporations control a large proportion of export activities. These remittances are listed in the national accounts statistics as factor payments abroad.[7] Table 1.A4 provides an estimate of how the changes in the terms of trade and income payments have directly affected the national income of different developing-country groups and, as a consequence, may have indirectly affected their domestic demand and growth.

Between 2003 and 2005, the deterioration in the terms of trade of manufacturing exporters (i.e. most of the East and South Asian economies) meant a relative loss of income for this group of close to 1 per cent of GDP per annum. However, this deterioration does not necessarily imply absolute losses in real product and income as long as it is accompanied by productivity gains and an expansion of export volume.

The impact of terms-of-trade changes has varied greatly among commodity exporters. Oil exporters obtained, on average, windfall revenues equivalent to 6.7 percentage points of their GDP, which dramatically improved their domestic income. In some countries, particularly the sub-Saharan oil-exporting countries, a sizeable proportion of these gains was offset by higher outflows of profit remittances and interest payments on external debt. In West Asia, on the other hand, where oil

Figure 1.A3

NET BARTER TERMS OF TRADE, SELECTED DEVELOPING COUNTRIES, 2000–2005[a]

(Index numbers, 2000 = 100)

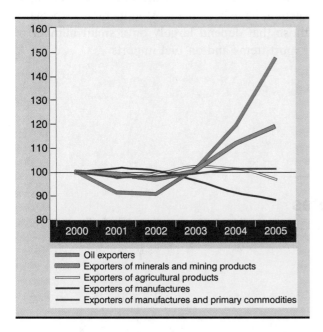

Legend:
- Oil exporters
- Exporters of minerals and mining products
- Exporters of agricultural products
- Exporters of manufactures
- Exporters of manufactures and primary commodities

Source: UNCTAD, secretariat calculations, based on UN COMTRADE; United States Department of Labor, Bureau of Labor Statistics, *Import/Export Price Indexes* Database (www.bls.gov/mxp/home.htm; Japan Customs, *Trade Statistics* Database (www.customs.go.jp); IMF, *International Financial Statistics* Database; UNCTAD, *Commodity Prices Bulletin*, various issues; and ECLAC, *Balance of Payments Statistics* Database.
a Preliminary estimates.

Countries exporting mining products have also benefited from significant income gains from terms of trade, amounting, on average, to close to 3 percentage points of GDP between 2003 and 2005. However, in this group of countries, the outflow of profit remittances appears to be particularly large due to the large share of mining activities controlled by TNCs and the fiscal benefits offered to private companies operating in that sector. It is estimated that two thirds of the income gains from terms-of-trade changes have been offset by higher net income payments abroad.

The group of commodity-exporting countries that are exporting neither oil nor mining products, on average, experienced neither substantial gains nor losses from the terms of trade, and the negative impact of net factor payments on their national income was mainly on account of interest pay-

Table 1.A4

IMPACT OF CHANGES IN TERMS OF TRADE AND NET INCOME PAYMENTS ON NATIONAL DISPOSABLE INCOME IN SELECTED DEVELOPING-COUNTRY GROUPS, AVERAGE FOR 2003–2005

(Per cent of GDP)

	Effects from changes in terms of trade	Effects from changes in net income payments	Net impact
Africa	2.1	-0.9	1.2
Latin America	1.4	-0.8	0.6
East and South Asia	-1.0	0.1	-0.9
West Asia	5.9	0.4	6.3
Exporters of manufactures	-0.8	0.0	-0.8
Oil exporters	6.7	-0.5	6.2
Exporters of mineral and mining products	3.2	-2.2	1.0
Other commodity exporters	0.2	-0.6	-0.4

Source: UNCTAD secretariat calculations, based on United Nations Statistics Division, United Nations Common Database (UNCDB); IMF, *Balance of Payments Statistics* Database; ECLAC, *Balance of Payments Statistics* Database; EIU, *Country Forecast*, various issues; national sources; and UNCTAD estimates of unit value and volume of exports and imports.

production is controlled to a greater extent by State-owned firms, outflows of profit remittances constituted a much smaller percentage of the gains from terms of trade. Moreover, net factor payments were positively influenced by inflows from returns on assets held abroad, including growing international reserves. In Venezuela, a reformulation of contracts with private companies has increased the share obtained by the producing country, bringing a positive "net income" effect. Other developing countries, as well as some developed countries, are also revising the terms of rent distribution. All in all, the huge income gains in most oil-exporting countries have boosted domestic spending, both private and public, and accelerated growth of GDP as well as imports.

ments on the relatively large stock of external debt accumulated by many countries within this group.

In sum, the terms of trade have evolved favourably for a large number of developing countries, and for many countries that registered terms-of-trade losses, these were compensated by higher export volumes. The resulting real income gains have been very substantial for exporters of fuels and ores and minerals, which is reflected in higher domestic expenditures. For this group, the related improvements in fiscal and external balances made it possible to pursue more expansionary economic policies. Countries that are exporters of primary commodities other than oil and mining products seem to have been the most vulnerable, especially those that depend largely on a small number of export items and on fuel imports. ■

Notes

1 For a more detailed analysis of short-term price developments by commodity, see UN-DESA/UNCTAD, 2006.

2 For more details, see Banks, 2005b.

3 Average of Dubai/Brent/Texas equally weighted (UNCTAD, *Commodity Price Bulletin*, various issues).

4 This corresponds to a 12.9 per cent increase in agricultural commodities, a 9.58 per cent rise in energy products and a 6.87 per cent fall in non-precious metals. The latter may reflect a market correction in early 2005 as mentioned above. However, there are indications that speculative activity had accelerated by the end of 2005 and early 2006.

5 For more detailed discussions of the recent interest of investors in commodities, see *Financial Times*, 2005; Acworth, 2005; Banks, 2005d; and Russell-Walling, 2005.

6 UNCTAD secretariat calculations, based on Banco Central de Chile, Series de Indicadores Database: www.bcentral.cl/esp/infoeconomica/seriesindicadores/index_aeg.htm.

7 For a more detailed analysis of the gains and losses from terms of trade and their distribution, see *TDR 2005*, chap. III.

References

Acworth W (2005). Going long on commodities. *Futures Industry Magazine*, May/June.

Banks J (2005a). Are high prices boosting mine production? *Ringsider eNewsletter*, 2, London Metal Exchange, Autumn.

Banks J (2005b). Striking while the non-ferrous is hot. *Ringsider eNewsletter*, 2, London Metal Exchange, Autumn.

Banks J (2005c). Growing energy costs remain a hidden problem for the base metals sector, *Ringsider eNewsletter*, 3, London Metal Exchange, Winter.

Banks J (2005d). Friend or foe? *Ringsider Metals Yearbook 2005*, London Metal Exchange.

Banks J (2006). Production costs supporting base metals prices, *Ringsider eNewsletter*, 4, London Metal Exchange, Spring.

Burghardt G (2006). Annual volume survey – 9,899,780,283 contracts traded. *Futures Industry Magazine*, March/April.

Dubois P (2006). Improving market conditions for coffee producers: the experience of ICO. Presentation at the WTO Committee on Trade and Development, Geneva, 11 May.

Financial Times (2005). World commodities. Business Reports, 22 November.

Financial Times (2006). Copper hits high on Codelco strike, 5 January.

Hansen MA (2006). The alternative appeal of commodities structured products. *Swiss Derivatives Review,* 31, Summer.

ICSG (2006). *Copper Bulletin*, 13 (4). International Copper Study Group, April.

IEA (2006). *Oil Market Report*. Paris, International Energy Agency, April.

IMF (2006). *World Economic Outlook*. Washington, DC, International Monetary Fund, April.

Metals Economics Group (2006). *World Exploration Trends*. A special report from the Metals Economics Group for the Prospectors and Developers Association of Canada International Convention, Toronto, 4–7 March.

Morrison K (2006a). Commodity prices look set to spiral even higher, *Financial Times*, 10 April.

Morrison K (2006b). Global investors push up prices. *Financial Times*, 10 April.

National Bureau of Statistics of China (2006). Statistical communiqué of The People´s Republic of China on the 2005 National Economic and Social Development, 28 February.

Russell-Walling E (2005). Commodities as a new institutional asset class, *Ringsider Metals Yearbook 2005*, London Metal Exchange.

UN-DESA/UNCTAD (2006). *World Economic Situation and Prospects*. New York, United Nations.

UNCTAD (various issues). *Trade and Development Report*, United Nations publication, New York and Geneva.

THE THEORETICAL BACKGROUND TO THE SAVING/INVESTMENT DEBATE

1. Introduction

Despite decades of intensive research, the underlying forces driving development and catching up are still relatively mysterious. Only a few facts can be taken for granted. One is the central role of the accumulation of capital and improvements in technology. The close correlation between overall growth and investment growth is evident, along with the simple fact that no country has ever jumped from agriculture-driven growth to industry-driven growth without largely expanding innovation and investment. About the main determinants of investment the jury is still out and on the academic battlefronts positions have hardly converged.

On the necessary conditions for investment much has been said. Obviously, in primitive societies and on Robinson Crusoe's island nobody could invest without reducing consumption of the available food and water beforehand. But does that mean that in more highly-developed societies people have to become thrifty first, reducing their expenditure to allow investment, or that the more they save the more is invested? Even if that were the case, why are some relatively thriftless societies prospering whereas others with a much lower propensity to consume are lagging behind? What are the sufficient conditions for investment-led growth?

2. The controversy

The theory of saving and investment is, up to the present time, rather rudimentary. Its core still is the more-or-less sophisticated breakdown of an identity. The gross domestic product of a closed economy (or the world) is split into a part that is consumed immediately (during the period of production) and a part that is saved to be consumed later. For a closed economy it is found what is assumed, namely, that saving equals investment (see box 1.A2).

For a single open economy, disposing of both national saving and foreign saving (with positive foreign savings being the logical correlate of a current-account deficit), the identity of saving and investment is given with total investment equalling foreign saving and national saving. Hence, according to the orthodox view prevalent during the last two decades, "if saving falls short of desired investment, ... foreigners must take up the balance, acquiring, as a result, claims on domestic income or output" (Obstfeld and Rogoff, 1996). Or, as Krugman puts it: "An external deficit *must* (italics in original) have as its counterpart an excess of domestic investment over domestic savings, which makes it natural to look for sources of a deficit in an autonomous change in the national savings rate" (Krugman, 1992: 5).

Statements like these suggest that the identity implies causality, giving "saving" a specific, leading role in the process. However, the crucial question behind these identities is about causality. Does the fact that – from an *ex-post* point of view – a gap has emerged between saving and investment in a single country even hint at an "autonomous" decision of any economic agent in any of the involved countries? Can the plans of one group of actors be realised without taking into account a highly complex interaction of the plans of other actors and price and quantity changes under conditions of uncertainty about the future? Do *a priori* judgements based on perfect foresight in models of "desired" saving and investment really account for the various possible outcomes and multiplicity of causal relationships in an "open society", namely a society that is not evolving on a predetermined inter-temporal path and a society that is open to international influences and shocks?

Obviously, splitting up consumption and investment among certain groups of actors like private households, the government or "foreign countries" does not add any information about causality to the identity. It still remains a simple definition. To give it informational content, the variables have to be identified that determine the movements of saving, consumption and investment, and in consequence the product (income), of the regional conglomerate under consideration, along with those of all its neighbouring regions. Moreover, the accounting identity does not give any indication about the efficiency of the process leading to *ex-post* equality of saving and investment, and thus cannot be treated as an equilibrium condition without explicitly naming the equilibrating factors and their role in the adjustment process.

The weakness of the orthodox approach becomes evident if it has to deal concretely with changes in the behaviour of economic agents in an economy subject to objective uncertainty, which means an economy where economic agents do not know much about the future; an economy that is exposed to unforeseeable shocks. For example, if the saving rate of private or public households or of other countries like oil producers suddenly rises, companies, faced with falling demand and falling profits, will react with falling investment if they do not possess more systemic information than just the information about the drop in demand.

Only if it is assumed that they expect growth to be higher later because of the rise in savings can they react in the "right" way, according to the orthodox approach. Hence, in this world they would increase their investment expenditure *because* demand is falling off. They just switch the financing of the higher amount of investment from equity (cash flow, profits) to interest-bearing loans. The mechanism for accomplishing this remarkable transition is a fall in interest rates. Obviously, in this world falling current profits do not impact negatively on profit expectations, because otherwise even falling interest rates would not induce a positive outcome.

The implication of this approach is paradoxical: after the increase of the savings rate of private households, companies can acquire the same level of profit as in a situation of unchanged consumption. But now they have to invest more than before – exactly the amount spent by consumers earlier and now saved – although final demand has dropped. The implication is that they demand interest-bearing credit to fill the profit gap opened by the decrease of consumption, which means that in this case exactly the same amount that investors are additionally demanding on the capital market they would have acquired "for nothing" if private or public households were spending as much as before.

A comparison of the two cases shows that the case with higher savings is clearly inferior to the case with lower savings of private households, since the funds that companies need to protect their profit rate are now more expensive than before. In other words, companies have to invest more than before, although they may have piled up unsold stock already as a result of involuntary investment and/or capacity utilization is lower. Only if we assume that – even in adverse eco-

nomic conditions – maintaining the level of profits is by all means what drives investors, the outcome is positive in the long run since a larger sum is invested in this economy than before and, at least according to some models of economic growth, the long run growth rate is higher.

Only if the assumption of constant or zero profits is accepted *a priori* can the system's dynamics be explained exclusively in terms of private consumption smoothing over time as investors and entrepreneurs passively adjust to any kind of microeconomic decision by households without ever endangering either the equilibrium values of the model or its inherent stability. In other words, such an economy is not only exclusively driven by autonomous consumer decisions; the model assumes totally reactive entrepreneurs who never take into account actual business conditions while deciding about investment. Instead, as a rule, the present deterioration of their business is taken as proof for a warranted (expected) improvement in the future.

The question for policymakers in any country is whether they should rely on this model or rather whether they should question its ability to grasp the most important ingredient of everyday economic life, namely, the role of time and the availability of information in affecting the sequence of decisions that economic agents take under conditions of objective uncertainty about the future. In a world of money and uncertainty, the decision to save more and consume less can have grave repercussions on the goods market before it impacts on the capital market. The decision "not to have dinner today" (Keynes, 1936: 210) depresses the business of preparing dinner today without immediately stimulating any other business.

Thus, any realistic sequencing would see the entrepreneurs' "saving" fall exactly and *uno actu* by the amount that the savings of private households increase (government dis-savings fall or foreign savings increase – or government deficits fall or a current-account deficit increases). That is why the secular decline in the saving rate of private households in the industrialized world starting at the beginning of the 1990s – the savings rate of the G-7 countries almost halved, falling from around 9 per cent in 1992 to 4.5 per cent in 2005 – is mirrored in the secular rise, from

Box 1.A2

TWO MODELS FOR CHOICE

The investment-saving theory has been extremely simple up until now. If Y is the gross domestic product and the income of a closed economy (or the world), then the whole product (or income) obviously can be split into a part C that is consumed immediately (in the period of production) and a part I (or S) which is not consumed in this period and therefore is invested or put on stock in order to increase the product Y in a later period (the sum of fixed investment and changes in inventories is total gross investment). We can write the product or the income as:

$$Y = C + I \text{ or } Y = C + S$$

And we "find" for the closed economy what was assumed, namely, that:

$$S = I$$

An open economy with international trade can dispose over national savings (S_n) and foreign savings (S_f), with the latter being the correlate of the current-account deficit if its value is positive. Hence:

$$S_n + S_f = I$$

The recent academic discussion has not focused on the underlying philosophy of the $I = S$ approach but simply returned to a rather uncritical use of the identities that characterized the discussion in the 1920s. This despite the fact that some 70 years ago, in his "fundamental equations" in the Pure Theory of Money, which forms the first volume of his "Treatise on Money", Keynes clarified the inherent logic of the classical approach. The famous equality of saving and investment is either true if the observer describes the situation of a certain economy from an *ex-post* point of view, or if the economy under consideration is in a state of perfect equilibrium. The latter describes a stationary economy, an economy where real income is constant and where there are no incentives for entrepreneurs to change the existing level of activity, as the level of profits is exactly zero. In all other cases, development and catching up included, it is not $S = I$ that rules the course of events but an equation like:

$$Q = I - S$$

with Q as profits or losses of entrepreneurs, i.e., the residual income that to a large extent rules the dynamics of the market system (Keynes, 1930: 136–138). In this world, any act of individual

---

8.5 per cent to 11.5 per cent of the savings of corporations. Hence, thrift of private households is not a virtue per se but has to be analysed in the context of all the other forms of saving by other agents, including company saving.

This implies that in a world of uncertainty, variable income and flexible profits, the intention

of individuals to save an absolutely higher sum than before may completely fail because the future income they realize at the end of the period may be lower than their expected income at the beginning of the period. Even if households succeed in raising the ratio of saving to actual income (the savings rate), the absolute amount of income saved (and invested) may be lower, as the denomi-

Box 1.A2 (concluded)

saving by the non-entrepreneurial sectors (governments, private households or the rest of the world) reduces profits, the saving of companies, because it decreases effective demand of the company sector as a whole.

The difference between the two models is remarkable and, unfortunately, very often not adequately reflected even in development theory or economic theory in general. With profits Q being the most important equilibrating force between saving and investment, the world changes fundamentally and the old perfect capital market model can no longer describe it. In Keynes' own words: "The classical theorists resemble Euclidean geometers in a non-Euclidean world ..." (Keynes, 1936: 16). In his discussion of "the classical theory of interest" (Keynes, 1936: 14–18) Keynes concludes that the classical theory is "... faulty because it has failed to isolate correctly the independent variables of the system. Saving and investment are the determinates ... not the determinants of the system" (Keynes, 1936: 183).

It is perplexing to see that much of the mainstream academic treatment of the development problem dismisses the dynamic approach by confusing it with a profoundly diminished, static Keynesian theory. Ros (2001: 8) puts it very clearly that "we should not confuse these development problems with the effective demand problems on which Keynes focused. Not much is lost, for example, by assuming Say's Law when looking at income differences across countries ... differences in resource utilization account for a very small fraction of the large gaps in income per capita across the world". Obviously, in a statement like this exactly the wrong question is asked. It is not the difference in income *per se* that has to be explained, but the ability of countries to enter a process of self-sustaining growth and the inability of others to trigger such a growth process. The result of these dynamic processes will be catching up or falling behind; but, and this is overlooked by this treatment of apparently short term phenomena, these processes are intractably intertwined with both demand problems and policy intervention in the long and in the short term.

To take Say's Law ("supply creates its own demand") for granted and to analyse development processes as if saving would always smoothly adjust to investment assumes away the most demanding of all economic problems. Contrary to modern interpretations J.S. Mill (1909), and along the same lines J.A. Schumpeter (1954), saw Say's Law just as a rule for rational behaviour of economic agents in the long term. In their interpretation, Say's Law simply states that the needs of people do not restrict supply because those needs are indefinite. It was meant as an argument against theories of need saturation that were quite popular at that time. David Ricardo, in his "Principles of economics" in 1814, already put it this way: "If people ceased to consume they would cease to produce" (Ricardo, 1814: 293). Hence, Say's Law does not exclude the kind of event that disturbs the process of economic development so fundamentally: shocks on the demand side of the economy, including shocks stemming from the deterioration of monetary conditions.

nator of the saving rate, real income, may have fallen due to the decline in demand and profits, with an induced fall in investment.

The economics of saving and investment in an international context follows the logic of their domestic treatment. In a non-stationary environment, any increase in expenditure (increase in a net debt position of one sector) increases profits and any increase in saving (net creditor position) reduces profits. Whether the act of saving or of investment happens here or there, whether the beneficiaries (or the disadvantaged agents) are located in the country where the shock originated or in other countries, does not change the course of events. The decision of a certain group of economic agents (private or public, domestic or foreign) to spend less (to save more) out of their current income diminishes profits and growth. The other way round, a drop in foreign savings may mean higher domestic profits and more investment instead of a drop in investment.

If a current-account deficit, or a growing "inflow of foreign saving", emerges in the wake of negative shocks on the goods market, for example due to falling terms of trade or a lasting real currency appreciation, the real appreciation directly diminishes the revenue of companies if market shares are protected by a pricing-to-market strategy. If companies try to defend their profit margins, a fall in market shares and, as a rule, a swing in the current account towards deficit, is unavoidable. Higher net inflows of foreign savings, which are logically associated with an increase of net imports (higher imports or lower exports), can by no means compensate for the fall in overall profits or even help the country to invest more than before. If the process leading to the swing in the current account reduces the real income of the economy under consideration (destroying profits or other income having repercus-sions on profits) then the situation before and after the swing cannot simply be compared by looking at capital flows in isolation. In this case a higher net capital inflow indicates a negative shock.

Generally, and this is very often forgotten in the theoretical dispute between the two models, the adjustment of saving to investment is overlaid by exogenous shocks of all kinds in the real world. Interest rates may not fall if monetary policy is fighting a higher price level stemming from a negative supply shock, as has been the case during the oil price explosions in the industrialised world in the 1970s and recently. Interest rates may even go up in a cyclical downturn if financial markets dictate higher interest rates to a developing country due to increasing risks of a default. The negative effects of falling private demand on profits may be aggravated by pro-cyclical fiscal policy in developing countries if "the markets" expect a quick reduction of public budget deficits (see "the confidence game" in chapter IV of this *Report*). An overvaluation of the real exchange rate may disturb the adjustment process by forcing monetary policy to react pro-cyclically or by directly enforcing the pro-cyclicality of monetary conditions.

3. The policy options in theory

The political consequences of the two theoretical approaches are totally different. In the dynamic model of flexible profits the implications of globalization, the opening of markets and of policy interventions can have tremendous effects on the overall outcome in terms of growth and jobs. By contrast, the fixed-profits model does not ask for much room for manoeuvre for economic policy, and where it considers economic policy options they are the direct opposite of those put forward under the flexible-profits model.

For policymakers in a developing country it is of vital interest to know on which model policy recommendations that they receive are based. Frequently it is argued that there is a rational choice between the two models and that economic policy in developing countries can opt for interest rate flexibility instead of flexibility of profits and real income:

> In one view, saving is seen as resulting from a choice between present and future consumption. Individuals compare their rate of

time preference to the interest rate, and smooth their consumption over time to maximize their utility. The interest rate is the key mechanism by which saving and investment are equilibrated. The other view sees a close link between current income and consumption, with the residual being saving. In this view, saving and investment are equilibrated mainly by movements in income, with the interest rate having a smaller effect (IMF, 1995: 73).

It is important to bear in mind that "utility maximization" in the fixed-profits-model describes an entirely different objective for the society under consideration than does "income generation" in the flexible-profit-model. Smoothing consumption may maximize utility in a very narrow and static sense in a world without entrepreneurial behaviour, that is, if the economy just moves along the consumption frontier or along a pre-defined growth path. Maximizing utility in a dynamic setting that allows, say, for temporary monopolies, new technological solutions and investment will shift the production (and thereby the consumption) frontier outwards by increasing potential output beyond the means created by the planned saving of private households.

If real income of the "open society" is treated as a variable that can be influenced by policy and exogenous shocks on the micro- as well as the macro-level, the search for variables "equating" saving and investment in a smooth way ends up "solving" the problem by assuming it away.[1] Applying strictly the idea of the interest rate as an equilibrating mechanism of saving and investment implies that real income (the product) of the economy under consideration is either constant or is growing with rates that cannot be systematically changed by policy interventions. In such a model the dynamics of the society are defined away, as economic agents have perfect foresight about the future and complete information about their economic environment. Can cycles, unexpected shocks and – most importantly – development driven by unexpected entrepreneurial innovation and investment and political decisions be explained by such an approach?

The direct comparison of the two models suggests that movements of income are as good as movements of the interest rate for equilibrating saving and investment. The "instruments" of a

change in real income and a change in the interest rate can only be seen as alternatives if it is assumed that the growth rate of real income cannot be influenced by any kind of (non-equilibrium) entrepreneurial or economic policy activity. But then the whole discussion is useless from the beginning. Consequently, governments have to choose whether their economic policy approach shall rest on the idea of investment induced by "thrift-savings" or on the idea of investment induced by profit-savings.

Obviously, depending on the model used by policymakers, the economic policy strategies of developing countries are totally different and reflect differing levels of need to define the room for national policy. In the orthodox model the adjustment of investment to savings is an automatic process that, without government or central bank intervention, brings about the optimal result in terms of growth and jobs. In the other model, there can be extra profits or losses of companies and the economy is inherently unstable. In this case, government and/or central bank intervention is needed to stimulate investment, as interest rate flexibility may not be sufficient to stabilize the economy and since the whole process may be overlaid by negative exogenous shocks.

If the movement (increase) of income is the main goal of economic policy, then economic policy should focus on a process where investment plans regularly exceed saving plans. In such a world, even with the private incentive to "thrift" left unchanged, the economy as a whole may expand vigorously. The "savings" corresponding to the increased investment are generated through investment and the original investment is "financed" through liquidity created by bank credit based on expansionary central bank policy. Increased investment stimulates higher profits, as temporary monopoly rents of the company sector rise. These profits provide for the macroeconomic saving required from an *ex post* point of view to "finance" the additional investment. In this approach that could be called the flexible profits approach "the departure of profits from zero is the mainspring of change in the ... modern world ... It is by altering the rate of profits in particular directions that entrepreneurs can be induced to produce this rather than that, and it is by altering the rate of profits in general that they can be induced to modify the average of their offers of remuneration to the factors of production" (Keynes, 1930: 141).[2]

Hence, in a world of uncertainty and of permanent deviation from the fiction of perfect competition, shocks on the goods and the capital market lead to quantity and profit adjustment rather than price adjustment. If labour is mobile or wages are determined in a way that the labour market is ruled by the law of one price, which means that wages of different skill groups are a given variable for each single company, companies compete by differing productivity performances. An innovation or a new product, as a rule, triggers a relative fall of unit labour costs for the innovating firm. The lower cost level may be passed on into lower prices, increasing the company's market share, or it may increase the company's profits directly if prices remain unchanged.

In such a world, the response of quantities and profits does not reflect a pathological "inflexibility" of prices and wages but rather introduces the main ingredient of real world market systems, namely, the fight for absolute temporary advantages of companies. In its inter-temporal dimension this fight is about the combination of higher productivity with given wages. In its international dimension it is about the combination of lower wages with a given high productivity (*TDR 2004*, annex 1 to chap. IV).

In a world of differing productivity performances of companies, prices of intermediary products and wages are given for the individual firm but profits are flexible. Seen the other way round, if prices and wages reacted flexibly to individual events on the company level, profits would be sticky. In a dynamic setting where prices and wages are determined by the market, the flexibility of individual profits provides the steering wheel and investment is the vehicle to drive the economy through time. In this world, the branch of industry, a particular region or a state are not the main actors, and any analysis focusing on these entities without leaving room for the role of profits and entrepreneurship does not capture the nature of the process of dynamic development.

Basically, the savings-based approach argues just the other way round. This model expects

shocks from trade or technology to be buffered by a flexible reaction of prices or wages, whereas quantities react less and may even remain constant. Profits do not respond to shocks, since the system of perfect competition – by assumption – is always steered so as to avoid any change in profits. In this approach, increasing imports from developing countries forces wages and unit labour costs in the North to fall and thus the prices of domestic products adjust to cheaper imports. A rise in unemployment can only be avoided by stretching the wage structure between workers of different skills as well as between branches and firms exposed to the new competition and those who are not.

The fundamental differences between the two models can easily be illustrated in the case of foreign direct investment (FDI). In the orthodox setting, capital moves from high-wage countries to low-wage countries to reduce the quantity of capital required as well as its overall cost by implementing a more labour-intensive technology in the latter. In the other view, the relocation of production to low-wage countries in most cases takes place by moving the existing capital-intensive technology of the high-wage country to a low-wage location. Thus, it is not the smaller quantity of capital and the reduction in overall capital costs that determines the relocation, but the chance to realize a temporary monopoly rent, which is higher the lower the wage level of the capital-importing country and the lower its overall growth rates of productivity and wages.

In conclusion, in a realistic setting of prices, wages and profits, economic policy attempts at improving growth performance and heading for catching-up are not in vain. The savings-lead approach favoured by the mainstream view in economics is misleading. If markets do not automatically deliver positive and stable growth rates of real income and catching up, then the dynamic view, highlighting the incentive of temporary monopoly rents for pioneering investors, is more than ever relevant for the development of the system as a whole. The orthodox approach, putting primary focus on the decision of consumers to "smooth consumption over time" under conditions of perfect foresight, offers an elegant version of Walrasian market clearing but hardly captures the main features of modern economies. ∎

Notes

1 The standard assertion of many authors is a notion of the kind that "In equilibrium, however, the world interest rate equates global saving to global investment" (Obstfeld and Rogoff, 1996: 31). But, as saving and investment are always identical *ex-post*, the notion of "equilibrium", as well as the associated equilibrating role of the interest rate, is misleading.

2 This is the position UNCTAD, in many *Trade and Development Reports*, has called the "profit-investment-nexus".

References

IMF (1995). *World Economic Outlook*. Washington, DC, International Monetary Fund, April.

Keynes JM (1930). A Treatise on Money-The Pure Theory of Money. In: Moggridge D, ed. (1973), *The Collected Writings of John Maynard Keynes*, vol. V. London and Basingstoke, Macmillan.

Keynes JM (1936). The General Theory of Employment, Interest and Money. In: Moggridge D, ed. (1973), *The Collected Writings of John Maynard Keynes*. vol. VII. London and Basingstoke Macmillan.

Krugman P (1992). Exchange Rates and the Balance of Payments. In: Currency and Crises, Cambridge, MA, MIT Press.

Mill JS (1909). *Principles of Political Economy*. In: Ashley WJ, ed. (1976), Reprints of Economic Classics. Fairfield, NJ, Augustus M. Kelley.

Obstfeld M and Rogoff K (1996). *Foundations of International Macroeconomics*. Cambridge, MA, MIT Press.

Ricardo D (1814). Principles of Political Economy. In: Sraffa P, ed. (1951), *The Works and Correspondence of David Ricardo*. Cambridge University Press.

Ros J (2001). *Development Theory and the Economics of Growth*. University of Michigan Press.

Schumpeter JA (1954). *History of Economic Analysis*. New York, Oxford University Press.

UNCTAD (various issues). *Trade and Development Report*, United Nations publication, New York and Geneva.

Chapter II

EVOLVING DEVELOPMENT STRATEGIES – BEYOND THE MONTERREY CONSENSUS

A. Introduction

Policy reforms undertaken by developing countries in the 1980s and 1990s were strongly influenced by the international financial institutions, which emphasized stabilization and liberalization. Through their lending activities and political support from the major industrialized countries, the International Monetary Fund (IMF) and the World Bank were able to exercise considerable leverage on the design and implementation of developing countries' macroeconomic and development policies. The new policy agenda, which came to be labelled the "Washington Consensus", evolved over time, incorporating additional elements in response to the disappointing outcomes of reform programmes and to criticism that emanated from the international policy debate.

The elements that were added to the standard reform programmes primarily addressed the initially neglected social implications of adjustment and the institutional requirements for the success of reforms. Advocacy by various international organizations and civil society highlighted the issue of poverty in the developing world, and its linkages with adjustment policies in a globalizing world economy began to receive increasing attention in the early 1990s. This culminated in the formulation of the Millennium Development Goals (MDGs) at the United Nations World Summit in 2000. The increasing belief that local governments should take ownership of reforms led to revisions in the operational design of reform programmes in low-income countries. Moreover, with the recognition that external constraints were inhibiting the success of policy reforms, the international community stepped up its efforts to establish a global partnership for development. This resulted in far-reaching debt relief initiatives, new commitments to greater bilateral official development assistance (ODA) and the exploring of new sources of international development finance.

In this chapter it is argued that although the different amendments to the standard reform packages placed stronger emphasis on specific institutions for developing countries, they did not imply a fundamental change in the orientation of the reform agenda. There was the continued belief that improved factor allocation through market liberalization and opening up to international trade and finance would be key to solving the problems of developing countries by strengthening their productive capacity, raising productivity and accelerating technological upgrading.

This chapter is not intended to provide a comprehensive evaluation of the wealth of literature on the subject. Rather, it attempts to provide an outline of the evolution of mainstream thinking on development strategies since the early 1980s, and its influence on practical policy-making in terms of its implications for capital accumulation, productivity growth and technological progress. It discusses how the various adjustments to the reform programme are reflected in the different initiatives taken by the United Nations since the beginning of the new millennium, without, however, succeeding in reducing the income gap between the majority of developing countries and the developed world. Despite the revisions of and additions to the standard policy prescriptions for developing countries, the dominating philosophy underlying development

> The standard reform agenda was built on the belief that improved factor allocation through market liberalization and opening up to international trade and finance would be key to solving the problems of developing countries.

policy, with its focus on efficiency gains from market-determined improvements in factor allocation, has remained unchanged. The experience of the past 25 years has shown that reliance on market forces alone is not enough to achieve the pace and structure of productive investment and technological upgrading necessary for catch-up growth and sustained poverty eradication. Inadequate attention has been paid to active government policies in favour of diversification and dynamic industrialization that take into account country-specific constraints, possibilities and capabilities. The chapter concludes with recommendations for a more fundamental reorientation of policy reforms, at both national and international levels, with a view to strengthening capital accumulation, innovation and productivity growth in developing countries – all prerequisites for better integration into the world economy and for reducing the income gap between rich and poor nations.

B. The emergence of the "Washington Consensus"

Development policies over the past 25 years have been shaped largely by policy prescriptions of the international financial institutions. Their influence on developing countries had increased considerably since the early 1980s following a dramatic rise in the current-account deficits of numerous developing countries over the course of the preceding decade. In the case of countries that had access to international financial markets, these deficits were initially financed by borrowing from those markets; the poorer countries that lacked such access had to rely on official loans, leading

to their increasing dependence on external financing and a rapid build-up of external debt. When the United States shifted to a monetary policy of aggressive disinflation from 1978 onwards, dollar interest rates rose dramatically, which increased the cost of their accumulated external debt; meanwhile their export earnings suffered from weakening global demand.

As a result of their widening current-account deficits developing countries' use of IMF credit rose sharply, as commercial banks were unwilling to maintain their pace of lending. In 1982, the IMF took the lead role in managing the debt crisis affecting many developing countries that were carrying large amounts of commercial bank debt. The number of IMF-supported programmes rose from an annual average of 10 during the 1970s to 19 in 1980 and to 33 in 1985 (Jespersen, 1992). When it became apparent that in most cases the short-term horizon of the stabilization programmes was inappropriate to bring a lasting solution to the problem, the IMF established the Structural Adjustment Facility (SAF) for low-income countries in March 1986. Then in November 1987 it created the Enhanced Structural Adjustment Facility (ESAF) to provide additional balance-of-payments assistance through the International Development Association (IDA) to eligible low-income developing countries that faced protracted balance-of-payments problems. Lending under the ESAF was designed to support comprehensive reforms and adjustments, as reflected in the stringent conditionality attached to such lending, including the standard ingredients of IMF stabilization packages, such as a reduction in public spending, restrictive monetary policies and exchange-rate adjustment, but also structural conditions, such as import liberalization, privatization and deregulation of the domestic economy.

As noted by Schadler et al. (1993: 9), "[t]he strategy underlying the structural reform programme was to strengthen the financial position of the public sector and reduce government interference in the allocation of resources" with the objective of containing inflation and attaining fiscal and current-account balance. However, it did not address the question of how to raise productive capacity for export growth and employment creation, which would have required a more balanced mix of monetary and fiscal measures (Lipumba, 1995: 38). While imprudent domestic policies in the 1970s had contributed in many countries to increased vulnerability to external shocks, the debt crisis itself had been triggered by global factors. Yet a case-by-case approach was adopted in attempting to solve the problems, based

on the belief that government failure was the sole cause of the crisis and that market discipline would prevent such failures in the future.

Earlier, in 1979, the World Bank, which had previously focused its lending activities on the financing of investment projects, had responded to the difficulties facing developing countries by introducing structural adjustment loans, designed to assist countries in overcoming structural – rather than cyclical – impediments to payments adjustment. Like IMF programmes, World Bank structural adjustment lending placed emphasis on greater macroeconomic stability, but also on a reduced role for the State, greater reliance on market forces and a rapid opening up to international competition as key to unlocking growth potential. Its policy prescriptions to achieve these objectives included liberalization of trade and foreign exchange allocation, deregulation of interest rates and prices, reduced public sector involvement in agricultural marketing, privatization of public enterprises and restructuring of public expenditures.

> Structural adjustment policies placed emphasis on greater macroeconomic stability, a reduced role for the State, greater reliance on market forces and a rapid opening up to international competition.

IMF operations helped the borrowing countries in their efforts to remain current on their debt service payments and to maintain a minimum level of crucial imports, but the conditionality attached to the lending by the international financial institutions restricted the policy options that could be used to provide support to capacity-enhancing investment. Entering into an agreement with the IMF soon became a prerequisite for debt restructuring, and the willingness of bilateral or private lenders to extend new loans to developing countries increasingly came to depend on how closely these countries' economic policies conformed with the standard reform packages advocated by the Bank and the Fund. As a result, the structural adjustment programmes not only shaped the economic policies of countries that had to resort to borrowing from the international financial institutions, they also came to be widely accepted as the standard reform package for countries that were reviewing their development strategies for achieving closer integration into the globalizing world economy.

In 1989, the term "Washington Consensus" was coined to signify the standard set of policy prescriptions of the Washington-based institutions (Williamson, 1990). They were initially formulated for Latin America but were subsequently extended to developing countries elsewhere, and from the early 1990s onwards, also to economies in transition. In addition to the elements listed above, other policy elements considered appropriate by the advocates of the Consensus included tax reforms to lower the marginal rates and to broaden the tax base, opening up to foreign direct investment (FDI) and protecting property rights.[1] Although the term Washington Consensus was subject to various interpretations and misinterpretations, it became a reference point for discussions on development policies.[2]

This policy orientation marked a shift from the development thinking and practice that had dominated the previous decades. Earlier approaches had advocated a more central role for government policies and the public sector in driving the development process. Thus, until the late 1970s, development strategies in most developing countries were built on a strong public sector and State intervention and regulation of economic activity. Many countries adopted a variety of price controls and State intervention in resource allocation, aimed at directing the economic process towards outcomes that were perceived to respond to prevailing social and human needs and the requirements of long-term development. State ownership of enterprises was often considered necessary in the absence of a critical mass of private, capitalist entrepreneurs. In addition, control over the financial sector and regulation of credit allocation were considered necessary in the absence of an efficient system of financial intermediation and sufficiently deep financial markets, and to ensure that the financial sector served the needs of the real economy and conformed with national objectives.

The diagnosis of "market failure" and the inherent instability of markets had provided an important theoretical basis to justify the need for government policies to correct such failures. This led to greater State intervention, not only as a provider of infrastructure and social services, but also as a capitalist investor in strategically important industries, and as a source of financing for private investment. This approach had been adopted not only in the economic and social policies of developing countries, but also by many developed countries. While sticking to market principles, they too had given a key role to various forms of State intervention: from active support for the private sector in post-war industrial reconstruction and State ownership of strategically important sectors – such as banking, energy provision and transportation – to an array of policy measures to support specific sectors and economic activities that were considered important for national economic security, for socially acceptable income distribution, for maintaining high employment and for meeting other fundamental objectives. Economic policies in developed and developing countries alike were still influenced by the Great Depression and by the experience that decentralized agents in the private sector, in their pursuit of self-interest, had not automatically been generating full-employment equilibrium and sustained growth.

In developing countries, igniting a process of industrialization was the central concern of economic policy. In Latin America during the Great Depression and the Second World War, previously imported manufactures that had become difficult to acquire were substituted by domestic production. Starting from this basis, inward-oriented industrialization was subsequently promoted by deliberate policies, including trade protection, directed credit and subsidies, and the creation of State-owned enterprises. Most development economists of the time generally regarded capital accumulation as the core process by which all other aspects of growth and economic transformation are made possible (Cairncross, 1955).[3] The importance of entrepreneurship, technical progress and innovation, and education and vocational training was well recognized, but it was also considered necessary for the "developmental State" to take the

> The Washington Consensus approach to development represented a shift away from the focus on capital accumulation to an almost exclusive reliance on improved factor allocation generated by market forces.

lead role. From this perspective, the reorientation of structural adjustment policies and the Washington Consensus approach to development represented a shift away from the focus on capital accumulation to an almost exclusive reliance on the efficiency-enhancing potential of improved factor allocation generated by market forces.

The previous orthodoxy of State-centered development strategies, with their high degree of interventionism, State *dirigisme* and protectionism, was considered responsible for market distortions leading to suboptimal resource allocation and underperformance of developing economies. The new approach recommended privatization, deregulation, trade and financial liberalization aimed not only to improve incentives for more efficient resource allocation, but also to reduce the need for State discretion. Even when there

were market failures resulting from externalities, the provision of public goods, imperfect and asymmetric information, imperfect competition and incomplete markets, little justification was seen for policy intervention, since the consequences of government failures were considered to be much more serious than those of market failures. Equally important was that the standard set of reform policies implied a shift from a national perspective on development towards outward orientation, price determination by global markets and, despite the problematic experience of the second half of the 1970s, a greater reliance on foreign capital inflows. Thus, efficiency enhancement in resource allocation was sought to be achieved through liberalization and deregulation at the national level and through opening up to competition at the global level, as underlined by the importance given to liberalization of trade and FDI.

C. The outcome of orthodox reforms

The performance of countries that undertook orthodox reforms, including the transition economies in the 1990s, rarely met the high expectations. It was especially disappointing in comparison with that of economies that had followed alternative strategies, in particular the fast-growing newly industrializing economies (NIEs) in East Asia (*TDR 2003*, chap. IV). Average annual GDP growth in these economies exceeded 7 per cent throughout the period from 1980 to 1996. In China it was even higher with an annual average exceeding 10 per cent between 1980 and 2000. Latin America, on the other hand, registered an average annual GDP growth of 1.8 per cent in the 1980s and 3.3 per cent in the 1990s, and sub-Saharan Africa's average annual GDP growth did not reach 3 per cent in either decade. Moreover, the dramatic slowdown in the latter two regions compared to the 1960s and

1970s was accompanied by much greater instability. By contrast, growth remained consistently high in Asia, and was associated with less instability than during the preceding decades (table 2.1).

In Latin America, stabilization policies in the 1980s helped to bring inflation, which had often taken the form of hyperinflation, under control and to achieve a reasonable degree of monetary and fiscal discipline. However, the policy prescriptions soon came under criticism because of the disappointing overall performance of the economies where they were implemented, especially in terms of growth dynamics and capital formation. Moreover, it soon became apparent that the programmes had undesirable social repercussions. The per capita income in Latin America fell on average by 0.3 per cent per annum between 1980 and 1990

Table 2.1

GDP GROWTH IN SELECTED DEVELOPING COUNTRIES AND REGIONS, 1960–2004

(Average annual percentage change)

Region/country	1960– 1965	1965– 1970	1970– 1975	1975– 1980	1980– 1985	1985– 1990	1990– 1995	1995– 2000	2000– 2004
Africa	5.4	4.9	4.4	3.8	2.2	2.6	1.1	3.4	3.9
Sub-Saharan Africa, excl. South Africa	3.9	3.9	3.9	1.9	1.7	3.2	1.5	3.7	4.2
Latin America	4.6	5.8	6.6	5.1	0.5	1.8	3.6	2.8	1.5
East Asia	5.0	7.5	6.8	7.6	7.1	8.2	8.8	4.9	6.2
China	2.1	5.3	5.1	6.1	11.0	7.8	12.9	8.5	9.4
First-tier NIEs	8.0	9.8	8.3	9.0	7.1	9.1	7.3	4.2	3.8
South Asia	4.5	4.9	2.3	3.6	5.3	5.9	5.0	5.3	5.7
India	4.2	4.9	2.4	3.0	5.3	6.6	5.3	5.8	6.1
Developing countries	4.8	6.0	6.4	5.1	2.9	4.3	5.4	4.1	4.4

Source: UNCTAD secretariat calculations, based on World Bank, *World Development Indicators*, various issues; United Nations Statistics Division (UNSD), *National Accounts Main Aggregates* Database; and Taiwan Province of China, *MacroEconomics* Database.
Note: Calculations are based on GDP in constant 1995 dollars.

(table 2.2), and income distribution deteriorated, in some countries dramatically. The decline in industrial output, combined with the compression of the public sector, implied a sharp increase in open unemployment and informal sector activities as well as a widespread deterioration in working conditions, including a significant fall in real wages, and a dramatic increase in poverty (Calcagno, 2001). The 1990s saw some recovery after the preceding "lost decade", but growth did not return to the levels experienced before the debt crisis and the poverty level remained unchanged.

In Africa, per capita income fell on average by 0.4 per cent in the 1980s, and thereafter scarcely any country returned to the pace of growth of the previous decades, even though they implemented structural adjustment programmes for many years. Of the 15 countries that the World Bank had identified as core adjusters in 1993, only three were classified by the IMF as strong performers by the end of the decade. Where there were improvements in growth performance, these could largely be explained by special circumstances that were unrelated to structural adjustment policies (*TDR 1998*,

Part Two, chap. I, table 34). As in Latin America, programme implementation was also accompanied by deteriorating social indicators: the proportion of the population living on less than $1 a day in the least developed countries (LDCs) of Africa increased continuously from the second half of the 1960s – from an average of 55.8 per cent to 64.9 per cent in 1995–1999 (UNCTAD, 2002: tables 19 and 20). Estimates by the UNCTAD secretariat for 20 LDCs, including 17 from Africa, on the impact of SAF/ESAF programmes on poverty, show that, comparing the three years before and after the adoption of the programmes, the overall incidence of poverty rose by nearly one percentage point (UNCTAD, 2002: table 40). As frustration with the results of the adjustment programmes intensified, the view gained ground that structural adjustment programmes were "part of the problem rather than part of the solution of the development crisis in Africa" (Lipumba, 1995: 52).

There are differing views on the causes of the failure, and varying experiences suggest a complex relation between different domestic and external factors.[4] A major cause of the failure of

Table 2.2

PER CAPITA GDP GROWTH IN SELECTED DEVELOPING COUNTRIES AND REGIONS, 1960–2004

(Average annual percentage change)

Region/country	1960– 1965	1965– 1970	1970– 1975	1975– 1980	1980– 1985	1985– 1990	1990– 1995	1995– 2000	2000– 2004
Africa	2.8	2.2	1.6	0.9	-0.7	-0.2	-1.5	1.0	1.6
Sub-Saharan Africa, excl. South Africa	1.3	1.2	1.1	-1.0	-1.2	0.2	-1.3	1.1	1.8
Latin America	1.7	3.1	4.0	2.7	-1.6	-0.2	1.9	1.2	0.1
East Asia	3.0	4.7	4.4	5.9	5.4	6.4	7.5	3.8	5.3
China	0.3	2.6	2.8	4.6	9.5	6.1	11.7	7.5	8.7
First-tier NIEs	5.0	7.2	6.1	7.1	5.5	8.0	6.1	3.2	3.2
South Asia	2.2	2.5	0.0	1.4	2.9	3.6	2.8	3.3	4.0
India	1.9	2.5	0.1	0.9	3.1	4.4	3.3	4.0	4.5
Developing countries	2.5	3.4	3.9	2.9	0.7	2.2	3.5	2.4	2.9

Source: UNCTAD secretariat calculations, based on World Bank, *World Development Indicators*, various issues; UNSD, *Population* Database and *National Accounts Main Aggregates* Database; and Taiwan Province of China, *MacroEconomics* Database.

Note: See table 2.1.

the reform programmes to meet expectations was probably that they were typically initiated during a situation of crisis, when domestic adjustment took a deflationary path. This necessitated a tightening of fiscal and monetary policy to bring down inflation, while global demand growth remained insufficient to give the needed expansionary stimulus. In addition, measures taken to deal with external shocks often aggravated pressure on the fiscal accounts (e.g. through the impact of currency devaluation on the domestic currency value of debt servicing and on the costs of imports for public investment). Rescue measures for the financial sector and the nationalization of private but publicly guaranteed external debt also represented a heavy additional burden on public finances (*TDR 1989*, chap. IV). Sizeable cuts had to be made in spending for productive infrastructure and social purposes as a result of the pressure for rapid fiscal adjustment. Stabilization policies adversely affected investment and brought the process of capital accumulation to a halt, in some cases even reversing it. In addition, the imposition of austerity measures led to serious social conflicts, thus contributing to growing instability.

Advocates of the orthodox policies attributed the unsatisfactory results to slippages in their implementation, partly reflecting lack of ownership by governments and other stakeholders in the countries undertaking the reforms. Indeed, the stringency of conditionality and the similarity of the reform programmes across countries often made it difficult for national policymakers to obtain the necessary support from domestic groups and institutions for implementation of reforms. By 1994, the World Bank officially recognized that the removal of distortions in product and factor markets alone would be insufficient to "put countries on a sustained, poverty-reducing growth path", and that it would require "better economic policies and more investment in human capital, infrastructures, and institution building, along with better governance" (World Bank, 1994: 2). The Bank did not, however, revise its definition of "good economic policies" by giving more weight to macroeconomic and sectoral policy measures aimed at strengthening productive private investment.

In most countries, the crisis was perpetuated by external constraints that became increasingly intrusive as economies opened up unilaterally to international trade and finance in the context of structural adjustment programmes. The fast pace of trade liberalization in many developing countries caused their trade deficit associated with any given rate of growth to become larger, adding to payments difficulties and increasing dependency on capital inflows. Since in open economies with flexible exchange rates, the interest rate and the exchange rate cannot be used as independent policy instruments, efforts to attract capital inflows involved a spiral of rising interest rates and an appreciating exchange rate. These negatively affected trade performance and fed into increasingly speculative capital inflows. In many developing countries and emerging market economies, the ensuing rising cost of capital hindered accumulation, and the loss of competitiveness induced a reduction in real wages. At the same time, high-interest-led capital flows generated credit expansion, consumption booms and speculative bubbles, which, owing to the lack of proper financial regulatory and supervisory institutions, were a source of financial instability and crisis (Eatwell and Taylor, 2002).

Contrary to orthodox expectations that the cuts in public sector deficits would crowd in private investment, and that a reduced State presence in economic activity would unleash a fresh wave of private entrepreneurial initiatives, private investment remained depressed. An "investment pause" had been expected to occur in the immediate aftermath of the reforms, but the situation persisted because of obvious inconsistencies between the various elements of the standard reform package. It did not pay sufficient attention to the importance of favourable monetary conditions for private investment, to the complementarity of public and private investment, and to the fact that State involvement – now drastically reduced –

> Private investment remained depressed, contrary to expectations that reduced State presence in economic activity would unleash a fresh wave of private entrepreneurial initiatives.

> Policies promoted with a view to getting relative prices "right" at the micro level failed, because in too many cases they got prices "wrong" at the macro level.

often ensures the provision of goods and services that private actors are unwilling to produce, but which create important positive externalities for a wide range of productive activities (*TDR 1993*, chaps. II and III).

In Latin American countries, more investment-friendly macroeconomic policies were constrained initially by the urgent need to combat inflation, and, later, by the need to remain attractive for external capital flows in a context of increasing current-account deficits, as discussed in chapter IV below. In Africa, dependence on private capital flows was less pronounced than in Latin America, but declining prices for primary commodity exports due to weak growth in global demand until the beginning of the new millennium, and the resulting deterioration in the terms of trade and the purchasing power of exports were the most constraining factors for capital accumulation and output growth. In the absence of external financing to compensate for the terms-of-trade losses, adjustment had to take the form of severe import compression and a sharp decline in investment.

As a result of these factors the share of investment in Latin American GDP, which had averaged over 25 per cent in the 1970s, had fallen to 18 per cent by the early 1990s, recovering to about 20 per cent at the end of the 1990s (figure 2.1; and *TDR 2003*, chap. IV). The standard policies geared to improving factor allocation did not succeed in bringing about an investment recovery in sub-Saharan Africa either: the average ratio of investment to GDP dropped from 24 per cent in the 1970s to 17 per cent at the beginning of the 1990s, a level from which it has barely recovered so far. This downward adjustment had an impact mainly on public investment, but contrary to conventional wisdom, this did not "crowd in" private investment. Indeed, the share of private investment in GDP continued to remain lower in the late 1990s than it had been in the 1970s.

In these circumstances, capital formation in most economies in Latin America and Africa was unable to keep pace with the increased need for productivity enhancement and technological innovation, which are basic requirements for the success of export-oriented development strategies. Consequently, they were ill-equipped to meet the challenges posed by opening up to international markets and exposing actual and potential domestic producers to international competition. In sub-Saharan Africa and Latin America, this meant not only sluggish growth and slow structural change, but also in some cases deindustrialization (*TDR 2003*, chap. VI).[5] Between 1980 and 1990 the share of manufacturing output in GDP fell, from 17.4 per cent to 14.9 per cent in sub-Saharan Africa, and from 28.2 per cent to 25 per cent in Latin America. By 2000, the share of manufacturing was still at the same low level in sub-Saharan Africa, while in Latin America it had fallen further, to 17.8 per cent.

Policies promoted with a view to getting relative prices "right" at the micro level failed, because in too many cases they got prices "wrong" at the macro level (i.e. the real interest rate and the real exchange rates). This meant that they did not create more incentives for investment, innovation and diversification of production, despite the retreat of government and the freeing of market forces. Indeed, they led to greater instability of the key macroeconomic prices due to continuing market failures resulting, for example, from asymmetric information and adverse selection in financial markets, as well as inadequate sequencing of liberalization of product and factor markets in an environment of weak institutions. Even in instances where microeconomic incentives were generated, macroeconomic disincentives, structural constraints and institutional weaknesses prevented them from creating a vigorous supply response. And whatever efficiency gains liberalization and deregulation generated, they did not produce faster growth, but led to growing inequality.

After more than a decade of liberalizing reforms, the payments disorders in many countries remained as acute as before, and their economies had come to depend even more on external financ-

Figure 2.1

GROSS FIXED CAPITAL FORMATION IN SELECTED DEVELOPING REGIONS AND CHINA, 1965–2004

(Per cent of GDP)

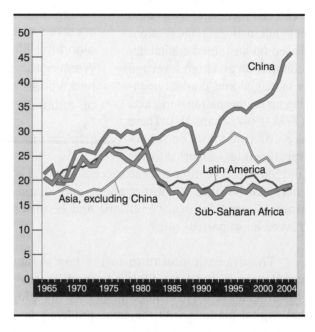

Source: UNCTAD secretariat calculations, based on World Bank, *World Development Indicators, 2005*.

Note: Latin America comprises Argentina, Bolivia, Brazil, Chile, Colombia, Ecuador, Mexico, Peru, Uruguay and Venezuela. Asia comprises China, India, Indonesia, Malaysia, Pakistan, the Philippines, the Republic of Korea, Thailand, Taiwan Province of China, and Turkey.

ing in their efforts to achieve the growth rates necessary to tackle their deep-rooted problems of poverty and underdevelopment. In Latin America, average growth was lower by 3 per cent per annum in the 1990s than in the 1970s, while trade deficits as a proportion of GDP remained constant. In sub-Saharan Africa, growth fell but deficits rose. But despite the lack of success, the "consensus" of the 1990s firmly stuck to the notion that there was no alternative to these policies.

Meanwhile, development successes occurred where prescriptions along the lines of the Washington Consensus had limited or no influence on national policies, notably in the East Asian economies. Their average growth rates exceeded 8 per cent per annum over many years, and, until the crisis in the late 1990s, the imposition of policies by the international financial institutions was avoided. The East Asian economies, which followed a more selective and gradual approach to liberalization than the developing countries that followed the orthodox reform agenda, achieved more stable and faster growth. They also achieved successful integration into international trade relations based on sustained capital accumulation at a high level and a managed and gradual opening up to international markets (*TDR 1999*, chap. IV). There are differing views on the respective roles of market forces and State intervention in these success stories, but there can be little doubt that policy and institutions tailored to local conditions and histories played an important role.[6]

The dramatic downturn in the East Asian economies in the late 1990s occurred because governments failed to manage integration into global capital markets with the same prudence and strategic reasoning they had previously adopted in managing trade liberalization. As in other countries earlier, especially in Latin America, capital-account opening made the economies of the region more vulnerable to financial disturbances. In 1997 massive capital outflows prompted a financial crisis, which resulted in IMF intervention with its standard reform packages applied in several crisis-stricken countries. Although the adjustment programmes were combined with massive financial assistance, they led to a sharp recession and a dramatic deterioration in the poverty situation. This inevitably prompted a questioning of the IMF's diagnosis before and after the crisis and, consequently, the appropriateness of its policy prescriptions. Nevertheless, owing to the structural strength of the productive sector and the strong position of their exporters on world markets, most of these countries recovered rapidly after a sharp real devaluation, and terminated their collaboration with the IMF.

> Development successes occurred where prescriptions along the lines of the Washington Consensus had limited or no influence on national policies.

D. Second-generation reforms and debt reduction

1. *A new focus on poverty and institutions*

The disappointing results of policy reforms in the 1980s and 1990s, and the related critiques emanating from the international policy debate led to the recognition in the 1990s that the initial reform package would have to be supplemented by measures to mitigate the adverse social effects of the reforms.

Almost two decades of focusing on price reform in product, labour and financial markets, as well as on external trade, increasingly led to the recognition that key to the success of policy was a better understanding of what the market mechanism could be expected to deliver in developing countries, or, as Rodrik (1999: 2) put it: "The encounter between neo-classical economics and developing societies served to reveal the institutional underpinnings of market economies."[7] Thus the enlarged policy agenda evolving in the 1990s placed greater emphasis on country-specific institutions and focused on good governance, including combating corruption as a major element, to make the State and non-market institutions more effective (Hayami, 2003). Strengthening property rights came to be regarded as the key institutional element for solving the problem of insufficient investment. Moreover, the enlarged policy agenda, sometimes called the "post-Washington Consensus" (Stiglitz, 1998) or "second-generation reforms" (Kuczynski and Williamson, 2003), emphasized the reduction of poverty and the mitigation of its effects as immediate objectives of development policies, requiring direct government involvement.[8]

In part, the new emphasis on health, education and infrastructure was also an outcome of the notion that development is more than economic growth – a notion that gained widespread acceptance in the 1990s (Cornia, Jolly and Stewart, 1987; Sen, 1999). It also found expression in the creation of the Human Development Index, used by the United Nations Development Programme (UNDP) since 1993 as a standard measure of human well-being, as well as in the World Social Summit held in 1995, which pledged to make the conquest of poverty, the goal of full employment and the fostering of social integration the overriding objectives of development.

There can be little doubt that the functioning of markets is strongly influenced by supporting institutions, and that capital accumulation is closely linked to the consolidation of property rights. However, the view that institutional shortcomings were the main reason why the policies of the Washington Consensus did not live up to their promises served to shift attention away from the shortcomings of the principles underlying those policies and their theoretical foundation. The quality of institutions in developing countries had been no better in previous decades when growth performance was more satisfactory. Similarly, poverty reduction was not an entirely new objective of development policies, as it had been a stated goal of the World Bank since the early 1970s (Hayami, 2003: 58); however, the assumption implicit in the initial structural adjustment approach was that it would occur as a trickle-down effect of growth.

The logic of market-oriented reforms was to improve efficiency and economic performance,

> The disappointing results of policy reforms led to the recognition that the initial reform package would have to be supplemented by measures to mitigate the adverse social effects.

leading to higher growth and overall living standards by redirecting resources from inefficient, non-tradable goods and import-substituting production to export activities with the help of new investment and productivity increases. This would be made possible by opening up to capital inflows. The restructuring process induced by more openness to international competition was expected to lead to only a temporary displacement followed by a rapid reabsorption of the labour force into activities where the economy had the greatest comparative advantages. Poverty would naturally be reduced by increased efficiency of labour allocation and income growth. As growth turned out to be insufficient in most countries to make even a dent on poverty alleviation, and the more efficient reallocation of resources lagged behind the speed of destruction of inefficient activities, the focus shifted to policies that would directly address the problem of poverty. The implicit assumption that the determinants of growth, the effects of trade, financial integration and market liberalization are independent of, or exert only a temporary effect on, poverty and income distribution was reflected in the reorientation of mainstream thinking; the modified approach added social policies to the standard measures of liberalization and to the operations of the IMF and the World Bank (Berg and Taylor, 2000).

By 1990, the World Bank had already recognized the need to develop special social funds, which, due to a number of factors, including limited funding, poor targeting and inadequate sequencing, only made a marginal contribution to reducing poverty and reversing adverse shifts in income distribution (Cornia, 1999: 132). The introduction of the Poverty Reduction Strategy Papers (PRSPs) in 1995 was a more significant step aimed at reducing poverty. The PRSP approach recognized that stabilization and adjustment policies exert, at least temporarily, an adverse impact on the poor, which can be mitigated through safety nets and targeted spending programmes.

This approach also responded to another weakness of the previous adjustment policies by strengthening ownership, partly through a re-orientation of conditionality and partly through a revision of procedures for programme implementation. PRSPs are to be prepared by national authorities in developing countries with the broad-based participation of civil society, including enterprises and representatives of the poor, but they are subject to joint approval by the Bank and the Fund. In the same context, and in line with the shift of emphasis towards measures that would directly address the incidence of poverty, the IMF replaced its Enhanced Structural Adjustment Facility (ESAF) with the Poverty Reduction and Growth Facility (PRGF). The preparation and implementation of PRSPs became a prerequisite for debt relief under the enhanced Heavily Indebted Poor Countries Debt Initiative (HIPC Initiative) of the IMF and World Bank (see chapter III, section C below) and for access to Poverty Reduction Support Credit (PRSC) introduced by the World Bank in 2001. Bilateral grants, concessionary loans and debt relief also became closely linked to the poverty reduction policies and strategies.

Compared to the ESAF conditions, the PRSP process gives countries greater autonomy in designing social safety nets and targeted spending programmes, but not in the formulation of their macroeconomic policies and development strategies. With respect to the latter, little autonomy is left to governments to define alternative paths to poverty reduction that would place more emphasis on measures to stimulate output growth and employment creation. Regarding the macroeconomic and structural adjustment contents of PRSPs, there has been no fundamental departure from the kind of policy advice espoused under former structural adjustment programmes (UNCTAD, 2002; ODI, 2001).

The PRSP approach emphasizes the reallocation of existing fiscal resources to areas that can

> The focus shifted to policies that would directly address the problem of poverty.

> Curing the symptoms of poverty can lead to intertemporal trade-offs if public spending is diverted away from broader development targets that would have a longer lasting impact on the causes.

have a direct impact on the well-being of the poor. Such a reallocation responds to an ethical imperative and can go some way in solving the most pressing social problems. However, there are limits to the extent this can be expected to achieve sustained poverty eradication. Despite the positive welfare impact of social spending, real progress in poverty reduction may be handicapped as long as macroeconomic and adjustment policies continue to push in the opposite direction, generating impulses that hamper capital formation and lead to regressive changes in income distribution. The World Bank noted that "most recipients consider the focus of the initiative to be excessive on social sectors, and too little on growth and 'wealth creation'" (World Bank, 2003: 46).

The new emphasis of PRSPs on achieving quick results by redirecting public expenditure to areas such as primary health care and education may not have a lasting impact on poverty as long as structural change remains slow and capital accumulation insufficient to boost growth and create productive employment. Although output growth alone is not enough for improving the living standards of all social segments, it is likely to be a necessary condition for a sustained reduction of poverty. Indeed, growth and sustained poverty reduction appear to be fundamentally dependent on the same forces and policies that lead to productive restructuring, capital accumulation and productivity increases. From this perspective, coordinated policies of capacity development in new industrial activities for enhancing efficiency and reducing the adverse effects of labour displacement can also eradicate poverty at its source. PRSPs, therefore, can give rise to serious intertemporal trade-offs to the extent that the cure of the symptoms involves a diversion of public spending away from broader development targets that would have a longer lasting impact on the causes, such as those discussed in chapter V of this *TDR*.

2. Debt relief and the proliferation of conditionality

The solution to the debt crisis of the 1980s was initially sought through ad hoc debt renegotiations. At the end of that decade the recognition that the success of policy reforms and structural adjustment was also contingent on external financial constraints provided the rationale for the Brady Plan, which addressed the debt servicing problems of middle-income developing countries. The plan represented an important change in focus for the resolution of these problems: from policies designed to create large trade surpluses to those that would reduce the debt burden and improve access of the debtor countries to the international capital markets in order to refinance their debts. After years of insistence by the international financial institutions on a country-by-country approach to deal with the debt overhang that had emerged simultaneously in many countries at the beginning of the 1980s, the Brady Plan represented an international effort to resolve the debt crisis. The plan was designed to give debtor governments additional "breathing space" by allowing them to divert part of their debt service payments to more productive uses, which in turn would eventually enable them to grow out of their debt problems.

Similarly, the launching of the HIPC Initiative in 1996 was designed to support policy reforms in the poorer countries that were primarily indebted vis-à-vis official creditors. It implied recognition that the debt problems of these countries were a major hindrance to their faster growth, and that the causes of their debt problems were at least partly systemic in nature. The HIPC Initiative advanced slowly, largely because fulfilling the conditions attached to it was an exercise that frequently exceeded the institutional and administrative capacities of the poorest countries.

The international initiatives to deal with the debt problem of developing countries improved the context for growth-oriented development policies. They enlarged the fiscal space to support domestic economic and social development, as well as the scope for importing the capital goods and technologies essential for a dynamic growth process and successful trade integration. However, the impact of debt reduction on the liquidity situation of the beneficiary countries has in many cases been limited, particularly where, prior to the granting of the debt relief, debt service payments were in arrears (see also chapter III, section C). Therefore, in most countries, official debt relief needs to be complemented by increased flows of official development assistance (ODA), as far as possible in the form of grants for the poorest countries, in order to increase the capacity of the State to provide essential public goods and infrastructure. This would also help prevent a new build-up of debt and maintain debt sustainability in the medium and long term in countries where faster capital formation is not possible without imports of capital and intermediate goods that exceed export earnings potential.

> The proliferation and widening scope of conditionality has faced growing criticism over the years.

The debt relief initiatives also served to perpetuate the key elements of the orthodox reform package and the Washington Consensus through the conditionality attached to them or through the increasing dependence of exchange rates and balance-of-payments performance on market sentiment. Although there was broad agreement that new lending by the international financial institutions and the provision of official debt relief should be linked to certain conditions, the conditionality actually applied came under growing criticism over the years, not only because of its deflationary bias, but also because of the proliferation and widening scope of the conditions (Goldstein, 2000; Kapur and Webb, 2000; and Buira, 2003).

The original rationale for conditionality by the Bretton Woods institutions was to protect their financial integrity and preserve the revolving character of their resources. But as the operations of the IMF and World Bank in developing countries expanded, their conditionality became tighter and more complex, encompassing areas which are within the purview not only of other international organizations but also of national development strategies. And with "second-generation reforms", conditionality expanded further, into issues of political and economic governance.

The average number of structural conditions, covering a wide range of policy areas – from trade and finance to public enterprises and privatization, and even labour market institutions and social safety nets – doubled between the 1970s and 1980s. At the end of the 1990s there were more than 50 structural policy conditions for a typical Extended Fund Facility programme, and between 9 and 15 for stand-by programmes. The number of structural performance criteria in the IMF programmes for the three Asian countries struck by the 1997 crisis was four times the average for all Fund programmes over the period 1993–1999, prompting assertions that there was a "temptation to use currency crises as an opportunity to force fundamental structural and institutional reforms on countries" (Feldstein, 1998). On a strict definition of conditionality used by Kapur and Webb (2000: 5–7), the number of conditions attached to lending by the Bretton Woods institutions at the end of the 1990s ranged between 15 and 30 for sub-Saharan Africa, and 9 and 43 for other regions. If conditionality is loosely defined, the number increases to between 74 and 165 for sub-Saharan Africa, and between 65 and 130 for the others.

Many observers, both within and outside the Bretton Woods institutions, have questioned the effectiveness of conditionality in preventing policy failures and improving economic performance.[9] Evidence shows that with the proliferation of structural conditions in the 1980s and 1990s, the degree of compliance with the programmes declined (Mussa and Savastano, 1999). More importantly, there has been very little correlation between compliance and economic performance. For instance, in 1993 the World Bank identified 15 countries in sub-Saharan Africa as a core group of adjusters on the basis of their compliance with the policies recommended, including their implementation of significant institutional changes.

However, the subsequent economic performance of these countries was quite disappointing. Only three were among what the IMF classified as strong performers towards the end of the 1990s. In other words, the majority of countries that accounted for much of the faster growth in sub-Saharan Africa in the second half of the 1990s were not among the high-compliers five years earlier; while most of the countries that were thought to be pursuing sound policies by World Bank criteria were not among the subsequent strong performers (*TDR 1998*: 124–125 and table 34).

The Fund's extensive use of structural conditions in its lending programmes is widely considered to be in violation of its own guidelines for conditionality established in 1979. These guidelines explicitly state that performance criteria should be confined to macroeconomic variables, and that they can relate to other variables only in exceptional cases when their macroeconomic impact is significant. As argued by a former Research Director of the IMF, these guidelines aimed at making conditionality "less intrusive by limiting the number of performance criteria, insisting on their macroeconomic character, circumscribing the cases for reviews, and keeping preconditions to a minimum. Yet, these restraining provisions have not prevented the intensification of conditionality in every direction that the guidelines attempted to block" (Polak, 1991: 53–54).[10]

There is a rationale for macroeconomic conditions to be formulated at aggregate levels, such as the volume of adjustment in public spending or in monetary aggregates, without going into what items should be involved; in other words, leaving these to the discretion of the national authorities. Such conditionality would be justified as a device for risk management by the lender (Kapur and Webb, 2000: 1–2), but it would not permanently circumscribe the space for development policy. Structural conditions by their nature are different, because they entail permanent changes in legislation and institutions, and circumscribe policies in such a way that their reversal may be extremely difficult and costly.[11]

> Structural conditions entail permanent changes in legislation and institutions, and circumscribe policies in such a way that their reversal may be extremely difficult and costly.

E. The MDGs and the Monterrey Consensus

Following several major international conferences in the course of the 1990s, all of which addressed, in one form or another, the issue of poverty and its social and human impact, the expression of international concern with the problem of persisting poverty culminated in the formulation of the Millennium Development Goals (MDGs). Seven of these eight goals address objectives to be pursued at the national level, with support by the international community. Only Goal 8 – Develop a global partnership for development – adds an international dimension to the agenda. The formulation of the MDGs by the Heads of State and Government at the United Nations Millennium Summit in 2000 reflects the degree of dissatisfaction with development progress and the setback in the fight against poverty under the policy conditions that had prevailed over the previous two decades. It is also a response to the lack of progress in achieving a truly global approach to closing the large and widening gaps in income and living standards by the turn of the millennium. Goal 8 has a number of subsidiary targets, which implicitly recognize the role of the external environment and the shared responsibility of the developed countries for the achievement of the other seven goals.

The targets under Goal 8[12] that have a direct bearing on the orientation of economic policies and development strategies are: to promote "an open trading and financial system that is rule-based, predictable and non-discriminatory"; to deal "comprehensively with developing countries' debt problems through national and international measures to make debt sustainable in the long term"; to "develop decent and productive work for youth"; and, "in cooperation with the private sector, [to] make available the benefits of new technologies."

The outcome of the subsequent International Conference on Financing for Development, the Monterrey Consensus of 2002, can be considered a programmatic complement to the MDGs. It acknowledged that the capability of developing countries to realize the MDGs is heavily influenced by external factors. In particular, concerns were expressed about the general steady decline in ODA during the 1990s. Indeed, at the beginning of the new millennium, total ODA provided by the member countries of the Development Assistance Committee (DAC) as a share of their combined GNI was only about 0.22 per cent, a historical low (OECD, 2006). The Monterrey Conference also recognized that a solution to the external debt problem and progress in dealing with the systemic issues of coherence and consistency of the international monetary, financial and trading system could make a significant contribution in support of development.

> There is no agreement as to what constitutes the necessary internal conditions for adequate levels of productive investment, and what role domestic policies could play to improve those conditions.

Box 2.1

THE MONTERREY CONSENSUS ON INVESTMENT-FRIENDLY POLICIES

In January 2002, Heads of State and Government gathered in Monterrey, Mexico, to address the challenges of financing for development. In the outcome document, the Monterrey Consensus, they agreed on a number of leading actions to eradicate poverty, achieve sustained economic growth and promote sustainable development. Considerable attention was given to the crucial role of investment for growth and development, and to policies in its support (United Nations, 2002).

The Monterrey Consensus recognizes the key role of capital accumulation for development, noting that in the "pursuit of growth, poverty eradication and sustainable development, a critical challenge is to ensure the necessary internal conditions for ... sustaining adequate levels of productive investment and increasing human capacity" (para. 10), and that "an enabling domestic environment is vital for ... increasing productivity (and) ... encouraging the private sector" (para. 10), leaving open the question of what constitutes an enabling environment.

When noting that "improvements in public spending that do not crowd out productive private investment" are necessary (para. 15), and that "investments in basic economic and social infrastructure, social services and social protection ... are vital for enabling people ... to better adapt to and benefit from changing economic conditions and opportunities" (para. 16), the Monterrey Consensus highlights the complementarity between public and private investment in the development of local capacities. This aspect of State involvement in economic activity was largely neglected in the standard reform packages until the mid-1990s; public finances were squeezed for many years and previously existing institutions that had provided social services were often dismantled.

Finally, the Monterrey Consensus points to the need for a "sound system of financial intermediation ... to foster productive investments" (para 17). It thereby addresses a major constraint to stronger domestic capital formation in many developing countries, made worse as a result of financial liberalization and deregulation. However, as the experience of today's developed countries shows, a sound system of financial intermediation takes many years to evolve. The question therefore arises as to the options available for the large number of countries that are still far from having such a

The Monterrey Consensus also addressed a number of questions in the areas of trade, financial and macroeconomic policies for development, and it explicitly pointed to the challenge facing developing countries to ensure the necessary conditions for adequate levels of productive investment. From the perspective of development strategy, the important point here is that, while the Consensus does not call into question the alleged beneficial effects of trade and financial openness, it draws attention to the necessity of favourable "internal" conditions for productive investment. Yet there is no overall agreement as to what constitutes the necessary internal conditions, and what role domestic policies could play to improve those conditions. In this respect, the

Monterrey Conference failed to recognize a major lesson that could be drawn from more than 20 years of orthodox policy reforms: the need to revise the role of monetary and fiscal policies to directly stimulate capital accumulation and growth, and to reconsider the possible contribution of sectoral policies and institutions to technological upgrading. Moreover, there is a remarkable imbalance in the Monterrey Consensus in terms of its bias in favour of FDI as compared to domestic investment (box 2.1). Yet FDI in Latin America and Africa has in general not been in sectors and technologies that are capable of generating sizeable growth and value added, and its impact on domestic income has often been limited because TNCs operating in tradable goods

Box 2.1 *(concluded)*

system. In the absence of a mature system of private financial intermediation it would be advisable for these countries not to wait for market forces to generate such a system; rather, they should identify locally viable instruments of public policy that would accelerate its development on the one hand, and provide risk capital to strengthen the productive sector of the economy on the other.

The text of the Monterrey Consensus cited above testifies to the considerable attention given at the Conference to the need to improve the conditions for domestic investment, although the policy conclusions against the background of the preceding 20 years remained rather vague. The text places even greater emphasis on FDI, thus paying tribute to the principles of the (post-) Washington Consensus. While five paragraphs of the Monterrey document address the issue of domestic investment, without going beyond general recommendations, seven paragraphs address the issue of FDI. They offer an array of recommendations that are much more concrete, especially with regard to measures aimed at attracting FDI. The Monterrey Consensus suggests that in order

> to attract and enhance inflows of productive capital, countries need to continue their efforts to achieve a transparent, stable and predictable investment climate, with proper contract enforcement and respect for property rights, embedded in sound macroeconomic policies and institutions that allow businesses, both domestic and international, to operate efficiently and profitably (para. 21).

It goes on to remind developing-country governments that

> special efforts are required in such priority areas as economic policy and regulatory frameworks for promoting and protecting investments, including in the areas of human resource development, avoidance of double taxation, corporate governance, accounting standards, and the promotion of a competitive environment. Other mechanisms, such as public/private partnerships and investment agreements, can be important (para. 21).

Finally, paragraph 22 points to the need for

> international, regional and national institutions in source countries to provide export credits, cofinancing, venture capital and other lending instruments, risk guarantees, leveraging aid resources, information on investment opportunities, business development services, forums to facilitate business contacts and cooperation between enterprises of developed and developing countries, as well as funding for feasibility studies.

sectors frequently use a high proportion of imported inputs. Policies in support of FDI have been found to benefit development only when embedded in a broader development strategy that ensures its complementarity with domestic investment and its creation of dynamic linkages with domestic activities as well as an appropriate regulatory framework (*TDR 2003*, chap. VI).

The Monterrey Consensus contributed to the evolution of development policy thinking by emphasizing the need for increasing ODA as a precondition for many developing countries to make decisive progress towards growth and achievement of the MDGs, especially through increased spending on education, health and basic

social infrastructure. However, like other new initiatives that had "augmented" the standard reform package before, the Monterrey Conference did not lead to a new consensus on a policy agenda geared at stimulating capital formation and structural change, leaving the take-off of a dynamic growth process to market forces alone. An "enabling environment" for economic development is certainly strongly influenced by the way markets operate, but it is also characterized by externalities of various kinds. Yet policy prescriptions focusing on "getting the prices right" have limited the scope for active government policies to address such externalities, which in many cases will be decisive for investment decisions (see chapters V and VI of this *Report*).

F. Beyond the Monterrey Consensus

On a more practical level, and with a greater focus on the role of governments, the report of the United Nations Millennium Project[13] of 2005, entitled *Investing in Development* (also known, as the *Sachs Report*), represents a further step in the same direction (UN Millennium Project, 2005). As the title indicates, the report's main emphasis is on investment, and indeed, more on domestic investment than on FDI. This is because it primarily addresses the problems of low-income countries that have very limited access to FDI, and because very little can be expected from FDI for solving social problems and reducing poverty. Thus the report makes a strong case for a substantial increase in public investment to achieve faster and socially acceptable growth, and it suggests financing the greater investment through a combination of higher domestic taxation and a substantial rise in official external financing, especially in the form of grants.

In the aftermath of the Millennium Summit and the Monterrey Conference, several developed-country governments had already made commitments for gradually but substantially increasing their ODA. This is in line with UNCTAD's call in 2000, for a doubling of ODA to sub-Saharan Africa, based on an estimate that a net capital inflow of at least an additional $10 billion per annum would be needed for a decade or so in order to lift the countries in that region onto a growth path that would allow a gradual narrowing of their income gap with the more advanced countries (UNCTAD, 2000, sect. E). UNCTAD had argued that a doubling of official capital inflows, in combination with policy measures to raise the efficiency of investment, could set off a process of accelerated growth that would reduce, in a decade or so, both the resource gap of the region and its dependence on aid. Subsequent estimates made by the World Bank, the Economic Commission for Africa (ECA) and others confirmed that a doubling of aid was indeed necessary to help initiate faster development in countries and sectors that do not attract private investment and that cannot afford to borrow extensively from commercial sources. The need for more aid has been well recognized by major donors, and various initiatives have been launched since 2002 to this end, which are also endorsed in the *Sachs Report*. These include a proposal for an international finance facility, or a special airport tax earmarked for the financing of health expenditures in the poorest countries. These initiatives signal serious efforts by the international community to strengthen the global partnership for development (see also chapter III, section C below).

The *Sachs Report* recognizes the importance of country-specific national policies and institutions in the development process,[14] thus rediscovering a significant role for the State in development. To some extent, this implies a reorientation away from the past orthodox approach, which considered dismantling the "inefficient" public sector to be the most important precondition for unleashing private economic activity. However, the *Report* does not offer a new approach to dealing with the problem of insufficient capital formation and growth. In line with the policy proposals of the "second-generation reforms", the *Sachs Report* also relies on investment in health, education and basic infrastructure for attaining the MDGs. By suggesting that in countries with extreme poverty

Box 2.2

ECONOMIC GROWTH IN THE 1990s - LEARNING FROM A DECADE OF REFORM: QUOTATIONS FROM THE WORLD BANK REPORT

- "Growth-oriented action, for example, on technological catch-up, or encouragement of risk taking for faster accumulation may be needed." (10)

- "There are many ways of achieving macroeconomic stability, openness, and domestic liberalization." (12)

- "Different policies can have the same effect, and the same policy can have different effects, depending on the context." (13)

- "Like that of policies, the effect of institutions depends on the context." (13)

- "The role of activist industrial policies is still controversial but is likely to have been important." (83)

- "The available evidence suggests that restrictions on short-term capital flows may have a role to play in the pursuit of outcomes-based macroeconomic stability in developing countries." (116)

Source: World Bank, *Economic Growth in the 1990s - Learning from a Decade of Reform,* Washington, DC, 2005.

PRSPs should be aligned with the MDGs, the *Sachs Report* again advocates implicitly the types of national policies and the same reliance on the "invisible hand" to guide private decisions on resource allocation and accumulation that had characterized the structural adjustment policies of the IMF and World Bank and the post-Washington Consensus.

Also in 2005, the World Bank published a study, entitled *Economic growth in the 1990s - Learning from a Decade of Reform*, which acknowledges a number of mistakes and shortcomings of the previous approach with structural adjustment policies, and draws lessons from these for the design of development strategies (box 2.2).[15] First, it suggests that "reforms need to go beyond the generation of efficiency gains to promote growth", as economic growth also "entails structural transformation, diversification of production, change, risk taking by producers, correction of both gov-

ernment and market failures, and changes in policies and institutions"; and it goes on to suggest that, consequently, "growth-oriented action, for example, on technological catch-up, or encouragement of risk taking for faster accumulation may be needed" (World Bank, 2005: 10, 11).

Second, it recognizes that there is no one-size-fits-all set of successful policies: "There are many ways of achieving macroeconomic stability, openness, and domestic liberalization ... Different policies can have the same effect, and the same policy can have different effects, depending on the context" (World Bank, 2005: 11, 13). It admits, for example, that for achieving macroeconomic stability it may be worth considering the imposition of restrictions on capital flows, because "notwithstanding the theoretical arguments in favour of capital account openness, the evidence on growth is inconclusive and volatility clearly increased" after capital-account opening

(World Bank, 2005: 17). The authors of the World Bank study, while laying strong emphasis on the important role of institutions, also underline the need for diversity in institutional development, because, "like that of policies, the effect of institutions depends on the context" (World Bank, 2005: 13). Third, the World Bank study recognizes that "Key functions to be fulfilled in sustained growth processes are the accumulation of capital, allocative efficiency, technological progress, and the sharing the benefits of growth", and that "the role of activist industrial policies is still controversial but is likely to have been important" (World Bank, 2005: 83, 85) in the successful experiences of growth and catching up.[16]

Thus, *Learning from a Decade of Reform* testifies to the growing uncertainty about the commitment to the Washington Consensus, including the different augmentations of that Consensus. But it is probably an exaggeration to interpret that study as a "radical rethink of development strategies" (Rodrik, 2006: 7), because the basic paradigm remains largely intact. The authors do not go very far in their redefinition of the role of public policies in support of capital accumulation and technological change. This is probably because they remain sceptical about the capacity of national governments to carry out effective discretionary policies. The experience of the 1990s leads them to suggest that "government discretion cannot be dispensed with altogether, so it is important to find ways in which it can be exerted effectively" (World Bank, 2005: 14). There can be no doubt that rendering discretionary government intervention more effective must itself be part of a comprehensive reform programme, but the World Bank study suggests that this be limited to certain activities "ranging from regulating utilities and supervising banks to providing infrastructure and social services" (World Bank, 2005: 14). It thereby excludes direct support measures to promote capital accumulation, or sectoral policies to help diversification, upgrading of the production structure and strategic integration into the international trading system.

G. Towards a fundamental policy reorientation[17]

Beyond the stocktaking and the propositions of the *Sachs Report,* and the translation of the *Learning from a Decade of Reform* into implementation of reforms, it will be necessary to analyse the range and kind of policy instruments that individual developing countries have at their disposal to remedy the widespread weakness of private capital formation, productivity growth and technological upgrading. For instance, the *Sachs Report* considers household savings as the most important source of financing investment, without reflecting on how these savings could be generated and to what extent such higher savings would imply lower domestic absorption, and, thus, a disincentive for investment and job creation, especially in the non-tradables sector. In this context, the provision of incentives for the self-financing of investment by firms and the productive use of rent from the exploitation of natural resources are likely to be much more relevant than household savings, which are only one element of national savings (Akyüz and Gore, 1994). The design of the tax system, for example, can play an important role in this regard. The *Sachs Report* considers taxation only as a potential source of the fiscal income required to finance an increase in public investment, whereas the major importance of the design of the tax system for the incentive structure, and thus for the propensity to invest in different production and trade activities, is neglected.

The varying experiences among developing countries, and the evidence provided in this regard in the World Bank study, *Learning from a Decade of Reform,* suggest that more proactive government policies in support of capital accumulation and productivity enhancement are needed for successful integration into international economic relations and as a basis for sustained improvements in the welfare and incomes of all groups of the population.

The market-based reforms pursued in a majority of developing countries since the early 1980s have not lived up to the promises of their proponents. It has not been possible to combine greater macroeconomic stability and external balance with rates of growth that are high enough to close the income gap with the more advanced countries, while at the same time reducing poverty and enabling people. In part, this is probably due to shortcomings in the model of the social and economic realities in the developing world that has been underlying the conventional reform agenda. Within this model, the potential impact on growth of efficiency gains, resulting from leaving adjustments in relative prices to autonomous market forces, has been overestimated. So also has the effect of "crowding in" of private investment as a result of reduced State economic activity. The failure is also likely to be partly due to an excessively deflationary macroeconomic policy stance, not least because savings are not as sensitive to higher interest rates, as assumed, and private investment does not rise in response to higher household savings (see also annex 2 to chapter I).

But in part, the explanation may be found in the reduced number of policy instruments available to policymakers under the development paradigm of the past 25 years. As discussed in the preceding sections of this chapter, much of the internation-

> More proactive government policies in support of capital accumulation and productivity enhancement are needed for successful integration into the global economy and for sustained improvements in the welfare and incomes of all groups of the population.

> To meet the challenges of open developing economies, the scope for national policymaking will have to be widened beyond what has been acceptable under the Washington Consensus approach.

ally supported liberal reform effort "sought to introduce policies that would limit the discretion of national authorities in growth strategies" (World Bank, 2005: 14). Indeed, a key problem faced by policymakers, as demonstrated by Tinbergen (1956) and Hansen (1967), is that there are not always an adequate number of effective instruments to attain all the objectives that they may wish to pursue, because, formally, it takes at least as many instruments to carry out a policy as there are linearly independent goals. This can lead to incompatibility of targets and create difficulties in formulating consistent policies, even in an economy that is not subject to external constraints.

For instance, deregulation of domestic financial markets reduces the ability of monetary authorities to control credit conditions through instruments such as caps on bank interest rates, or restrictions on the volume and direction of credits. Similarly, as integration into global markets is deepened through the removal of restrictions over the movement of goods and services, money and technology, the range of policy instruments shrinks. This is because external influences over national policy targets become stronger, and the trade-offs between internal and external objectives intensify. For instance, it would not be possible to control both the interest rate and the exchange rate while maintaining free capital movement. In an open capital-account regime the exchange rate and the interest rate are both potential policy instruments, but only one of the two can actually be employed independently.[18] From this perspective, economic opening up involves not only the elimination of barriers to the movement of goods and services, money and capital, and labour and technology, but also commitment to obligations and acceptance of rules set by international economic governance systems and institutions, thereby weakening na-

Box 2.3

ECONOMIC OPENNESS AND NATIONAL POLICY AUTONOMY

Economic openness is not only about the elimination of barriers to the movement of goods and services, money and capital, and labour and technology, but also about integration into international economic governance systems and institutions. Both these processes have often overlapped and reinforced each other. On the one hand, liberalization of markets has reduced the number of instruments under the control of policymakers, much in the same way as sovereign policy-making is circumscribed by enhanced multilateral disciplines. On the other hand, multilateral rules and practices have generally weakened the influence of national policy instruments on national policy objectives by promoting liberalization and closer integration into world markets. The figure below attempts to illustrate the potential impact of openness on national policy autonomy, notwithstanding the potential positive effects of trade integration.

IMPACT OF ECONOMIC OPENNESS ON NATIONAL POLICY AUTONOMY

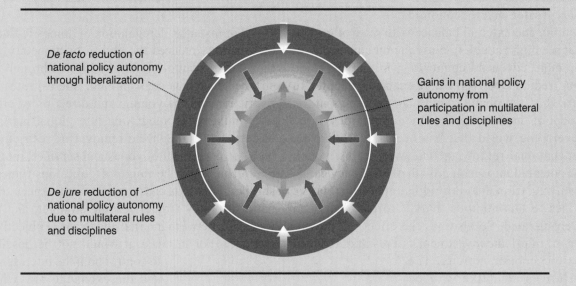

De facto reduction of national policy autonomy through liberalization

Gains in national policy autonomy from participation in multilateral rules and disciplines

De jure reduction of national policy autonomy due to multilateral rules and disciplines

tional policy control over domestic economic variables and development targets (box 2.3).

The autonomy of national economic policy is often defined in terms of the effectiveness of domestic policy instruments in influencing national targets.[19] Even in a closed economy this autonomy is constrained, since formal command over policy instruments does not automatically translate into full control over national targets.

This *de facto* constraint is due to a number of factors. First, the relationships between instrument and target variables are often unstable, and knowledge and information about these relationships are sometimes insufficient. Second, there can be trade-offs in the effectiveness of different instruments, as well as in the objectives sought, and it may not be possible to attain all of them simultaneously with the instruments available. Such trade-offs can exist in many areas of policy, for example, be-

Box 2.3 (concluded)

It shows that in the process of integration into the global economic system, policy autonomy in developing countries is restricted at two levels, but it can also gain from such integration, as the policy autonomy of other countries is also restricted.

(i) Liberalization of markets and dismantling of restrictions on cross-border movements of goods and services, money, capital and labour weakens the *de facto* policy autonomy and influence of national policy instruments over macroeconomic and development policy objectives, as indicated by the outer ring in the figure. This is the case, for example, when capital-account opening reduces the autonomy of national monetary policy, or when opening up to international trade reduces the effectiveness of sectoral support measures as an instrument of income distribution policy.

(ii) Multilateral rules, disciplines and obligations, as well as commitments resulting from bilateral agreements reduce *de jure* sovereign control over policy instruments, as indicated by the second ring of the figure. This is the case, for example, when conditionality attached to assistance from the multilateral financial institutions reduces the autonomy of governments to determine the size and structure of public expenditures, or when accession to the WTO reduces the scope for import protection through tariffs.

(iii) This loss of policy autonomy can be compensated to a certain extent by the gains that can be had from participating in the system of multilateral rules and disciplines, as indicated by the third ring. Examples of such gains are the possible impacts of improved access to external markets on the effectiveness of national policies aimed at increasing supply capacity and productivity in certain sectors, or the benefits of multilateral surveillance over exchange rates for gearing monetary policy to domestic objectives. And, ideally, the possibility to influence in some way the choice and design of the multilateral rules and disciplines could help safeguard, if not promote, national interests.

The extent to which economic openness influences policy autonomy in an individual country, and the extent to which a loss of autonomy in one area can be compensated by gains in another depends on the nature of the rules and disciplines, which in turn largely depends on the way in which the rules and disciplines are created and how they are adapted to changing circumstances. Where this balance lies largely depends on each country's specific conditions. This pattern is, in principle, valid for all countries, although countries with less bargaining power in international processes and with less economic weight in the world economy are likely to experience a greater net reduction of policy autonomy than those with more influence. Thus, there is an "optimum degree of openness" (Bhaduri, 2005) for each country, at which the net benefits of integration are maximized.

tween full employment and price stability, growth and income distribution or, more generally, between efficiency and equity. Third, policy instruments can only be used within certain boundaries or are constrained by certain policy decisions taken in the past which might limit the policy space available for the present. For instance, there is a limit on how far nominal interest rates can be lowered – a problem faced in Japan in recent years – or discretionary action in fiscal policy can be restricted by debt service obligations resulting from debt accumulation over the years (Akyüz, 2006a).

This gap between *de jure* sovereignty of national economic policy and *de facto* control over national economic development widens with the degree of economic openness, with similar consequences.[20] While external liberalization narrows policy autonomy by weakening *de facto* control over national economic development, insertion into international economic governance systems and institutions does so by reducing the *de jure* sovereignty of national economic policy. For instance, there is little difference between loss of autonomy to use tariffs as a means of curbing imports because of WTO rules and commitments on the one hand, and loss of ability to use the exchange rate as an effective instrument for external adjustment because of capital-account liberalization on the other.

If the average developing country is to reach the MDGs, and if the income gap between rich and poor nations is to be narrowed, developing countries will have to grow much faster than they did in the past 25 years. Therefore, the scope for policies to meet the challenges of open developing economies will have to be widened beyond what has been acceptable under the Washington Consensus agenda. In this context lessons could well be drawn not only from the cases of successful catching up in East Asia, but also from the policy practices that formed the basis for private sector development in practically all of today's developed market economies, especially with respect to the instruments employed and intermediate targets they pursued to sustain a dynamic growth process (see, for example, Chang, 2002). Central to these successful strategies were investment-friendly macroeconomic policies, the use of a broad array of fiscal and regulatory instruments in support of capital accumulation, technological upgrading and structural change, and the existence of effective institutions to support and coordinate private and public-sector activities.

Meanwhile, globalization has advanced further – itself the result of policy decisions – but its outcome for development and income distribution, both among and within countries, is dependent on global economic governance and national policies. Against this background, active policies in support of economic development and industrialization must be designed, and their instruments adapted to an outward-oriented strategy. Such a strategy in turn can be nurtured by integration into the global trading and financial systems, provided that national policies and the rules and procedures governing these systems are coherent.

Since a global partnership for development has generally been accepted as a policy imperative for the new millennium, appropriate policy instruments at the national level should be complemented by some operating and controlled at the international level. Examples are ODA grants to improve global income distribution, international macroeconomic policy coordination for managing global demand, or global collective action in the form of multilateral disciplines designed to minimize negative externalities and maximize the positive ones resulting from interdependence. Multilateral discipline is a form of global collective action whereby governments voluntarily agree to reduce sovereignty on a reciprocal basis by subjecting their policies in specified areas to certain rules in the expectation that such an action would lead to a net benefit.

Indeed, interdependence provides the principal rationale for multilateral disciplines because it gives rise to externalities, spillovers and arbitrage opportunities. For example, financial crisis in a country can spread across several other countries through contagion, including to economies with sound policies and good fundamentals. Lax financial standards or excessively liberal tax policies could give rise to regulatory arbitrage and migration of businesses at the expense of countries with more prudent regulations or progressive tax systems. In such cases, the main objective of multilateral disciplines would be to prevent negative externalities or minimize global public "bads".[21] But multilateral cooperation and discipline can also help maximize global public goods. For example, countries may be unwilling to undertake unilateral trade liberalization even when they believe that it would bring efficiency gains, for fear of its adverse repercussions for balance of payments, aggregate demand and employment, but collectively they may be able to do so by securing reciprocal market ac-

> Lessons can be drawn not only from the cases of successful catching up in East Asia, but also from the policy practices that formed the basis for private sector development in practically all of today's developed market economies.

cess.[22] Greater stability of the international financial system is another global public good that can result from multilateral disciplines. It would liberate national monetary policy from the task of stabilizing capital flows and exchange rates thereby providing additional flexibility for macroeconomic policy geared to improving the environment for domestic investment and technological change.

An additional case for policies at the international level is that, with the opening up to international trade, external demand conditions have become increasingly important determinants of national investment decisions. Output and employment growth require an expansion of demand, both at the aggregate level and at the level of sectors that serve as engines in a dynamic growth process. Although the potential of domestic markets to support diversification and industrialization from the demand side in an appropriate macroeconomic setting should not be underestimated, in most developing countries, diversification and industrialization in many sectors implies a strong outward orientation, because domestic markets are too small to achieve the economies of scale required to make industrial production viable. The need to rely on external demand for growth and employment creation is stronger, the smaller the domestic market and the greater the degree of openness. Therefore, policies pursued in other countries and competition with producers in other countries become co-determinants of growth. Appropriate multilateral rules and regulations in trade and finance can thus be of considerable benefit for launching and sustaining a dynamic growth process in developing countries to the extent that they ensure access to markets of other countries, reduce the scope of unfair competition and provide for stability of external monetary and financial conditions.

> An outward-oriented strategy can be nurtured by integration into the global trading and financial systems, provided that national policies and the rules and procedures governing these systems are coherent.

At present two asymmetries in multilateral arrangements merit particular attention. First, international trade is organized around a rules-based system, with certain core principles applying to all participants, but this is not the case in international money and finance. This asymmetry is all the more important because adverse international spillovers and arbitrages generated by self-centred national monetary and financial policies can be much more damaging than those created by trade and trade-related policies, particularly for developing countries (see *TDR 2004*, chap. IV). Second, there is an asymmetry between developed and developing countries in terms of the extent to which multilateral rules and practices restrain policy autonomy. The choice of which aspects of international economic interactions should be brought under multilateral disciplines and which rules and practices should be established in areas subject to such disciplines is not neutral in terms of how the requirements of the development trajectories of industrial and developing countries are accommodated, even when there is a level playing field in the application of the rules. In the current international set-up the more advanced countries have more influence on these choices than the developing countries.[23] The absence of a rules-based system in money and finance is one dimension of this asymmetry, since it permits developed countries which have a disproportionately large impact on global monetary and financial conditions to escape multilateral discipline, while allowing considerable leverage over weaker countries through conditionalities attached to multilateral lending by the Bretton Woods institutions. Another dimension is the existence of rules and regulations in support of the free movement of industrial goods, money, capital and enterprises, which favour advanced countries, but not labour, agricultural products or technology –

> There is an asymmetry between developed and developing countries in terms of the extent to which multilateral rules and practices restrain policy autonomy.

areas that would bring greater benefits to developing countries.

At the national level, additional policy instruments should be explored to support actual or potential domestic producers in their efforts to integrate into the international trading system, and to achieve and maintain international competitiveness in a dynamic process. Examples of such national policy instruments include more flexible fiscal instruments, such as public investments or subsidies on the expenditure side of the public budget, and taxation or tariffs on the income side. However, the success of such instruments also depends on how monetary policies and capital-account management shape the macroeconomic environment. Also at the national level, different forms of heterodox, non-monetary instruments, such as an incomes policy, could free monetary and fiscal policy from the task of domestic stabilization, while sectoral policies (which also offer a strong potential for regional cooperation) could be part of a consequent upgrading strategy.

> In a dynamic process of structural change, the targets and instruments of economic policy must themselves evolve over time.

The choice of national policy instruments needs to take into account the fact that in a dynamic process of structural change, the objectives, targets and the instruments themselves evolve over time. For example, the objective of diversification of primary production will typically be followed by greater diversification into manufacturing, and industrial upgrading and diversification of activities into industrial services, although not all countries will have to follow precisely the same pattern. Or certain economic activities may merit a country-specific form of State support at a promising initial stage, but that support may no longer be warranted when those activities have matured, and at some point in the future their phasing out may actually need to be supported by publicly sponsored social and rehabilitation programmes. At the same time, new, promising activities may merit infant-industry support. Similarly, State intervention in one form or another for credit allocation to support enterprise development and structural change may diminish over time as the financial sector deepens and improves its capac-

ity for intermediation of risk capital, which may itself be a target of active government policies. Therefore, a pragmatic approach will be needed, aimed at solving problems as they emerge in the process of achieving national objectives. This calls for considerable flexibility in the policy-making process, including in the selection and application of policy instruments.[24]

Widening the scope of policy instruments beyond those that were deemed acceptable under the development paradigm of the past 25 years would not only allow the pursuit of additional goals, it would also increase the number of potential combinations of instruments, which in many cases will be decisive for the success or failure of a strategy. For example, public expenditure for research and development is unlikely to fuel growth when the results of these activities are not translated into innovation at the product or production level, particularly when monetary or financing conditions for investment are unfavourable. Similarly, productivity-enhancing measures in agriculture will not translate into significant acceleration of growth and alleviation of poverty if rural workers that eventually become redundant cannot be absorbed into industrial production due to unfavourable exchange-rate developments that hamper exports. These examples illustrate a key aspect of successful catch-up experiences, which seems to have been "the connection between macropolicy and structural policy, in which the links between sectoral policies, trade and macroeconomic growth contributed significantly to economic dynamism" (Bradford, 2005: 14). Moreover, administrative and institutional capacities are a key determinant of the effectiveness with which available policy instruments can be applied.

Strengthening multilateral rules and regulations on the one hand, and national policies in support of capital accumulation and strategic integration into the world economy on the other, may not always be easy to reconcile, because policy-making at the international level has to serve the interests of a large number of countries. In order to ensure coherence between national and international policies, including the setting of rules and regulations, each set of policies has to be designed with a view to its implications for the other. While the options for national policies will be circumscribed by international policies, the latter should be designed in such a way that they allow maximum scope and flexibility for the application of domestic instruments. This is especially true for countries where growth and development are severely handicapped by their governments' inability to use policy instruments that are essential for their successful integration into the international trading and financial systems.

Options for active government policies to encourage investment and technological progress in support of a dynamic process of growth and structural change that benefits from – rather than being constrained by – integration into the world economy are discussed in subsequent chapters of this *Report*. ∎

Notes

---

1   There is a large body of literature that explains, justifies or criticizes the Washington Consensus. Notable among the more recent contributions are Kanbur, 1999; Naim, 2000; Rodrik, 2006; and Williamson, 2000 and 2002a.

2   In the words of Williamson, who first introduced the term, the Washington of the Consensus was "both the political Washington of Congress and senior members of the administration and the technocratic Washington of the international financial institutions, the economic agencies of the US government, the Federal Reserve Board, and the think tanks" (Williamson, 2002b: 1). He added that Washington itself "does not, of course, always practice what it preaches to foreigners." It may be added that the Consensus also included leading international banks and the majority of governments of creditor countries.

3   For a detailed analysis of the relationship between capital accumulation, economic growth and structural change, see *TDR 2003*, especially chaps. IV and V.

4   It is difficult to establish a strong causal link between individual elements of the reform programme, such as trade liberalization, and the outcome for growth and income distribution, not only because of the complex relationship between each element of the reforms, but also because the effects of various reform elements and stabilization measures influence each other. For the controversies over the relationship between trade and growth, see for example Srinivasan and Baghwati, 1999; and Krueger, 1998, on the one hand, and Rodrik, 1998; and Ocampo and Taylor, 1998, on the other.

5   In terms of the Schumpeterian concept of "creative destruction" as the driving force in the capitalist economy, the strategy implied a "destroy first" approach to economic and structural change. Trade liberalization was intended to "free" up productive resources from "inefficient" activities, and it was assumed that these resources would spontaneously be redeployed to more efficient activities. This is the opposite of the Schumpeterian approach, in which "creation" has the lead role, and it also differs from the experience of structural change in the East Asian catch-up process.

6   There is an extensive literature on the role of trade and industrial policy, as well as institutions, in the East Asian cases of successful development. See, for example, Akyüz, 1999; Amsden, 1989; Bradford, 1994; Chowdhury and Islam, 1993; Rodrik et al., 1994; and World Bank, 1993. The lessons that can be drawn from East Asian experience have also been discussed extensively in past TDRs, in particular *TDR 1989*, Part One, chap. V; *TDR 1994*, Part Two, chap. I; *TDR 2002*, chap. III; *TDR 2003*, chaps. IV and V.

7   In Rodrik's view, "three sets of disparate developments conspired to put institutions squarely on the agenda of reformers. One of these was the dismal

failure in Russia of price reform and privatization in the absence of a supportive legal, regulatory, and political apparatus. A second is the lingering dissatisfaction with market-oriented reforms in Latin America and the growing realization that these reforms have paid too little attention to mechanisms of social insurance and to safety nets. The third and most recent is the Asian financial crisis which has shown that allowing financial liberalization to run ahead of financial regulation is an invitation to disaster" (Rodrik, 1999: 3).

8   The term "second-generation reforms" refers to a set of reforms, not clearly standardized, but including the following elements in addition to what is generally understood to be stipulated by the Washington Consensus: improvement of corporate governance, fighting corruption, introducing greater flexibility in the labour market, accession to WTO agreements, introducing financial codes and standards, prudent capital-account opening, application of non-intermediate exchange-rate regimes, ensuring independence of the central bank together with inflation targeting, creation of social safety nets, and targeted poverty reduction.

9   See, for example, Stiglitz, 2002b: chap. 2; Gilbert, Powell and Vines, 1999: 616–619; Ocampo, 2001: 13–14; International Financial Institutions Advisory Commission Report, 2000: 43–62; and Kapur and Webb, 2000.

10 In response to mounting criticism, the IMF issued new guidelines in 2002 (IMF, 2005) without, however, addressing the fundamental problem of intrusiveness of structural conditionality. See also IMF/IEO, 2005.

11 A case in point is trade liberalization, which, since the 1980s, has become an essential component of IMF surveillance and conditionality. It is generally recognized that unilateral trade liberalization undertaken mainly by low-income countries working under Fund programmes put them at a disadvantage in multilateral trade negotiations (WTO, 2004). A country liberalizing unilaterally acquires no automatic rights in the WTO vis-à-vis other countries, but it could become liable if it needs to take measures in the context of Fund programmes that are in breach of its WTO obligations.

12 The targets are: (a) Develop further an open trading and financial system that is rule-based, predictable and non-discriminatory, including a commitment to good governance, development and poverty reduction – nationally and internationally; (b) Address the least developed countries' special needs. This includes tariff- and quota-free access for their exports; enhanced debt relief for heavily indebted poor countries; cancellation of official bilateral debt; and more generous official development assistance for countries committed to poverty reduction; (c) Ad-

dress the special needs of landlocked and small island developing States; (d) Deal comprehensively with developing countries' debt problems through national and international measures to make debt sustainable in the long term; (e) In cooperation with the developing countries, develop decent and productive work for youth; (f) In cooperation with pharmaceutical companies, provide access to affordable essential drugs in developing countries; (g) In cooperation with the private sector, make available the benefits of new technologies – especially information and communications technologies.

13 The United Nations Millennium Project was established in 2002 as an independent advisory body to identify strategies to achieve the MDGs, particularly in those countries deemed to be far off-course in progress. The *Sachs Report* synthesizes the analyses prepared by the 10 task forces established under the project.

14 The *Sachs Report* contains 10 recommendations for policy action to achieve the MDGs: (1) Developing country governments should adopt the MDG-based poverty reduction strategies (MDG-BPRSs) bold enough to meet the MDG targets; (2) The MDG-BPRSs should provide a framework for strengthening governance, promoting human rights, engaging civil society, and promoting the private sector; (3) Developing country governments should craft and implement the MDG-BPRSs in transparent and inclusive processes, working closely with civil society organizations, the domestic private sector, and international partners; (4) International donors should identify at least a dozen MDG "fast-track" countries for a rapid scale-up of ODA in 2015; (5) Developed and developing countries should jointly launch a group of Quick Win actions to save and improve millions of lives and to promote economic growth; (6) Developing countries should align national strategies with such regional initiatives, and direct donor support for regional projects should be increased; (7) High-income countries should increase ODA from 0.25 per cent of donor GNP in 2003 to 0.44 per cent in 2006 and 0.54 per cent in 2015 to support the MDGs, particularly in low-income countries, and debt relief should be more extensive and generous; (8) High-income countries should open their markets to developing countries' exports and help Least Developed Countries (LDCs) raise export competitiveness through investment in critical trade-related infrastructure, including electricity, roads and ports; (9) International donors should mobilize support for global scientific research and development to address special needs of the poor in areas of health, agriculture, natural resource and environmental management, energy and climate; (10) The UN Secretary-General and the UN Development Group should strengthen the coordi-

nation of UN agencies, funds, and programmes to support the MDGs, at headquarters and country level.

15 Similarly, a report by the World Bank's Independent Evaluation Group, issued in March 2006, found that Bank support for trade over two decades helped open markets but "was not as effective in boosting exports and growth, and alleviating poverty as anticipated". As a consequence the report suggests that "If developing countries are to reap larger gains from trade liberalization, the reforms need to be combined better with investments and institution building and measures to mitigate adverse effects" (World Bank/IEG, 2006: Press release at: www.worldbank.org/ieg/trade/docs/press_release_trade_evaluation.pdf).

16 For a discussion of the positive effects of industrial policy in East Asia, and a methodological critique of quantitative tests that fail to identify such positive effects, see Rodrik et al., 1994; and Wade, 1996.

17 This section draws in large part on Akyüz, 2006b.

18 For the distinction between potential and actual policy instruments, see Bryant, 1980: chap. 2.

19 The distinction between instruments and targets constitutes the basis of the theory of economic policy first elucidated by Tinbergen, 1952; see also Hansen, 1967; and Bryant, 1980: chap. 2.

20 The impact of openness on policy autonomy goes back to Tinbergen, 1956; see also Cooper, 1968. For the distinction between *de facto* control over national development and *de jure* sovereignty of national economic policy, see Bryant, 1980: chaps. 10–12.

21 Interdependence creates opportunities for individual countries to use commercial, macroeconomic, financial or exchange-rate policies in pursuit of certain national objectives, such as accelerating industrial development or creating jobs at the expense of the others. This could trigger retaliatory policy action by those affected. In the absence of multilateral disciplines and cooperation, this process can easily create instability and disruptions in international economic relations, leaving all countries worse off. In economic policy, the provision of international economic stability as a global public good appears to be one of the most compelling reasons why multilateral discipline is needed.

22 The increased significance of international externalities associated with growing interdependence among countries has resulted in the broadening of the concept of global public goods and growing public interest in their provision, which often requires global collective action. Global security, international economic and financial stability, global environment, knowledge, humanitarian assistance and global health are now typically included among global public goods; see Kaul et al., 1999; Phillips and Higgott, 1999; Stiglitz, 2002a; Bryant, 2003; and Kaul et al., 2003.

23 The need to strengthen the voice and participation of the developing countries in global economic governance has been noted in six paragraphs of the Monterrey Consensus: paras. 8, 38, 53, 57, 62, and, in greater detail, para. 63.

24 This seems to be the reasoning behind the argument by Rodrik (2004: 3) that "the analysis of industrial policy needs to focus not on policy *outcomes* – which are inherently unknowable ex ante – but on getting the policy *process* right. We need to worry about how ... private and public actors come together to solve problems in the productive sphere ... and not about whether the right tool for industrial policy is, say, directed credit or R&D subsidies."

References

Akyüz Y, ed. (1999). *East Asian Development - New Perspectives*. London, Portland, OR, Frank Cass.

Akyüz Y (2006a). From liberalization to investment and jobs: Lost in translation. Paper prepared for the International Labour Organization, Geneva.

Akyüz Y (2006b). Multilateral disciplines and the question of policy space. Mimeo. Forthcoming.

Akyüz Y and Gore C (1994). The investment-profits nexus in East Asian industrialization. UNCTAD Discussion Paper 91. Geneva, UNCTAD.

Amsden A (1989). *Asia's Next Giant: South Korea and Late Industrialization*. Oxford, Oxford University Press.

Berg J and Taylor L (2000). External liberalization, economic performance, and social policy In: Taylor L, ed., *External Liberalization, Economic Perform- ance, and Social Policy.* Oxford, Oxford Univer- sity Press.

Bhaduri A (2005). Toward the optimum degree of open- ness. In: Gallagher K, ed., *Putting Development First. The Importance of Policy Space in the WTO and International Financial Institutions.* London, Zed Books.

Bradford Jr CI (1994). The East Asian development ex- perience. In: Grilli E and Salvator D, eds., *Economic Development: Handbook of Comparative Economic Policies,* 4. London, Greenwood Press.

Bradford Jr CI (2005). Prioritizing economic growth: Enhancing macroeconomic policy choice. G-24 Discussion Paper no. 37, New York and Geneva, UNCTAD, April.

Bryant RC (1980). *Money and Monetary Policy in Inter- dependent Nations.* Washington, DC, The Brookings Institution.

Bryant RC (2003). *Turbulent Waters. Cross-Border Fi- nance and International Governance.* Washington, DC, The Brookings Institution.

Buira A (2003). An Analysis of IMF Conditionality. G- 24 Discussion Paper no. 22. New York and Geneva, UNCTAD.

Cairncross AK (1955). The place of capital in economic progress. In: Dupriez LH, ed., *Economic Progress.* Papers and proceedings of a round table organized by the International Economic Association. Louvain, Belgium.

Calcagno AF (2001). Ajuste estructural, costo social y modalidades de desarrollo en América Latina. In: Sader E, ed., *El ajuste estructural en América Latina.* Buenos Aires, Consejo Latinoaméricano de Ciencias Sociales: 75–97.

Chang HJ (2002). *Kicking Away the Ladder - Develop- ment Strategy in Historical Perspective.* London, Anthem Press.

Chowdhury D and Islam I (1993). *The Newly Industrial- izing Economies of East Asia.* London, Routledge.

Cooper RN (1968). *The Economics of Interdependence: Economic Policy in the Atlantic Community.* New York, McGraw Hill for the Council on Foreign Re- lations.

Cornia GA, Jolly R and Stewart F (1987). *Adjustment with a Human Face: Protecting the Vulnerable and Promoting Growth.* Oxford, Clarendon Press.

Cornia GA (1999). Social funds in stabilization and ad- justment programmes. *International Monetary and Financial Issues for the 1990s, XI.* United Nations publication, sales number E.99.II.D.25, New York and Geneva.

Feldstein H (1998). Refocusing the IMF. *Foreign Affairs,* 77 (2): 20–33, March/April.

Eatwell J and Taylor L (2002). *International Capital Markets.* New York and Oxford, Oxford University Press.

Gilbert C, Powell A and Vines D (1999). Positioning the World Bank. *Economic Journal,* 109 (459): 598–633.

Goldstein M (2000). IMF structural programs. Paper pre- pared for the NBER Conference on Economic and Financial Crises in Emerging Market Economies. Woodstock, Vermont. October 19–21. Available at: www.iie.com.

Gore C (2000). The rise and fall of the Washington Con- sensus as a paradigm for developing countries. *Word Development,* 28 (3): 780–804.

Hansen B (1967). *Lectures in Economic Theory, Part II: the Theory of Economic Policy and Planning.* Lund, Sweden.

Hayami Y (2003). From the Washington Consensus to the post-Washington Consensus: Retrospect and prospect. *Asian Development Review,* 20 (2): 40– 65.

International Financial Institution Advisory Commission Report (Meltzer Report) (2000). Washington, DC, March.

IMF (2005). Review of the 2002 Conditionality Guide- lines – Selected Issues. March 4. Washington, DC.

IMF/IEO (2005). Evaluation of structural conditionality in IMF-supported programs. Issues paper for an evaluation of the Independent Evaluation Office, Washington, DC, May. Available at: www.imf.org/ External/NP/ieo/2005/sc/051805.pdf.

Jespersen E (1992). External shocks, adjustment policies and economic and social performance. In: Cornia GA, van der Hoeven R and Mkandawire T, eds., *Africa's Recovery in the 1990s: From Stagnation and Adjustment to Human Development.* Basingstoke, United Kingdom, Macmillan.

Kanbur R (1999). The strange case of the Washington Consensus: a brief note on John Williamson's 'What should the World Bank think about the Washington Consensus?' Ithaca. July. Available at: http:// people.cornell.edu/pages/sk145.

Kapur D and Webb R (2000). Governance-related conditionality of the International Financial Insti- tutions. G-24 Discussion Paper no. 6. United Na- tions, New York and Geneva, August.

Kaul I, Grunberg I and Stern MA, eds. (1999). *Global Public Goods: International Cooperation in the 21st Century.* New York, Oxford University Press.

Kaul I, et al., eds. (2003). *Providing Global Public Goods: Managing Globalization.* New York, Oxford Uni- versity Press.

Krueger AO (1998). Why trade liberalization is good for growth. *The Economic Journal,* 108 September: 1512–1522.

Kuczynski PP and Williamson J, eds. (2003). *After the Washington Consensus: Restarting Growth and Reform in Latin America.* Washington, DC, Insti- tute for International Economics.

Lipumba N (1995). Structural adjustment policies and economic performance of African countries. *Inter-*

national Monetary and Financial Issues for the 1990s, V. United Nations publication, sales no. E.95.II.D.3, New York and Geneva: 35–64.

Mussa M and Savastano M (1999). *The IMF Approach to Economic Stabilization*. IMF Working Paper 99/104. Washington, DC, 13 September.

Naim M (2000). Washington Consensus or Washington Confusion? *Foreign Policy,* 118, Spring. Washington, DC, Carnegie Endowment for International Peace.

Ocampo JA (2001). Recasting the international financial agenda. G-24 Discussion Paper no. 13. New York and Geneva, UNCTAD.

Ocampo JA and Taylor L (1998). Trade liberalization in developing economies: Modest benefits but problems with productivity growth, macro prices, and income distribution. *The Economic Journal,* 108 (450): 1523–1546, September.

OECD (2006). Aid from members. Reference DAC Statistical Tables. Available at: www.oecd.org/dac/stats/dac/reftables.

Overseas Development Institute (ODI) (2001). *PRSP Institutionalization Study: Final Report*. Submitted to the Strategic Partnership for Africa, London.

Phillips N and Higgott R (1999). Global governance and the public domain: Collective goods in a Post-Washington Consensus era. CSGR Working Paper 47/99, University of Warwick.

Polak JJ (1991). The changing nature of IMF conditionality. Princeton Essays. *International Finance*, no. 184. Princeton, Princeton University.

Rodrik D (1998). Globalization, Social Conflict and Economic Growth. *Journal of Development Perspectives*, 6: 87–105.

Rodrik D (1999). Institutions of high-quality growth: What they are and how to acquire them. Paper prepared for the IMF Conference on Second Generation Reforms. Washington, DC, 14 October. Available at: www.imf.org/external/pubs/ft/seminar/1999/reforms.

Rodrik D (2004). Industrial policy for the twenty-first century. Discussion Paper no. 4767, Centre for Economic Policy Research, London. November.

Rodrik D (2006). *Goodbye Washington Consensus, Hello Washington Confusion*? Paper prepared for the *Journal of Economic Literature*. Available at: http://ksghome.harvard.edu/~drodrik/.

Rodrik D et al. (1994). *Miracle or Design? Lessons from the East Asian Experience*. Washington, DC, Overseas Development Council.

Schadler S et al. (1993). Economic adjustment in low-income countries: experience under the Enhanced Structural Adjustment Facility. IMF Occasional Paper, no. 106. Washington, DC, June.

Sen AK (1999). Development as Freedom. New York, Alfred A. Knopf.

Srinivasan TN and Bhagwati J (1999). Outward-orientation and development: Are revisionists right? Eco-

nomic Growth Center, Discussion Paper 806. New Haven, CT, Yale University, September.

Stiglitz JE (1998). More instruments and broader goals: Moving toward the post-Washington consensus. The WIDER Annual Lecture, Helsinki, 7 January.

Stiglitz JE (2002a). Globalization and the logic of institutional collective action: Re-examining the Bretton Woods institutions. In: Nayyar D, ed., *Governing Globalization*. New York, Oxford University Press.

Stiglitz JE (2002b). *Globalization and its Discontents*. New York, WW Norton & Company.

Tinbergen J (1952). *On the theory of economic policy*. Amsterdam, North Holland.

Tinbergen J (1956). *Economic Policy: Theory and Design*. Amsterdam, North Holland.

UNCTAD (2000). *Economic Development in Africa: Capital Flows and Growth in Africa*. United Nations document UNCTAD/GDS/MSPB/7, New York and Geneva.

UNCTAD (2002). *Economic Development in Africa: From Adjustment to Poverty Reduction: What is New?* United Nations publication, sales no. W.02.II.D.18, New York and Geneva.

UNCTAD (2005). *UNCTAD Handbook of Statistics 2005*. United Nations publication, sales number E/F.05.II.D.29, New York and Geneva.

UNCTAD (various issues). *Trade and Development Report*. United Nations publication, New York and Geneva.

United Nations (2002). Report of the International Conference on Financing for Development. Monterrey, Mexico, 18–22 March. United Nations document A/CONF.198/11), New York.

UN Millennium Project (2005). *Investing in Development: A Practical Plan to Achieve the Millennium Development Goals (Sachs Report)*. London and Sterling, VA, Earthscan.

Wade R (1996). Japan, the World Bank and the art of paradigm maintenance: the East Asian miracle in political perspective. *New Left Review*, 217: 3–36.

Williamson J, ed. (1990). *Latin American Adjustment: How Much has Happened?* Washington, DC, Institute for International Economics.

Williamson J (2000). What should the World Bank think about the Washington Consensus? *World Bank Research Observer,* 15 (2): 251–264, August.

Williamson J (2002a). Did the Washington Consensus fail? Outline of remarks at the Center for Strategic and International Studies. Washington, DC, Institute for International Economics, 6 November.

Williamson J (2002b). What Washington means by policy reform. Update of chapter 2 of *Latin American Adjustment: How Much has Happened*? Washington, DC, Institute for International Economics, November. Available at: www.iie.com/publications/papers/williamson1 102-2.htm.

World Bank (1993). *The East Asian Miracle: Economic Growth and Public Policy*. Oxford, Oxford University Press.

World Bank (1994). *Adjustment in Africa: Reforms, Results and the Road Ahead.* New York, Oxford University Press.

World Bank (2003). *Debt Relief for the Poorest: An OED Review of the HIPC Initiative.* Operations Evaluation Department. Washington, DC.

World Bank (2005). *Economic Growth in the 1990s: Learning from a Decade of Reform.* Washington, DC.

World Bank/IEG (2006). Assessing World Bank Support for Trade 1987–2004: An IEG Evaluation. Independent Evaluation Group. Washington, DC.

WTO (2004). Coherence in global economic policymaking and cooperation between the WTO, the IMF and the World Bank. WT/TF/COH/S/9. Geneva, World Trade Organization.

Chapter III

CHANGES AND TRENDS IN THE EXTERNAL ENVIRONMENT FOR DEVELOPMENT

A. Introduction

The external environment for development continues to be determined by the growth performance, cyclical and structural changes as well as economic policy decisions of developed countries. In recent years, fast and sustained growth in the two developing countries with the largest populations, China and India, has added another dimension to this aspect of interdependence. However, although the growth dynamics of these two large Asian economies are increasingly exerting an influence on other developing countries, they themselves depend to a large extent on cyclical and structural changes in the industrialized countries.

The effects of the emergence of China and India as key players in the world economy on the pattern of globalization and the prospects for other developing economies were examined at length in *TDR 2005*. The extent to which China's output and import growth and its export drive influence the external environment for other developing countries in the coming years will depend not on China alone, but also largely on the way in which global imbalances are corrected, as discussed in chapter I of this *Report*. In addition to the evolu-

tion of demand from the industrialized countries and the impact of China's and India's growth, the overall external environment is also shaped by structural changes in other areas, such as international trading arrangements, and external debt and finance. These are areas in which the contribution of developed countries to the global partnership for development finds expression. This chapter looks at a number of these areas, which have evolved considerably over the past two decades.

There is widespread agreement that improved export opportunities can contribute significantly to economic development and the alleviation of poverty. The chapter therefore first examines in section B the nature and extent of improvements in export opportunities for developing countries over the past 15 years as a result of trade liberalization in developing countries' trading partners, the evolution of market entry conditions and non-tariff measures, and changes in income-related import demand in their main trading partners' markets.

One factor that has inhibited investment and growth in many developing countries has been their debt overhang. Recognizing the constraining and systemic nature of the debt problem, the international financial institutions and bilateral donors have launched various initiatives to address the problem, partly through the provision of debt relief. The progress achieved in the area of debt relief, especially under the HIPC Debt Initiative of the World Bank and IMF, and its relationship with recent trends in official development assistance (ODA) are discussed in section C. While ODA remains a key element in the global partnership for development, it is smaller than both private capital flows and migrants' remittances. The latter have been gaining importance as a source of foreign exchange for a number of developing countries, exceeding ODA flows by an increasing margin and prompting questions about the potential impact they could have on development in the receiving countries, as discussed in section D of this chapter.

Another important feature of the world economy in recent decades has been the growth of foreign direct investment (FDI) and related internationalization of production by transnational corporations (TNCs). A number of developing countries and economies in transition have been recipients of these increased flows and are progressively participating in international production networks. Indeed, a few of them are also assuming an increasingly important role as sources of FDI for other developing countries. Consequently, FDI and internationalization of production present new opportunities for developing countries and economies in transition, which they need to consider in their development strategies. But there are also new challenges for policymakers in terms of balancing private sector interests with national economic objectives and development priorities. Against this background, section E takes a closer look at trends and patterns in FDI to developing countries over the past quarter century, the potential of FDI to enhance growth and structural transformation in host countries, and the implications for policies aimed at strengthening the contribution of FDI to the development process. The chapter ends with a summary of conclusions.

> The external environment for development is mainly determined by the growth performance, cyclical and structural changes as well as economic policy decisions of developed countries, but growth in China and India has added another dimension to these determinants.

B. Export opportunities for developing countries

There is widespread agreement that improved export opportunities can significantly help promote economic development and alleviate poverty. The Monterrey Consensus (paragraph 26) emphasizes the potential role of "international trade as an engine for development" and affirms that a "universal, rule-based, open, non-discriminatory and equitable multilateral trading system, as well as meaningful trade liberalization, can substantially stimulate development worldwide, benefiting countries at all stages of development".

The aim of this section is to assess improvements in export opportunities for developing countries over the past 15 years. External conditions for increasing developing-country exports include: (i) trade liberalization in developing countries' trading partners through multilateral trade negotiations or regional and unilateral measures to give them enhanced market access; (ii) the lowering of market entry barriers and other non-tariff measures (NTMs); and (iii) an increase in import demand in trading partners' markets as a result of rising incomes.[1]

1. Market access conditions

(a) Market access following the Uruguay Round Agreements

Although developing countries are increasingly trading among themselves (*TDR 2005*, chap. IV), market access conditions in developed countries continue to be a major determinant of their export opportunities.[2] It was not until the launch of the Uruguay Round that major sectors and products

of export interest to developing countries, such as agriculture, and textiles and clothing, were included in the multilateral trade negotiations. However, to date, progress towards improving market access for developing countries' exports has been modest.[3] High levels of protection continue to be applied against those products that are produced mainly by developing countries, such as labour-intensive manufactures, as well as primary commodities.

An analysis of the evolution of the post-Uruguay Round tariff structure, between 1994 and 2005 (table 3.1) shows that the products of export interest to developing countries face the highest tariff barriers in developed-country markets:[4]

- Applied tariffs on agricultural products and labour-intensive manufactures, which include textiles, clothing, footwear, leather and travel products, are higher than those on non-labour-intensive manufactures.

- Overall, developed countries apply higher average tariffs to developing countries' products than to those from other developed countries, signifying that there is a bias against export opportunities for developing countries. This is the case particularly for labour-intensive manufactures.

- Between 1994 and 2005, developed countries reduced weighted average tariffs on their imports from other developed countries by more than on their imports from developing countries. This difference in tariff reductions is especially significant for agricultural products and labour-intensive manufactures.

Table 3.1

EFFECTIVELY APPLIED TARIFFS IN DEVELOPED AND DEVELOPING COUNTRIES BY SELECTED PRODUCT GROUP, 1994 AND 2005

(Per cent)

Exporting regions

Products and markets	Simple Average						Weighted average					
	1994		*2005*		*Percentage change*		*1994*		*2005*		*Percentage change*	
	Developed countries	*Developing countries*	*Developed countries*	*Developing countries*	*Developed countries*	*Developing countries*	*Developed countries*	*Developing countries*	*Developed countries*	*Developing countries*	*Developed countries*	*Developing countries*
All products												
Developed countries	5.43	5.73	2.54	3.80	**-53.2**	**-33.7**	3.32	4.47	1.29	2.12	**-61.1**	**-52.6**
Developing countries	18.83	19.96	9.14	9.87	**-51.5**	**-50.6**	13.15	14.71	5.85	4.88	**-55.5**	**-66.8**
Agriculture												
Developed countries	5.09	3.11	5.19	3.02	**2.0**	**-2.9**	4.88	2.83	2.98	2.48	**-38.9**	**-12.4**
Developing countries	19.92	18.98	15.55	11.59	**-21.9**	**-38.9**	11.20	14.04	12.62	12.12	**12.7**	**-13.7**
Manufactures												
Developed countries	5.49	6.21	2.28	3.94	**-58.5**	**-36.6**	3.25	5.18	1.14	2.39	**-64.9**	**-53.9**
Developing countries	18.76	20.13	8.52	9.68	**-54.6**	**-51.9**	13.65	16.83	5.13	4.38	**-62.4**	**-74.0**
Labour-intensive manufactures												
Developed countries	9.35	11.59	4.94	8.44	**-47.2**	**-27.2**	8.90	11.19	4.33	9.32	**-51.3**	**-16.7**
Developing countries	26.07	26.74	11.95	13.86	**-54.2**	**-48.2**	23.55	31.96	6.92	7.33	**-70.6**	**-77.1**
Other manufactures												
Developed countries	4.56	3.81	1.64	2.13	**-64.0**	**-44.1**	2.98	2.83	1.03	0.88	**-65.4**	**-68.9**
Developing countries	17.85	18.47	8.06	8.60	**-54.8**	**-53.4**	13.36	14.31	5.10	4.03	**-61.8**	**-71.8**

Source: UNCTAD, *Trade Analysis and Information System* (TRAINS) Database at the World Integrated Trade Solution (WITS).
Note: Based on the nearest year for which tariff data are available.

- The highest tariffs are to be found in labour-intensive manufactures. The implementation of the Agreement on Textiles and Clothing (ATC) led to a progressive elimination of quotas in international trade of this product category, culminating in their complete removal by 1 January 2005.[5] But the ATC did not affect tariffs, which for textiles and clothing continue to be much higher than the average for other manufactured exports from developing countries.

Average tariff levels conceal the level of effective protection against developing countries' exports. Products of particular export interest for developing countries are often subject to specific tariffs, tariff peaks and tariff escalation in developed-country markets. In the case of specific tariffs that are non-ad-valorem tariffs of a fixed amount, widely used in agriculture, the protection level rises when international prices fall. These kinds of tariffs offer higher protection against lower-priced exports from developing countries. Additionally, the proportion of specific tariffs tends to increase with the degree of processing. In the Quad,[6] over 30 per cent of the tariff lines in agriculture contain non-ad-valorem tariffs of this kind (Aksoy, 2005).

Tariff peaks[7] are applied mainly to agricultural products and labour-intensive manufactures. Between 1994 and 2005 the number of international tariff peaks applied by developed countries to developing countries' exports increased by over 13 per cent, the corresponding maximum levels of tariffs increasing from 800 to 1,235 per cent. Tariff peaks on agricultural exports of developing countries to developed countries more than doubled during this period, accounting for 29 per cent of total tariff peaks in 2005. The number of peaks in labour-intensive manufactures, which in 2005 accounted for almost 90 per cent of total peaks in manufactured exports, increased by 10.5 per cent between 1994 and 2005 (UNCTAD TRAINS database).

Developing countries' exports are also negatively affected by tariff escalation in developed countries,[8] which is extensively applied on processed food products. Elamin and Khaira (2003) note that tariff escalation is more pronounced in commodities such as meat, sugar, fruit, coffee, cocoa and hides and skins, which are of export interest to many of the poorer developing countries.

Other forms of agricultural protection in developed countries are domestic support and export subsidies. Progress in reducing these forms of protection in OECD countries has been limited, but there have been positive steps towards decoupling support from production. According to the OECD (2005), the level of support to OECD producers remains high, having changed little since the mid-1990s. As a share of gross farm receipts, producer support fell from an average of 37 per cent in 1986–1988 to an average of 30 per cent in 1995–1997, and since then it has not changed much. Total support to agriculture declined from 2.3 per cent of GDP in 1986–1988[9] to 1.2 per cent of GDP in 2002–2004. In absolute terms, the total support estimate increased from an average of $305 billion in 1986–1988 to $378 billion in 2004, and the producer support estimate increased from $243 billion to $279 billion.

The impact of each of the three pillars of protection on agricultural trade differs, with market access having by far the greatest effect.[10] Domestic support and export subsidies are normally less trade distorting than border measures. However, domestic support is known to significantly distort trade in selected commodities such as sugar and cotton. And export subsidies are small compared with trade-distorting domestic farm support (Hufbauer and Schott, 2006).[11] Therefore, even drastic reductions in export subsidies, which are the least distorting of these forms of agricultural protection, may not have major consequences for the export opportunities of developing countries.[12]

In conclusion, although better market access conditions in developed countries have somewhat improved developing countries' export opportu-

> Although better market access conditions in developed countries have somewhat improved developing countries' export opportunities, those conditions continue to be biased against developing countries.

nities, under the multilateral trading system those conditions continue to be biased against developing countries.

(b) Market access under regional and bilateral trade agreements

In addition to developments in the multilateral trading system, developing countries may benefit from improved export opportunities through regional trade agreements (RTAs) and non-reciprocal preferential trading agreements with developed countries. The number of RTAs and their share in world trade has considerably increased over the past few years.[13] The main instrument used by developed countries to grant non-reciprocal, preferential market access to developing countries has been the Generalized System of Preferences (GSP), under which selected products originating in developing countries are granted lower than most-favoured nation (MFN) tariff rates. LDCs receive special and preferential treatment for a wider range of products, as well as deeper tariff cuts. The EU's GSP system was revised in 2005 and streamlined into three schemes: a general scheme with increased product coverage; a new "GSP plus" scheme for particularly vulnerable economies with special development needs and which have ratified a number of international conventions on sustainable development and good governance; and the "Everything but Arms" (EBA) scheme. Some preferential schemes have a specific focus on particular countries. For example, the EBA initiative, which the EU adopted in 2001, grants duty-free access to imports of all products from LDCs without any quantitative restrictions, except on arms and munitions. In 2000, the United States' African Growth and Opportunity Act (AGOA) amended the basic GSP programme in favour of designated sub-Saharan African countries, providing duty-free treatment for a much wider range of products, including textiles and apparel.

Although preferences were expected to lead to increased export earnings and promote diversification in the preference-receiving countries, evidence shows that developing countries, and particularly the poorest ones, have not been able to fully benefit from them. The preferences are not fully utilized by the LDCs and a significant proportion of their exports are outside the preferences. For example, in 2003, the sectors in LDCs' economies that relied on market access preferences accounted for an estimated 33 per cent of the total foreign exchange earnings of these countries (UNCTAD, 2005a). Moreover, the actual utilization of trade preferences is concentrated in a few country/product pairs (UNCTAD, 2003). For instance, in 2005 petroleum accounted for over 92 per cent of AGOA imports (including GSP) into the United States.[14]

The underutilization of preferences and their limited benefits are due to uncertainty surrounding the schemes, restrictive rules of origin, insufficient product coverage and supply-capacity constraints. Moreover, many products of major export interest to developing countries are regarded as "sensitive" and are therefore excluded from preferential schemes. For example, the GSP scheme of the United States covers only about 50 per cent of the tariff lines and excludes articles such as textiles, watches, footwear, handbags, luggage, steel, glass and electronic equipment (Amiti and Romalis, 2006). Under the EBA initiative, there are temporary exceptions for rice, sugar and bananas, but market access restrictions are to be phased out between 2006 (for bananas) and 2009 (for rice and sugar).

In addition to non-reciprocal preferential agreements, for those developing countries that are not generally included in the preferential schemes some free-trade agreements (FTAs) can offer better market access conditions than multilateral agreements. However, reciprocity in these agreements in many instances implies concessions by developing countries that go beyond their multilateral obligations; that is, they do not have the "less than full reciprocity" approach of multilateral agreements or the non-reciprocal character of preferential schemes such as GSP, EBA and AGOA. Many bilateral agreements also cover more areas than trade in goods, such as services, investment and competition, which developed countries tried to incorporate in the multilateral trade agenda, but with limited success.[15]

(c) Potentially new export opportunities from multilateral trade liberalization

Benefits resulting from a global reduction of market access barriers are often assessed on the basis of computable general equilibrium (CGE) models. These measure the welfare[16] benefits from efficiency gains and terms-of-trade effects that result from trade liberalization. The results of these models are highly dependent on fairly restrictive assumptions[17] and therefore need to be interpreted with caution. Simulation results can only provide a general idea, rather than accurate projections, of the impact of trade liberalization on different sectors and regions in the world. Moreover, these models often misinterpret the difference between two equilibrium states as representing a change from one to another (Akyüz, 2005).

CGE models were widely used to estimate the benefits that would result from the Uruguay Round of WTO negotiations. However, actual benefits from that Round have been much smaller than those prior estimates (Panagariya, 1999). This has contributed to increasing scepticism among developing countries regarding estimates of the gains they could obtain from multilateral trade negotiations. In recent years, a number of studies have also included CGE model estimations to assess the potential benefits expected from the Doha Round of multilateral trade negotiations.[18] A recent World Bank study by Anderson, Martin and van der Mensbrugghe (2005)[19] arrives at considerably lower estimates for the overall benefits of trade liberalization than earlier simulations by the World Bank that were published just after the launching of the Doha Round (World Bank, 2002). The earlier simulations used 1997 data while the later study used 2001 data, which reflect the current conditions of the global economy much better.[20] Indeed, the results using this updated database, compared to the results of earlier studies, show a decline in the estimated share of developing countries in those benefits (van der Mensbrugghe, 2005: fig. 1).[21]

Although Anderson, Martin and van der Mensbrugghe (2005: 385) conclude that "a great

Export and income gains expected to result from the Doha Round appear to be modest, and concentrated in a few countries.

deal can be gained from liberalizing merchandise – especially agricultural – trade under … [the likely Doha scenario], with a disproportionately high share of that potential gain available for developing countries (relative to their share in the global economy)", a closer analysis of the potential gains for developing countries leads to a less optimistic conclusion. In per capita terms, the global gains of $96 billion by 2015 resulting from the likely Doha scenario[22] amount to only $3.13 per year, or the equivalent of less than a cent per day for those living in developing countries (Ackerman, 2005). Similarly, as a share of GDP, this scenario would lead to an overall rise in income of just 0.16 per cent in developing countries.

Among the developing countries, there is a high concentration of the welfare benefits. In the likely Doha scenario, only six countries (Argentina, Brazil, China, India, Indonesia and Thailand) would receive 73.3 per cent of developing-country benefits. Brazil alone would account for 22.4 per cent of the gains for developing countries. On the other hand, some countries, such as Bangladesh, Mexico and Viet Nam would stand to lose.

By sector of economic activity, reforms in agriculture would account for most of the global potential gains from full multilateral trade liberalization (63 per cent). Additionally, a decomposition of the effects by policy instrument shows that almost all the welfare gains from liberalization of agriculture would stem from a reduction in market access barriers. Only minor gains would accrue from the other two pillars of the multilateral trade negotiations (i.e. removal of domestic support and export subsidies). Agricultural liberalization in developed countries could even harm some, particularly food-importing, developing countries, because it may lead to higher food prices.

As for expected trade effects, according to estimations by Anderson, Martin and van der Mensbrugghe (2005), under the likely Doha scenario, by 2015 developing countries' total exports will be higher by $78 billion, which is about 37 per cent of the estimated global increase in exports. On a sectoral basis, about 55 per cent of the global increase would be in manufacturing exports (excluding textiles and clothing), 26 per cent in agricultural and food exports and 19 per cent in textiles and clothing exports. In developing countries, agricultural and food exports would contribute the most (53 per cent) to export expansion. Textiles and clothing would represent 32 per cent of the export expansion for developing countries, while other manufacturing would account for only 15 per cent. This is in contrast with the results for developed countries, where the manufacturing sector, excluding textiles and clothing, would contribute over 77 per cent to export expansion.

The estimated rise in total developing-country exports is concentrated in a few countries, particularly China for manufactures and Brazil for agricultural products. For example, simulation results by Polaski (2006: 42–43) indicate that liberalization based on the framework set out in the Ministerial Declaration of the WTO Ministerial Conference in Hong Kong (China) in December 2005 would "lead to most East and South Asian developing countries exporting more labor-intensive manufactured goods and electronic equipment and importing more manufactured intermediates and capital intensive products. Brazil and Argentina would see a broad decline in manufactured exports offset by growth in food and agricultural exports. However, a number of the poorest developing countries experience an overall decline in exports, dominated by declines in labor-intensive exports and processed food."

Fernandez de Cordoba and Vanzetti (forthcoming) show that any of the likely scenarios for non-agricultural market access liberalization under the Doha Round negotiations will cause substantial adjustment pressure in terms of employment and output losses for individual economic sectors. For example, according to their simulation results, an ambitious application of a Swiss-type formula would lead to an output decline of 36 per cent in the motor vehicle sector in South Asia, excluding India, and of 14 per cent in those countries' electronic equipment sector; in Mexico, output would decline by 15 per cent for textiles and by 20 per cent for wearing apparel, and India's non-ferrous metal sector would experience an output decline of 25 per cent. The potential adjustment costs associated with trade liberalization and the unequal distribution of the benefits that may arise from

new export opportunities have been recognized, leading to the "Aid for Trade" initiative, under which increased trade-related international assistance will be made available to developing countries (IMF and World Bank, 2005a).

While the numbers referred to above are not accurate projections of the increase in developing countries' export opportunities, it may be useful to put their magnitude in perspective by comparing them with projections for other variables related to the external sector, such as ODA flows and migrants' remittances. According to Anderson, Martin and van der Mensbrugghe (2005) total annual exports of developing countries will be higher by $78 billion by the year 2015 under the Doha scenario, and annual exports of developing countries to the developed countries will be higher by $62 billion. This compares with ODA inflows that can be expected to be higher by around $50 billion by 2010 thanks to new commitments by members of the OECD Development Assistance Committee (OECD, 2006: table 2), and to a level of migrants' remittances that by 2015 can be estimated to be $100 billion higher than in 2005, on the basis of recent World Bank estimates (World Bank, 2005).[23] In light of these comparisons the expected export gains from a successful conclusion of the Doha Round again appear relatively modest.[24]

2. Non-tariff measures (NTMs)

The reduction in tariff barriers has in recent years been accompanied by an increase in the use of NTMs, most notably in the form of technical measures.[25] These are technical regulations and standards that can be mandatory or voluntary, and they may be applied by the government or by the private sector. In principle, technical measures are aimed at accomplishing the legitimate policy objectives of human safety and health protection, as well as environmental protection.[26] Problems arise when the purpose of these technical measures goes beyond their legitimate protection policy objectives. Some countries may strategically abuse them as an instrument of trade policy, so that in effect they become a disguised form of protectionism by unfairly restricting imports, thereby discriminating against foreign producers in favour of domestic ones.

The quantification of NTMs, and particularly their impact on trade, remains a difficult task, as they are hard to define and detect. They may be measured in different ways, none of which seems entirely satisfactory.[27] One possible illustration of the increasing importance of technical measures, obtained from the UNCTAD TRAINS database, is to count the tariff lines affected by each type of NTMs and to calculate the percentage distribution for all countries for which data were available at the end of 1994 and 2004. This shows that the use of technical measures almost doubled, from 31.9 per cent to 58.5 per cent over that 10-year period. The most recent trends in NTMs indicate an increasing use of technical measures, as well as quantitative measures associated with technical measures (i.e. non-core measures), from 55.3 per cent to 84.8 per cent, and a decreasing use of all other measures (core measures), from 44.7 per cent to 15.2 per cent (UNCTAD, 2005b). Indeed, 10 years after the conclusion of the Uruguay Round, there has been a sevenfold increase in government-mandated testing and certification requirements (UNCTAD, 2006a).

Other evidence of the increasing use of technical measures is the number of technical barriers to trade (TBTs) and sanitary and phytosanitary (SPS) measures that have been the subject of notifications to the WTO since 1995. As can be seen in figure 3.1, the number of TBT notifications shows a slightly increasing trend, but not to the same extent as the number of SPS notifications. An analysis of the notifications by developing countries to the Negotiating Group on Non-Agricultural Market Access (NAMA) of the Doha Work Programme also shows that of all the NTMs, the highest number of notifications involved TBTs. Together with SPS notifications they represent over 55 per cent of all notifications (Flies and Lejarraga, 2005). The number of disputes over TBT and SPS measures could also be considered an indicator of the use of technical measures as trade barriers. However, as develop-

> The reduction in tariff barriers has in recent years been accompanied by an increase in the use of non-tariff measures.

> Anti-dumping measures have emerged as the most widespread impediment to international trade over the past 25 years.

ing countries lack the appropriate capacities to initiate these disputes, this number may be an underestimation. This shows that while it may be relatively straightforward to report on the frequency of use of technical measures, it is not easy to measure the extent of their trade restrictiveness.[28] In general, this would require a case-by-case analysis.[29] In business surveys, which are another approach used to assess the importance of NTMs, technical measures are among the most frequently reported NTMs and they are considered a major obstacle to exports.[30]

Anti-dumping has emerged as the most widespread impediment to international trade over the past 25 years. There is the danger that increasing recourse to anti-dumping measures will erode the predictability and non-discriminatory application of trade policies that have been achieved through successive rounds of multilateral trade negotiations. The number of anti-dumping investigations grew considerably during the 1990s, and the composition of the countries initiating anti-dumping cases, as well as those targeted by anti-dumping investigations, changed radically.[31] The number of anti-dumping initiations per year more than doubled between the late 1980s and the late 1990s, reaching a peak of 364 initiations in 2001, but falling subsequently to 191 in 2005.[32] Until the beginning of the 1990s, anti-dumping measures were used mainly by developed countries. Indeed, the so-called "traditional users" (including Australia, Canada, the EU, and the United States) accounted for more than 80 per cent of the total number of anti-dumping initiations. But in recent years, Argentina, Brazil, India, Mexico, the Republic of Korea, South Africa and Turkey within the group of "new users" have initiated a large number of investigations, their share increasing to between 50 and 60 per cent from virtually none in the early 1980s.

The growing number of investigations as well as users of anti-dumping measures has been ac-

Figure 3.1

**TBT AND SPS NOTIFICATIONS
TO THE WTO SINCE 1995**

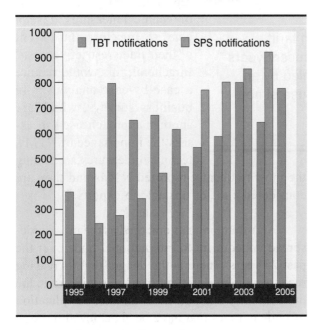

Source: WTO, 2006; and Pay, 2005.

and technical equipment required to effectively defend their interests in an anti-dumping investigation.

3. Import demand growth in developing countries' trading partners

With growing global trade integration across countries, a developing country's export opportunities are strongly influenced by the economic fortunes of its trading partners. In this context, a country's export opportunities depend on the extent of its trade with high-performing countries, and the economic size, import propensity and rate of aggregate income growth of its trading partners.

The first step in examining which developing countries have been best placed to benefit from strong import demand conditions in their trading partners is to measure export weights. These weights can be used to calculate weighted average changes in each developing country's export opportunities stemming from changes in the economic fortunes of its trading partners. Measuring export weights (i.e. each trading partner's share in a developing country's total exports) for three successive five-year intervals over the period 1990–2004, using a sample of 91 exporting developing countries that accounted for 99.7 per cent of total developing-country exports during the period 2000–2004, reveals a number of interesting facts.

First, most developing countries rely on a narrow range of countries as export destinations. The share of developing countries' five most important trading partners in their total exports was, on average, 66.9 per cent for the period 1990–2004. This high concentration changed little during this period, as the respective numbers for the three 5-year sub-periods are 67.7 per cent (1990–1994), 65.8 per cent (1995–1999), and 67.2 per cent (2000–2004).[33] However, these averages mask wide variations. While the five most important export destinations accounted for about 95 per cent of the total exports of a number of countries (which, over the past 10 years, comprise especially Mexico, but also Brunei Darussalam, the Dominican Republic, the Democratic Republic of the Congo and

companied by a rising number of countries targeted by dumping charges. Among individual countries, Asian countries have increasingly been subject to anti-dumping investigations, their share rising from about 30 per cent in the late 1980s to over 70 per cent in 2005. China has become the most investigated country, accounting for about 30 per cent of all anti-dumping investigations in 2005.

Most of the investigations concern the base metals and chemicals sectors, which accounted for almost half of total investigations between 1995 and 2005. Other sectors where the number of investigations is high are plastics and rubber, machinery, electrical and electronic equipment, textiles, and pulp and paper.

Developing-country exporters are particularly vulnerable to the adverse impact of anti-dumping actions, because often they are new entrants to international markets and thus are more exposed to uncertainty and unpredictability in international trading relations than well-established exporters. They also lack the expertise, financial capacities

Iraq), they absorbed only about 40 per cent of the total exports of other countries (including, over the past 10 years, Bahrain, Lebanon, India, the United Republic of Tanzania, Viet Nam and Zambia). Perhaps more importantly, for a variety of developing countries one single destination accounted for the vast majority of their exports during the period 2000–2004 (table 3.2). Mexico tops this list, with almost 90 per cent of its exports going to the United States. Many of the developing countries geographically close to the United States ship a very large share of their exports to that market. It should, however, be borne in mind that these results, as well as the results reported below, rely on export data expressed in gross value terms. This means that the data are inflated for countries that have a high import content in their exports due to, for example, their active participation in international production networks.[34] Many of the countries listed in table 3.2 have preferential access to the United States markets, including through outsourcing agreements.

Second, looking at the single most important export destination for developing countries more generally shows a number of interesting features (table 3.3). First, unsurprisingly, large economies rank at the top. This is true for both the developed and the developing countries that were the most important destinations for developing-country exports. However, the importance of Japan, and particularly that of the large European developed economies, has declined over the past 10 years (reflecting their lacklustre economic performance during this time),[35] whereas the importance of the United States and rapidly growing developing countries – especially China, but also India – as the main trading partner of developing countries has increased.[36] Second, the already considerable importance of the United States as developing countries' major export destination in the mid-1990s has further increased over the past few years, and that country is now the main export destination for almost half of the developing countries in the sample. As already mentioned, geographical closeness is a key determinant, which would explain why the majority of the developing countries for which the United States is the

> A country's export opportunities are strongly influenced by the economic fortunes of its trading partners.

Table 3.2

DEVELOPING COUNTRIES WITH THE HIGHEST CONCENTRATION OF EXPORTS TO A SINGLE DESTINATION, 2000–2004

Exporter	Destination	Market share of destination (Per cent)
Mexico	United States	88.9
Dominican Republic	United States	80.1
Trinidad and Tobago	United States	67.7
Sudan	China	67.4
Nicaragua	United States	66.8
El Salvador	United States	65.9
Mozambique	Netherlands	64.6
Venezuela	United States	63.8
Gabon	United States	59.1
Cambodia	United States	55.9

Source: UNCTAD secretariat calculations, based on IMF, *Direction of Trade Statistics*, October 2005.

most important export destination are in Central and South America. The number of countries in South and Central America for which the United States is the most important export destination has remained virtually unchanged. It has also remained the most important export destination of large African fuel exporters (such as Angola, Gabon and Nigeria) over the entire period 1990–2004. Between 1994 and 1999 it temporarily gained in importance for a number of Asian economies (e.g. Cambodia, Iraq, Myanmar and Nepal). Moreover, in 2004 the United States was the most important export destination for some additional fuel exporters from Africa (e.g. Algeria and Equatorial Guinea).[37]

Several factors affect the kind of impact that trading partners' economic fortunes will have on a country's export opportunities. A first group of factors can be characterized as determining whether two countries are a "good match". These factors,

Table 3.3

MAIN MARKETS FOR DEVELOPING-COUNTRY EXPORTS AND NUMBER OF DEVELOPING COUNTRIES FOR WHICH THEY ARE THE MOST IMPORTANT MARKET

1994		*1999*		*2004*	
United States	33	United States	40	United States	40
Japan	11	Japan	9	China	9
France	7	France	5	Japan	8
Italy	5	Italy	5	France	3
Brazil	4	Brazil	3	India	3
Germany	4	China	3	Italy	3
United Kingdom	3	India	3	Netherlands	3
Australia	2	United Kingdom	3	Brazil	2
Belgium and Luxembourg	2	Australia	2	South Africa	2
China	2	China, Taiwan Province of	2	Thailand	2
Russian Federation	2	Germany	2		
Saudi Arabia	2	Saudi Arabia	2		
Spain	2	South Africa	2		
Thailand	2	Spain	2		

Source: See table 3.2.
 Note: Includes all developing countries whose cumulated average exports accounted for 99.7 per cent of total developing-country exports during the period 2000–2004, and for which comprehensive data are available (i.e. 90 countries for 1994, and 91 for 1999 and 2004). The table lists only those countries that were the main export destinations of at least two developing countries in the respective years.

which include geographic distance (which has a strong impact on trading costs), the overlap between one country's export composition and the other country's import composition, and the exporter's competitiveness relative to other countries exporting the same product palette, are reflected in the export weights discussed above. A second group determines the extent to which changes in a trading partner's economic performance influence a country's export opportunities. This influence is reflected in the trading partner's relative economic size (measured by its share in world aggregate income),[38] a change in the trading partner's economic activity (measured by the rate of the country's aggregate income growth, in constant dollars), and the trading partner's import/ GDP ratio, which measures that partner's import propensity and its import price elasticity.

Taking account of both these groups of factors, the 15 developing countries whose export opportunities have evolved the most favourably, and the 15 whose export opportunities have evolved the least favourably, in response to changes in world economic conditions during the period 1990–2004 are shown in table 3.4. Three features of the table are noteworthy. First, only a narrow range of developing countries appears in the table for all three sub-periods. The main beneficiaries include economies in Central and South America that are geographically close to the United States, as well as Angola, Gabon and Macao (China). Those that benefited the least include four African countries,[39] as well as Cuba, Lebanon and Paraguay. Second, in each of the three five-year periods, more than half of the main beneficiaries were those that are geographically close to the United States, with the other half comprising small economies that have a strong concentration of exports in fuels or clothing. Some of the economies benefiting the least either have a small neighbouring country as their main trading partner (e.g. Lebanon and Syria,

Table 3.4

RANKING OF DEVELOPING ECONOMIES WITH THE LARGEST AND SMALLEST INCREASES IN EXPORT OPPORTUNITIES FROM WORLD IMPORT DEMAND GROWTH, 1990–2004

1990–1994	*1995–1999*	*2000–2004*

The 15 developing economies with the largest increase in export opportunities

1990–1994	1995–1999	2000–2004
Mexico	Mexico	Mexico
Angola	Dominican Republic	Dominican Republic
Honduras	Angola	Cambodia
Dominican Republic	Gabon	El Salvador
Venezuela	Honduras	Venezuela
Costa Rica	Venezuela	Gabon
Trinidad and Tobago	China, Macao	China, Macao
Ecuador	Jamaica	Guatemala
Nepal	Guatemala	Angola
Congo	Bangladesh	Trinidad and Tobago
Panama	Sri Lanka	Honduras
Philippines	Nicaragua	Iraq
Nigeria	Philippines	Panama
Gabon	Colombia	Colombia
China, Macao	Trinidad and Tobago	Nicaragua

The 15 developing economies with the smallest increase in export opportunities

1990–1994	1995–1999	2000–2004
Jordan	Jordan	Togo
Iraq	Benin	Paraguay
Benin	Togo	Benin
Lebanon	Paraguay	Senegal
Mali	Senegal	Uganda
Cuba	Lebanon	Lebanon
Togo	Cuba	Mozambique
Paraguay	Mali	Cuba
Cambodia	Yemen	Zambia
Mongolia	Sudan	Mali
Kenya	Kenya	Yemen
Myanmar	Dem. People's Rep. of Korea	Dem. People's Rep. of Korea
Zambia	Mozambique	Papua New Guinea
Bahrain	Uruguay	Iran, Islamic Rep. of
Senegal	Syrian Arab Republic	United Republic of Tanzania

Source: UNCTAD secretariat calculations, based on IMF, *Direction of Trade Statistics*, October 2005; UN COMTRADE; and UNCTAD *Handbook of Statistics*, various issues.

Note: Calculations based on a sample of 94 developing countries whose cumulated average exports in 2000–2004 accounted for 99.7 per cent of total developing-country exports; due to missing data on export weights for some of these countries, the sample covered 90 countries for 1990–1994 and 1995–1999, and 91 countries for 2000–2004. The ranking is based on the magnitude of change in export opportunities.

Uganda and Kenya), or their main export product is a primary commodity that experienced extended periods of low prices (e.g. cotton for Benin, Mali and Togo; coffee for Uganda; copper for Zambia; and sugar for Cuba). To the extent that commodity price movements have been responsible for the evolution of developing countries' export opportunities, the recent commodity price rise has substantially improved their opportunities for higher export earnings. Finally, for all of the 15 major beneficiaries in all three sub-periods, the United States was the most important export destination, with the exception of Nepal, for which Germany was the most important export destination in the period 1990–1994. The 15 developing countries that benefited the least have a wide variety of trading partners and their main export destination has been frequently changing.

The results of this first measure of changes in developing countries' export opportunities, shown in table 3.4, are strongly influenced by the economic size of their main trading partners. Using a second measure, which excludes the economic size variable and the import propensity variable from the calculation, and calculating the improvement in export opportunities arising from changes in world income conditions only on the basis of export market shares and export partners' aggregate income growth, strongly increases the importance of developing countries, especially China but also a few other Asian economies such as Malaysia, Thailand and Taiwan Province of China, as trading partners that provide the fastest increase in export opportunities. This is evident particularly for the period 2000–2004, when the main export destination for the exports of nine out of the ten developing countries with the largest increase in export opportunities calculated on this basis was a developing country, and for six out of nine it was China, as shown in table 3.5.[40] This is additional evidence of China's rising importance as a destination of developing-country exports, as discussed in some detail in *TDR 2005*.

The table also shows that those countries for which the United States is the main export desti-

> The economic ascendance of the Asian drivers has become an important determinant of developing countries' export opportunities.

nation tend to have a highly concentrated destination pattern. While this is undoubtedly beneficial as long as the main trading partner is a large economy with robust economic growth, it also strongly increases the risk of being adversely affected when the trading partner's economic fortune turns. This risk became manifest during the Asian financial crisis, when the trade channel was one of the main mechanisms of contagion (*TDR 2004*), and it is also reflected in the sensitivity of Mexico's GDP to changes in United States import demand (see, for example, EIU, 2005a).

Table 3.5 also shows that those developing countries identified as the main beneficiaries of improved export opportunities due to changes in world import demand (i.e. the second measure) tend to experience significantly higher rates of export growth. However, the absolute value of exports is significantly higher for those countries identified on the basis of the first measure (i.e. the economic size of the main trading partner). This is probably due to the fact that the import composition of those economies that have experienced rapid growth over the past few years, especially China, significantly differs from that of very large economies, such as the United States. Hence, the economic ascendance of the Asian drivers has come to be an important determinant of developing countries' export opportunities.

The increasing significance of Asian developing countries in world imports is also likely to be the main reason for the growing importance of the "old" economy in product-specific dynamism of developing-country exports over the past few years. Between 2000 and 2003, which is the latest year for which comprehensive data are available, the export values of many products in the category of high-technology-intensive manufactures, and in particular the electronics products of the "new" economy, continued to experience a rate of growth above the average for all products. There was also robust growth in the export values of an increasing number of primary commodities, as well as of manufactures in the low- and medium-technology-intensive categories (table 3.6). Although much

Table 3.5

INCREASE IN EXPORTS DUE TO RISING EXPORT OPPORTUNITIES FROM WORLD IMPORT DEMAND GROWTH, 2000–2004

| Exporting economy | Destination providing biggest improvement in export opportunities, 2004 | | Exports | | Memo item: Purchasing power of exports, 2004 (Index number, 2000=100) |
	Destination	Market share	Average annual change 2000–2004 (Per cent)	Total value 2004 ($ million)	
First variant[a]					
Mexico	United States	88.4	3.0	189 083	109
Dominican Republic	United States	80.1	8.9	1 299	121
Cambodia	United States	55.9	14.5	2 415	..
El Salvador	United States	65.9	2.4	1 474	99
Venezuela	United States	63.8	2.0	36 200	92
Gabon	United States	59.7	11.4	3 970	151
China, Macao	United States	49.9	-2.1	2 160	..
Guatemala	United States	53.6	1.8	2 938	98
Angola	United States	38.0	16.6	13 550	157
Trinidad and Tobago	United States	67.7	5.6	5 103	..
Memo item:					
Average		62.3	6.4	25 819	118
Second variant[b]					
Mongolia	China	47.8	9.3	770	..
Sudan	China	67.4	20.7	3 778	194
China, Hong Kong	China	44.1	6.9	259 314	135
Yemen	Thailand	33.9	6.3	5 109	112
Dem. Republic of the Congo	China, Taiwan Prov. of	27.8	7.3	3 115	115
Oman	China	29.5	3.9	13 342	125
Dem. People's Rep. of Korea	China	41.8	8.9	1 035	..
Cuba	Netherlands	22.8	-0.8	1 730	..
Mali	China	32.7	18.2	1 123	145[c]
Myanmar	Thailand	41.4	12.6	2 921	156
Memo item:					
Average		38.9	9.3	29 224	140
Average excl. Hong Kong (China)		38.3	9.6	3 658	140

Source: See table 3.4.

Note: See table 3.4. The ranking is based on the magnitude of improved export opportunities.

a Magnitude of improved export opportunities measured by export market share multiplied with export partner's composite index (economic size * import propensity * GDP growth).

b Magnitude of improved export opportunities measured by export market share multiplied with export partner's GDP growth.

c 2003.

Table 3.6

DYNAMIC PRODUCTS IN DEVELOPING-COUNTRY EXPORTS
BY CATEGORY, 1995–2003

(Number of products)

	1995–2000		2000–2003		**Memo item:** 1995–2003	
	Above-average growth	Below-average growth	Above-average growth	Below-average growth	Above-average growth	Below-average growth
Primary commodities	20	71	47	44	19	72
Labour- and resource-intensive manufactures	10	25	12	23	9	26
Low-technology-intensive manufactures	6	15	18	3	7	14
Medium-technology-intensive manufactures	18	18	27	9	25	11
High-technology-intensive manufactures	20	23	31	12	27	16

Source: UNCTAD secretariat calculations, based on UN COMTRADE; and UNCTAD estimates.
Note: For the composition of the product categories, see *TDR 2002*: 87–92. The dynamism of an individual product refers to its rate of export value growth relative to the average rate for all products.

of the dynamism in developing countries' exports of primary commodities (e.g. a range of cereals, as well as silver) over the past few years has occurred from a low base, the export values of commodities that figure more prominently in these countries' export baskets (e.g. cocoa, rubber and vegetable oils) have risen rapidly. Between 2000 and 2003, among low- and medium-technology-intensive manufactures, export values grew the most rapidly for iron and steel, transport equipment and machinery.

In sum, the evolution of import demand in developing countries' main trading partners has had a significant impact on developing countries' export opportunities. The structure of this demand growth has also strongly influenced the product-specific pattern of developing countries' export

dynamism since 1995. Thus, by implication, there appears to be only a weak link between changes in developing countries' market access conditions and their export opportunities. Nevertheless, evidence suggests that even a slight easing of such conditions could provide a sustained improvement in developing countries' export opportunities. By contrast, demand growth in developing countries' main trading partners can significantly increase their export opportunities, but it also has a strong cyclical component and may therefore eventually prove to be unsustainable. The challenge for developing countries is to translate these improvements in export opportunities into faster export growth. For this, it will be necessary to improve supply-side conditions, in particular through rapid productivity growth and technological upgrading, as discussed in chapter V below.

C. Debt relief and official development assistance

For developing countries, cross-border debt financing is considered an important vehicle for mobilizing resources for public and private investment. External financing from international capital markets or official sources enables countries to import more inputs for domestic production than the current level of their export earnings would normally allow. Where the official external financing takes the form of grants, it will not create any repayment obligation in the future, and its use for social and humanitarian purposes is therefore appropriate. By contrast, external borrowing leads to debt service obligations in the future, and the question as to whether developing-country borrowers will be able to service their debts as scheduled is at the core of debt sustainability analysis, which has received increasing attention in recent years.

In principle, the productive use of external debt will itself create the capacity for servicing that debt to the extent that it generates additional income and foreign exchange through either higher export earnings or reduced dependence on imports. However, experience from the last three decades shows that, in addition to inappropriate domestic policies, exogenous shocks such as terms-of-trade deterioration, interest rate hikes or natural disasters, can seriously undermine a country's ability to service its external debt. With the rapid build-up of the stock of debt during the 1970s and 1980s, debt rescheduling became more frequent, and analysis of the debt problem of devel-

> Exogenous shocks can seriously undermine a country's ability to service its external debt.

oping countries began to evolve from the traditional view that it was strictly a liquidity problem, towards the view that in many countries it was a structural one.

This section briefly reviews the considerable progress made in recent years by the international community in dealing with the debt problems of the poorest countries, which are mainly or exclusively indebted vis-à-vis official creditors. It also takes up some issues relating to the debt problems of low- and middle-income countries that have obligations to private creditors, for which little progress has been made in finding satisfactory solutions.

1. The framework for official debt relief

The rescheduling of official bilateral debt takes place under the aegis of the Paris Club, a voluntary, informal group of creditors that coordinates agreements with debtor countries to redress debt service difficulties. The incidence of Paris Club reschedulings rose dramatically among the poorest countries over the period 1976–1988, when 24 of the countries that later were identified as heavily indebted poor countries (HIPCs) were granted 77 reschedulings: 10 under ad hoc[41] treatments and 67 under the classic terms. These reschedulings led to a postponement of debt service

Table 3.7

PARIS CLUB TERMS AND RESCHEDULINGS

	Paris Club terms	Debt reduction[a] (Per cent)	Number of reschedulings		Number of debtor countries involved in reschedulings	
			Total	HIPCs	Total	HIPCs
1956–present	Classic terms (non-concessional)	-	169	68	58	27
	1976–1982	-	27	20	15	10
	1983–1990	-	101	47	43	23
Sept. 1990– present	Houston terms	-	34	5	20	5
Oct. 1988–June 1991	Toronto terms	33	28	27	20	19
Dec. 1991–Dec. 1994	London terms	50	26	24	23	22
Jan. 1995–present	Naples terms					
	Jan. 1995–Sept. 1999	50	6	5	4	3
	Jan. 1995–present	67	44	40	31	28
Dec. 1996–Nov. 1999	Lyon terms	80	7	7	5	5
Nov. 1999– present	Cologne terms	90	42	42	28	28

Source: UNCTAD estimates, based on the "breakdown by year of agreements already concluded by Paris Club creditors" at www.clubdeparis.org.
Note: Data for HIPCs cover the countries identified under the HIPC Initiative, including countries that were deemed to have potentially sustainable debt following traditional debt relief (Angola, Kenya, Viet Nam and Yemen); they do not refer to the newly identified countries included under the extended sunset clause.
a Debt reduction may apply to either debt service or stock.

payments to a later date, thereby causing debt stocks to rise (IMF, 1999).

The evolution of the terms granted by the Paris Club creditors since the late 1970s reflects the increasing realization that repeated rescheduling of debt service flows was not the solution to the debt problems of developing countries (table 3.7). The turning point occurred with the adoption of the Toronto terms in 1988, which first introduced debt stock reduction for poor countries. Under these terms, eligible countries obtained a 33 per cent reduction of their debt stock. During the period 1988–1991, 19 countries (now classified as HIPCs) underwent 27 debt reschedulings under the Toronto terms. The Houston terms, which were adopted in 1990, did not provide for any debt stock reduction. These terms were intended to address the debt of lower-middle-income countries and were also applied in a few cases to countries presently classified as HIPCs.

Despite these new measures, it soon became evident that they were insufficient to avert the continued and unsustainable increase in debt stocks. Consequently the London terms replaced the Toronto terms in late 1991, increasing the debt stock reduction granted to eligible countries to 50 per cent. Despite this debt stock reduction, an additional 22 countries presently classified as HIPCs underwent 24 debt reschedulings under the London terms in the subsequent three years. Clearly, the frequency of reschedulings was not declining. Debt reduction efforts were further enhanced in 1994 with the adoption of the Naples terms, which provided a 67 per cent reduction of the debt stock.

While the official creditors were reducing the stock of bilateral debt of the poorest countries, there was no mechanism to address their rising stocks of multilateral debt, which continued to increase as a percentage of their external debt position. It was soon recognized that the repeated rescheduling process was not addressing the problem of debt overhang, and that a more comprehensive scheme would be necessary to successfully tackle the debt problem of these countries.

Consequently, in 1996 the proposal for the HIPC Debt Initiative was put forward at the G-7 Summit in Lyon. It was designed to coordinate the efforts of the involved creditors through broad and equitable participation. The Initiative represented a major step towards comprehensively addressing the debt problems of the poorest countries in that it sought to find a lasting solution to the problem of debt overhang through a reduction of debt to a sustainable level. A major feature was the inclusion, for the first time, of multilateral debt in the international debt relief effort. Further, the proposal increased the net present value (NPV) of debt stock reduction accorded to eligible countries by Paris Club creditors to 90 per cent under the Cologne terms. The architects of the Initiative envisaged that a simultaneous treatment of both official and multilateral debt, accompanied by a large debt stock reduction, would provide a permanent exit for HIPCs from repeated debt rescheduling operations.

The rationale behind the HIPC Initiative was that debt overhang has a negative impact on growth and investment because high debt service obligations reduce the flexibility of fiscal policy and the scope for public investment; moreover, they create uncertainty about future macroeconomic developments among potential domestic and foreign investors, and therefore raise the cost of borrowing.[42] This is because creditors tend to require a higher marginal return when there is uncertainty over a country's future debt servicing capacity. The higher cost of borrowing reduces the willingness of governments to undertake public investment, with attendant effects on private investment and growth. In addition, as governments are forced to divert resources to servicing debt and away from investment and social expenditure, the presence of a severe debt overhang can undermine a country's ability to pursue the Millennium Development Goals (MDGs). Debt service obligations can create fiscal constraints that distort effective resource utilization, and they diminish a government's

capacity to form and shape a national development strategy (Moss and Chiang, 2003: 9). An underlying principle of the HIPC Initiative, therefore, was to use the newly freed public resources from lower debt service payments to increase social expenditures aimed at reducing poverty.

After 10 years of implementation, the HIPC Initiative has not succeeded in meeting all its goals. One of the main obstacles to solving the current debt problem of HIPCs, and minimizing the risk of their plunging into a new debt crisis, remains the limited participation of non-Paris Club creditors in the write-offs and litigation by some private creditors who refuse to accept any write-off on their claims. Moreover, some lenders are not following the World Bank's principle of extending highly concessional loans or grants to post-HIPC countries, thus paving the way for new debt servicing difficulties for these countries a few years from now. The process for countries to benefit from the Initiative is lengthy, slow and complex, which places a burden on their already weak institutions. By the third quarter of 1999 only seven of the eligible countries had reached the "decision point" – the stage of the Initiative at which the international community commits to providing additional assistance beyond traditional debt relief to assist countries in reaching the debt sustainability thresholds defined under the Initiative. At the end of 1999, the HIPC Initiative was broadened,[43] and by the end of 2000, 22 countries had reached the decision point under the enhanced Initiative.

> After 10 years of implementation, the HIPC Initiative has not succeeded in meeting all its goals.

Despite these efforts, the Initiative has constantly faced financing problems, making a quick resolution to the debt problems of HIPCs impracticable. While the HIPCs as a group have made progress in terms of a number of debt indicators, such as the ratio of debt service to exports and debt service to government revenue, a number of completion point countries continue to have unsustainable levels of debt. According to World Bank estimates based on 2003 NPV debt ratios of 13 countries for which data was available, the debt ratios of 11 countries have deteriorated; of these, 8 countries have exceeded the sustainability thresholds. Moreover, one third of the completion point countries – Burkina Faso, Ethiopia, Guyana, Nicaragua, Rwanda and Uganda – are expected to exceed the sustainability thresholds in the medium term of the post-completion period (World Bank, 2006a: 18–19).

In an additional push to resolve the debt problem of the poorest countries, in July 2005 the G-8 announced the Multilateral Debt Relief Initiative (MDRI), which provides countries that have reached the completion point under the HIPC Initiative with 100 per cent debt cancellation of claims from multilateral financial institutions.[44] The objective of the G-8 proposal is to complete the HIPC debt relief process by freeing additional resources to support countries' efforts to achieve the MDGs. It is estimated that the MDRI will reduce the NPV debt-to-export ratio from 140 per cent post-HIPC relief to approximately 52 per cent (IMF and World Bank, 2005b). The cancellation of the multilateral debt of these countries is expected to have a profound impact on the burden of their debt overhang and on the pursuit of their development objectives.

2. Extent and impact of the HIPC Initiative

Estimating the amount of debt relief accorded to countries under the HIPC Initiative and assessing its impact is not straightforward. Debt relief can take the form of concessional debt restructuring – which leaves the nominal debt stock unchanged – or various forms of debt cancellation, with different implications on future debt service obligations (Chauvin and Kraay, 2005: 7–8). Behind a given nominal value of the debt forgiven there is a structure of interest and principal payments, which determines the degree to which the nominal debt relief will reduce future debt service payments, and the impact on future debt service payments of forgiving a nominal amount of concessional debt will differ greatly from the same amount of forgiveness on non-concessional debt.

In 2004, the nominal stock of debt of the HIPCs that had begun to receive debt relief after reaching the decision point under the enhanced Initiative, was roughly the same as it had been

Figure 3.2

TOTAL EXTERNAL DEBT OF HIPCs, 1970–2004

(Billions of dollars)

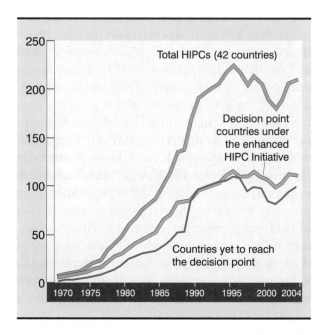

Source: UNCTAD secretariat calculations, based on World Bank, *Global Development Finance* Database.
Note: The decision point countries include data for the 27 HIPCs that reached the decision point by end 2004. For a listing of the decision point countries, see annex table 3.A1 of this chapter.

in 1996, the year of the launch of the Initiative (fig. 3.2). What is apparent, though, is that the accumulation of debt decelerated, and even declined from 1998 to 2001, before rising again from 2002 onwards. This could lead to the conclusion that the enhanced Initiative has not adequately addressed the problem of debt overhang for the countries that have reached the decision point (listed in annex table 3.A1). However, it is important to note that there have been steady improvements in the terms of the new loan commitments for the countries that had reached the decision point by the end of 2004. These trends are apparent with respect to the average interest rate, the average maturity and the proportion of the grant element in the terms of the new commitments (fig. 3.3). The improvements are more pronounced when compared to the terms for the countries that have been identified as potentially

Figure 3.3

DECISION POINT HIPCs: TERMS OF NEW LOAN COMMITMENTS, 1980–2004

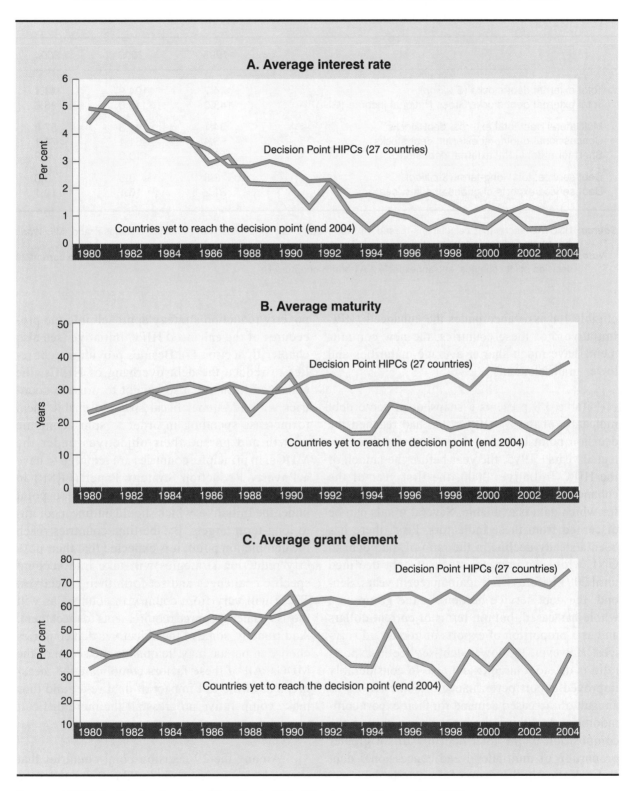

A. Average interest rate

Decision Point HIPCs (27 countries)

Countries yet to reach the decision point (end 2004)

B. Average maturity

Decision Point HIPCs (27 countries)

Countries yet to reach the decision point (end 2004)

C. Average grant element

Decision Point HIPCs (27 countries)

Countries yet to reach the decision point (end 2004)

Source: UNCTAD estimates, based on World Bank, *Global Development Finance*, May 2006.

Note: Figures reflect a simple average. The countries that had yet to reach the decision point by end 2004 are Burundi, Congo and the countries identified as potentially eligible for assistance under the enhanced HIPC Initiative, including the Central African Republic, Comoros, Côte d'Ivoire, Eritrea, Haiti, Kyrgyzstan, Liberia, Nepal, Somalia, Sudan and Togo. Due to lack of data, Eritrea and Kyrgyzstan are not included in the group averages.

Table 3.8

DEBT INDICATORS OF DECISION POINT HIPCs, 1995–2004

(Weighted average, per cent unless otherwise indicated)

	1995	2000	2004
Total external debt stocks (*$ billion*)	114.7	104.9	111.1
Total external debt stocks/Gross National Income (GNI)	143.0	115.8	86.8
Multilateral debt/total external debt stocks	34.1	41.8	57.8
Concessional debt/total external debt stocks	55.4	61.4	74.1
Short-term debt/total external debt stocks	9.8	10.0	4.9
Debt service, total long-term (*$ billion*)	3.8	3.5	3.3
Debt service/exports of goods and services	31.2	16.1	10.1

Source: UNCTAD secretariat calculations, based on World Bank, *Global Development Finance* Database; and IMF, *World Economic Outlook* Database.

Note: The table presents data for the 27 HIPCs that reached the decision point by end 2004. For a listing of the current 29 decision point countries, see annex table 3.A1 of this chapter.

eligible for assistance under the enhanced HIPC Initiative. For these countries, the new commitments have much shorter average maturities and lower grant elements.

Table 3.8 presents a snapshot of some debt indicators of the 27 HIPCs that had reached the decision point by the end of 2004, for three selected years: 1995, the year before the launch of the HIPC Initiative; 2000, the first year of the enhanced HIPC Initiative; and 2004, the last year for which data is available. Several trends can be discerned from these indicators. First, there has been a steady decline in the ratio of total debt to GNI, while the nominal stock of debt declined until 2001 before rising again in recent years. Second, the debt service burden for the group as a whole has eased, both in terms of current dollars and as a proportion of exports of goods and services. However, the lower debt-service-to-exports ratio is due to a large extent also to considerably improved export performance of some HIPCs as a result of increased demand for their export commodities. And third, there has been a shift in the composition of the total debt towards a greater proportion of multilateral and concessional debt and a decline in the share of short-term debt.

In 1999, the IMF and the World Bank introduced "country owned" poverty reduction strategies as the basis for future lending, and incorporated the poverty reduction strategy approach into the procedures of the enhanced HIPC Initiative (see also chapter II, section D). Besides providing debt relief to reduce the debt overhang of HIPCs, the enhanced Initiative also sought to provide countries with additional fiscal space to enable them to increase spending in order to spur economic growth and pursue their objectives under the MDGs. In principle, countries are required to have a Poverty Reduction Strategy Paper (PRSP) in place by the time they reach the decision point under the Initiative, which should outline medium- to long-term targets. By the time countries reach the completion point, it is expected that their poverty reduction strategies will take into account specific challenges and set forth their objectives. These will vary from country to country, as will the associated resource requirements to meet them. Additionally, some of the objectives that countries choose to pursue may lie outside the scope of the MDGs. All of these factors complicate the measurement of the full impact of debt relief and thus make comparative progress all the more difficult to gauge.

Among the 29 decision point countries that reached the decision point by May 2006 under the enhanced HIPC Initiative, there has been a rise in poverty reduction expenditures and a fall in debt service, measured as a ratio of government revenue (fig. 3.4). This is not surprising, as the provision

Figure 3.4

DECISION POINT HIPCs: DEBT SERVICE AND POVERTY REDUCING EXPENDITURES AS A PERCENTAGE OF GOVERNMENT REVENUE, 1998–2008

(Weighted average)

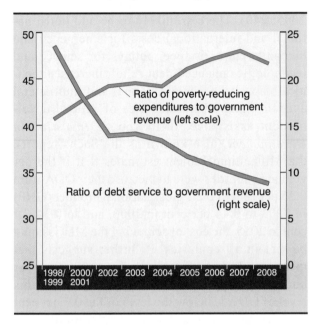

Source: IMF, *HIPC Statistical Update*, March 2006.
  Note: See figure 3.2. The ratio of poverty-reducing expenditures to government revenue for 1998/1999 is only for 1999. Data for 1998/1999 and 2000/2001 are averages.

achieving and maintaining higher levels of economic growth over the long term. The launching of the HIPC Initiative coincided with an upward swing in average per capita GDP growth in those countries that had reached decision point by the end of 2004, from a negative rate of around -2 per cent between 1980 and 1995 to a positive one in the order of 1.5 per cent in 1996–2004 (fig. 3.5). Although the swing occurred too early to be attributable to the economic effects of the HIPC Initiative, the expectation and actual provision of debt relief is likely to have been a contributory factor. In any case, in order to reap the benefits from debt relief for growth and employment creation, due consideration has to be given to the context of spending within a country's national development strategy and to the overall impact of investment (particularly in infrastructure) on growth (UNCTAD, 2004a). Further, the vulnerability of

Figure 3.5

DECISION POINT HIPCs: PER CAPITA GDP GROWTH AND RATIO OF TOTAL DEBT TO GNI, 1980–2004

(Weighted average)

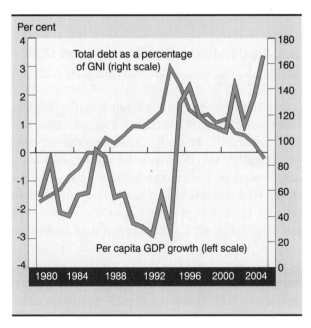

Source: UNCTAD secretariat calculations, based on United Nations Statistics Division, United Nations Common Database (UNCDB); and World Bank, *Global Development Finance* Database.
  Note: See figure 3.2.

of such expenditures was incorporated into the PRSP process. However, despite the increase in these expenditures, the additional resources resulting from debt relief remain below what is needed for these countries to achieve the MDGs. Many of the countries have made only modest progress towards attaining some of the goals, with the majority of countries likely to fall considerably short of the targets set for 2015 (annex table 3.A2). As a group, these countries have made some progress towards achieving the goals under gender equality, improved sanitation facilities and child mortality, although individual performance varies widely. It is evident that these countries will require a sizeable increase in development assistance if they are to reach the targets.

Elimination of a debt overhang is a necessary but certainly not sufficient condition for these countries to exogenous shocks, such as adverse weather conditions, exchange rate changes, or commodity price movements, and their degree of export diversification should also be taken into account when considering their long-term growth prospects. Underestimation of this vulnerability has been one of the reasons why estimates of export earnings and economic growth in the context of the implementation of the HIPC Initiative tended to be overly optimistic in the past (USGAO, 2004). There is thus a need for caution in making economic projections that serve to assess future debt sustainability.

It is also necessary to bear in mind that traditional debt indicators only give a partial picture of the foreign exchange obligations resulting from external financing; they do not reflect the root cause of many of the debt problems of developing countries. As such problems frequently retard progress in economic development and structural change, so that countries continue to remain vulnerable to adverse changes in the external environment, it is important to incorporate systematic debt management in national development strategies. This would help ensure that progress is made not only towards poverty reduction, but also in areas that support diversification, output growth and technological progress.

3. Additionality of debt relief and ODA

Even after reaping the full benefits of debt relief under the HIPC Initiative, countries continue to be faced with the challenge of maintaining debt sustainability while seeking the additional financing needed to pursue the MDGs. One-off debt relief will not provide a universal solution to broader structural problems, and it certainly will not ensure against a recurrence of debt problems.

According to the OECD, ODA to developing countries, including debt forgiveness grants, provided by DAC rose to $106.5 billion in 2005, representing an increase of 31.4 per cent over 2004. However, ODA is expected to fall again in 2006 and 2007, since the sharp increase in 2005 was mainly due to exceptionally high debt relief accorded to Iraq ($14 billion) and Nigeria ($5 bil-

lion), and emergency aid to tsunami-affected countries ($2.2 billion) (OECD, 2006b).

In comparison, the total donor cost of supporting the MDG financing gap in investment for every low- and middle-income country is estimated to be $73 billion for 2006, increasing to $135 billion by 2015 (UN Millennium Project, 2005: 240). There are likely to be additional national and international costs for emergency and humanitarian assistance, outlays for science and technology, enhanced debt relief, increased technical capacity needs of bilateral and multilateral agencies, and other categories of official development assistance. In its report, *Investing in Development* (also known as the Sachs report), the Millennium Project estimates that if the developed countries were to increase their ODA from 0.25 per cent of their gross national product (GNP) in 2003 to 0.44 per cent in 2006, and to 0.54 per cent in 2015, the cost of achieving the MDGs could be met in all countries. It further suggests that these should largely take the form of grants for budgetary support. It should be noted that this level of ODA is below the level of the 0.7 per cent of GNP that donors had already committed to reach by 2015 to support the MDGs and other development assistance priorities.

Most HIPCs will need greater grant-based financing if they are to achieve the MDGs by 2015 without encountering further debt servicing difficulties. However, in cases where additional loans are necessary to finance investment for development, there is a need to promote responsible lending and borrowing, and to link the grant element of such loans to the capacity to pay, which, in the poorest countries is often subject to externally induced fluctuations, given the high dependence of these countries on commodity export earnings. In this context, the question arises as to how a country can strike the proper balance between grants and concessional loans, which would allow it to achieve its development objectives without the risk of getting into an unsustainable external debt position.[45]

The obvious benefit of grants is that they will not lead to potential debt servicing problems at a later stage, while providing the valuable fiscal space and resources needed to achieve national development objectives. The HIPC completion point countries, in particular, will not have enough resources to finance development expenditures without a sizeable increase in aid, preferably in the form of grants. There is concern, however, that a significant shift to grants from loans may increase uncertainty with regard to future aid flows.

Once the debt relief initiatives are complete, countries will have to find additional means to finance the MDGs. The main concern is that the HIPC Initiative makes only a modest contribution to alleviating a government's budgetary constraints. While the modalities of debt relief may have an impact on a country's balance of payments – in the sense that debt stock relief, unlike debt service relief, eliminates the need to mobilize foreign exchange for repayment to the creditor – it will not ease the budgetary burden, as the amount previously scheduled for debt service payments will instead be transferred into a special account that is drawn upon to finance social expenditures under the country's PRSP. Where countries had accumulated significant arrears before benefiting from the HIPC Initiative, governments will thus have to incur additional expenditures to "clear" these arrears in the form of higher social spending. These additional expenditures will have to be financed by reducing expenditure on other categories of public sector outlays or by finding ways of increasing government revenue. Hence, to what extent debt relief can provide additional fiscal space to enable the beneficiary government to take measures to achieve the MDGs, and to what extent the conditions attached to the programme impose additional constraints on public spending and investment or on measures in support of growth and structural change in the longer term, is a matter of interpretation.

Moreover the provision of debt relief, which was intended to free up resources for increased public expenditures, was based on the assumption that such relief would be in addition to aid flows that may have been provided in the absence of debt relief. Again, the judgement about additionality in this sense is largely a matter of interpretation and assumptions about the counterfactual. But a decomposition of nominal ODA flows from DAC members suggests that, so far, debt relief has not been fully additional under the Initiative. As can be seen from figure 3.6, for the countries that reached the decision point by the end of 2004,

Figure 3.6

DECISION POINT HIPCs: ODA FLOWS AND DEBT RELIEF, 1990–2004

(Billions of dollars)

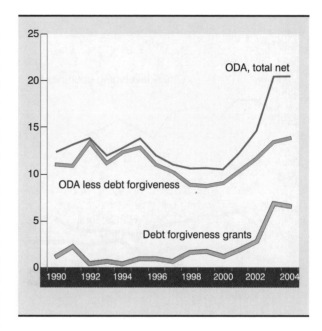

Source: UNCTAD secretariat calculations, based on OECD, *Development Assistance Committee* Database.
Note: See figure 3.2.

there was a continuous decline in aid flows, after deduction of debt forgiveness, following the launch of the HIPC Initiative in 1996 until 2000. This trend was reversed in 2001, with a continuous rise in the level of aid. A recent evaluation by the World Bank (2006a) points out that HIPC debt relief was significantly additional to non-debt transfers in the period after 1999. However, it is important to note that this rise of ODA, less debt forgiveness, only meant a return to the level prevailing before the launch of the HIPC Initiative.

ODA flows from DAC members, after deduction of debt relief grants, rose faster from 2001 to 2004 for developing countries that are not among the beneficiaries of the HIPC Initiative (55 per cent) than for the HIPCs (27 per cent) and the transition economies of South-East Europe and the CIS (10 per cent) (fig. 3.7). This could lead to the conclusion that bilateral HIPC debt relief has partly been at the expense of other ODA flows to HIPCs as a group. However, a large proportion of

Figure 3.7

ODA LESS DEBT RELIEF BY DAC MEMBERS, 1990–2004

(Billions of current dollars)

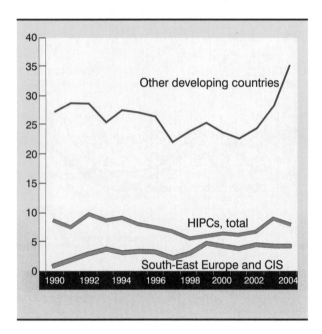

Source: UNCTAD secretariat calculations, based on OECD, *Development Assistance Committee* Database.

the increase in ODA flows, excluding debt forgiveness, to non-HIPCs was due to a substantial increase in aid flows to only two countries with exceptional reconstruction needs: Afghanistan and Iraq (OECD, 2006c).

4. Debt problems of middle-income countries

In addition to calling for measures to assist the poorest countries, the Millennium Declaration also underlined the need for national and international measures to help make the debt of low- and middle-income developing countries more sustainable in the long term. While the 1990s were marked by a major effort to deal with the debt sustainability problems of the poorest countries, those of the middle-income countries did not receive the same attention. It was only after the Argentine default in 2001 that both private and

official creditors turned their attention to improving the existing mechanisms for dealing with the debt problems of these countries.

The fact that a number of non-HIPCs also face serious problems of debt sustainability was recognized in the Evian approach proposed in 2003. This approach provides a framework for treatment by the Paris Club of the official debt of low- and middle-income countries, which have not been eligible for debt relief under the HIPC Initiative but have accumulated similar debt overhangs as the HIPCs. Under this approach, the standard terms of flow reschedulings will be applied to countries with a liquidity problem but an otherwise sustainable debt. For countries that have an unsustainable debt situation, but are committed to policies implemented within the framework of IMF programmes, the Evian approach allows a comprehensive treatment of their debt problem by the Paris Club, including flow rescheduling, stock re-profiling, or stock reduction. It also reinforces the principle of comparable treatment by other creditors, including private creditors.

So far the Evian approach has been applied only to six countries, two of which were considered to have an unsustainable debt situation.[46] Although no new terms of treatment have emerged from the Evian approach, the Paris Club considers it an improvement over past practices in debt renegotiations with middle-income countries. However, there are a number of problems with this approach: first, the factors which allow a distinction to be made between liquidity and solvency problems are not clearly identified; second, the case-by-case treatment of debtor countries is not entirely transparent in terms of the criteria or methodology underlying the treatment of the individual case; and, third, the debt sustainability analysis that serves as a basis for determining the treatment focuses on macroeconomic policies while paying little attention to the links between development policies and sustainability, or between vulnerability factors and sustainability.

During the 1990s there was considerable progress in solving the debt problems of the 1980s that were related to obligations vis-à-vis commercial bank creditors, but at the same time new debt problems built up that came to haunt the international financial markets by the end of the decade.

The improved external position of a number of middle-income countries, coupled with their reliance on capital inflows to finance investment and accelerate growth led to a rapid expansion of international bond issuance by middle-income countries.

Finding a solution to debt servicing problems related to bond debt is more complex than that concerning problems related to international syndicated bank lending, which was the most frequent form of private external financing before the 1990s. This is because bond lending involves diversified groups of bondholders, including domestic residents, and can be issued under different jurisdictions. In case of crisis, an orderly and collaborative debt restructuring agreement will be difficult to achieve, and aggressive creditor litigations and protracted negotiations can lead to a stalemate, or produce an outcome which would not correspond to the financial needs of the debtor countries.

The Argentine crisis once again showed the need for the development of an orderly international mechanism for solving sovereign debt default. In hindsight, it would seem that it would have been in the interest of both Argentina and the bondholders to seek an earlier resolution to the crisis within a well-established and internationally recognized structure. This issue is not new, but little progress has been made to devise an internationally agreed and institutionalized work-out mechanism for sovereign debt since the debt crisis of the 1980s. Against the background of that crisis and the slow progress in solving the debt problems of the countries indebted vis-à-vis commercial banks in the first half of the 1980s, *TDR 1986* highlighted the lack of a fair and efficient mechanism in the international financial system for resolving sovereign debt problems:

> The lack of a well articulated, impartial framework for resolving international debt problems creates considerable danger, which has in part already materialized, that international debtors will suffer the worst of both possible worlds: they may experience the financial and economic stigma of being judged *de facto* bankrupt, with all the consequences that this entails as regards credit-

worthiness and future access to financing. At the same time, they are largely without the benefits of receiving the financial relief and financial reorganization that would accompany a *de jure* bankruptcy handled in a manner similar to chapter 11 of the United States Bankruptcy Code (*TDR 1986*, annex to chapter VI).

It was only after a number of financial crises in emerging-market countries that the idea of an international framework for dealing with sovereign debt received greater attention in the IMF in 2002, in the form of a proposal for a sovereign debt restructuring mechanism (SDRM) (Krueger, 2001). In parallel with discussions about the SDRM, which sought a statutory solution comprising elements of national bankruptcy legislations, the IMF also supported further analysis of the effects of the incorporation of collective action clauses (CACs) into newly issued emerging-market bonds. Such clauses are cooperative arrangements that facilitate a restructuring of the debt resulting from individual bond issues, should the need arise, and they are relatively easy to implement. They have been used in recent years by an increasing number of developing-country issuers, and experience has shown that initial fears that an inclusion of CACs in new bond issues could send a wrong signal to potential investors and make external borrowing more costly were unwarranted.

However, CACs have little in common with the initially proposed framework that was intended to bring debtors and creditors together to resolve problems with the overall servicing of sovereign debt, secure greater transparency, and provide a mechanism for dispute settlement. Thus the problem of an orderly debt work-out, which would also ensure a fair sharing of the burden of financial crises between creditors and debtors, as well as between the private and public sectors, remains unsolved. Involving private creditors in crisis management and resolution would also help to prevent such crises, as creditors would have to bear the risks they take with speculative investments in emerging markets (see also *TDR 2001*, chap. III). In contrast to the procedures outlined in national

> Little progress has been made to devise an internationally agreed and institutionalized debt work-out mechanism.

bankruptcy laws, the current international financial architecture still does not ensure independent mediation and arbitration with regard to the required level of debt relief necessary for a country to regain a sustainable debt position. There is still a need to develop a comprehensive, fair and efficient international system for the resolution of a sovereign debt crisis.

D. Migrants' remittances

1. Recent trends in migrants' remittances

Recorded migrants' remittances[47] to developing countries have considerably increased since the early 1990s. They quadrupled between 1990 and 2004, becoming an increasingly important source of foreign exchange for these countries (fig. 3.8). In 1990, the level of remittances was about half that of ODA inflows, and close to that of FDI inflows. Subsequently, they grew more slowly – albeit more steadily – than FDI but faster than ODA, and since 1996 they have been exceeding ODA by an increasing margin.

Because of incomplete reporting, which is mainly due to the fact that a large proportion of migrants' remittances goes through informal channels, their actual value is believed to be much higher than what is recorded in balance-of-payments statistics. Minimum thresholds for official recording also mean that many countries do not register all their remittance inflows. Indeed, it is estimated that unrecorded remittances amount to at least 50 per cent of the recorded flows (World Bank 2006b: ix).

Overall, remittance inflows into developing countries have been more stable than their export earnings, FDI inflows, other private capital inflows and ODA. Unlike private capital flows, they do not fluctuate with the mood of capital markets or decline when the performance of the domestic economy of the receiving countries worsens. In fact remittances continued to increase at the beginning of the millennium when FDI showed considerable volatility as a result of the weak outlook of the global economy (fig. 3.8). Indeed, remittances often behave in a countercyclical pattern, as remitters tend to increase their transfers in times of economic crisis or natural disasters in their countries of origin. However, to some extent migrants' remittances are also undertaken for portfolio diversification reasons, in which case they tend to behave procyclically.

> Migrants' remittances to developing countries have become an important source of foreign exchange, exceeding ODA by an ever-increasing margin.

China and the Philippines provide two examples of how remittances can respond to dramatic changes in economic activity and the investment climate in recipient countries in the same manner as capital flows. Remittance inflows into China in the past few years have in part been motivated by speculation about the exchange rate of the renminbi and have behaved procyclically due to fast economic growth in that country. Similarly, remittance flows to the Philippines rose steadily as the investment climate improved in the early 1990s, but they became more volatile following the financial crisis in the late 1990s. Cross-country comparisons also reveal that remittances are affected by the investment climate in recipient countries (OECD, 2003), but, overall, remittance flows have been found to be less volatile and procyclical than foreign exchange inflows from other sources (IMF, 2005b).

Another particularity of migrants' remittances is that they typically constitute a form of additional household revenue in the recipient countries and the government has little control over their use. This makes it difficult to integrate their use into a strategy for the financing of development. On the other hand, they are less costly for the recipient country than foreign exchange inflows from other sources, because they do not create liabilities vis-à-vis the country of origin, such as interest payments in the case of debt instruments, conditionality in the case of official grants, or profit remittances in the case of FDI.

The rapid expansion of recorded remittance flows since 1990 has been due to three factors. First, migration from developing countries has been increasing owing to a confluence of conditions, such as labour shortages in some activities in a number of advanced and dynamic economies (United Nations, 2006), wage differentials and demographic disparities between source and destination countries, as well as lower costs of migration, including transportation. Second, the share of skilled workers and immigrants with higher educational attainment has risen significantly in the past three decades. Their resultant higher earning power has also contributed to larger remittances (Burgess and Haksar, 2005). The third factor is a purely statistical one: both receiving and sending countries have significantly improved their tracking and recording of remittances in recent years, and there has also been a shift from informal to formal channels of transferring in response to lower transaction costs and technological advances. The share of unrecorded remittances is also likely to have shrunk as a result of stricter controls since September 2001. In addition, a number of developing countries have changed their foreign exchange control policies, which has

Figure 3.8

MIGRANTS' REMITTANCES AND FINANCIAL FLOWS TO DEVELOPING COUNTRIES, 1990–2004

(Billions of dollars)

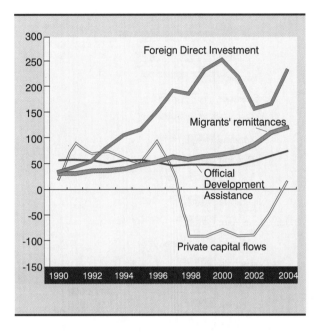

Source: UNCTAD secretariat calculations, based on *UNCTAD Handbook of Statistics,* online; IMF, *Balance of Payments Statistics*, CD-ROM, June 2006, and *World Economic Outlook* Database, April 2006; OECD, *OLISnet* Database.

Note: Migrants' remittances are workers' remittances, compensation of employees and migrants' capital transfers; data for 2004 are estimates. Private capital flows are net private portfolio flows and other private capital flows.

reduced the black market premium for foreign exchange. Therefore, while the actual value of remittances may still be considerably underestimated, the actual year-on-year increase over the past few years is likely to be smaller than what the official records suggest.

Although migrants' remittances vary considerably across countries, they are spread more evenly among developing countries than FDI flows. Nevertheless, the inflow of remittances has grown much faster in Latin American and Caribbean countries and in Asian developing countries than in Africa. Between 1990 and 2004 these flows multiplied by a factor of 12.4 in East Asia and the

Figure 3.9

MAJOR REMITTANCE-RECEIVING DEVELOPING COUNTRIES, 1995, 2000 AND 2004

(Per cent of GDP)

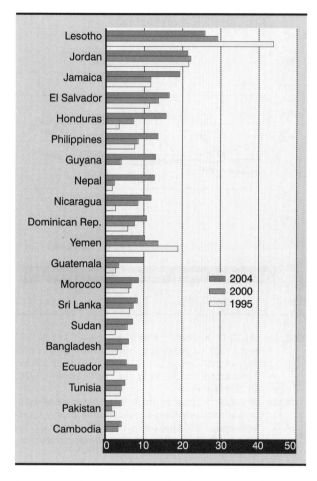

Source: UNCTAD secretariat calculations, based on United Nations Statistics Division, *National Accounts Main Aggregates* Database; and IMF, *Balance of Payments Statistics*, CD-ROM, June 2006.

Note: Tonga, Lebanon and Haiti also appear to receive large inflows of remittances, as a proportion of GDP (World Bank, 2005: 90). However, these are not included in the figure due to inconsistencies in available data.

plains, for example the high level of remittance inflows, in absolute terms, for Mexico, and, in relation to GDP, for Lesotho, Jordan or Yemen. In absolute terms, the largest remittance-receiving countries are the two developing countries with the largest population, China and India. However, in terms of their share of GDP, remittances are of particular importance for smaller countries (fig. 3.9). In 2004, they accounted for more that 15 per cent of GDP in 5 developing countries and for 10 per cent or more in 10 countries. In exceptional cases (Jordan and Lesotho) remittances represent over one fifth of GDP. For some small countries, remittances have exceeded FDI inflows by a wide margin. But the same is also true for India, where they reached $20.5 billion in 2005 – almost twice the total inflow of portfolio investment and FDI combined, which was $11.9 billion (EIU, 2005b).

2. The economic impact of migrants' remittances

Remittances have many facets and can have various effects at the microeconomic and macroeconomic level. There is broad agreement that they have a direct positive impact on poverty alleviation, since they frequently flow directly to poor recipients and allow them to meet basic needs, such as food and clothing, and to purchase other consumer goods. The effects of migrants' remittances on economic growth and development are less clear. They depend on a variety of factors, including the pattern of utilization of remittances by recipient households, the size of remittance streams over time and the motivation for remittances, as well as the efficiency of domestic financial intermediation and national monetary conditions. The contribution to growth and development of the receiving economy would be greater the larger the proportion of remittance inflows that can be channelled into investment in physical and human capital, either directly by the receiving individuals or indirectly through financial intermediation in the recipient country.

Pacific, by 7 in Latin America and the Caribbean and by 5.6 in South Asia, but only by 4 in sub-Saharan Africa, where recorded remittances are far less significant (World Bank, 2006b).

Geographical or cultural proximity to countries with much higher per capita income is one of several factors influencing migration from, and hence remittances to, developing countries. It ex-

Evidence on the actual utilization of remittances at the micro level is anecdotal, but it is estimated that 80 to 85 per cent of remittances are used to cover basic everyday needs of the recipient households (de Vasconcelos, 2005: 5). Remittances are an important social insurance against shocks for low-income households, and they help to smooth consumption. Where many of these households face difficulties in borrowing for the acquisition of land or residential construction, remittances can play an important role in easing private credit constraints and, to some extent, substitute for shortcomings in the domestic financial system (Giuliano and Ruiz-Arranz, 2005).

Although remittances generally add to household income and consumption, sometimes they are also used for investment in capacity- or productivity-enhancing investment in agriculture or to start or expand small-scale entrepreneurial activities in manufacturing or services. Some studies indicate that remittances have facilitated the capitalization of migrant-owned businesses (Buch, Kuckulenz and Le Manche, 2002). Their contribution to capital formation is likely to increase with the level of per capita income of the recipient country: once basic consumption needs are satisfied, a growing share of remittances is used for investment in physical and human capital. There are also examples of joint efforts by groups of migrants to provide grants for investment in local infrastructure projects, such as schools, in their countries of origin.

It is well known that while emigration can alleviate the unemployment burden and generate remittance income, it costs the country in terms of a loss of skilled workers and talent, rendering it more difficult to develop local manufacturing activities. On the other hand, over and above remittances, emigrants can also benefit their home countries when they return with additional professional skills and, sometimes, entrepreneurial spirit.

Parallel to the microeconomic impact on income and welfare of the receiving households, remittances can have significant macroeconomic effects in the recipient economies. As remittances are a major source of foreign exchange, they can help alleviate the balance-of-payments constraints of developing countries, so that a trade deficit does not result in higher indebtedness. By providing additional foreign exchange for the acquisition of imported inputs for domestic production they constitute a source of financing for development. However, this effect depends on how the receiving households use their remittance income. To the extent that the latter is spent directly on imported consumer goods, the positive balance-of-payments effect will be offset.

It has been argued that the potential positive effects of migrants' remittances can be reduced by their impact on the exchange rate (Amuedo-Dorantes and Pozo, 2004). However, to have such an effect, the share of remittances in the recipient country's foreign exchange transactions would have to be particularly large; moreover, the size of remittances would have to increase dramatically within a short period of time, and not be matched by a similar increase in imports.[48] These conditions are likely to occur only in exceptional cases. In general, as noted earlier, migrants' remittances are the most stable form of financial flows to developing countries, often changing against the cycle and frequently accompanied by changes in imports. There is even some evidence that in countries that receive both large private capital flows and large remittances, the latter can help reduce the probability of current-account reversals and financial crises (Bugamelli and Paterno, 2005).

An indirect effect of a stable and large inflow of migrants' remittances for the recipient countries appears to be better access to international capital markets. Expectations of higher future remittance inflows tend to lead to improved creditworthiness and higher bond ratings of the country. On the one hand, this opens or strengthens the possibility to "leverage" the impact of remittance inflows on development by additional external borrowing for the financing of imports that are essential for diversification, creation of additional productive capacity and technological progress. On the other hand, this effect may also lead to external borrowing for non-productive purposes, thereby contributing to the build-up of debt that will have to be serviced from future national income.

> Remittances have a direct positive impact on poverty alleviation, but their effects on economic growth and development are less clear.

3. National and international policies to enhance remittances' impact

Current world demographic trends and the widening gap in standards of living between most developing and developed countries point to an intensification of labour migration from developing to developed countries for a number of years to come. From a longer-term perspective on development, remittances should be considered a temporary source of additional foreign exchange which can help solve the problems that have been causing emigration in the first place. That is, they can push domestic growth and development and generate increasingly productive domestic employment.

Developing countries, especially those for which migrants' remittances constitute a major source of foreign exchange income, should therefore aim at integrating migration and migrants' remittances into a broader development strategy. Such a strategy could include the provision of incentives for migrants, or for the recipients of their remittances, to channel these transfers to the largest extent possible into productive uses.[49] From this perspective, such remittances could have a similar effect as "diaspora" investment, which can play an important role in the development process. This is because the diasporas are often better informed about local conditions than other potential foreign investors.

The potential of migrants' remittances has been increasingly recognized in the international debate on development policies. In order to increase remittances per migrant, the importance of reducing the cost of remittance transfers and making transfer channels more efficient, for example through a common electronic platform to facilitate remittance transfers, has been stressed. Furthermore, the impact of remittances could be enhanced by efforts to strengthen the domestic financial system in developing countries (Kapur, 2004).

Another approach to addressing development concerns in relation to emigration would be the provision of incentives in home countries to encourage the return of talented migrants after several years of work abroad. They may bring home valuable skills acquired in destination countries, thus turning the "brain drain" into "brain gain". With internationally managed cross-border labour mobility as an element of the global partnership for development, several objectives could be pursued in parallel: an increase in remittance flows to developing countries, meeting labour demand in some segments of the international labour market, and ensuring "productive repatriation" of migrants are some possibilities.

There have been proposals to "multilateralize" immigration rules as a global public good (Rodrik, 2001). Coordination between source and destination countries, on the basis of bilateral agreements and temporary foreign labour schemes could be part of managed migration policies. For instance, Rodrik (2004) has suggested the creation of a temporary labour mobility scheme as an instrument to spark development and growth in the home country. Under such a scheme, migrants would leave their home countries for a period of 2 to 5 years, while both the home and host country would provide incentives for their return and for a new round of migrants to replace them. It is expected that those who return would bring back some financial capital, as well as various skills and professional competencies that could be employed in support of economic and social development in their home country. Obviously, such a scheme can only function if it is supported by a number of other institutional features at the international level, as well as at the national level in both the home and host country. One step in the direction of greater international labour mobility is the so-called Mode 4 proposal for supplying services that is under consideration in the current round of GATS negotiations at the WTO. This recognizes that a regulated temporary movement of skilled persons could create welfare benefits for both the home and host countries by turning the brain drain into managed brain circulation to benefit development. It could also enhance predictability and transparency (UNCTAD, 2004b).

> Coordination between source and destination countries, bilateral agreements and temporary foreign labour schemes could be part of managed migration policies.

E. A strengthened role for FDI?

1. FDI in developing countries: trends and patterns

FDI flows to developing countries including "greenfield" as well as portfolio investment rose consistently from the mid-1980s until the late 1990s. While maintaining their level, they have become less stable since the turn of the millennium. Since the early 1990s, FDI has been the largest component of financial flows to developing countries (UNCTAD, 2005c: 7), accounting for over half of all financial resource flows to them as a group in 2003. All developing regions have seen an increase in their FDI inflows over the past two and a half decades (fig. 3.10). However, flows to different regions have been rising at different rates, resulting in changes in the relative positions of different host regions in terms of their shares of FDI stock (fig. 3.11).

Before the 1980s Latin America and the Caribbean received by far the largest share of FDI flows to developing countries. This changed when output growth in that region declined dramatically and macroeconomic instability increased in the context of the debt crisis of the 1980s, while a number of East Asian economies continued to grow fast and to integrate successfully into the world economy. As the differences in the macroeconomic conditions and domestic investment widened between Asia and Latin America, Asia became the most important developing host region for FDI at the beginning of the 1980s. Since then, its relative importance has increased further, as favourable conditions for both domestic and foreign investment in several East and South-East Asian countries have attracted additional FDI. China has accounted for a rapidly increasing share of the total since the 1990s, and has emerged at the beginning of this century as the largest FDI recipient among all developing countries.

Although Latin America saw much smaller FDI inflows than Asia, its share in developing-country FDI stock remained stable during the period 1980–2004. FDI inflows to the region rose during the 1990s, in large part in response to large privatization programmes, but declined after 1999 as the potential for privatization shrank and the macroeconomic conditions remained unfavourable. Since 2004, there has been a resurgence of inflows to some countries, driven mainly by prospects for greater earnings potential in the primary sector, especially in the extractive industries.

By contrast, Africa's share in developing-country FDI stock declined steadily from the early 1980s, although inflows increased significantly in the 1980s and 1990s. Since 2001, there has also been a considerable rise in FDI flows to some, mainly oil- and metal-exporting, countries as a result of improved prospects in international raw material

> The role that FDI inflows can play in national development strategies differs considerably from one country to another.

Figure 3.10

FDI INFLOWS TO DEVELOPING ECONOMIES BY REGION, 1980–2004

(Billions of dollars)

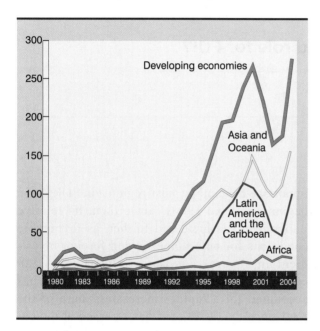

Source: UNCTAD, *FDI/TNC* Database (www.unctad.org/
fdistatistics).

markets. Overall, not only FDI, but also domestic investment has been lower in Africa for the past 25 years; the latter fell from more than 25 per cent of GDP in the mid-1970s to around 18 per cent in 2000–2004 (UNCTAD, 2005d, section B).

Cross-border mergers and acquisitions (M&As) in developing countries, although much fewer than in developed countries, have increased significantly since the mid-1990s. Privatization in industries such as electricity and telecommunications in Latin America and the Caribbean – especially Argentina and Brazil – accounted for a major proportion of the sales of local firms until 2000 (UNCTAD, 2000: 123). Acquisitions by foreign firms of enterprises in Asian countries affected by the financial crisis of 1997–1998, such as Indonesia and the Republic of Korea, also contributed to the growth of M&As in developing countries. More recently, there has been a significant increase in cross-border M&As in China and India (UNCTAD, 2005c: 9), suggesting that this mode of FDI entry to developing countries – with its

underlying motivations of rapid entry and acquisition of created or strategic assets in the form of enterprises – may be extending its scope beyond privatizations (as in Latin America and Africa) or special circumstances (as during the East Asian financial crisis).

Although the bulk of FDI flows are among developed countries, the share of developing countries in world FDI stock is growing. In 2004 they accounted for 25 per cent of that stock and for 39 per cent of the inflows (tables 3.9 and 3.10). Outward FDI from developing countries has risen sharply over the past two and a half decades, from annual outflows of less than $20 billion in the 1980s to over $40 billion in the mid-1990s and to a peak of $100 billion in 2000 (UNCTAD, 2005c: 6). TNCs from China, Malaysia and South Africa, for instance, are among the most important foreign investors in Africa (UNCTAD, 2005d, section B; UNCTAD, 2005e), and in developing Asia and Oceania more than 40 per cent of FDI flows are intraregional, with Hong Kong (China), China and Singapore as the leading investors. According to a study by Aykut and Ratha (2003), South-South FDI is estimated to have risen from 5 per cent of all FDI flows to the South in 1994 to 30 per cent in 2000.[50]

While the attitude of TNCs towards investment in developing countries is an important factor in the external environment for development, the role that FDI inflows can play in national development strategies differs considerably from one country to another. Changes in aggregate figures on FDI flows and stocks in developing countries or regions give an imprecise picture of their role in individual countries. It is well-known that FDI stocks and inflows are highly concentrated in a relatively small number of developing countries: in 2004, the top 10 recipients had almost two thirds of developing-country FDI stocks, and China and Hong Kong (China) accounted for almost one third (table 3.10). In the same year, 8 of the 10 major hosts of FDI stocks were also among the 10 major recipients of new flows, which accounted for about 70 per cent of all FDI flows to developing countries that year (with China and Hong Kong (China) alone receiving over 34 per cent). Thus there is a continuing trend towards the concentration of FDI and related TNC activities in a minority of developing countries.

Figure 3.11

SHARES IN INWARD FDI STOCK OF DEVELOPING ECONOMIES
BY REGION, 1980, 1990, 2000 AND 2004

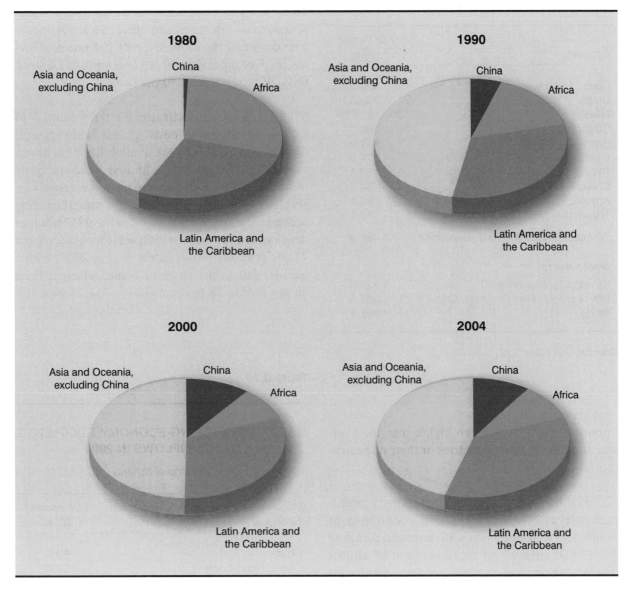

Source: See figure 3.10.

However, the absolute amount of FDI inflows does not give a clear picture of the importance or the potential impact of FDI in an individual country. A better picture is obtained by indicators relating the volume of FDI to some national variable, such as gross fixed capital formation (GFCF) or the size of GDP (table 3.11).[51] From this perspective, FDI plays a less important role in Asia, and in particular in South Asia, than in Africa and Latin America. A comparison of FDI inflows with

GFCF and FDI stocks with GDP also puts into perspective the distribution across countries: in 2004, only three economies (Chile, Hong Kong (China) and Singapore) that were among the ten major recipients of FDI inflows and among the ten major hosts of FDI stock had a ratio of FDI inflows to GFCF of more than 20 per cent and a ratio of FDI stock to GDP of more than 40 per cent. By contrast, in many smaller economies in Africa and Latin America and the Caribbean the

Table 3.9

MAJOR DEVELOPING HOST ECONOMIES OF FDI IN 2004

(Billions of dollars)

Economy	FDI inward stock
China, Hong Kong	456.8
China	245.5
Mexico	182.5
Singapore	160.4
Brazil	151.0
Bermuda	77.6
Republic of Korea	55.3
Chile	54.5
Argentina	53.7
Thailand	48.6
10 major developing host economies	*1 485.9*

Memo items:

Developing economies	2 225.9
Developing economies, excl. China	1 980.5
World	8 895.3

Source: See figure 3.10.

ing China, and 9.1 per cent for China. FDI stocks as a percentage of GDP stood at 21.5 per cent in 2004, compared to 29.1 for the developing countries excluding China, where the stock has been accumulated over a much longer period of time, and 14.9 per cent for China. Azerbaijan and Kazakhstan, where oil and other extractive industries dominate the economy, both had ratios of FDI to GFCF of more than 20 per cent and of FDI stock to GDP of more than 40 per cent.

A significant indicator for the potential of FDI to contribute to development is its sectoral distribution. Although the availability of continuous, comprehensive data is limited, there are strong indications that FDI has grown more rapidly in services than in the primary and manufacturing sectors. The share of services in the FDI stock of developing countries is estimated to have risen from 47 per cent in 1990 to 55 per cent in 2002, with a parallel fall in the share of manufacturing, from 46 per cent to 38 per cent (UNCTAD, 2004c: 30).

importance of FDI is much higher than the average of all developing countries or their respective regions.

FDI has come to play an increasingly important role also in the transition economies of South-East Europe and the CIS. Between 2000 and 2004, FDI inflows to these economies almost quadrupled and expectations are for a further increase (UNCTAD, 2005c: 74–78). During the same time the FDI stock almost tripled, after having grown during the 1990s from practically zero to $70 billion, to a large extent in the context of large-scale privatizations. The Russian Federation and Romania had inflows in 2004 on the same scale as the major developing country recipients, at $15.4 and $6.5 billion, respectively, and Azerbaijan and Kazakhstan also received inflows of over $3.5 billion. The quantitative importance of FDI for the transition economies is evident from the ratio of FDI inflows to GFCF, which averaged 15.9 per cent for the group in 2002–2004, compared to 9.9 per cent for the developing countries exclud-

Table 3.10

MAJOR DEVELOPING-ECONOMY RECIPIENTS OF FDI INFLOWS IN 2004

(Billions of dollars)

Economy	FDI inflows 2004
China	60.6
China, Hong Kong	34.0
Mexico	18.7
Brazil	18.1
Singapore	14.8
Bermuda	14.8
United Arab Emirates	8.4
Republic of Korea	7.7
Chile	7.2
India	5.5
10 major developing-economy recipients	*189.8*

Memo items:

Developing economies	275.0
Developing economies, excl. China	214.4
World	703.7

Source: See figure 3.10.

Within the services sector, the traditionally dominant subsectors of finance and trade appear to have declined in relative importance in developing countries' inward FDI, while activities such as electricity, gas and water, construction, transport, storage and communications, have attracted larger shares of FDI, some of them as a result of privatization of public utilities (UNCTAD, 2004c: 99). FDI in business activities, which include holding companies and consultancy firms, accounted for one third of total FDI in services in 2001–2003, with more than two thirds of these flows destined for Hong Kong (China) (UNCTAD, 2004c: 262). Although the shift towards services has taken place in all developing regions, the sectoral and industrial patterns of inward FDI differ considerably among the three major regions.

In Asia, the share of FDI stock in services is estimated to have risen from 43 per cent in 1995 to 50 per cent in 2002, while that in manufacturing fell from 51 per cent to around 44 per cent, and it remained small in the primary sector (UNCTAD, 2004c: 52). In Latin America and the Caribbean, over half of the inward FDI stock in 2002 was in the services sector, following a sharp rise from about 20 per cent in the mid-1980s to about 50 per cent in 1996 (UNCTAD, 2004c: 64–65). The primary and manufacturing sectors each accounted for around 20 per cent of the total FDI stock in Latin America in 2002. The share of the manufacturing sector has shrunk considerably since the late-1980s, while that of the primary sector has more than doubled (UNCTAD, 2004c: 65). Recently, there have been signs of a reversal in this trend, as several TNCs have been selling their foreign affiliates or shareholdings to local investors in line with changes in their global investment strategies and in host countries FDI policies and regulations, but also in response to changes in the privileges accorded to foreign investors. The shift in the sectoral composition of FDI in Latin America and the Caribbean may also be due to the apparent growth of FDI in the primary sector in response to the boom in markets for primary commodities, especially oil and gas. However, it is not clear to what extent these recorded investments constitute a reinvestment of profits for the enlargement or upgrading of productive capacities, or just undistributed profits added to the reserves of the international firms that have been benefiting from the commodity boom since 2002,

Table 3.11

FDI IN RELATION TO GROSS FIXED CAPITAL FORMATION AND GDP IN SELECTED REGIONS AND ECONOMIES IN 1990 AND 2004

	Inflow of FDI as a percentage of GFCF	Inward stock of FDI as a percentage of GDP	
	2002–2004[a]	1990	2004
Developed economies	8.3	8.2	20.5
Developing economies	9.6	9.8	26.4
Developing economies, excl. China	9.9	10.2	29.1
Africa	13.5	12.7	27.8
Angola	57.1	10.0	88.8
Chad	56.2	14.4	72.9
Congo	34.7	20.6	66.7
Gambia	52.5	49.4	85.9
Mauritania	47.4	5.8	64.2
Nigeria	34.0	30.0	44.0
Seychelles	35.8	55.4	114.7
Unit. Rep. of Tanzania	24.3	9.1	48.0
Zambia	18.0	31.1	55.8
Asia	8.0	8.7	23.2
East Asia	9.0	9.7	28.4
China	9.1	5.8	14.9
China, Hong Kong	52.6	60.3	277.6
China, Macao	41.3	86.4	52.1
Malaysia	14.8	23.4	39.3
Rep. of Korea	2.6	2.1	8.1
Singapore	43.3	83.1	150.2
Thailand	3.8	7.0	29.7
South Asia	3.4	1.1	6.3
India	3.2	0.5	5.9
Latin America	14.6	10.5	34.1
Argentina	13.9	6.2	35.3
Belize	45.6	22.1	66.2
Bermuda	-	869.7	1793.5
Brazil	15.4	8.0	25.2
Chile	28.4	33.2	58.2
Guyana	24.3	10.6	120.9
Jamaica	23.9	18.6	66.4
Mexico	11.2	8.5	27.0
Nicaragua	20.4	12.4	49.7
Trinidad and Tobago	45.1	41.3	83.3

Source: See figure 3.10.
a Annual average.

as it seems to have been the case in the Chilean copper sector. In Africa, depending on the country, between 50 and 80 per cent of FDI is in natural resource exploitation; FDI in manufacturing has been lagging behind that in services, with some exceptions (UNCTAD, 2004c: 45; UNCTAD, 2005d). It has been increasing in services – just as it had done earlier in Latin America – particularly in telecommunications, electricity, management and trade, partly as a result of privatization programmes in the case of the first two.

If the sectoral structure of FDI stocks and inflows varies considerably among regions, it varies even more among countries, where the level and type of FDI depends on income levels and consumption patterns, initial or acquired comparative advantages, technological capabilities and infrastructure, as well as policies relating to FDI. Thus, as some countries have grown and strengthened their human resources and technological capabilities, they have been able to attract FDI in more technology-intensive industries and more sophisticated activities and functions within TNCs' integrated international production systems, including R&D in manufacturing and services.

2. The role of international production systems and networks

FDI in manufacturing and services in developing countries in part continues to aim at serving local markets, particularly in the larger economies of Latin America and Asia, but to an increasing extent it is motivated by the low-cost, unskilled or skilled labour and other cost advantages these countries offer. The latter type of FDI is intended to serve global and regional markets, often in the context of international production networks. Beginning in the 1960s with export-oriented investments in the textiles and clothing industry in East Asia, FDI has diversified and expanded into other countries and regions, to more industries and to a wider range of activities or functions located in host countries. Increased competition in a globalizing world economy, combined with advances in transport and, especially, in information technology (IT) and telecommunications,

> To an increasing extent, FDI is intended to serve global and regional markets, often in the context of international production networks.

have increased pressures and provided new incentives for TNCs in the manufacturing sector to fragment and spread their value chains globally or regionally, or to develop a network of closely related suppliers or contract manufacturers, some of whom in turn undertake FDI to enhance their efficiency. Several Asian countries are locations for this efficiency-seeking kind of FDI, especially in the electrical, electronics and automobile industries, in addition to textiles. China has also attracted FDI in a range of low-value-added, export-oriented consumer industries. Latin American and Caribbean countries are hosts to efficiency-seeking FDI in textiles and clothing and, in the case of Costa Rica and Mexico, in electronics and automobiles respectively. Some African countries have attracted FDI in garment manufacturing for export.

More recently, efficiency-seeking FDI has also expanded to the services sector. Service functions that can be digitized, separated from related activities and exported via telecommunication links from cheaper locations are being offshored by TNCs, either as parts of their own internationally integrated value chains or for delivery (as "contract service providers") to other firms. While many services still need to be produced where their customers are located, IT-enabled, back-office and front-office work in areas such as accounting, billing, software development, design, testing and customer care is increasingly being relocated abroad by TNCs, including to some developing countries (UNCTAD, 2004c). The skill intensity of these offshored tradable services is generally higher than that of TNC activities in manufacturing or natural resource exploitation in developing countries.

Since the late 1990s, there has also been a trend towards the internationalization of R&D by TNCs, leading to increasing FDI in this area in some developing countries. However, such investment is still small (accounting for only 3 per cent of total FDI flows of United States parent companies to developing countries) and even more concentrated than total FDI, with five countries (Brazil, China, Mexico, the Republic of Korea and Singapore) accounting for an estimated 70 per cent of the total FDI to developing countries (UNCTAD, 2005c: 129). Nevertheless, the share of developing countries in total overseas R&D expenditure by United States parent companies rose from about 8 per cent to more than 13 per cent between 1994 and 2002 (UNCTAD, 2005c: 129). Moreover, there are indications that such R&D activities are no longer only confined to adapting technologies to local conditions; increasingly they also involve "innovative" R&D, including developing technologies for regional and world markets (UNCTAD, 2005c: 138). But to what extent such R&D investment in developing countries spills over into the domestic economy in terms of both local application of innovative technology and strengthening of local R&D capacities (see also chapter V, section D below) is still unclear. And the policy instruments developing countries are able to use in order to enable such spillovers differ from country to country, not least because of different negotiating power vis-à-vis foreign investors.

> The potential impact of FDI on development depends on the strategy of the TNCs involved and on the national policies and characteristics of the host economy.

3. The potential impact of FDI on development

The growth of FDI in many developing countries relative to other variables, such as domestic capital formation or GDP, suggests that inward FDI has come to play a more significant role in developing economies than it did some two decades ago. If integrated into a strategic concept for productive capacity building and upgrading, FDI inflows can have a direct impact on domestic income creation, including fiscal income, and an indirect impact by positively influencing domestic investment.

In some countries, especially in Africa and Latin America and the Caribbean, where the indicators presented in table 3.11 hint at a quantitatively important role played by FDI in their economies, such investment is still heavily concentrated

in extraction and exploitation of natural resources with weak potential linkages to the domestic economy. In other countries, it has expanded to a range of manufacturing and service industries, where the potential for linkages with and spillovers to domestic industries is larger. But to what extent this larger quantitative presence of FDI amounts to a strengthened role in the development process of the countries that host more production activity by foreign firms depends on the balance between TNCs' private business interests and national development objectives.

FDI may be viewed as a package of tangible and intangible resources and assets, many of them firm-specific, that can contribute to economic development in host countries. Key elements of the package include capital, technology, skills and management techniques. FDI can also be a vehicle for host economies to access international markets by integrating into the international production, marketing and distribution networks of TNCs. What matters most from a dynamic perspective is the extent to which such investment brings modern technologies and know-how that might not otherwise be available to developing countries, and the extent to which it raises the efficiency with which existing technologies are used, improving productivity and strengthening technological capabilities in the host countries. The role of FDI and its impact on host-country development in these respects are likely to depend on two factors. One is the motivation and strategy of the TNCs involved and the specific assets they bring to a host country; another is the national policies and characteristics of the host economy.

The effects of FDI on domestic investment and growth in individual countries depend to a large extent on the mode of entry (UNCTAD, 2000). For example, FDI in new plant equipment ("greenfield investment") adds to the existing capital stock, and it is more likely than portfolio investment to involve a longer-term commitment by the foreign investor to produce in the host country. In contrast, portfolio investment allows easier exit or repatriation of capital. FDI in the form of M&As may involve transfer of know-how and technology and improved market access in the future, but it does not add to the host country's stock of productive capital.

On the other hand, host-country regulations, including contractual obligations with regard to technology transfer, special incentives for entry in targeted economic sectors, and performance requirements related to purchases of intermediate inputs from local suppliers, can influence the creation of linkages between domestic producers and foreign affiliates and the extent to which FDI contributes to technology transfer. Moreover, the existence of a physical, scientific and institutional infrastructure, and of a dense network of potential domestic input suppliers, as well as support policies designed to create such a network, can be an important means to attract or retain TNCs. Such support policies are important not only because they influence the quantity and kind of FDI that a country attracts, but also because of the possible indirect effects that can be had from linkages with, and spillovers to, host-country firms and institutions.

Belief in the positive impacts of FDI on economic growth, technology transfer and productivity has led many countries to adopt investment regimes that offer special fiscal or other financial incentives to foreign enterprises. However, macroeconomic studies on the relationship between FDI and growth have yielded diverging results, and empirical evidence points to considerable variation in the benefits that host countries actually reap from FDI inflows (UNCTAD, 1999, Part Two; Moran et al., 2005). According to Kumar (2005: 179–186), a multitude of recent empirical studies show that knowledge spillovers from FDI have been rare, and in some cases FDI may have the negative effect of crowding out domestic investment. While the crowding out of the least efficient firms from an industry may not matter if incoming FDI

> Host-country regulations can influence the creation of linkages between domestic producers and foreign affiliates and the extent of technology transfer.

> The development of local industry can be jeopardized if FDI crowds out domestic investment.

raises average productivity and domestic value added across foreign-owned and domestic firms, crowding out of most of the competitors (and suppliers linked to them) as a result of the overwhelming market power of the incoming TNC may severely compromise the opportunities for favourable effects and externalities. Moreover, there is a tendency for TNC affiliates to acquire the bulk of their inputs from their parent companies or other already associated suppliers, and hence generate few domestic linkages. One study suggests that the effectiveness of FDI depends on the stock of human capital in the host country (Borensztein, De Gregorio and Lee, 1998). Significant positive effects of FDI on growth have been found in samples of countries with higher skill levels (Xu, 2000).

Other studies have concluded that FDI does not exert an independent and robust influence on growth once other factors such as trade openness are accounted for (Moran et al., 2005). A major problem for empirical research on the contribution of FDI to growth, and thus a reason for the mixed results, may be the difficulty of capturing, in multi-country macroeconomic studies, the different factors that influence the impact of FDI, such as the type of FDI, firm characteristics, as well as host countries' economic conditions and policies. While the evidence for the impact of FDI on income growth is mixed, there are strong indications that high and stable income growth based on high rates of domestic investment attracts FDI. As a result, FDI that supports manufacturing activities tends to by-pass countries that are most in need of external capital and know-how for diversification and industrialization, while benefiting economies where domestic forces for growth are already vigorous.

A varied picture also emerges from studies based on firm-level data (Lipsey and Sjoholm, 2005; Blalock and Gertler, 2005). A number of analyses have concluded that productivity and wages in foreign firms are higher than in domestic firms, and that these have positive spillover effects on domestic firms. Spillovers are found to be highest in sectors where there is vigorous competition, and to be greater when the technological gap between foreign and domestic firms is not too wide. On the other hand, some studies have found that productivity growth in domestic firms is lower than it would have been without the presence of foreign firms, suggesting the absence of positive spillovers. More generally, it is clear that FDI alone cannot provide opportunities for sustained growth unless there is a minimum level of domestic industrial capabilities and the technological capacity necessary to benefit from eventual externalities of TNC activity (Narula and Lall, 2004). The growth of South-South FDI, with its distinctive characteristics that may be closer to those of enterprises in host developing countries, may provide increased opportunities for host countries to benefit from inward FDI. However, much depends on host-country policies.

The varied experiences of host developing countries with respect to the role played by FDI and its impact on the development process, and the importance of host-country absorptive capacities for benefiting from FDI, highlight the need for FDI policies to be in line with the identified development objectives of a country. Such policies should also aim at maximizing the potential benefits of FDI while minimizing the negative effects, such as those that could result from crowding out of domestic firms and the abuse of market power. Government intervention may be motivated by two main types of market failure: (i) information or coordination failures in the investment process; and (ii) the divergence of the private interests of investors from the economic and social objectives of the host economies. To optimize the impact of inward FDI, governments need to address the following four sets of issues (UNCTAD, 1999: 317–328):

- Information and coordination failures in the international investment process. Addressing such failures can enable governments to pursue effective policies to attract the volume and type of FDI that can best serve domestic objectives of sectoral development, on the one hand, and protect themselves against FDI that is not desirable from the point of view

of their overall development strategy, on the other. Effective promotion should go beyond simply "marketing a country"; it should also coordinate the supply of immobile assets with specific development needs to attain national development targets.

- Infant industry considerations for the development of local enterprises, which can be jeopardized if inward FDI crowds out those enterprises. Addressing these requires striking the right balance between policies that regulate and those that permit or attract FDI entry. A few economies (such as the Republic of Korea and Taiwan Province of China) have built impressive domestic capabilities and innovative systems while restricting the access of TNCs, but many others have not succeeded in these respects, despite restricting foreign entry.

- The static nature of advantages transferred by TNCs in situations where host-country domestic capabilities are low and do not improve over time, or where TNCs fail to invest sufficiently in improving the relevant capabilities. Addressing these requires adopting an appropriate trade and competition policy regime; developing appropriate policies with regard to the operations of foreign affiliates, such as local content requirements, incentives for local training or R&D, and pressures to diffuse technologies; influencing TNCs' location decisions by targeting investors; inducing upgrading through specific measures and incentives; and improving local factor markets, firms and institutions.

- Weak bargaining and regulatory capabilities on the part of host-country governments, which can result in an unequal distribution of benefits or an abuse of market power by TNCs. This is of particular relevance for major resource extraction projects and for the privatization of large public utilities and industrial companies. Addressing these issues requires strengthening host-country bargaining and regulatory capabilities to ensure that appropriate standards are set in areas such as competition and environmental protection, and that a race to the bottom in the provision of fiscal incentives is avoided.

To conclude, developing countries have responded to the challenges of rapid technological change, globalization and increased competition by opening up their economies to trade and foreign investment. However, differences persist in the ability of countries to draw on the potential technological and other contributions that FDI can make to the process of development. This underlines the need for effective policy interventions with a view to maximizing the benefits of FDI for host-country development in an open environment.

F. Conclusions

The review of some structural elements that have shaped the global environment for development in the first decade of the new millennium gives a mixed picture. In several respects there have been improvements in the external environment, but not all initial promises or expectations have been fulfilled, and in some areas new constraints have emerged.

External conditions for export growth in developing countries are shaped mainly by import demand from the developed countries, resulting from income growth and shifts in the structure of domestic production. But the extent to which such income growth translates into higher exports of developing countries also depends on market access conditions in developed countries, as well as the evolution of market entry conditions and the use of non-tariff measures.

While better market access conditions in developed countries can provide lasting improvements in developing countries' export opportunities, there have been very few improvements in such conditions for developing countries since the conclusion of the Uruguay Round. Indeed, market access conditions in developed countries continue to be biased against developing countries. Moreover, the link between changes in these conditions and the actual export opportunities of developing countries appears to be relatively weak compared to their dependence on demand growth in their main trading partners. The potential gains from growing import demand for developing countries' exports are likely to be much larger, but this demand also has a strong cyclical component, and depends on improved global macroeconomic management, especially with regard to correcting the global imbalances that have built up in recent years (see chapter I).

Although preferences were expected to improve export earnings and promote diversification in the preference-receiving developing countries, especially the poorest ones, these countries have not been able to reap large benefits from them. The main reasons for the underutilization of preferences and their limited benefits are the uncertainty of the schemes, restrictive rules of origin, the often limited product coverage, and supply capacity constraints. Similarly, the export gains that can be expected to result from the Doha Round appear to be relatively modest when compared to other sources of foreign exchange, such as expected ODA inflows or migrants' remittances. The decline in tariffs has in recent years been accompanied by an increase in the use of non-tariff measures, particularly in the form of technical barriers to trade and anti-dumping measures. The latter have emerged as the most widespread impediment to international trade in the past 25 years, and there is the danger that increasing recourse to such measures will erode the predictability and non-discriminatory application of trade policies that have been achieved through successive rounds of multilateral trade negotiations.

The progress achieved under the HIPC Initiative and additional bilateral debt relief, as well as faster GDP growth and higher budget revenues have alleviated developing countries' external debt burden in recent years. However, despite an overall improvement, many low- and middle-income countries remain severely indebted. Indeed, 10 years after the launch of the HIPC Initiative, only 29 of the 42 eligible countries have reached the decision point, at which countries qualify for interim debt relief, and only 19 countries have reached the completion point, which qualifies them for the full amount of debt relief possible under the Initiative. In the spirit of a global partnership for development, it is therefore imperative to mobilize additional efforts at the national and international level to enable more expeditious implementation of the HIPC Initiative and the Multilateral Debt Relief Initiative, so that all eligible countries can benefit from the debt reductions.

Commitments for multilateral debt relief and considerably increased bilateral ODA could improve the prospects for the poorer developing countries to achieve the MDGs and reduce the income gap with the more advanced economies. In order for these countries to avoid falling back into unsustainable debt situations, it will also be essential to ensure that the pledged rise in ODA is additional to debt relief, and that increased official financing is made available, in particular for social and humanitarian purposes, in the form of grants. Bolder debt reductions for middle-income countries could also be envisaged under the Paris Club's Evian terms.

Large-scale outward migration is one of the symptoms of slow progress in development and low expectations of employment and higher living standards at home. Nevertheless, for many developing countries, remittances of migrants working abroad have become an important source of foreign exchange. They are private income and a means to improve the living conditions of many poor households in the receiving countries. While the ultimate policy objective must be to remedy the root causes of the migration through output and productivity growth and job creation in the home countries, remittances are to some extent a potential contribution to the external financing needs of the migrants' home countries. A challenge for policymakers is to use this potential within the framework of a broader development strategy and channel the remittances, as far as possible, to productive uses. Developed countries can support efforts to maximize the developmental impact of migrants' remittances by reducing the cost of remittance transfers and making the transfer channels more efficient. Home and host countries could also cooperate to create incentives for talented migrants to return home after several years of work abroad so as to strengthen the local human resource base, by using the experience and skills acquired abroad. Indeed, managing international labour mobility, especially between the developed and the more advanced developing countries, on the one hand, and the poorer countries or economies with large amounts of excess labour, on the other, could constitute a key element of the global partnership for development.

In contrast to migrants' remittances, FDI flows are the outcome of a global assessment of profit opportunities. If well managed, FDI, especially in the manufacturing sector, can help the recipient developing economies to seize opportunities presented by globalization. From the point of view of developing countries with a small domestic market or excess labour, FDI offers one possibility to participate in international production networks. Accordingly, in recognition of this potential, many countries have liberalized the entry of TNC affiliates and stepped up efforts to attract FDI by offering fiscal, financial and material incentives. But more FDI does not automatically result in higher domestic income, enhanced productive capacity or faster growth. Its impact depends in

> In several respects there have been improvements in the external environment, but not all initial promises or expectations have been fulfilled, and in some areas new constraints have emerged.

large part on the extent to which the investment actually adds to existing productive capacity and increases productivity, and on the sectors in which the investment is made. It also depends on whether the profit motives underlying TNC investment decisions can be brought in line with the broader national economic and development objectives of the host countries. This requires appropriate macroeconomic and sectoral policies to create an environment that is conducive to private investment in general and to entrepreneurial risk-taking in sectors strategically important for domestic structural change and beneficial integration into international trade relations. Increasing FDI should not be regarded as an objective in its own right or as a yardstick for successful integration into the globalizing world economy. Rather, it is an instrument that can help achieve successful integration, and success should be measured against the benefits actually accruing in terms of higher per capita income.

There is considerable scope for further improvements in the external environment, especially in the areas of trade and aid, and strengthened global economic governance that takes into account the needs and specificities of different developing countries. The various factors that have shaped the changing external environment for development since the mid-1980s, some of which are examined in this chapter, can contribute to faster growth and poverty alleviation by providing new opportunities for trade and sectoral development, or by alleviating financial constraints. Even though there have been improvements in the external environment as a result of a strengthened global partnership for development or other factors, such as the rise in primary commodity prices discussed in chapter I, the challenge for developing countries is to translate these positive developments into faster growth of domestic output, employment and income. As discussed in chapter II, meeting this challenge will require more than a reliance on market forces complemented by a stronger focus on social policies. There is a greater likelihood of obtaining long-term benefits for growth and poverty alleviation from existing and possible future improvements in the external environment by the adoption of a development strategy that incorporates good macroeconomic and sectoral policies in support of investment, productivity growth and technological change. ∎

Notes

1 Integration into global production networks, whose importance in international trade flows has increased considerably in the last few years, is another factor that improves developing countries' export opportunities (not discussed here, however, as it was already discussed in detail in *TDR 2002*).

2 The discussion in this section is limited to commercial policies relating to merchandise trade.

3 The UR also agreed on increasing transparency by converting NTMs into tariffs, but as the rules of tariffication allowed significant increases in tariffs, these remained high even after implementation of the agreed tariff reductions.

4 The table provides simple and weighted averages of effectively applied tariffs that take into account unilateral and/or reciprocal preferences. Although weighted averages take better account of the relative importance of various tariff lines, they may have a downward bias because there will be lower imports of products that are subject to higher tariffs (a prohibitive tariff would give a zero weight).

5 However, both the EU and the United States have introduced quota restrictions on exports from China under safeguard agreements (Brenton and Hoppe, 2005).

6 Canada, the EU, Japan and the United States.

7 International tariff peaks are tariffs that exceed 15 per cent.

8 Under tariff escalation, tariffs increase with the degree of processing.

9 The period 1986–1988 was the reference period used in the Uruguay Round agreements.

10 According to Anderson, Martin and Valenzuela (2006), if all forms of support to farmers and to agricultural processors globally are taken into account, 75 per cent of total support is provided by market access barriers and only 19 per cent by domestic farm subsidies.

11 Outright export subsidies amount to less than $5 billion, versus $80 billion of "amber box" subsidies worldwide, in applied terms.

12 The Hong Kong Ministerial Declaration of December 2005 agreed "to ensure the parallel elimination of all forms of export subsidies and disciplines on all export measures with equivalent effect to be completed by the end of 2013" (WTO, 2005a). Meanwhile, the EU had already planned to phase out most export subsidies, which account for almost 90 per cent of all OECD export subsidies (Aksoy, 2005).

13 More than one third of all global trade takes place between countries that have some form of reciprocal RTA – a share more than three times that of 1990 – with the EU and the United States playing a prominent role (World Bank, 2004).

14 See AGOA Fact Sheet, accessed at: http://www.agoa.gov/ on 11 April 2006.

15 At the 2003 Cancun Ministerial Conference, WTO member States failed to reach an agreement on the so-called "Singapore issues", which included investment, competition, government procurement and trade facilitation.

16 Welfare is measured as the equivalent variation, which is the increase in income that would have the same impact on the welfare of households as the removal of the tariff. For a detailed, non-technical explanation on how these models work, see Piermartini and Teh, 2005.

17 As Stiglitz and Charlton (2005: 69) recognize "much of the analysis… relies on a particular model of the economy, the neo-classical model, which assumes full employment of resources, perfect competition, perfect information, and well-functioning markets, assumptions which are of questionable validity for any country, but which are particularly problematic for developing countries."

18 Recent reviews of these kinds of studies can be found in Charlton and Stiglitz, 2005; UN-DESA, 2005; and FAO, 2005.

19 The study provides simulations that use an updated version of the *Global Trade Analysis Project* (GTAP) database, which refers to 2001 rather than 1997. They include China's recent trade liberalization (particularly in the context of its WTO acces-

sion), the termination of the ATC Agreement, and the recent enlargement of the EU. Most importantly, a more comprehensive picture of trade protection is provided, as it incorporates preferential arrangements, both reciprocal and non-reciprocal. It also contains effective tariff rates, MFN tariff rates and bound rates, which allows measurement of the relative importance of the "binding overhang" between bound and applied tariff rates. For other recent studies, see Francois, van Meijl and van Tongeren, 2005; Bouet et al., 2005; and Polaski, 2006.

20 For a detailed, critical assessment of the new World Bank estimates, see Ackerman, 2005; Wise and Gallagher, 2005; and Suppan, 2005.

21 Van der Mensbrugghe (2005) analyses the changes in the results of the estimations by comparing the results using the GTAP5 database with those using the new GTAP6 database, first under MFN tariff rates, then including preferences, and finally, incorporating other policy commitments, such as China's WTO accession.

22 The results of the simulations are provided for a set of scenarios, starting with full liberalization. The likely Doha Round liberalization scenario corresponds to a harmonizing formula for agricultural market access, with smaller tariff cuts for developing countries and none for LDCs, plus a 50 per cent cut in all tariffs on non-agricultural products for developed countries, 33 per cent for developing countries, and none for LDCs (Anderson, Martin and van der Mensbrugghe, 2005: 360).

23 The estimates by Anderson, Martin and van der Mensbrugghe (2005) also show that by 2015 under the Doha liberalization scenario annual developing country imports from developed countries will be $55 billion higher. In the past, trade liberalization has caused trade deficits associated with any given rate of income growth to become larger, adding to payments difficulties, increasing dependency on capital inflows, and heightening the risk for financial crises (*TDR 1999*).

24 Moreover, these additional exports would occur after the reduction in tariffs, with attendant adverse effects on developing countries' fiscal revenues. Developing countries' tariff revenues amounted to $156 billion in 2001 (Laird, 2006). According to the IMF (2005a), trade tax revenues represent one quarter to one third of the total tax revenue of low- and middle-income countries.

25 As defined in the UNCTAD *Trade Analysis and Information System (TRAINS)* database, which is the most comprehensive database on technical measures, such measures refer to product characteristics such as quality, safety or dimensions, including the applicable administrative provisions, terminology, symbols, testing and test methods, packaging, mark-

ing and labelling requirements as they apply to a product. They may also refer to different aspects of production processes.

26   They are also intended to facilitate trade in the context of globalization, as they improve compatibility among products and enable a degree of homogenization and harmonization. According to the *WTO World Trade Report 2005*, the use of standards and technical regulations can help markets operate effectively by addressing market failures in three major ways: first, they enhance compatibility between complementary goods in consumption and production in the presence of network externalities, where the value of the product depends on the availability and variety of complementary goods and/or the number of people using the same product; second, they solve the problem of asymmetric information about quality (e.g. safety standards); and third, they reduce negative environmental externalities. While in the first case they help increase trade, in the other two cases they may reduce trade. Technical measures are more frequently applied in developed countries since they are used more intensively as incomes rise. Consumers in developed countries tend to demand higher quality products. In the food sector, this trend has been accelerated by the worldwide dispersion of different food diseases. Additionally, as a result of their greater awareness of environmental and social issues, consumers in developed countries are increasingly demanding products that fulfil certain relevant criteria, such as organic agricultural and fair trade products.

27   At the UNCTAD Expert Meeting on Methodologies, Classifications, Quantification and Development Impacts of Non-Tariff Barriers which took place in September 2005, the Secretary-General of UNCTAD announced the setting up of a Group of Eminent Persons on NTMs to address this issue, among others related to NTMs. For a more elaborate discussion on the problems related to the quantification of NTMs, see UNCTAD, 2005b.

28   A recent study by the World Bank indicates that standards and technical regulations in developed countries affect the propensity of developing-country firms to export (Chen, Otsuki and Wilson, 2006).

29   Jaffee and Henson (2005) illustrate the potentially disruptive impact of food safety and agricultural health measures on exports from developing countries with examples relating to fish bans, limits on mycotoxins and horticultural product standards.

30   See UNCTAD, 2005b and 2006b; and Fliess and Lejarraga, 2005.

31   The data are compiled by the WTO secretariat and include anti-dumping measures taken only by members of the WTO. Zanardi (2004) shows that Taiwan Province of China has been a long-standing user of anti-dumping measures, and that the Rus-

sian Federation and Ukraine have recently joined the ranks of new users.

32   Data on anti-dumping are obtained from the WTO *Antidumping Statistics* website at: http://www.wto.org/english/tratop_e/adp_e/adp_e.htm#dol for the period 1995–2005, and from Miranda, Torres and Ruiz (1998) for earlier years.

33   These data refer to the 91-country sample less South Africa for which comprehensive data were not available.

34   On the other hand, gross export data usually provide the basis for assessments of developing countries' participation in world trade and of their ability to take advantage of newly arising export opportunities.

35   The decline in Brazil's importance as a major export destination for developing countries probably reflects the devaluation and slow income growth. But there could well be a reversal following the more recent economic upswing.

36   This finding contrasts markedly with the result in Arora and Vamvakidis (2005: 27) that "for most countries, the set of most important trading partners remains relatively stable over time." However, the examination here differs from theirs by including only developing countries (rather than all countries) as exporters, looking at the period 1990–2004 (rather than 1960–1999), and, given the strong concentration of export destinations – which raises some doubts as to the appropriateness of the approach taken by them – looking at only five (rather than ten) of the most important trading partners.

37   Thus, the strategy to diversify the origin of its fuel imports, combined with the coming on-line of oil reserves in a number of African countries, are important factors in the growing importance of the United States as developing countries' main export destination.

38   From the results of an analysis based on a gravity model, the IMF (2002: 124) concludes that "differences in economic size account for 80 percent of the difference in average bilateral trade flows."

39   Moreover, Kenya and Zambia rank 16th in the subperiod for which they are not among the 15 least benefiting countries.

40   Moreover, China has become the second most important destination for Yemen and Congo, almost as important as their leading destinations.

41   Ad hoc treatment used to be provided when a country did not fit into previous categories but required a global, comprehensive and exceptional treatment. Such treatment has been rationalized for non-HIPCs under the Evian approach, which is discussed in greater detail later in this section. Since 1988, only two HIPCs have received such treatment, Kenya (1994, 2000) and Guyana (2004).

42   For a review of the extensive literature on the macro-

economic implications of a debt overhang, see Patillo, Poirson and Ricci, 2002.

43 The Initiative employs several key benchmarks as indicators of debt sustainability, one of which is the ratio of the net present value (NPV) of debt to exports. Under the original initiative, countries were required to bring this ratio to a range of 200 to 250 per cent; this was amended under the enhanced Initiative to 150 per cent. The sustainability indicator – the ratio of debt to government revenue – was also lowered from 280 per cent to 250 per cent, and the eligibility thresholds for the export-to-GDP ratio and the revenue-to-GDP ratio were reduced to 30 per cent and 15 per cent respectively.

44 HIPCs will not benefit equally from this new initiative, as the only regional financial institution participating in debt relief under the Initiative is the African Development Bank. The inclusion of other regional financial institutions should therefore be considered, so as to be able to offer similar (equal) treatment for all completion point countries under the HIPC Initiative.

45 Daseking and Joshi (2005) suggest that projects of high social value but with low financial returns may be better suited to funding by grants, while other projects that may generate more immediate proceeds may be more effectively financed through loans.

46 The countries that have received assistance under the Evian approach are the Dominican Republic, Gabon, Georgia, Iraq, Kenya and Kyrgyzstan. Iraq and Kyrgyzstan were deemed as having an unsustainable debt.

47 Remittances refer to workers' remittances, migrants' capital transfers and compensation of employees.

48 Amuedo-Dorantes and Pozo (2004: 1414) refer to a "…doubling of transfers in the form of workers' remittances", which, according to their findings, can "result in real exchange rate appreciation of about 22% in our panel of 13 Latin American and Caribbean nations."

49 Some governments of developing countries which are among the main recipients of remittances, such as India, Morocco, Pakistan and Turkey, already appear to be providing different types of incentives to channel those remittances into the domestic financial system, including various interest and tax advantages (see, for example, Ennin, 2006).

50 In the study by Aykut and Ratha (2003), the definition of South includes not only developing economies, but also some economies in Central and Eastern Europe.

51 These measures of the relative importance of FDI should not be understood as reflecting the part of fixed investment that is undertaken by foreign investors, since FDI figures also include the acquisition by foreigners of already existing real capital.

References

Ackerman F (2005). The shrinking gains from trade: a critical assessment of Doha Round projections. Working Paper 05-01, Tufts University, Global Development and Environment Institute, Medford, MA.

Aksoy MA (2005). Global agricultural trade policies. In: Aksoy MA and Beghin JC, eds., *Global Agricultural Trade and Developing Countries*. Washington, DC, World Bank: 37–53.

Akyüz Y (2005). The WTO negotiations on industrial tariffs: What is at stake for developing countries? Penang, Malaysia, Third World Network, May.

Amiti M and Romalis J (2006). Will the Doha Round lead to preference erosion? Working paper, WP/06/10, International Monetary Fund, Washington, DC.

Amuedo-Dorantes C and Pozo S (2004). Workers' remittances and the real exchange rate: a paradox of gifts. *World Development*, 32 (8): 1407–1417.

Anderson K, Martin W and Valenzuela E (2006). The relative importance of global agricultural subsidies and market access. World Bank Policy Research Working Paper 3900, Washington, DC, April.

Anderson K, Martin W and van der Mensbrugghe D (2005). Market and welfare implications of Doha reform scenarios. In: Anderson K and Martin W, eds., *Agricultural Trade Reform and the Doha Development Agenda*. Washington, DC, World Bank and Palgrave Macmillan, 333–399.

Arora V and Vamvakidis A (2005). How much do trading partners matter for economic growth? IMF Staff Papers, 51 (1): 24–40.

Aykut D and Ratha D (2003). South-South flows: How big are they? *Transnational Corporations*, 13 (1), 149–176.

Blalock G and Gertler PJ (2005). Foreign direct investment and externalities: The case for public intervention. In: Moran T, Graham E, and Blomstrom M, eds., *Does Foreign Direct Investment Affect Economic Growth?* Washington, DC, Institute for Economic Growth and Center for Global Development, 73–106.

Borensztein E, De Gregorio J and Lee JW (1998). How does foreign Direct Investment Affect Economic Growth. *Journal of International Economics*, 45 (1): 115–135.

Bouet A et al. (2005). Multilateral agricultural trade liberalization: The contrasting fortunes of developing countries in the Doha Round. *The World Economy*, 28 (9): 1329–1354, September.

Brenton P and Hoppe M (2005). Life after quotas? Early Signs of the New Era in Trade of Textiles and Clothing. In: Newfarmer R, ed., *Trade, Doha, and Development: Window into the Issues*. Washington, DC, World Bank: 155–164.

Buch C, Kuckulenz A and Le Manche MH (2002). *Worker Remittances and Capital Flows*. Working Paper no. 1130. Kiel, Germany, Institute for World Economics, June.

Bugamelli M and Paterno F (2005). Do workers' remittances reduce the probability of current account reversals? World Bank Policy Research Working Paper no. 3766. Washington, DC. November.

Burgess R and Haksar V (2005). Migration and foreign remittances in the Philippines. IMF Working Paper, WP/05/111. Washington, DC, International Monetary Fund, June.

Charlton A and Stiglitz JE (2005). A development-friendly prioritization of Doha Round Proposals. *The World Economy*, 28 (3): 293–312, March.

Chauvin N and Kraay A (2005). What are 100 billion dollars worth of debt relief done for low-income countries? Mimeo. Available at: http//:economics.uchicago.edu/download/ChauvinKraazWhatHasDebtRelief AccomplishedSept2005.pdf.

Chen MX, Otsuki T and Wilson JS (2006). Do standards matter for export success? World Bank Policy Research Working Paper 3809, Washington, DC, January.

Daseking C and Joshi B (2005). Debt and new financing in low-income countries: looking back, thinking ahead. Paper presented at the IMF seminar on Foreign Aid and Macroeconomic Management, held in Maputo, Mozambique, March. Available at: www.imf.org/external/np/seminars/eng/2005/famm/pdf/bikas.pdf.

de Vasconcelos P (2005). Improving the development impact of remittances. UN/pop/mig/2005/10, United Nations, New York, 5 July.

EIU (2005a). *Country Profile 2005, Mexico*. Economist Intelligence Unit.

EIU (2005b). *Country Report: India*. Economist Intelligence Unit, September 2005. Available at: www.eiu.com.

Elamin N and Khaira H (2003). Tariff escalation in agricultural commodity markets. *Commodity Market Review 2003-2004*, 101–120. Rome, Food and Agricultural Organization of the United Nations.

Ennin B (2006). *Making Ghana competitive*. Available at Ghana home page: www.ghanaweb.com/GhanaHomePage/features/artikel.php?ID=100748 (accessed on 10 March).

FAO (2005). *The State of Food and Agriculture 2005*. Rome, Food and Agricultural Organization of the United Nations.

Fernández de Córdoba S and Vanzetti D (forthcoming). Now what? Searching for a solution to the WTO industrial tariff negotiations. In: Laird S and Fernandez de Cordoba S, eds., *Coping with Trade Reforms: A Developing-Country Perspective on the WTO Industrial Tariff Negotiations*. Basingstoke: Palgrave MacMillan.

Fliess B and Lejarraga I (2005). Non-tariff barriers of concern to developing countries. In: OECD, *Looking Beyond Tariffs: The role of Non-Tariff Barriers in World Trade*. Paris, Organisation for Economic Co-operation and Development: 227–296.

Francois J, van Meijl H and van Tongeren F (2005). Trade liberalization in the Doha Development Round. Gauging the WTO negotiations' potential gains. *Economic Policy*, 20 (42): 349–391, April.

Giuliano P and Ruiz-Arranz M (2005). Remittances, financial development and growth. IMF Working Paper, WP/05/234. Washington, DC, International Monetary Fund, December.

Hufbauer GC and Schott JJ (2006). The Doha Round after Hong Kong. *Policy Briefs in International Economics* no. PB06-2. Washington, DC, Institute for International Economics, February.

IMF (1999). From Toronto Terms to HIPC Initiative: a brief history of debt relief for low-income countries. IMF Working Paper WP/99/142, Washington, DC, International Monetary Fund, October.

IMF (2002). Trade and financial integration. *World Economic Outlook*. Washington, DC, International Monetary Fund, September.

IMF (2005a). Dealing with the revenue consequences of trade reform. Background paper for *Review of Fund Work on Trade*. Washington, DC, International Monetary Fund, February.

IMF (2005b). *World Economic Outlook*. Washington, DC, International Monetary Fund, April.

IMF and World Bank (2005a). Doha Development Agenda and Aid for Trade. Washington, DC, 19 September. Available at: www.imf.org/external/np/pp/eng/2005/091905.pdf.

IMF and World Bank (2005b). Note on the G8 debt relief proposal: assessment of costs, implementation issues, and financing options. DC2005-0023, Washington, DC, Development Committee, Joint Ministerial Committee of the Boards of Governors of the Bank and the Fund, 21 September. Available at: *http://siteresources.worldbank.org/DEVCOM MINT/Documentation/20656508/DC2005-0023(E)-DebtRelief.pdf*.

Jaffee SM and Henson S (2005). Agro-food exports from developing countries: the challenges posed by standards. In: Aksoy M and Beghin JC, eds., *Global Agricultural Trade and Developing Countries*. Washington, DC, World Bank: 91–114.

Kapur D (2004). Remittances: The new development mantra? G-24 Discussion Paper no. 29, April.

Krueger AO (2001). International financial architecture for 2002: A new approach to sovereign debt restructuring. Address to the American Enterprise Institute, Washington, DC, 26 November. Available at: www.imf.org/external/np/speeches/2001/112601.htm.

Kumar N (2005). Performance requirements as tools of development policy: lessons from developed and developing countries. In: Gallagher KP, ed., *Putting Development First: The Importance of Policy Space in the WTO and International Financial Institutions*. London and New York, Zed Books: 179–194.

Laird S (2006). Coping with trade reforms. Presentation at the Commission of Trade in Goods and Services, and Commodities. Geneva. 6–10 February.

Lipsey R and Sjoholm F (2005). The impact of FDI on host countries: Why such different answers? In: Moran T, Graham E. and Blomstrom M, eds., *Does Foreign Direct Investment Affect Economic Growth?* Washington, D.C, Institute for Economic Growth and Center for Global Development, 23–44.

Miranda J, Torres RA and Ruiz M (1998). The international use of antidumping: 1987–1997. *Journal of World Trade*, 32 (5): 5–71.

Moran T, Graham E and Blomstrom M, eds., (2005). *Does Foreign Direct Investment Promote Development?* Washington, DC, Institute for International Economics.

Moss TJ and Chiang HS (2003). The other costs of high debt in poor countries: Growth, policy dynamics, and institutions. *Issue Paper on Debt Sustainability* no. 3, Washington, DC, Center for Global Development, August.

Narula R and Lall S (2004). Foreign Direct Investment and its Role in Economic Development. In: Narula R and Lall S, eds., Understanding FDI-Assisted Economic Development, Special Issue of the *European Journal of Development Research*, 16 (3): 447–464.

OECD (2003). *Trends in International Migration 2003*. Paris, Organisation for Economic Co-operation and Development.

OECD (2005). *Agricultural policies in OECD countries: Monitoring and evaluation*. Paris, Organisation for Economic Co-operation and Development.

OECD (2006a). *Aid rising sharply, according to final ODA figures for 2004*. Paris, Organisation for Economic Co-operation and Development.

OECD (2006b). Aid flows top USD 100 billion in 2005. 4 April. Available at: www.oecd.org/documentprint/30.

OECD (2006c). OECD Development Assistance Committee Database online. Available at: www.oecd.org/dataoecd/50/17/5037721.htm.

Panagariya A (1999). On the "extravagant" predictions of benefits from the Uruguay Round. *Economic Times*, 25 August.

Patillo C, Poirson H and Ricci L (2002). External debt and growth. IMF Working Paper WP/02/69, Washington, DC, International Monetary Fund, April 2002.

Pay E (2005). Overview of the Sanitary and Phytosanitary measures in Quad countries on tropical fruits and vegetables imported from developing countries, *South Centre T.R.A.D.E. Research Papers*. Geneva, November.

Piermartini R and Teh R (2005). Demystifying modelling methods for trade policy, World Trade Organization, Discussion Paper no.10, Geneva.

Polaski S (2006). *Winners and Losers: Impact of the Doha Round on Developing Countries*. Washington, DC, Carnegie Endowment for International Peace.

Rodrik D (2001). Comments at the Conference on Immigration Policy and the Welfare State. Trieste, 31 July.

Rodrik D (2004). Development Round: A marketing gimmick? *South Bulletin*, no. 73. Geneva, South Centre.

Stiglitz JE and Charlton A (2005). *Fair* Trade *For All: How Trade Can Promote Development*. Oxford, Oxford University Press.

Suppan S (2005). Policy coherence and agricultural trade liberalization: Lessons for the Doha Round. In: *Sailing Close to the Wind: Navigating the Hong Kong WTO Ministerial*. Minneapolis, Institute for Agriculture and Trade Policy: 45–58.

UN Millennium Project (2005). *Investing in Development: A Practical Plan to Achieve the Millennium Development Goals* (*Sachs Report*). London and Sterling, VA, Earthscan.

UNCTAD (1999). *World Investment Report 1999: Foreign Direct Investment and the Challenge of Devel-*

opment. United Nations publication, sales no. E.99.II.D.3, New York and Geneva.

UNCTAD (2000). *World Investment Report 2000: Cross-border Mergers and Acquisitions and Development*. United Nations publication, sales no. E.00.II.D.20, New York and Geneva.

UNCTAD (2003). Trade preferences for LDCs: An early assessment of benefits and possible improvements. UNCTAD/ITCD/TSB/2003/8, New York and Geneva.

UNCTAD (2004a). Debt sustainability: oasis or mirage? *Economic Development in Africa*. UNCTAD/GDS/AFRICA/2004/1, United Nations publication, sales no. E.04.II.D.37, New York and Geneva.

UNCTAD (2004b). *Trade and Development Aspects of Professional Services and Regulatory Frameworks*. TD/B/COM.1/EM.25/2, Geneva.

UNCTAD (2004c). *World Investment Report 2004: The Shift towards Services*, United Nations publication, sales no. E.04.II.D.36, New York and Geneva.

UNCTAD (2005a). Erosion of preferences for the Least Developed Countries: Assessment of effects and mitigating options, TD/B/52/4, 4 August.

UNCTAD (2005b). Methodologies, classification, quantification and development impacts of Non-Tariff Barriers, TD/B/COM.1/EM.27/2, Geneva, 25 June.

UNCTAD (2005c). *World Investment Report 2005: Transnational Corporations and the Internationalization of R&D*, United Nations publication, sales no. E.05.II.D.10, New York and Geneva.

UNCTAD (2005d). *Economic Development in Africa - Rethinking the Role of Foreign Direct Investment*. United Nations publication, sales no. E.05.II.D.12, New York and Geneva.

UNCTAD (2005e). Policy issues related to investment and development. United Nations document TD/B/COM.2/64, Geneva, 4 February.

UNCTAD (2006a). Market access, market entry and competitiveness, TD/B/COM.1/76, Geneva.

UNCTAD (2006b). *Trade and Environment Review 2006*, United Nations publication, sales no. E.05.II.D.27, New York and Geneva. .

UNCTAD (various issues). *Trade and Development Report*. United Nations publication, New York and Geneva.

UN-DESA (2005). *World Economic and Social Survey 2005*, New York.

United Nations (2006). International migration and development. Report of the United Nations Secretary-General, A/60/871. 18 May.

United States General Accounting Office (USGAO) (2004). Achieving Poor Countries Economic Growth and Debt relief targets faces significant financing challenges. GAO-04-0405. Washington, DC.

van der Mensbrugghe D (2005). Estimating the benefits of trade reform: Why the numbers change. In: Newfarmer R, ed., *Trade, Doha, and Development: Window into the Issues*. Washington, DC, World Bank: 59–75.

Wise TA and Gallagher KP (2005). The Hong Kong Ministerial: What's at stake for the Poor? Bridges, no. 10, Geneva, International Center for Trade and Sustainable Development, December.

World Bank (2002). *Global Economic Prospects 2002*. Washington, DC, World Bank.

World Bank (2004) *Global Economic Prospects 2005*. Washington, DC, World Bank.

World Bank (2005) *Global Economic Prospects 2006*. Washington, DC, World Bank.

World Bank (2006a). Debt relief for the poorest: an evaluation update of the HIPC Initiative. Washington, DC, Independent Evaluation Group, World Bank.

World Bank (2006b). *Global Economic Prospects: The Economic Implications of Remittances and Migration*. Washington, DC, World Bank.

WTO (2005a). *Doha Work Programme Ministerial Declaration*, WT/MIN(05)/DEC, Hong Kong, 22 December.

WTO (2005b). *World Trade Report 2005*. World Trade Organization, Geneva.

WTO (2006). Eleventh Annual Review of the Implementation and Operation of the TBT Agreement, Committee on Technical Barriers to Trade, World Trade Organization, G/TBT/18, 17 February.

Xu B (2000). Multinational Enterprises, Technology Diffusion and Host Country Productivity Growth. Journal of Development Economics 62 (2): 477–493, August.

Zanardi M (2004). Antidumping: what are the numbers to discuss at Doha? *World Economy,* 27 (3): 403–433.

Annex tables to chapter III

Table 3.A1

PROGRESS UNDER THE HIPC INITIATIVE, 1997–2006

	Original HIPC Initiative		Enhanced HIPC Initiative	
	Decision point	*Completion point*	*Decision point*	*Completion point*
1997	Bolivia (Sept.) Burkina Faso (Sept.) Guyana (Dec.) Uganda (April)			
1998	Côte d'Ivoire (March) Mali (Sept.) Mozambique (April)	Bolivia (Sept.) Uganda (April)		
1999		Guyana (May) Mozambique (June)		
2000		Burkina Faso (July) Mali (Sept.)	Benin (July) Bolivia (Feb.) Burkina Faso (July) Cameroon (Oct.) Gambia (Dec.) Guinea (Dec.) Guinea-Bissau (Dec.) Guyana (Nov.) Honduras (June) Madagascar (Dec.) Malawi (Dec.) Mali (Sept.) Mauritania (Feb.) Mozambique (April) Nicaragua (Dec.) Niger (Dec.) Rwanda (Dec.) Sao Tome and Principe (Dec.) Senegal (June) U. Rep. of Tanzania (April) Uganda (Feb.) Zambia (Dec.)	Uganda (May)
2001			Chad (May) Ethiopia (Nov.)	Bolivia (June) Mozambique (Sept.) U. Rep. of Tanzania (Nov.)
2002			Ghana (Feb) Sierra Leone (March)	Burkina Faso (April) Mauritania (June)
2003			Dem. Rep. of the Congo (July)	Benin (March) Guyana (Dec.) Mali (March)
2004				Ethiopia (April) Ghana (July) Madagascar (Oct.) Nicaragua (Jan.) Niger (April) Senegal (April)
2005			Burundi (Aug.)	Honduras (April) Rwanda (April) Zambia (April)
2006			Congo (March)	Cameroon (May)

Source: *IMF Survey*, various issues.

Table 3.A2

PROGRESS OF THE 29 DECISION POINT HIPCs TOWARDS
VARIOUS MILLENNIUM DEVELOPMENT GOALS

	Poverty and hunger		Universal primary education		Gender equality	
Target:	**Halve**, between 1990 and 2015, the proportion of people who suffer from hunger.		Ensure that, by 2015, **all** children will be able to complete a full course of primary schooling.		**Eliminate** gender disparity in primary and secondary education, preferably by 2005, and all levels of education by 2015.	
Indicator:	Malnutrition prevalence, weight for age (percentage of children under 5)		Primary completion rate, total (percentage of relevant age group)		Ratio of girls to boys in primary and secondary education (per cent)	
	Percentage point change[a]	Per cent	Percentage point change 1990/91–2004[b]	Per cent short of achieving the goal	Percentage point change 1991–2004	Per cent short of achieving the goal
Benin	-6.3	-21.6	30.4	51.2	21.9	28.6
Bolivia	-3.5	-31.5	28.8[b]	-0.2	..	1.6
Burkina Faso	5.0	15.3	9.1	70.5	14.6	23.7
Burundi	..	..	-7.9	66.9	0.1	18.2
Cameroon	3.0	19.9	6.3	36.7	4.0	13.3
Chad	-2.1	-5.4	12.9	70.5	16.5	42.0
Congo	..	..	7.3	33.6	..	..
Dem. Rep. of the Congo	-3.4	-9.9	..	..	..	..
Ethiopia	0.5	1.0	37.0	49.4	4.4	27.2
Gambia	-9.0	-34.4				
Ghana	-5.2	-19.0	2.6[b]	34.6	12.1	9.4
Guinea	5.9	22.0	29.8	51.5	26.7	27.5
Guinea-Bissau	..	..	..	..	..	..
Guyana	-4.7	-25.7	5.7	4.7	..	..
Honduras	-1.4	-7.8	14.7[b]	20.6	..	..
Madagascar	1.0	2.4	10.4	54.7	..	..
Malawi	-5.7	-20.7	29.4	41.5	17.3	1.5
Mali	6.3	23.4	33.5	56.0	15.5	25.6
Mauritania	-15.8	-33.2	13.9	56.9	28.0	4.5
Mozambique	-3.3	-12.2	4.1	71.0	10.8	17.7
Nicaragua	-1.4	-12.7	29.5	26.5	-6.6	-2.7
Niger	-2.5	-5.9	9.8	75.0	13.9	28.9
Rwanda	-5.1	-17.3	-8.0	62.6	4.1	-0.1
Sao Tome and Principe	..	..	..	25.1	..	..
Senegal	1.1	4.8	3.6	54.8	20.9	10.2
Sierra Leone	-1.5	-5.2	..	46.3	..	..
Uganda	-2.6	-10.2	..	42.9	15.4	2.9
United Rep. of Tanzania	0.5	1.7	10.1	43.5	..	..
Zambia	-2.2	-8.7	..	33.8	..	6.9
Average	*-2.1*	*-7.6*	*14.1*	*45.4*	*12.9*	*15.1*

Source: UNCTAD secretariat estimates, based on World Bank, *World Development Indicators* database 2006.
  Note: The series presented in the table were selected based on data availability.
   a Due to the inconsistent reporting periods across countries for this indicator, changes reflect the difference between the latest and earliest reported figures.
   b Data for 1991 were used for countries which did not have data reported for 1990.

Table 3.A2 (concluded)

PROGRESS OF THE 29 DECISION POINT HIPCs TOWARDS VARIOUS MILLENNIUM DEVELOPMENT GOALS

Reduce child mortality	**Environmental sustainability**			
Reduce the under-five mortality rate by **two thirds**, between 1990 and 2015.	**Halve** the proportion of people without sustainable access to safe drinking water and basic sanitation by 2015.			
Mortality rate, age under-5 (per 1 000)	Improved sanitation facilities (percentage with access)		Improved water source (percentage with access)	
Change (per 1 000) 1990–2004	Per cent	Percentage point change 1990–2002	Per cent	Percentage point change 1990–2002	Per cent
---	---	---	---	---	---
-21.4	-19.3	21.0	190.9	8.0	13.3	Benin
-35.0	-39.3	12.0	36.4	13.0	18.1	Bolivia
-16.2	-14.3	-1.0	-7.7	12.0	30.8	Burkina Faso
0.0	0.0	-8.0	-18.2	10.0	14.5	Burundi
2.2	2.6	27.0	128.6	13.0	26.0	Cameroon
0.0	0.0	2.0	33.3	14.0	70.0	Chad
-2.0	-2.4	..	..	..	..	Congo
0.0	0.0	11.0	61.1	3.0	7.0	Dem. Rep. of the Congo
-20.6	-15.7	2.0	50.0	-3.0	-12.0	Ethiopia
-14.0	-13.6	..	..	..	..	Gambia
-7.0	-9.3	15.0	34.9	25.0	46.3	Ghana
-44.0	-30.3	-4.0	-23.5	9.0	21.4	Guinea
-27.4	-17.9	..	..	..	..	Guinea-Bissau
-16.0	-25.0	..	..	..	..	Guyana
-12.6	-28.6	19.0	38.8	7.0	8.4	Honduras
-27.0	-26.2	21.0	175.0	5.0	12.5	Madagascar
-36.2	-24.8	10.0	27.8	26.0	63.4	Malawi
-19.0	-13.6	9.0	25.0	14.0	41.2	Mali
-7.0	-8.2	14.0	50.0	15.0	36.6	Mauritania
-53.6	-33.9	..	..	..	..	Mozambique
-21.2	-40.8	19.0	40.4	12.0	17.4	Nicaragua
-39.2	-20.5	5.0	71.4	6.0	15.0	Niger
15.0	14.6	4.0	10.8	15.0	25.9	Rwanda
0.0	0.0	..	..	..	..	Sao Tome and Principe
-12.4	-13.8	17.0	48.6	6.0	9.1	Senegal
-9.6	-5.5	..	..	..	..	Sierra Leone
-12.8	-13.8	-2.0	-4.7	12.0	27.3	Uganda
-23.6	-23.1	-1.0	-2.1	35.0	92.1	United Rep. of Tanzania
1.0	1.0	4.0	9.8	5.0	10.0	Zambia
-15.8	*-14.5*	*8.9*	*44.4*	*11.9*	*27.0*	*Average*

Chapter IV

MACROECONOMIC POLICY UNDER GLOBALIZATION

A. Introduction[1]

Globalization is permanently changing the framework of national macroeconomic policy, offering opportunities as well as posing challenges and constraints. Many developing countries and economies in transition that opened their borders to international trade and private capital flows over the last quarter of a century have experienced crises triggered by the vagaries of the international financial markets. The "creative destruction" expected from the new openness has often been much more destructive than creative, leading to deep recessions and political crises.

Closer integration of national economies into the international trading and financial systems by an increasing number of countries has created a new environment for national policy action. Although countries have lost some degree of freedom in designing and implementing their own economic policies, there has been considerable diversity in macroeconomic policies, both in developed and developing economies, in response to the new challenges arising from globalization and increased interdependence. There has also been a wide variety

of outcomes. By designing and implementing policies at the national, regional and multilateral levels, countries shaped the globalization process itself. From this perspective, globalization is not just the penetration of national markets by internationally-produced goods and foreign capital flows, but is likewise a reflection of policy decisions taken at the national, regional and international levels, including in multilateral processes.

The process of globalization and national policies mutually determine each other, though in an asymmetric way. Smaller industrialized countries, developing countries and economies in transition are less able than the major industrialized economies to influence globalization trends and global economic governance. This asymmetry is particularly noteworthy in the sphere of international monetary and financial relations, where the absence of a rules-based system permits developed countries, with their disproportionate impact, to determine global monetary and financial conditions. The latter include as well the conditionalities attached to the lending operations of the international financial institutions. Furthermore, existing rules and practices seek to promote the free movement of industrial goods, money, capital and enterprises, movements that favour advanced countries. They do not encourage the movement of labour, agricultural products or technology, areas where the benefits would be greater for developing countries.

The chapter will discuss the main challenges that globalization and structural reforms are posing to macroeconomic policies in developing countries. It will discuss the macroeconomic policies needed to provide an environment supportive of growth, investment and technological upgrading, contrasting that environment with recent experiences in a large number of developing countries. In those countries, it will be argued, macroeconomic policies often do not promote progress in development but actually hinder it. Finally, the feasibility of pro-active macroeconomic policies in support of capital accumulation and growth in the era of globalization will be examined.

B. Coping with the macroeconomic implications of liberalization and globalization

1. Financial integration and capital inflows

Financial integration is the aspect of globalization that has had the most critical influence on macroeconomic policy in developing and transition economies. It has not only largely determined the framework for macroeconomic policies, especially monetary and exchange-rate management, but it has also set new parameters for thinking on development policies in the broader sense.

During the 1970s, the abandonment of the Bretton Woods exchange-rate system, the expansion of international banking activities, the huge trade imbalances in the wake of the oil shocks and the concomitant increase of international liquidity radically changed the external environment for development. This new environment considerably enlarged the access of many middle-income countries to external finance, which previously had been provided primarily by official development assistance (ODA), credits from international financial institutions and foreign direct investment (FDI). The Bretton Woods system was based on the premise that large and continued imbalances in the current account were unacceptable and had to be prevented or rectified by adjustments of domestic expenditure and/or by currency devaluation. From the mid-1970s onwards, however, many developing countries were able to obtain credit from private lenders abroad, credit that was then used to finance current-account deficits. The result of this was a rapid accumulation of external debt, which made the indebted countries more vulnerable to external monetary shocks, leading to the debt crisis of the early 1980s.

In spite of this experience, the pressure towards full liberalization of international capital flows persisted, a policy shift that was even more pronounced in the developing economies than in most developed countries (Williamson and Mahar,

1998). Many developing countries substantially reduced or removed capital controls, although they could have retained such measures according to IMF rules. In the mid-1990s the IMF actively promoted an amendment to its Articles of Agreement that would make it compulsory for IMF members to open their capital accounts. This initiative was supported by the IMF Interim Committee at the Annual Meeting of 1997, but the Asian financial crisis and the perceived role played in that crisis by capital account deregulation weakened the support for such a reform. Although opening of capital accounts was not mandatory for IMF members, it was nonetheless undertaken by many developing countries, leading to their effective integration into the international financial markets. This led to two big waves of gross capital inflow, in 1976–1981 and 1990–1997, which were both followed by periods of retraction (1982–1988 and 1998–2002) (fig. 4.1).

The first wave of private capital inflows consisted primarily of bank lending and financed a large part of the current-account deficits resulting from the oil shocks of the 1970s. These deficits increased considerably when interest rates in developed countries soared at the beginning of the 1980s. The subsequent debt crisis forced a severe adjustment of current-account balances through devaluations, particularly in Latin America.

During the second wave, private capital flows to the developing countries occurred in greater part in the form of portfolio investment but, as in the first wave, had as a counterpart increasing current-account deficits. Private capital inflows contracted considerably after the financial crises in Asia and in the Russian Federation. Since 2003, gross private capital inflows have been expanding again but this time the counterpart is not a widening of current-account deficits. Rather, the private capital inflows are accompanied by current-account surplus in many developing countries, and both factors have led to massive reserve accumulation in the receiving countries, implying a large official capital outflow, as these reserves are held in dollar- or euro-denominated assets.

> Financial liberalization in Latin America did not increase savings and led to extended banking crises, while active financial policies in East Asia enhanced investment and growth.

2. Domestic financial liberalization

Deregulation of domestic financial markets, including the elimination of credit controls, deregulation of interest rates and the privatization of banks, was a key element in the reform agenda of the 1980s and 1990s and increased the influence of private sector interests on the performance of the financial sector, something considered to be beneficial for economic growth (Patrick, 1966; Shaw, 1973; McKinnon, 1973).[2] This was based on the belief that lifting "financial repression" in the form of interest ceilings would give the right signals for inter-temporal resource allocation, enhance willingness to save and attract additional resources to the banking system. It was assumed that the banking system, following market principles, would allocate these resources most efficiently. Combining this with a liberalized capital account, developing countries would attract financial savings originating in more prosperous economies and thus overcome a major barrier to growth.

Financial deregulation was not applied with the same intensity and rapidity everywhere, yet it had a marked impact on the functioning of the economies concerned. The Latin American experience of early and radical financial liberalization in several countries refuted the idea that such liberalization and the ensuing rise in interest rates would automatically raise the level of savings and improve their allocation. In particular, the bad experiences with financial reforms in the Southern Cone countries during the 1970s might have provided an early warning. These reforms proved to be counterproductive and led to widespread bankruptcies, massive government intervention, nationalization of private institutions and low domestic savings (Díaz-Alejandro, 1985). High interest rates raised the cost of finance for domestic business and investment, while the deregulated banking sector, rather than channelling more credit towards the most profitable investment opportunities, allocated it in large part to non-productive uses such as private and public consumption and speculative activities.[3]

Figure 4.1

CAPITAL FLOWS AND CURRENT-ACCOUNT BALANCE
IN EMERGING-MARKET ECONOMIES,[a] 1976–2004

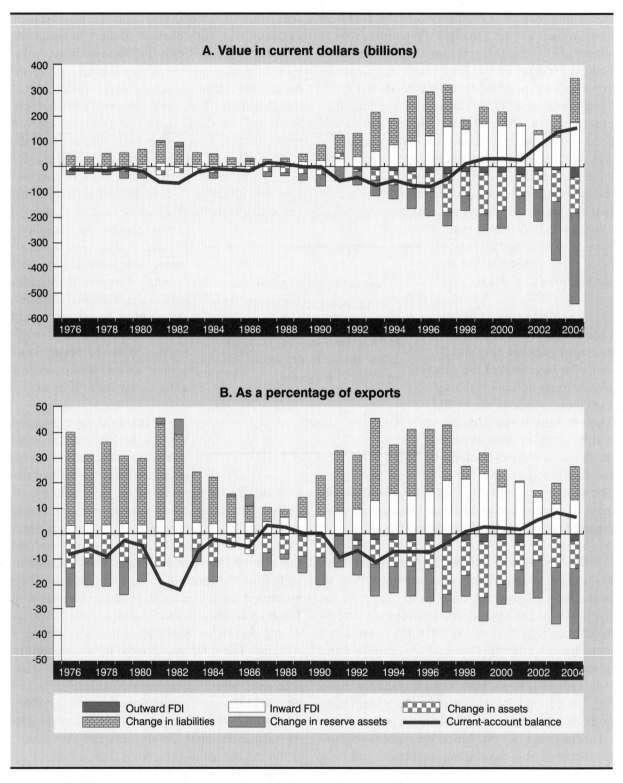

Source: UNCTAD secretariat calculations, based on IMF, *Balance-of-Payments* Database.

   a Argentina, Brazil, Chile, China, Colombia, Ecuador, India, Indonesia, Kuwait, Malaysia, Mexico, Morocco, Nigeria, Pakistan, Peru, the Philippines, Poland, the Republic of Korea, Romania, Saudi Arabia, Singapore, South Africa, Thailand, Tunisia, Turkey, Uruguay and Venezuela.

In contrast, active government policies in support of financial sector development, rather than deregulation, played an important role in the Asian NIEs: "In most of the rapidly growing economies of East Asia government has taken an active role in creating financial institutions, in regulating them, and in directing credit, both in ways that enhance the stability of the economy and the solvency of the financial institutions and in ways that enhance growth prospects" (Stiglitz, 1994: 50). Credit was directed towards providing long-term investment financing and cheap export financing, while restrictions were placed on consumer credit and the financing of real estate and stock market speculation. Interest rates and bank spreads were subject to government control, and the government also had a direct influence on credit allocation through State-owned commercial and development banks (World Bank, 1993: 225–227 and 273–287).

> Increased interest payments and the loss of fiscal income created serious problems for attaining fiscal equilibrium and compromised public investment.

3. Changes in the fiscal structure

The scope of macroeconomic policies has also been influenced by the impact that financial integration and reforms undertaken under the aegis of the Washington Consensus had on public sector finances of developing countries. A central element in the reform agenda was a drastic reduction of budget deficits with the intent of achieving fiscal equilibrium. This was seen not only as a key element in stabilization policies, since fiscal deficits and their monetary financing were viewed as one of the main causes of inflation, but also as a key tool for gaining creditworthiness and lowering country-risk spreads in international capital markets.

The composition of fiscal income and expenditure varies widely among developing countries, but it is possible to identify some trends shared by many countries since the 1970s. The most important of these is that the weight of interest payments in total current public expenditure has increased in many countries (table 4.1) as capital account

and financial liberalization led typically to increased public debt at higher real interest rates. Public debt increased dramatically during currency and financial crises, not only because these crises were accompanied by very high interest rates and currency depreciation but also because, in many cases, the Government nationalised private liabilities and provided costly rescue packages to the financial sector.

Governments had to undertake fiscal reforms in order to adjust to lower income from import taxes resulting from trade liberalization (table 4.1) and in some cases to reduced social security contributions resulting from reforms of the social security system. Privatization led to a reduction of fiscal revenue in a number of countries. The alternative sources of revenue that increased their share in total current income were value-added tax and other indirect taxes on goods and services, especially in Latin America, and taxes on income and profits, especially in Asian developing countries.

The effects of these structural changes on fiscal balances and on the ability to pursue active fiscal policies have been mixed. While fiscal administration improved in several countries, increased interest payments and the loss of fiscal income in many cases created serious problems for attaining the objective of fiscal equilibrium and compromised public investment. As a result, several governments are revising some of their previous choices, in particular those regarding taxation of firms exploiting natural resources. They are also re-thinking the question of the direct participation of the State in these activities (see *TDR 2005*, chap. III).

4. Exchange-rate and monetary policy

The liberalization of international trade and finance in developing countries during the 1980s and 1990s was undertaken under the heading of "getting the prices right". However, one of the reasons

Table 4.1

CENTRAL GOVERNMENT[a] INTEREST PAYMENTS AND TAXES ON INTERNATIONAL TRADE IN SELECTED DEVELOPING COUNTRIES, 1971–2004

(Annual averages)

	Interest payments (Percentage of current expenditure)				Taxes on international trade (Percentage of current revenue)			
	1971–1980	*1981–1990*	*1991–2000*	*2001–2004*	*1971–1980*	*1981–1990*	*1991–2000*	*2001–2004*
Argentina	8.3	12.6	12.3	28.2	14.6	14.0	6.7	12.5
Chile	5.5	6.6	4.9	5.7	8.0	8.6	8.7	3.7
Dominican Republic	3.4	5.9	8.4	8.5	41.5	33.0	39.6	27.8
El Salvador	2.4	9.3	14.8	11.8	40.8	24.0	13.6	7.9
Uruguay	2.2	7.0	5.9	14.5	10.1	11.4	4.5	4.6
Venezuela	4.4	14.8	18.0	16.8	6.3	12.7	9.0	5.3
Congo	2.1	36.8	36.6	30.0	22.5	12.9	..	6.5
South Africa	8.2	13.1	17.5	14.2	5.2	4.4	3.0	2.7
Tunisia	5.6	10.0	12.6	10.5	23.5	27.1	21.5	8.4
India	13.1	19.5	27.4	27.8	18.2	25.9	22.5	14.9
Indonesia	5.7	18.3	18.0	21.5	12.1	5.2	4.3	3.2
Malaysia	2.6	5.9	3.4	2.9	32.5	20.5	11.8	5.4
Pakistan	1.8	3.6	6.0	6.5	34.2	30.3	21.6	9.5
Philippines	5.8	27.4	27.7	27.0	26.7	23.8	24.1	17.2
Republic of Korea	4.8	7.3	4.2	6.2	14.0	14.2	6.0	4.2
Thailand	10.1	16.7	5.5	7.1	26.9	20.8	14.3	9.7
Turkey	3.8	14.5	24.3	53.5	13.6	6.9	2.9	0.9
Simple average	5.3	13.5	14.6	17.2	20.6	17.4	13.4	8.5

Source: UNCTAD secretariat estimations, based on IMF, *Government Financial Statistics* Database.

a Fiscal data are presented on a cash basis, with the exception of some recent figures that are only available from the IMF sources on an accrual basis. These are the cases of South Africa (since 2000), Chile and Congo (since 2001), Argentina, El Salvador, Uruguay and Venezuela (since 2002), and Thailand (since 2003). For these countries, the most recent figures are not strictly comparable with the rest of the series.

why the liberalization process may not have delivered the expected benefits for many countries has been the absence of a clear concept of how the most important international price, the exchange rate – and the closely related interest rate –, should be determined or regulated. Many academic observers favoured a market-based determination, arguing for a system of floating exchange rates, but the major financial institutions did not give clear guidance on this key issue. Absolutely fixed exchange rates were found to be as acceptable as systems of adjustable pegging or pure floating. In the late 1990s, however, following the experience of the Mexican and Asian financial crises, intermediate regimes were increasingly found to be inadequate. For example, in the view of Lawrence Summers – then United States Secretary of the Treasury – "a fixed, but not firmly institutionalized exchange rate regime holds enormous risks for emerging-market economies in a world where fast-flowing capital and insufficient developed domestic financial systems coincide". It should therefore "increasingly be the norm that countries involved with the world capital market avoid the 'middle ground' of pegged exchange rates with discretionary monetary policies" (Summers, 1999).

The two options for national exchange-rate policy that were considered viable, i.e. completely free floating and a completely fixed exchange rate ("hard peg") came to be known as the "corner solutions". For a fixed exchange-rate regime to be viable it must be backed by very strong institutional commitments (such as those involved in a currency board) and the country must give up its monetary independence. If the government is not willing to do so, it must opt for a system of free floating. From this perspective, financial globalization presents stringent limits to macroeconomic policy since it is incompatible with an autonomous monetary policy or with the targeting of an exchange-rate level.

The view that emerging-market economies with intermediate exchange-rate regimes were vulnerable to speculative attacks and should move towards either hard pegs or very flexible systems was widely shared, including by the IMF (Mussa et al., 2000: 21–31; Fischer, 2001). It was acknowledged, though, that developing countries could not normally accept sharp variations in their exchange rates with "benign neglect" and might therefore have to intervene in the currency market in order to smooth out exchange-rate movements. However, such interventions were not supposed to tar-

get a pre-determined exchange-rate level or range because this would result in a *de facto* pegging. Such "tightly managed floats" would be susceptible to speculative attacks just like other intermediate regimes. Only free or loosely managed floating would be acceptable as one of the viable exchange-rate regimes in economies integrated into international capital markets. In such a regime, the exchange rate is not providing a nominal anchor to the economy, a role that would need to be played by a quantitative money supply target or an inflation target included as elements of national monetary policy.

Several countries, both developed and developing, that chose a flexible exchange-rate regime adopted "inflation targeting" as the framework for their monetary policy. This entailed not only the definition of a quantitative target for price changes that are considered acceptable, but also a certain pattern for the assignment of available policy instruments to different goals: the central bank is exclusively in charge of price stability, while other economic goals, such as external balance, growth and high employment, which can be in conflict with price stability, have to be pursued with other policy instruments such as variations in fiscal revenues or expenditures. Against this background, a complementary institutional arrangement consisted in granting the central bank independence from the government (or "operational autonomy") in order to ensure the credibility of the commitment of the central bank to focus on attaining the inflation target.

> Trade and financial liberalization were achieved without a clear concept of how the exchange rate should be determined or regulated.

C. Macroeconomic policies in support of a dynamic investment and growth process

Capital accumulation is a key variable in sustained growth and structural change. It simultaneously generates income, creates employment, expands productive capacity and carries forward technological progress and productivity gains. However, the occurrence of innovative investment and, more importantly, the occurrence of waves of such investment, is not just the result of the right set of incentives on the microeconomic level; it needs a conducive structural and institutional framework and an appropriate macroeconomic environment that encourages entrepreneurial risk taking and the creation or expansion of productive capacity, with the attendant provision of employment opportunities for increasingly higher qualified workers.

There is a widespread belief that, apart from price stability, the key macroeconomic prerequisite for investment is the availability of savings, and that "foreign savings" are a desirable complement to national savings, allowing the investment rate of developing countries to rise without a reduction in consumption. This static view, which has determined the orientation of macroeconomic policies in many countries over the past quarter century, is not only theoretically flawed (see annex 2 to chapter I), but has also misled governments in their expectations of gains from capital account liberalization.

> A significant part of capital inflows to developing countries was not channelled towards investment in real productive capacity.

1. Monetary policy and interest rates

An increase in net capital inflows following capital account liberalization can temporarily relax balance-of-payments constraints and offers the opportunity to increase imports without a parallel rise in exports. However, experience has shown that such inflows are frequently not used for enhancing productive capacity through higher investment and/or imports of capital goods, practices that would generate the required income to meet debt service obligations. Rather, a significant part of capital inflows to developing countries was channelled through the domestic financial system of emerging-market economies into credit expansion. Rather than helping raise investment in real productive capacity, this boosted consumption or other activities that were either unproductive or not associated with the kind of production that in one way or another could generate the foreign exchange required for debt service.

In the case of Latin America, the expansion of bank lending based on the inflow of foreign savings in the 1990s was accompanied by a shift of such lending from producers of tradable manufactures to the service sector and to households (ILPES, 1998). In other cases, particularly in the

East and South-East Asian countries before their crises in the late 1990s, a higher part of foreign financing reached non-financial agents directly, and in many emerging-market economies domestic credit expansion resulting from increased capital inflows fed speculative bubbles in the stock and real estate markets. This generated highly volatile wealth effects that further encouraged private consumption. Abundant foreign capital was not associated with higher investment rates and better growth performances compared to countries with less dependence on that kind of finance. (Aizenmann, 2005: 973).[4]

In an alternative view, higher investment does not depend on the *ex-ante* availability of either domestic or foreign savings, but on the effectiveness of financial intermediation that not only allocates existing financial capital but also channels credit based on newly created money into productive and non-inflationary uses. Indeed, in an economy with a well-functioning banking system, it is the power to create money, and not the supply of loanable funds that generates the power to command the use of real resources for investment purposes. From this perspective, therefore, investment expenditure does not depend on the decisions of savers but on the decisions of central banks and bankers to provide finance to firms that is used to generate investment, higher income and, ultimately, higher savings from that higher income (*TDR 1991*: 93).

Against this background, monetary policy takes on a much broader responsibility than is usually stipulated, as it is playing a key role not only in price and exchange-rate stability but also in the performance of the real sector through its influence on the monetary aggregates and interest rates that determine the availability and cost of investment financing. Moreover, monetary authorities also play a central role through credit regulation and financial supervision. Since all these objectives cannot rely on a single policy instrument, monetary policy has to be complemented by other policies such as fiscal policy, various forms of incomes policy and capital account regulations.

> With additional instruments being employed to achieve price stability, monetary policy could be put at the service of the stimulation of investment and growth.

In many countries the traditional monetary rule of following a pre-established quantitative target for money supply has been replaced by inflation targeting. To the extent that the inflation target is credible it provides a "nominal anchor" to price expectations, preventing self-fulfilling inflation anticipation. Although inflation targeting does not exclude in principle that monetary policy decisions also take into account other objectives, especially high employment (Bernanke, 2003: 12), in practice it has led price stability to dominate other goals related to growth, employment or the exchange rate. Policymakers often fear that with multiple targets the credibility of the commitment to achieve the inflation target would be undermined, jeopardising the "confidence building" component of the inflation targeting approach.

While monetary policy alone cannot achieve multiple and potentially conflicting objectives, in a pragmatic approach policy priorities may change according to the economic situation, especially with cyclical developments, and monetary policy instruments may be employed for different purposes at different points in time (Frenkel, 2006). Moreover, if additional instruments were employed to achieve price stability, monetary policy could also be put at the service of other objectives, in particular the stimulation of investment and growth. Additionally, with a scheme that rigidly targets the change of the *general* price level, the central bank may over-adjust because changes in certain prices, especially in situations where inflationary pressure results from external price shocks, may not respond to its tools. To avoid excessive adjustment of interest rates and exchange rates, with the attendant adverse effects on the real economy, a more flexible and efficient approach might be to consider the use of "supply side" tools including, for example, government influence on income negotiations and/or the redefinition of the inflation target depending on the origins of the inflationary pressure.

Monetary authorities in developing countries have to manage a financial sector intrinsically susceptible to boom-and-bust episodes, a propensity that has been reinforced in many countries by financial deregulation and capital account liberalization. The central bank has a key role to play in preventing the succession of episodes of excessive credit expansion followed by excessive contraction. It must not only control the quantity of credit distributed, but also determine how it is used and in which currency it is denominated. Moreover, financial solvency and sustained growth depend on the extent to which credit is financing investment in productive capacity, consumption or the acquisition of real estate and financial assets. Prudential regulation does not always cover exchange rate risks appropriately; for instance, the requirement of a balanced currency composition in banks' assets and liabilities does not keep solvency problems from arising in the case of a sizeable devaluation if borrowers' revenues are derived from domestic sources and their debt is denominated in foreign currency. In other words, monetary authorities have to regulate the quantity of credit and its use by discouraging non-productive and speculative uses within fragile currency systems.

> The exchange rate must be flexible enough to avoid misalignments that harm the competitiveness of domestic producers and overall trade performance.

During recessions and crises, the central bank must play its role as lender of last resort to avoid widespread bankruptcies. One of its main objectives should be to avoid systemic financial crises. Tightening monetary policy and raising interest rates in order to attract capital inflows – or to stop capital outflows – has proved to be an extremely costly way of managing crises. Counter-cyclical monetary policy in developing countries is needed as much as it is in the developed world. This does not mean that monetary authorities should be indifferent to capital outflows and currency depreciation, but they should be flexible in both policy instruments and nominal targets by using ad-hoc policy instruments, including capital controls, for curbing capital outflows and by following a flexible exchange-rate policy.

The usual prudential regulations, if rigidly enforced, very often introduce a pro-cyclical bias into the monetary policy stance in emerging-

market economies. In a situation where banks lose deposits and face higher levels of non-performing loans and defaults, banks have to restore their asset/capital and liquidity ratios. However, in a crisis situation it is difficult for banks to raise new capital, and as a result lending typically contracts. "This naturally further weakens the economy, leading to more bankruptcies and lower net worth, and perhaps an even greater shortfall in capital adequacy" (Stiglitz, 1999: 320).

The more recent modifications of capital requirements introduced in the "Basle II" agreements (BIS, 2005) do not solve this problem. By fixing banks' capital requirements according to the risk of their assets, this prudential rule reinforces the pro-cyclical bias of bank credit: as the risk of default is negatively related to the economic cycle, the capital needed to meet the requirement will be low and the supply of credit high during expansions, while during recessions, with higher risks, the capital needed to meet the requirement will increase and the supply of credit will contract. A more proper precautionary rule should be to include a supplementary capital provision during expansions in order to constitute a reserve for use during recessions (Aglietta and Rebérioux, 2004: 265–269). Rules that are useful for managing the problems of individual banks in normal times may thus amplify those problems during times of crisis and contaminate the whole financial system. Hence, monetary authorities must avoid aggravating recessions and transforming individual problems into a systemic crisis.

2. The exchange rate

The exchange rate is the most important single price for both international financial markets and international trade in goods and services, and it has a strong impact on the domestic price level in small open economies. The exchange rate must be flexible enough to avoid persistent misalignments that would harm the competitiveness of domestic producers and overall trade performance. But at the same time, excessive volatility of the exchange rate must be avoided, as this discourages long-term investment, heightens domestic inflation and encourages financial speculation. Hence, an optimal exchange-rate system must allow different and to some extent conflicting demands to be managed. The choice of an exchange-rate regime reflects not only the policy priorities of a government or a central bank, but also the assumptions about the way in which financial and product markets function.

The exchange rate plays a central role in orientating investment and in determining an economy's balance of payments. As a result of international financial integration, changes in cross-border capital flows, which have reached a considerable magnitude and are often unrelated to investment or international trade in goods and services, increasingly influence the level and variability of exchange rates. Massive inflows of capital exert pressure for revaluation of the local currency. In some cases such exchange-rate appreciation has been welcomed as a means of curbing inflation, and the exchange rate has been used as a nominal anchor for inflation expectations. Sometimes currency appreciation has also been interpreted as an indication of the confidence that participants in the international financial markets have in the respective currency. On the negative side, however, revaluation of the real exchange rate, i.e. currency appreciation overshooting cost and price level differentials, has frequently impacted negatively on competitiveness and growth prospects (Bresser-Pereira, 2004: 16). Exchange-rate misalignment had a particularly negative impact on the outcome of trade liberalization, as local producers were massively handicapped by an overvalued currency (*TDR 2004*).

The "bipolar" view of the options for choosing an exchange-rate regime discussed in the previous section implied that international financial markets would always smoothly adjust exchange rates to their "equilibrium" level. In reality, however, exchange rates under a floating regime have proved to be highly unstable, leading to long waves of under- or over-valuation with dire consequences for the real economic activity of the economies involved. Moreover, sharp changes in the exchange rate of countries holding a significant external debt tend to generate debt servicing difficulties, liquidity and solvency problems (*TDR 2001*: 114). Due to the specific functioning of financial markets, floating exchange rates produce a most unstable external price level and the price signals for the "real" economy are a substantial source of uncertainty even if hedging for short-run purposes could be further developed. As a result, exchange-rate volatility tends to reduce growth and developing countries are correct in their "fear of floating" (Obstfeld and Rogoff, 1998; Aghion et al., 2006).

On the other hand, "hard pegs" were also based on an unrealistic view of economic adjustment in both product and financial markets. As the exchange rate could not be corrected in case of shocks or clear misalignment, the full weight of adjustment fell on the real sector of the domestic economy: exchange-rate rigidity had to be fully compensated by stronger adjustments in all other markets, mainly via movements in prices and wages. An overvalued exchange rate, for instance, calls for a general deflation in domestic prices and nominal wages. The most consequent forms of a fixed exchange-rate system are a currency board arrangement or full dollarization of the economy. The entry of foreign banks into the domestic banking system was mostly welcomed in this context, since foreign banks were supposed to obtain, in case of a lack of domestic liquidity, foreign financing from their parent company, which would play the role of a lender of last resort, otherwise non-existent under currency board or dollarization.

Experience has shown that fixed exchange-rate systems often end up sacrificing not only growth and employment stability, but also interest rate stability and the stability of the banking system more generally in order to obtain exchange-rate and price stability (ECLAC, 1999: 24). The

> The exchange-rate regime should provide room for manoeuvre in the presence of instability in international financial markets and allow governments to target a real exchange rate that is in line with their development strategy.

exchange rate, rather than serving as a policy instrument, becomes the central goal of macroeconomic policy, which then also requires fundamental structural changes. The collapse of the
currency board in Argentina in 2001 has considerably reduced the attractiveness of this strategy
and has given rise to a reconsideration of the exchange rate as an instrument variable.

Against the background of experience with
both rigidly fixed and freely floating exchange
rates, "intermediate" regimes have become the
preferred option in most developing countries.
According to a recent IMF report, "[t]he persistent popularity of intermediate regimes ... suggests
that such regimes may provide important advantages
... that ... are able to capture some of the benefits of
both extremes while avoiding many of the costs"
(Rogoff et al., 2004: 14). Indeed, developing countries require an exchange-rate regime that provides
sufficient room for manoeuvre in the presence of
instability in international financial markets, and
allows them to target a real exchange rate in line
with their development strategy. None of the "corner solutions" offer these possibilities. There is
an "impossible trinity": combining a *completely*
open capital account with *full* autonomy in monetary policy and *absolute* exchange-rate stability
is indeed impossible. But, given the shortcomings
of free floating, developing countries are faced with
an "impossible duality" (Flassbeck, 2001): with
open capital markets, neither fixed nor flexible
exchange rates give developing countries the *de
facto* autonomy to conduct monetary policy with
an exclusive orientation toward domestic needs.
Thus, aiming at a second-best combination appears
to be a feasible approach in practice: "It is possible to engage in *selective* capital controls and a
managed-intervention exchange rate regime which
reclaims *some* monetary policy autonomy. *These
moves away from the corners create more policy
space*" (Bradford, 2005: 5; emphasis in original).

In a world where developing countries focus
on creating favourable monetary conditions for the
domestic economy rather than on attracting foreign savings, the exchange rate should be com-
patible with a sustainable balance of payments,
i.e. it should allow domestic producers to achieve
and maintain international competitiveness so
that a surplus in the trade balance can be achieved
that is high enough to meet obligations resulting

from debt service and profit remittances.[5] Such
a policy could be labelled the "development strategy approach" to exchange-rate management
(Williamson, 2003).[6]

Countries trying to maintain the real effective exchange rate within an adequate range will
have to intervene frequently in the foreign exchange market even when capital controls are
applied. Such intervention may lead to an accumulation of international reserves and the need
for sterilizing the effect of this accumulation on
domestic monetary aggregates. In the case of massive and prolonged sterilization, the accumulation
of public domestic debt resulting from that sterilization could impinge upon a government's ability
to react flexibly to future crises and could involve
substantive fiscal cost if there were a significant
interest rate differential between the central bank
assets and liabilities (Harberger, 1989; Rodrik,
2006).[7] There may also be good reasons to accumulate reserves for "precautionary" purposes, for
example as a buffer against the impact of external
shocks that today are more likely to result from
the capital account than from the trade account of
the balance of payments.[8]

3. Confidence game or counter-cyclical policies?

In an economic policy approach that focuses
on foreign saving as a vital complement to national saving, attracting foreign capital becomes
a major policy goal. This is why many countries
have set up specific policies to attract foreign capital, including favourable tax conditions for FDI
and portfolio investment, and have played "the
confidence game" by taking macroeconomic
policy measures "that may not make sense in and
of themselves but that policymakers believe will
appeal to the prejudices of investors" (Krugman,
1998). In Latin America, for example, policies
were seen as "credible" only if the international
financial markets believed in their consistency and
adequacy (Bresser-Pereira, 2001) and responded
with increased lending and lower country-risk
premia. Typically, policies aimed at gaining confidence among financial market participants were
trying to provide profitability and predictability

in this area through market-established interest rates, low inflation and stable exchange rates. Strong domestic growth and the soundness of the development strategy were not necessarily part of that strategy. Confidence-building of this kind also determined the policy response in situations of financial and macroeconomic crises, so that policies frequently became pro-cyclical in the midst of economic depression.

Specifically, one of the central elements in IMF-supported programmes designed to cope with a crisis has been fiscal tightening. The Independent Evaluation Office of the IMF found recently that fiscal stances may have been unnecessarily contractive (IMF-IEO, 2003). It was found that adjustment programmes were overoptimistic in their estimates of growth, investment rates and fiscal balance, and that they were overly pessimistic concerning current-account adjustment and reserve accumulation, especially in the "capital-account crisis cases".[9] Consequently, the targeted external adjustment could have been reached with a much smaller dose of domestic demand restriction. Fiscal balances also fell short of expectations: instead of a planned improvement from 3.3 to 1.8 per cent of GDP, fiscal deficits actually increased to 4.3 per cent of GDP the first year and 3.7 per cent the second year. Thus, measures aimed at reducing fiscal deficits did not only end up with a much higher-than-expected contraction in GDP and investment, but also with higher fiscal deficits.

Seeking the reasons of such miscalculations in gauging the results of the programmes, the IEO did not find a clear rationale supporting pro-cyclical fiscal tightening.[10] Apparently, IMF-supported programmes considered that even in the midst of a crisis lower public expenditure would rapidly crowd-in private investment: "Programs typically assume rapid recovery, and therefore push for greater fiscal adjustment to make room for private investment, whereas a more realistic recognition of the negative impact of crises on in-

> Policies primarily aimed at gaining the confidence of foreign investors frequently tend to introduce strong pro-cyclical biases.

> Restoring confidence in an economy that is going deeper into recession is an almost impossible task.

vestor expectations would call for a more relaxed stance." (IMF-IEO, 2003: 47). Generally speaking, the rationale for the pro-cyclical responses during economic crises was to maintain or recover the confidence of financial markets, since the resumption of capital inflows was considered indispensable for stabilizing financial markets, exiting the crisis and resuming growth (Bradford, 2005).

As a supplementary way of building confidence, some countries have tried to enhance the credibility of their macroeconomic orientations by establishing legal restrictions to their policy management. This has been the case, in particular, with fiscal policy: the commitment to fiscal discipline has been instituted in national laws fixing limits to fiscal expenditure and/or to fiscal imbalances, sometimes on a multi-annual basis. An extreme example of such commitments was the "Zero-deficit Act" in Argentina, in 2001, which was intended to ban any fiscal deficit and ensure the servicing of the public debt by automatically adjusting primary fiscal expenditure (excluding interest payments) to current fiscal income. However, if the fiscal rule is excessively rigid, it introduces a strong pro-cyclical bias into macroeconomic management. In effect, if an economic recession affects fiscal income, the "fiscal rule" would command cutting public expenditure, which might aggravate the economic recession. Since this further reduces fiscal earnings, such a strategy is self-defeating and obtains neither fiscal balance nor credibility.

Explicit commitments aimed at gaining credibility also involved, in several countries, monetary and exchange-rate policies. In currency boards the exchange rate is "irrevocably" pegged to a currency (usually the dollar or the euro) and the Central Bank is committed to "back" the entire monetary base with international reserves. This means that, in principle, monetary supply expands exclusively with the accumulation of international reserves and contracts if those reserves diminish. This strict monetary rule is supposed to guarantee the sustainability of the exchange rate peg and create confidence again.

However, such a passive monetary rule may put the banking system in a dangerous position and unleash speculative attacks instead of preventing them. It is always possible to expand the monetary base as international reserves accumulate while maintaining an unchanged nominal exchange rate. On the other hand, it is impossible to keep selling international reserves beyond the moment they dry out. Most observers expected that a currency board regime would never reach this point since "all the money" is backed by Central Bank reserves. This, however, is only true for the monetary base but is false for wider monetary aggregates, which include time deposits. If domestic investors wish to change their bank deposits into dollars in a critical situation, the loss of deposits would cause a brutal credit deflation, along with further interest rate increases, and would aggravate the economic crisis. Sooner or later, then, the monetary rule must be abandoned and with it the fixing of the exchange rate.

In general, institutional regulations seeking to build credibility by showing the policymakers' strong commitment to sticking to the announced goals and policies will be unsustainable if these rules introduce a pro-cyclical bias, amplifying growth phases with fiscal and monetary expansions, and aggravating recessions with fiscal expenditure cuts, high interest rates and credit restrictions. Restoring confidence in an economy that is going deeper into recession is an almost impossible task (Stiglitz, 1999: 323).

On the fiscal side, in particular, stabilizing mechanisms should be enhanced or restored. Automatic stabilizers can play an increasingly important role in developing countries. They limit the reduction of demand and output growth in times of recession, when tax revenues normally decrease and social expenditure increases, provided that such changes are not accompanied by offsetting measures such as expenditure cuts in response to lower tax income. Strengthening the stabilizing role of public finances would require a flexible definition of budgetary targets, using expenditure instead of deficit targets (Martner, 2000). Such targets would allow for wider defi-

cits during recessions, and smaller deficits, or surpluses, during expansions. However, this rule should not be applied too rigidly either. Its proper application requires a distinction between cyclical elements of a possible deficit, elements which are transitory and should be permitted; and structural ones, which would not disappear during an upswing and should be avoided. Moreover, it may not be appropriate to save all the extra revenues that occur during upswings. Depending on the state of development and the specific situation of an economy, using such revenues for the acceleration of public investment projects can be critical to enhance supply capacities and, thus, long-term growth perspectives. In other situations, by contrast, the "automatic" element in the fiscal stance may have to be complemented with discretionary measures, especially in countries where institutions do not provide strong automatic fiscal stabiliszers.

Reinforcing automatic stabilizers should be a long-term institutional objective, even if it is difficult to implement at early stages of development and in economies with a large informal sector. Another institutional instrument for improving the working of counter-cyclical policies is fiscal stabilization funds, which have been established in several countries.[11] They would accumulate public sector revenues resulting, for example, from temporary commodity booms and release them for sustaining expenditure during slowdowns or in times of depressed prices.

4. Capital controls

Macroeconomic policies in countries closely integrated into international markets have to cope with several risks at the same time: that of the misalignment of macroeconomic prices – particularly that of the exchange rate and interest rates; the orientation of a substantial share of capital inflows and domestic credit towards financing consumption and non-tradable production; economic instability arising from the volatility of capital movements and credit-led cycles; and the creation of a debt overhang that may durably hamper both investment and growth.

Globalization has increased the need for pro-active macroeconomic policies in support of growth, but it has also introduced constraints to implementing them. Some of these are *de facto* constraints on monetary and exchange-rate policies in an environment of free capital movements, the "impossible duality" referred to above. Given these constraints, it may be necessary to protect the domestic economy against the impact of the instability of international financial markets on capital accumulation and growth by applying controls on capital inflows or outflows, actions that are within the formal "rules of the game" since they are allowed by the IMF Articles of Agreement.[12]

In a recent survey of 30 empirical studies on the effects of capital controls, four main reasons for their introduction have been identified. First, avoiding exchange-rate appreciation that would reduce competitiveness; second, avoiding an accumulation of "hot money" ready to leave the country at the first perceived sign of difficulties; third, avoiding too-large inflows that might generate asset price bubbles and over-consumption as well as dislocations in the financial system; and, fourth, avoiding the loss of monetary autonomy (Magud and Reinhart, 2006).[13] It is frequently argued that capital controls cannot be effective because they can be easily bypassed. However, Epstein et al. (2004) dismiss four frequent criticisms against capital controls, based on the positive experiences made with such controls, under different circumstances, in Chile, Colombia, Malaysia and Singapore. These experiences do not confirm the belief that the costs of controls in terms of distortions of factor allocation would outweigh the benefits of greater capital account stability. Moreover, the experience of Singapore refutes the argument that capital controls only work in the "short run", while that of Chile contradicts the notion that such controls have to be increasingly restrictive. Finally, the experiences of Malaysia and the Republic of Korea during the Asian financial crisis have shown that capital controls can be effective not only when applied to capital inflows, but also when they are applied temporarily to outflows.

Capital controls can take many different forms. Controls of the administrative type using prohibition, quotas or selective permission, depending on the use of capital, were practiced in many developed countries until the 1980s. Administrative measures can also take the form of minimum-stay requirements or, as in Colombia, outright prohibition of inflows for specific purposes such as investment in real estate. In developing countries over the last two decades, capital controls have frequently been of the market-based type, using disincentives in the form of taxation or specific reserve requirements.

The better known and most widely accepted form of capital control is the one that was introduced first by Chile and Colombia and more recently by the Russian Federation and Argentina, where a mandatory reserve requirement was imposed on some or all capital inflows. Under this system a significant proportion of the inflow has to be held in a non-interest-bearing deposit at the central bank so that short-term capital movements become less profitable. Thus, surges of capital inflows and the financial fragility resulting therefrom could be tempered, and "policy space" for fiscal and monetary policy was gained.[14] The imposition of temporary restrictions on capital outflows played an important role in stabilizing the exchange rate in Malaysia in 1998, and in Argentina after the 2002 devaluation.

There is a consensus that the Chilean type of capital control did manage to alter the composition of capital inflows in favour of FDI and at the expense of speculative capital movements (Le Fort and Lehmann, 2000). An alternative form was used

> Globalization has increased the need for pro-active macroeconomic policies in support of growth, but it has also introduced constraints to implementing them.

> Capital controls have in many cases alleviated pressure on exchange rates, making monetary policy more independent, and altered the composition of capital flows towards the longer-term variety.

by Argentina during the second half of the 1990s, imposing high non-interest-bearing liquidity requirements on domestic financial institutions receiving foreign capital, which discouraged at least those inflows passing through the banking system.

In sum, while capital controls are certainly not a panacea, they have in many cases succeeded in alleviating pressure on exchange rates, making monetary policy more independent, and reducing the instability of capital flows by altering the composition of these flows towards the longer-term variety. This, in turn, also helped reduce the pressure on exchange rates. Even if intervention to control capital inflows or outflows may to some extent be circumvented, these controls have served as dams to capital flows, avoiding massive flooding and helping to channel capital flows into more productive uses (Stiglitz, 1999: 327).

D. Towards a new assignment of policies

Overcoming the old interventionist developmental state with a revival of markets and market forces, as put forward in the Washington Consensus, has proved to be inappropriate in light of the challenges for developing countries and the imperfections of the global market system. Today, governments in developing countries have to make a distinct choice regarding the economic model on which to build their development strategy.

The history of economic ideas offers two main approaches in the context of a market economy. One centres around the apparent dependence of developing countries on the inflow of foreign savings to support their own limited means to invest and catch up. The other stresses the need to have the right macroeconomic policies and the right institutions in place to create savings in a process of dynamic development. These approaches tend to be mutually exclusive (see annex 2 to chapter I).

The perception that uncompromising stabilization of the price level is the most important condition for satisfactory growth performance dominated for a long time the debate on the sustainable assignment of macroeconomic policy instruments in both developed and developing countries. Under the heading of "sound macroeconomic policies", the orthodox monetarist approach that called for measures to avoid inflationary acceleration in the course of cycles and in the wake of shocks, with monetary policy playing the role of a guardrail for any combination of fiscal and structural policy, was widely accepted. The role of fiscal policy in this assignment was limited to assisting monetary policy by keeping budget deficits low and by minimizing government intervention.

In the most successful cases of economic catch-up price stabilization has also been a key target. However, this target was pursued not only with monetary policy tools but also with heterodox, non-monetary instruments such as incomes policy or direct intervention into the goods and labour markets (Flassbeck et al., 2005). Monetary and fiscal policy was at the service of fast growth and high investment. The preferred instruments were low interest rates and, at least since the Asian financial crisis, a slightly undervalued exchange rate. Fiscal policy was used pragmatically to stimulate demand whenever this was required in light of cyclical developments. Budget outcomes were not considered to be a direct policy target by themselves but were accepted as the result of an investment-led growth process.

The point of departure of such policies is that investment does not depend on savings that exist at the outset. Therefore, economic policy has to focus on raising investment and income, which will ultimately create the savings required for achieving macroeconomic equilibrium. This approach requires a monetary policy that breaks the orthodox rules, as it provides financing possibilities to enterprises that do not yet exist. As already observed by Schumpeter, it is potentially inflationary but does not actually lead to inflation to the extent that the newly created liquidity finances pioneering companies, real investment and output growth rather than consumption at a given level of income (Schumpeter, 1911).

There is thus a narrow link between catching up and structural change over time, on the one hand, and a country's monetary system on the other. Rapid economic development, initiated and pushed forward by pioneering firms in product markets, is only possible if monetary policy finances this process of capital accumulation in advance. Or as Friedrich von Hayek, one of the leading anti-Keynesian economists put it:

> By creating additional credits in response to an increased demand, and thus opening up new possibilities of improving and extending production, the banks ensure that impulses towards expansion of the productive apparatus shall not be so immediately and insuperably balked by a rise of interest rates as they would be if progress were limited by the slow increase in the flow of savings (Hayek, 1933: 177).

This perspective confirms the critical importance of price stabilization: in countries that are prone to high inflation it is much more difficult to start and sustain a process of development and catching up because of the frequent need to tighten the creation of money and credit. Without a sufficient number of policy instruments that can be

used effectively, the attempt to finance development through this creation is likely to fail as inflation rapidly flares up.

Conversely, in countries cultivating a highly disciplined attitude towards price stability by means of heterodox instruments such as incomes policy or the formation of a national consensus on reasonable wage claims, monetary policy can serve to make that kind of financing possible. The crucial task is then to reach social consensus to avoid struggles over income distribution, which become inflationary insofar as unit labour costs overshoot the inflation target. Such a consensus raises the likelihood of rapid economic development and the creation of savings through profits, even if the amount of household savings is negligible. Increasing profits, on the other hand, are made tolerable and sustainable when they are re-invested in large part and when it is ensured that all groups in society receive an adequate share in the rising national income. Monetary policy would step in only under exceptional circumstances, for example when the consensus is threatened during long periods of full or over-employment.

External financing remains necessary to the extent that increasing imports of capital goods as a result of higher investment lead to current-account deficits. But the successful cases of economic catching up, most recently seen in China, have shown that such deficits are not inevitable and that domestic sources of financing investment, including reinvested profits and credit creation in the Schumpeterian sense, can go a long way towards raising growth rates without calling on foreign savings. The decisive factor for catching-up is domestic accumulation of capital as the result of investment, consumption and the creation of rising real income for all groups in the society. If savings are understood to be the result of growth and not its precondition, opening up to the inflow of foreign capital is not always a necessary condition for successful catching-up. However, developing countries need to be able to determine long-term monetary conditions that are conducive to growth and investment. Premature capital ac-

> **Economic policy has to focus on raising investment and income, which will ultimately create the savings required for achieving macroeconomic equilibrium.**

count liberalization can be an important hindrance to the successful implementation of the profit-investment nexus and to catching up.

However, in low-income developing countries, the domestic financial system often does not allow for an effective transmission of central bank impulses through the banking system to the financing of investment, so that financing through reinvestment of profits or specially-designed development banks has to play the key role. Moreover, most of these countries also depend, either to a large extent or entirely, on imports of capital goods to carry out real productive investment and achieve productivity growth, and these imports have to be financed. As it is precisely these countries that have least access to private financial flows, except for some exporters of hydrocarbons and mining products, they should not play the "confidence game" in order to seek external financing mainly from private capital markets. Rather, the international community should step in with sufficient official financing to fill the gap. The largest possible independence from international capital markets allows central banks to use their instruments for actively pursuing development targets, provided that an acceleration of inflation is checked by non-monetary measures. This is all the more important since these countries, distinct from those that have already acquired a certain manufacturing supply capacity, are also having limited scope to use exchange-rate management as a tool of their development strategy as most of their exports have a relatively low elasticity with respect to price and exchange-rate changes.

In the absence of effective multilateral arrangements for exchange-rate management, macroeconomic policy in many developing countries in the past few years has been geared increasingly toward avoiding currency overvaluation. This has not only been a means for maintaining or improving international competitiveness, but also a necessary condition for low interest rates and an insurance against the risk of future financial crises. By contrast, a regime of current-account deficits has proved to be very costly in the past, as it has frequently resulted in financial crises. Interest rate hikes, huge losses of real income and rising debt burdens have been common features of all recent financial crises.

A case in point is the policies pursued in China after the financial crisis the country experienced in 1994 (Flassbeck et al., 2005). The absolute and unilateral fixing of the renmimbi against the dollar for more than ten years was possible because China, notwithstanding large inflows of FDI, did not become dependent on net capital inflows. China was able to fix its exchange rate and at the same time keep its interest rates extremely low despite very high growth rates. It pursued an extremely accommodating monetary policy over the long term, holding interest rates low and intervening massively in the foreign exchange market to keep the exchange rate at a competitive or even undervalued level (fig 4.2).

Many other developing countries were most of the time faced with the uneasy choice between low interest rates fuelling inflation and intervening in a costly way in the currency market to keep the exchange rate stable. Intervention, combined with relatively high domestic interest rates, means paying international speculators with tax-payers' money or ending up with real currency appreciation and a loss of competitiveness.

China, and before it other newly industrialized economies in Asia, found ways of avoiding an acceleration of inflation with non-monetary instruments and institutional arrangements, consisting of an array of different measures ranging from incomes policy to many other kinds of direct government inter-

> If savings are understood to be the result of growth and not its precondition, opening up to the inflow of foreign capital is not always a necessary condition for successful catching-up.

> The various examples of non-monetary measures to curb inflation illustrate that there is no "one-size-fits-all" rule regarding such measures.

vention into the process that determines prices and, even more importantly, nominal wages. Reacting to an inflationary acceleration in 1994 the Chinese Government, for example, extended its influence on the wage finding process by discontinuing backward looking indexation of wages to inflation and by coupling nominal wage increases much closer to productivity growth. Additionally, price controls and direct intervention into the price setting for crucial prices like electricity, coal and transportation services have been applied.[15]

Along the same lines, Argentina after the recovery following its dramatic currency crisis, rejected recommendations to increase interest rates and to allow for an appreciation of its currency when in the course of its strong recovery the inflation rate rose from 6 per cent in 2004 to 12 per cent in 2005. Instead, the authorities continued to target the exchange rate and the interest rate and sought to control inflation by a variety of instruments like temporary price moderation agreements with associations of producers and wholesale as well as retail distributors. They also intervened into wage negotiations, promoting rather moderate real wage increases. Moreover, the Government restricted meat exports for 180 days to curb the significant domestic price increase of these products, which are of great importance for the consumer price index. Despite the fact that all these measures were applied on a temporary basis, they have succeeded in moderating price expectations and have made it likely to reach the official inflation target between 8 and 11 per cent in 2006.

There are other examples in economic history of such an approach: Japan and Germany in the 1950s and 1960s also successfully combined an expansionary monetary policy stance with undervaluation and heterodox stabilization policies, mainly based on political pressure to keep nominal wage increases in line with productivity growth and the inflation target. The various examples of non-monetary measures to curb inflation illustrate that there is no "one-size-fits-all" rule regarding such measures. The selection of such heterodox measures very much depends on institutional arrangements on the labour and goods markets. For example, the degree of centralization of the wage bargaining mechanism and, closely related, the mobility of the labour force, is decisive for the

Figure 4.2

MONETARY CONDITIONS AND GDP GROWTH IN CHINA, 1980–2005

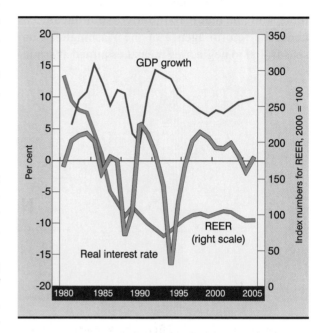

Source: UNCTAD secretariat estimates, based on IMF, *International Financial Statistics* Database.
Note: Interest rates refer to deposit interest rates. REER stands for real effective exchange rate.

effectiveness of government intervention in the labour market. The producer structure of the market for utilities, on the other hand, may be crucial to decide whether intervention in this area may help to achieve the overall inflation target.

The policy mix applied by the Asian NIEs has been complemented by some forms of capital account regulation. While such regulation may help contain and also prevent crises to some extent, the prime objective must be to avoid situations where such regulation becomes necessary, i.e. preventing the emergence of large interest rate differentials, arbitrage possibilities and incentives for speculation in the first place. Low domestic inflation, combined with low domestic interest rates, greatly facilitates the management of short-term capital flows with or without capital controls in place. However, since speculation on currency appreciation, with its concomitant destabilizing inflows of hot money, can never be fully avoided, the hands-on approach towards capital account management as it has been practiced in the Asian NIEs can be helpful. It is also important for developing countries to use the instruments they have at their disposal for short-term macroeconomic management. Overemphasis on structural problems and on macroeconomic "soundness", as under the reform agenda of the Washington Consensus, led to neglecting measures aimed at stimulating business activity and investment in the short run. The example of the successful emerging-market economies, including China with its largely incomplete structural reform agenda, also shows that effective macroeconomic management can compensate for many shortcomings in the functioning of markets as well as make up for structural weaknesses.   ∎

Notes

1   This chapter benefited from a background paper prepared by Arturo O'Connell (2006).

2   Patrick (1966) distinguished between financial development as a result of economic growth ("demand-following") and expansion of financial intermediation leading to economic growth ("supply-leading"), while the protagonists of the anti-financial repression literature, McKinnon and Shaw, focused exclusively on the latter.

3   At the conceptual level, one of the main academic supporters of financial liberalization, McKinnon, later acknowledged the weak effect of higher interest rates on savings (McKinnon, 1991).

4   Aizenman defines a self-financing coefficient as the ratio between gross national savings and gross investment, and finds a direct and econometrically well-established relation between a higher self-financing ratio and higher rate of growth. Latin American countries, with lower self-financing coefficients than the Asian NIEs, also registered lower rates of growth.

5   The accumulation of reserves for preserving a competitive exchange rate is what some authors call the "mercantilist view" on foreign exchange accumulation (Aizenmann and Lee, 2005).

6   There is, of course, a "fallacy of composition" if all countries were pursuing such exchange-rate targets, i.e., there are only n-1 degrees of freedom to set the exchange rates of the n currencies in the world (see also *TDR 2004* and chapter I of this *Report*).

7   This strategy can be sustained more easily the lower the interest rate on the sterilization bond. In China, which has massively accumulated foreign exchange reserves over the past few years, that rate is presently even lower than the interest earned from dollar assets.

8   It has been recommended that a level of reserves equivalent to at least the external debt maturing in the coming 12 months should be maintained in order for a central bank to be able to prevent financial crises (Bussière and Mulder, 1999; and Hviding et al., 2004).

9   The cases of capital-account crisis considered in this study are Argentina, 1995 and 2000; Brazil, 1998; Indonesia, 1997; Mexico, 1995; the Philippines, 1997; the Republic of Korea, 1997; Thailand, 1997; Turkey, 1994 and 1999. In these countries, GDP contracted (on average) by 5 per cent during the first year of the programme instead of growing by 1.6 per cent as had been envisaged; the investment rate was three percentage points lower than projected; but the current account shifted in just one year from a deficit of 3.4 per cent of GDP in the year before the programme to a surplus of 2.4 per cent, almost five percentage points of GDP more than scheduled in the programmes (which targeted, on average, a deficit of 2.4 per cent of GDP).

10 "Surprisingly, the rationale for the proposed fiscal adjustment is not very clear when we look at the 15 individual programs studied in this evaluation. An in-depth examination of staff reports and other Executive Board papers related to these programs often do not explain adequately how the magnitude and pace of the programmed fiscal adjustment have

been determined. Nor do most of the documents explain how the fiscal targets relate to the rest of the program, in particular to assumptions about recovery in private sector demand and short-term growth prospects" (IMF-IEO, 2003: 4).

11 In the Russian Federation and Norway the accumulation of financial resources from hydrocarbons in public funds greatly exceeds what may be needed for smoothing public expenditure, and actually constitutes a strategic asset for obtaining financial revenues to be used in the long term. In other cases, extra revenues from exports have been earmarked for the early repayment of public debts (Ecuador), financing development projects or constituting a fund for "future generations" (Chad). In all these cases, containing public expenditure in times of bonanza is intended to stabilize economic growth in the medium term and to avoid the appearance of fiscal deficits in the future, as it may be difficult to reduce fiscal expenditure when windfall revenues disappear. However, these rules may not be tenable if remaining government income is insufficient for coping with more urgent needs, as appeared to be the case in Chad and Ecuador.

12 Art. VI (Capital Transfers) Section 3 (Controls of Capital Transfers) states "Members may exercise such controls as are necessary to regulate international capital movements ...".

13 For a comprehensive survey of capital controls, see also Neely, 1999.

14 An alternative proposal, put forward in Chile when capital inflows started gaining momentum in the early 1990s, was to compensate for the ensuing increase in private demand by reducing government expenditure. The introduction of the "encaje" allowed the government to sustain, and even increase slightly, social expenditures while avoiding an excessive increase in domestic demand, thus gaining autonomy in fiscal policy.

15 For more details on non-monetary measures to curb inflation, see Flassbeck et al., 2005.

References

Aghion P, Bacchetta P, Rancière T and Rogoff K (2006). Exchange Rate Volatility and Productivity Growth: The Role of Financial Development. NBER Working Paper no. 12117. Cambridge, MA, National Bureau of Economic Research.

Aglietta M and Rebérioux A (2004). *Dérives du Capitalisme Financier*. Paris, Albin Michel.

Aizenman J (2005). Financial Liberalisations in Latin America in the 1990s: A Reassessment. *World Economy*, 28 (7): 959–984.

Aizenman J and Lee J (2005). International Reserves: Precautionary versus Mercantilist Views, Theory and Evidence. Mimeo.

Bernanke BS (2003). A Perspective on Inflation Targeting, *Business Economics*, 38 (3): 7–15, July.

BIS (2005). *International Convergence of Capital Measurement and Capital Standards, A Revised Framework*. Basel Committee on Banking Supervision. Basel, Bank of International Settlements, November.

Bradford Jr CI (2005). Prioritizing economic growth: Enhancing macroeconomic policy choice. G-24 Discussion Paper 37, New York and Geneva, UNCTAD, April.

Bresser-Pereira LC (2001). Incompetência e Confidence Building Por Trás de 20 Anos de Quase Estagnacao da América Latina. *Revista de Economia Política*, 21 (1): 141–166, January–March.

Bresser-Pereira LC (2004). The Growth cum Foreign Savings Strategy and the Brazilian Economy since the Early 1990s. Paper presented to the panel *Alternative Development Strategies for Latin America* at UNCTAD XI Conference, Sao Paulo, June 12–18. Available at: www.bresserpereira.org.br.

Bussière M and Mulder C (1999). External Vulnerability in Emerging Market Economies: How High Liquidity Can Offset Weak Fundamentals and the Effect of Contagion, IMF Working Paper WP/99/98. Washington, DC, July.

Diaz-Alejandro C. (1985). Good-bye Financial Repression, Hello Financial Crash. *Journal of Development Economics* 19: 1–24.

ECLAC (1999). *Proyecciones Latinoamericanas 1999–2000. División de Estadística y Proyecciones Económicas*, LC/R.1946, 1 December.

Epstein G, Grabel I and Jomo KS (2004). Capital Management Techniques in Developing Countries: an assessment of experiences from the 1990s and lessons for the future. G-24 Discussion Paper 27, New York and Geneva, UNCTAD, May.

Fischer S (2001). *Exchange Rate Regimes: Is the Bipolar View Correct?* Lecture at the meetings of the American Economic Association, New Orleans, 6 January.

Flassbeck H (2001). The Exchange Rate: Economic Policy Tool or Market Price? G-24 Discussion Paper 157, New York and Geneva, UNCTAD, November.

Flassbeck H, Dullien S and Geiger M (2005). China's spectacular growth since the mid-1990s: Macroeconomic conditions and economic policy challenges. In: UNCTAD, *China in a Globalizing World*. Forthcoming. Geneva, United Nations Conference on Trade and Development.

Frenkel R (2006). El esquema de 'inflation targeting' y las economías en desarrollo. Presentation to the *Jornadas Monetarias y Bancarias del Banco Central de la República Argentina*, June. Available at: www.bcra.gov.ar.

Harberger A (1989). Welfare Consequences of Capital Inflows. In: Findlay R et al. eds., *Debt, Stabilization and Development: Essays in Memory of Carlos Diaz-Alejandro*. Blackwell, Oxford.

Hayek FA (1933). *Monetary Theory and the Trade Cycle*. London.

Hviding K, Nowak M and Ricci LA (2004). Can Higher Reserves Help Reduce Exchange Rate Volatility? IMF Working Paper, WP/04/189. Washington, DC, October

ILPES (Instituto Latinoamericano y del Caribe de Planificación Económica y Social) (1998). *Reflexiones sobre el desarrollo y la responsabilidad del Estado*. Santiago de Chile.

IMF-IEO (2003). *Fiscal Adjustment in IMF-Supported Programs (Evaluation Report)*. International Monetary Fund - Independent Evaluation Office. Washington, DC.

Krugman P (1998). The confidence game. How Washington worsened Asia's crash, *The New Republic*. October.

Le Fort G and Lehmann S (2000). El Encaje, los Flujos de Capitales y el Gasto: Una Evaluación Empírica. Banco Central de Chile, Documentos de Trabajo, 64. Santiago de Chile.

Magud N and Reinhart C (2006). Capital Controls: An evaluation, NBER Working Paper 11973. Cambridge, MA, National Bureau of Economic Research.

Martner R (2000). Estrategias de política económica en un mundo incierto. Cuadernos del ILPES, 45. Santiago de Chile.

McKinnon R (1973). *Money and Capital in Economic Development*. Brookings Institution, Washington, DC.

McKinnon R (1991). *The Order of Economic Liberalisation: Financial Control in the Transition to a Market Economy*. Baltimore, John Hopkins University Press.

Mussa M, Masson P, Swoboda A, Jadresic E, Mauro P and Berg A (2000). Exchange Rate Regimes in an Increasingly Integrated World Economy. IMF Occasional paper, 193. Washington, DC.

Neely CJ (1999). An Introduction to Capital Controls. *Federal Reserve Bank of St. Luis Review*, 81 (6): 13–30.

Obstfeld M and K Rogoff (1998). Risk and Exchange Rates, NBER Working Paper no. 6694. Cambridge, MA, National Bureau of Economic Research.

O'Connell A (2006). Macroeconomic Policy in Developing Countries within the Current International Financial Architecture. Mimeo. Background paper prepared for UNCTAD's *Trade and Development Report 2006*.

Patrick H (1966). Financial Development and Economic Growth in Developing Countries, *Economic Development and Cultural Change,* 14 (2).

Rodrik D (2006). The Social Cost of Foreign Exchange Reserves. Presented to the American Economic Association meetings in Boston, MA. January.

Rogoff KS, Husain AM, Mody A, Brooks R and Oomes N (2004). Evolution and Performance of Exchange Rate Regimes, IMF Occasional Paper, 229. Washington, DC.

Schumpeter JA (1911). The Theory of Economic Development: An Inquiry into Profits, Capital, Credit, Interest, and the Business Cycle. Cambridge, MA, Harvard University Press (English Translation 1934).

Shaw E (1973). *Financial Deepening in Economic Development*. New York, Oxford University Press.

Stiglitz JE (1994). The role of the State in Financial Markets. Proceedings of the World Bank Annual Conference on Development Economics 1993, March.

Stiglitz JE (1999). Lessons from East Asia. *Journal of Policy Modelling* 21 (3): 311–330.

Summers LH (1999). Priorities for a 21st century global financial system: remarks at Yale University. New Haven, CT, 22 September. Available at: www. ustreas.gov/press/releases.

UNCTAD (various issues). *Trade and Development Report*. United Nations publication, New York and Geneva.

Williamson J (2003). *Exchange Rate Policy and Development*. Initiative for Policy Dialogue. Barcelona, June.

Williamson J and Mahar M (1998). A Survey of Financial Liberalisation. *Essays in International Finance* (211). International Finance Section, Department of Economics, Princeton University, Princeton, NJ.

World Bank (1993). *The East Asian Miracle, Economic Growth and Public Policy*. Oxford University Press, New York.

Chapter V

NATIONAL POLICIES IN SUPPORT OF PRODUCTIVE DYNAMISM

A. Introduction

The widening gap in relative income levels between rich and poor countries has been a major trend in the world economy over the past 250 years. On one estimate, the difference in per capita income between the richest and the poorest country in the world was about 5:1 before the Industrial Revolution; today this difference has increased to 400:1 (Landes, 1998). While the exactitude of these numbers is debatable, there can be little doubt that the world economy has been on a long-term path of substantial and growing divergence in relative productivity levels and living standards, both between developed and developing countries and among developing countries themselves.

The slow per capita income growth in developing countries has left millions of people in poverty. Nevertheless, recently the growth performance of many developing countries has improved, especially since the beginning of the current commodity price boom in 2002. Rapid growth in a few highly populated developing countries, especially China and India, has helped lift a substantial number of people out of poverty, in these countries themselves as well as in other developing countries that have benefited from spillovers of fast growth in Asia. But improved growth performance in the developing world will need to be more broad-based and sustained over a long period of time if there is to be more substantial progress towards achieving the Millennium Development Goals (MDGs) and eradicating poverty.

Around the long-term trend towards divergence in relative productivity and per capita income levels, a number of initially backward countries have succeeded, at different times, in catching up to the productivity and income levels prevailing in the frontier countries. It is well known that the current global technology leader – the United States – was itself once on a catch-up path with respect to the then economically and technologically leading country, the United Kingdom. Australia, Canada, New Zealand, some Latin American and many Western European and Scandinavian countries began catching up about 50 years prior to the First World War. Japan is a prominent example of catch-up during the decades before and after the Second World War, as are the East Asian newly industrializing economies (NIEs) since the 1960s (*TDR 1997*, Part Two, chap. II), and China and India more recently (*TDR 2005*). Fast growth in these Asian developing countries, particularly in China, has even succeeded in pulling along some of the lagging economies in Latin America and Africa.

Explaining this diversity in the pattern of development and determining what government policy can do to help achieve economic catch-up is among the oldest and most controversial issues in economics. There is no clear-cut policy prescription for success, but investment, technology adoption and structural change have traditionally been considered among the main critical factors for sustained economic catch-up. Giving support to earlier findings (Levine and Renelt, 1992), recent empirical analyses underline the importance of investment in physical capital as a "very strongly" robust growth determinant (Sala-i-Martin, Doppelhofer and Miller, 2004; Tsangarides, 2005). But for sustainability of economic growth, it is important that output expansion be based not merely on capital accumulation, but also on a continuous rise in labour productivity and the maintenance of productive dynamism over time, as is obtained through the acquisition of technological mastery over a broad range of activities, especially in manufacturing. The development of a strong manufacturing sector has been at the core of all successful catch-up experiences over the past 250 years, which suggests that achieving a lasting productivity-based increase in manufacturing is indispensable for a sustained rise in income levels and, ultimately, the eradication of poverty.[1]

Industrialization strategies have varied widely across developing countries over the past 50 years. Especially during the 1960s and 1970s, much of Latin America, Africa and parts of South Asia employed import-substituting industrialization strategies oriented towards the domestic market and based on a plethora of protective measures and other government interventions. Many of these countries subsequently abandoned those strategies for a variety of reasons, including their failure to promote development and because of the policy conditionality of multilateral lending institutions. Consequently, they began to view unfettered market forces and deep integration into the world economy as the most promising means to economic development during the 1980s and 1990s. There is some dispute as to the merits of the import-substituting industrialization strategy as a paradigm (Bruton, 1998), while the outcome of the liberalization strategy is generally judged disappointing (*TDR 2003*; World Bank, 2005). In any case, the annual rate of real economic growth averaged about 2.0–2.5 per cent in Africa and Latin America during the 1980s and 1990s, which is only about half that of these countries' growth performance during the 1960s and 1970s.

By contrast, the East Asian NIEs recorded an average annual rate of real economic growth of almost 9 per cent during the 1960s and 1970s and more than 7 per cent during the 1980s and 1990s. Their successful economic catch-up and industrialization, in particular until the mid-1990s, have been associated with outward-oriented industrialization strategies and strategic integration into the world economy. Proactive trade and industrial policies[2] played a key role in the pace and direction of structural change and economic growth particularly in the Republic of Korea and Taiwan Province of China (*TDR 1996*). Similarly, the recent star performers among developing countries in terms of economic growth, particularly China, India and Viet Nam, have not followed orthodox policy prescriptions of relying on unfettered market forces, broad-based liberalization and deep integration into the world economy.

Given that economic policies relying on unfettered market forces have failed to deliver the expected development results over the past two decades, many developing countries that had closely followed the prescriptions of the Washington Consensus have begun to reconsider the use of proactive trade and industrial policies in their development strategies. Arguing that "it is fair to say that nobody really believes in the Washington Consensus anymore" (Rodrik, 2006: 2) appears to be an exaggeration. Nonetheless, the reasoning put forward by Rodrik (2004), along with the establishment of a task force on Industrial Policies and Development within the Initia-

> Exclusive concentration on allocative efficiency implies that too little attention is paid to stimulating the dynamic forces of markets.

tive for Policy Dialogue directed by Nobel laureate Joseph Stiglitz at Columbia University, and the publication of a recent study by the World Bank (2005: xiii) whose "central message ... is that there is no unique universal set of rules ... [and that we] need to get away from formulae and the search for elusive 'best practices'", have given new vigour to the industrial policy debate.

In spite of the revitalization of the debate, much controversy remains in development policy discourse concerning the rationale for proactive trade and industrial policies and the feasibility for developing-country governments to adopt them. Some have questioned the efficacy of such policies, tending to associate them with failed inward-looking, import-substituting strategies, a comprehensive range of open-ended interventions and a strong bias towards protectionism (Krueger, 1990). Others have argued that sectoral policies conferred only modest benefits in the economic catch-up experiences in East Asia after the Second World War and that, due to the associated high risk of protracted rent-seeking and other potentially adverse effects, developing countries "should be exceptionally cautious before embarking on such policies" (Pack, 2000: 64). By contrast, most of the recent development literature argues that industrial policies were indeed an important supportive factor for East Asia's economic catch-up. For example, according to the World Bank (2005: 83) "the role of activist industrial policies is still controversial but is likely to have been important."

The rationale for proactive trade and industrial policies has been questioned also because of their possible adverse effects on efficient resource allocation (Bora, Lloyd and Pangestu, 2000; Pack and Saggi, 2006). But a major theme in historical analyses of economic catch-up in mature and late industrializers (Amsden, 2001; Chang, 2002; Rodrik, 2006) is that exclusive concentration on allocative efficiency implies that too little atten-

> Many believe that the new international trading rules reduce the degree of freedom available to developing country policymakers ...

> ... causing them to relinquish policies that favour industrial development.

tion is paid to stimulating the dynamic forces of markets that underlie structural change and economic growth. As widely argued in the recent literature (Akyüz, 2005; Chang, 2005; Gomory and Baumol, 2000; Hausmann and Rodrik, 2003; Rodrik, 2004; Singh, 2005; Stiglitz, 2005; World Bank, 2005), industrialization and economic catch-up are not generally the result of a natural process simply based on an efficient allocation of resources. As recently stated by Rodrik (2006: 5), "market or government failures that affect accumulation or productivity changes are much more costly, and hence are more deserving of policy attention, than distortions that simply affect static resource allocation." A recent study by the World Bank (2005: 10) also argues that "growth entails more than the efficient use of resources". This is particularly true for developing countries where economic growth entails dynamic changes in the structure and technology-content of production.

From this perspective, successful industrialization and economic catch-up need to be interpreted as a process of cumulative causation. Supportive national economic policies advocated by this interpretation focus on strengthening the dynamic forces of markets related to information externalities in the context of innovative investment, coordination externalities associated with complementarities in investment, production and consumption, and dynamic economies of scale resulting from cumulative production experience. Strategic integration into the world economy helps to maximize the benefits of these externalities at the level of the national economy. But all of these externalities are intimately linked to departures from the competitive equilibrium ideal of conventional economic theory; if unsupported by proactive national economic policies, such externalities cause a suboptimal provision in the volume and industry composition of investment.

Another aspect of the argument that questions the wisdom of adopting proactive trade and industrial policies as an integral element of development strategies relates to the feasibility for developing-country governments to implement such policies. There is indeed a widespread belief that the new international trading rules and regulations, which have emerged following both the conclusion of the Uruguay Round of multilateral trade negotiations and the rising number of regional and bilateral trade arrangements, reduce the degree of freedom available to developing-country policymakers to the point that they are required to relinquish policies that favour domestic industrial development and associated trade-related strategies (see, for example, Das, 2003; Gallagher, 2005; Chang, 2006).[3]

This raises the following questions: What are the principles on which developing-country policymakers should base their formulation of in-dustrialization and technological upgrading strategies? Which principles would they need to heed in formulating the set of policy instruments appropriate to the specific conditions of their economies? And what degree of freedom remains for policy implementation, given the increased importance of international rules and commitments stemming from international trade agreements? Sections B and C address these questions. Section D discusses the main features of industrial development and technological upgrading in developing countries over the past decade with a view to examining whether and to what extent commitments from international trade agreements have required developing countries to abandon the use of policy instruments on which they had previously relied, what kinds of policies they have adopted instead, and with what effect on industrial development. The final section draws conclusions on options for policy innovation at the national and international level.

B. Stimulating the dynamic forces of markets

1. Maintaining productive dynamism

Countries at the earliest stages of economic development can increase per capita income and living standards simply by capital accumulation that allows a fuller use of underutilized labour and natural resources. This is the case in particular for countries seeking to diversify away from the production of primary commodities. But sustained economic success to enable countries to go beyond these early stages depends on continuous improvements in productivity. The basic policy questions facing these developing countries are how to maintain productive dynamism and technological upgrading as the key to successful eco-nomic development and structural change, and how best to promote trade and investment to that end. From this perspective, when formulating economic policies related to industrialization and structural change, developing-country policymakers need to take into account the interrelationship between income growth, productivity gains and changes in production structure in an open economy.

Four arguments[4] in favour of a proactive national economic policy designed to support productive dynamism and technological upgrading have received the most attention:[5] (i) the presence of dynamic scale economies that gives rise to increasing returns of scale at the firm level; (ii) complementarities in investment, production and consumption that, if unchecked, result in coordination failures; (iii) information externalities associated with investment in goods or modes of production that are new for the respective economy; and (iv) strategic trade integration, which describes the open-economy pattern of public support policies that is motivated by the above three arguments. This form of integration represents a mix of import substitution through temporary protection and export promotion using temporary subsidies, and embeds industrial policy in a wider, outward-oriented industrialization strategy.

(a) Strengthening the creative functions of markets

Dynamic scale economies are important in that substantial productivity growth can result from an increase in investment. This is because investment in physical capital includes the components of technological change that are embedded in machinery and equipment and investment in human capital allows for the efficient use of increasingly sophisticated technologies. Moreover, learning by doing, resulting from cumulative experience with a production process, facilitates incremental improvements in product design and organizational practices that support productivity growth. These productivity gains in turn, combined with productivity growth resulting from other factors – for example, increased specialization of production within firms and the introduction of more specialized capital equipment – drive the profitability of a firm's activities and its further investment.

> Substantial productivity growth can result from an increase in investment.

Demand is an important incentive for investment by entrepreneurs. Only when they expect to have a large enough market for their new activities to be profitable will they engage in new investment. Developing countries with a large population and some minimum level of domestic purchasing power may be able to generate domestically a substantial part of the demand needed to support industrialization.[6] But most developing countries will need to generate exports as a vent for output, because a small economy is hardly able to maintain the circular causal links between productivity growth and large-scale output and investment simply by trying to meet domestic demand. It is thus the interaction of supply and demand factors in the investment process that translates productivity growth into further investment and maintains productive dynamism and technological upgrading.

Changes in the production structure influence the intensity of the interrelationship between income and productivity growth. Traditionally, the belief has been that industrialization, particularly the development of manufacturing activities, offers the greatest scope for productivity growth. This is because manufacturing provides a large potential for the division of labour as well as virtually unlimited scope for technological change. Moreover, the income and price elasticity of demand of most manufactures exceeds that for other products.

Turning to the second argument in favour of industrial policies, the presence of complementarities in investment, production and consumption is also generally considered to be greater in manufacturing than in other sectors because manufacturing activities give rise to more and stronger forward and backward linkages. For example, investment and profits of one manufacturing firm depend not only on its own output and factor inputs, but also on the output and factor inputs of other manufacturing firms that provide intermediate production inputs or use the firm's output as production inputs in their own production.

This type of interdependence among different individual firms, which increases the profits of both of them, has been referred to as "pecuniary external economies" in the economic literature. When investment creates pecuniary external economies, its economy-wide impact exceeds its private profitability. Hence, profitable investment can fail to develop unless investment in upstream and downstream activities occurs at the same time.[7] In this sense, a key problem of entrepreneurs, acting as independent agents and only in their self-interest, is how to coordinate investment so as to exploit external economies. As noted by Scitovsky (1954: 150), market prices are not capable of providing a signalling device to transmit information about present investment plans and future production conditions when there are reciprocal pecuniary external economies.

The above two arguments in favour of industrial policy have generally been interpreted as providing a rationale for temporary protection. By contrast, the third argument supporting the adoption of industrial policy stresses that protection of the manufacturing sector per se does not provide an incentive for an entrepreneur to undertake innovative investment and create new production capacity at an internationally competitive level of productivity.[8] Following Meade (1955) and Baldwin (1969), Rodrik (2004) argues that large uncertainties related to the profitability of investment associated with the manufacture of products or the adoption of modes of production which are new for the respective economy, as well as to the speed of entry of imitative entrepreneurs, give rise to information failures.

This information problem results from the fact that each potential investor that creates production facilities for new products or introduces new modes of production faces fixed start-up costs. But the investor usually does not know the cost function of these new activities, and therefore whether they will be profitable and whether the sunk costs can be recovered, because the production costs of modern, non-traditional activities can be determined only after the initial investment has been made.[9] In addition, an entrepreneur who discovers the best way to produce a particular product incurs the risk of potential imitators entering the market too quickly to allow the realization of sufficient profits to cover the initial sunk cost.[10] Hence, imitative entry reduces the private return that the innovative investor can realize, but at the same time it increases its social return because of the spillovers

> A key problem of entrepreneurs is how to coordinate investment to exploit external economies.

> Large uncertainties related to the profitability of investment in new activities give rise to information failures.

from imitation that allow the newly discovered cost structure of the economy to be exploited by a wide range of entrepreneurs. Moreover, if the investment fails, the innovative entrepreneur will bear the full cost of the mistake. Thus, the potential innovative entrepreneur's initial lack of knowledge of the cost structure of new products or the use of new production processes causes an information failure. If unchecked, this information failure results in a suboptimal provision in the volume and industry composition of investment.

According to this argument, the main task of public support policies is to address the information externalities entailed in discovering the cost structure of an economy (Meade, 1955: 256–257; Baldwin, 1969; Rodrik, 2004). Acquiring knowledge of the underlying cost structure of an economy that determines the evolution of production patterns over time is a discovery process (Zeira, 1997; Hausmann and Rodrik, 2003). In this sense, industrial policy needs to be defined not in terms of an expected outcome (i.e. an altered sectoral structure of production), but in terms of a process – "one where firms and the government learn about underlying costs and opportunities and engage in strategic coordination ... with the aim of uncovering where the most significant obstacles to restructuring lie and what type of interventions are most likely to remove them" (Rodrik, 2004: 3).

This reasoning on the role of policy implies a shift in emphasis concerning policy instruments. In terms of supporting innovative investment, protection is a rather blunt instrument. But, as noted by Meade (1955) and Rodrik (2004), and succinctly stated by Baldwin (1969: 298), "[w]hat is needed, of course, is a subsidy to the initial entrants into the industry for discovering better production techniques".

From this perspective, economic development, technological upgrading and structural change amount to a cumulative process of emerging new and more dynamic economic sectors, with traditional activities being phased out or performed in more productive ways. This process goes through several stages, distinguished by the changing relative importance of economic sectors and activities. Empirical evidence shows that in the course of economic development the sectoral allocation of employment changes. In a study covering a wide cross-section of countries, Imbs and Wacziarg (2003) note that during the earlier stages of economic development countries diversify (i.e. they spread economic activity more equally across sectors), but relatively late in the development process, at around a per capita income of $9,000, they start specializing again. They suggest that an increase in a country's productivity level, relative to the rest of the world, drives the tendency towards diversification, while a decline in trading costs – stemming from a decline in transport costs or tariffs, or from an increase in agglomeration economies resulting from forward and backward linkages – leads to a shrinking range of goods produced domestically, thus fostering specialization (Imbs and Wacziarg, 2003: 82–83). They also emphasize that "increased sectoral specialization, although a significant development, applies only to high-income economies. Countries diversify over most of their development path" (Imbs and Wacziarg, 2003: 64). Thus economic development appears to be closely related to the acquisition of technological mastery over an increasing range of products.

Rodrik (2004) provides a powerful restatement of the need to address information problems related to the key importance of innovative investment for diversification and technological upgrading in developing countries. This restatement complements the other two arguments, mentioned earlier, that provide a rationale for industrial policy: the need to support dynamic economies of scale and overcome coordination failures.

A frequent argument made against industrial policy is that if there are industries with a potential comparative advantage, but domestic private investors fail to develop the necessary activities

because of insufficient financing possibilities, government policy should be directed at the full development of domestic financial markets, rather than providing industrial policy support. In other words, policy should address the financial market imperfections with a view to moving the economy towards fully developed factor markets and competitive equilibrium. However, this reasoning is valid only when investment is actually financed from sources external to the firm. It has been shown that much of the investment that drove successful industrialization in East Asia relied on profits as a source for investment (*TDR 1996*).

Moreover, the full development of domestic financial markets takes time. As a result, the above argument has led to the suggestion that the task of determining whether the prospects for the domestic infant industry are profitable be left to foreign investors whose decisions are based on production experience elsewhere. Some authors (e.g., Pack and Saggi, 2006) argue that the promotion of foreign direct investment (FDI) should play a key role in industrial development and national economic policies should be limited to the creation of locational advantages – such as the provision of appropriate physical infrastructure and assuring appropriate education and health services for the labour force – with a focus on the provision of incentives to attract FDI. This view considers FDI not only as eliminating information constraints regarding the profitability of innovative investment, but also as delivering a bundle of assets that includes additional capital investment, productivity-enhancing technology and best corporate norms and practices. Moreover, it is assumed that the knowledge initially transferred to an enterprise through FDI will spill over to other firms in the same industries.

Such optimism about the economic growth, technology transfer and productivity consequences of FDI has led many countries to adopt investment regimes that offer special financial incentives to foreign enterprises. However, empirical evidence points to considerable variation in the benefits that host countries actually reap from FDI

> In the cumulative process of technological upgrading and structural change the relative importance of economic sectors and activities changes.

inflows, and much depends on the establishment of an appropriate regulatory and fiscal framework.

Kumar (2005: 179–186) cites a number of recent empirical studies showing that knowledge spillovers may not take place, especially in developing countries, and domestic enterprises may actually be affected adversely. In some cases FDI may be immiserizing by crowding out domestic investment. Moreover, the interests of a transnational corporation (TNC) may diverge from the host country's developmental objectives, due to the TNC's strategy of pursuing global profit maximization. Thus its decisions to source production inputs locally or from international suppliers may not be taken on the basis of efficiency considerations alone. Also, TNC affiliates in developing countries tend to buy the bulk of their inputs from their parent companies or other associated suppliers, and hence generate few domestic linkages.

One explanation for this variation in FDI-related developmental benefits is that the effects of FDI on domestic investment and growth partly depend on the mode of entry (UNCTAD, 2000). For example, FDI in new plant equipment (i.e. "greenfield investment") adds to the existing capital stock and may indicate a longer-term commitment of the foreign investor to producing in the host country. However, in the poorer countries that are most in need of external financing of investment, much of the greenfield investment has occurred in fuel and mineral industries, thus making little contribution to the diversification and development of competitive manufacturing activities. In other cases, FDI has often taken the form of mergers and acquisitions, thus making no addition to the host country's productive assets.[11]

Apart from the nature of FDI inflows themselves, national policies also determine the extent to which FDI contributes to technology transfer and linkage creation. Restrictions on entry in the form of contractual obligations on technology transfer, ownership ceilings, the provision of incentives only for entry in specific targeted economic sectors, and performance requirements related to purchases of intermediate inputs from local suppliers can play an important role in increasing the developmental impact of FDI. These measures try to establish positive, complementary interactions between foreign and domestic investment so that they can have a favourable impact on the host country's productivity performance. To what extent such attempts are successful often depends on the leverage of host countries over foreign firms. It is clear that the larger a host country's domestic market and the more developed its industrial production structure, the better it will be able to offer auxiliary activities that foster the profitability of TNC activities. It will therefore be in a good position to demand concessions in terms of technology transfer and input sourcing from domestic suppliers in exchange for access to a large domestic market and a large domestic network of input suppliers.

> Developing-country policymakers need a pragmatic and strategic perspective on how FDI can fit into their wider development agenda.

National policies that aim to create locational advantages based on cost differentials, for example through favourable tax treatment or relatively low unit labour costs, rapidly risk becoming ineffective as a result of small cost changes or the emergence of alternative host countries. By contrast, support policies designed to create a dense network of intermediate input suppliers can be an important means to attract or retain TNC activities, develop domestic supply capacity and foster technological upgrading. Local availability of high-quality intermediate inputs at world market prices provides pecuniary externalities for TNC activities. The profit incentive for the TNC to produce in the host country will be higher, the more intensively it uses intermediate inputs, and the higher will be the savings stemming from lower imports and the associated lower trade costs of such production inputs. As explained in the literature related to new economic geography models (e.g. Puga and Venables, 1996, 1999), a similar mechanism applies when the host country provides a large market for the output of the TNC: TNC profits will increase because of the scale effects of additional demand.[12] Thus, support policies designed to provide a network of competitive input suppliers or output users can be a key factor in a host country's locational advantage.

Thus there is a need for investment policies to mobilize domestic resources as well as FDI. Such policies should be combined with an appropriate regulatory and fiscal framework to ensure that the expected development gains will be obtained. An excessive focus of national industrialization policies on attracting FDI would bias the national economic policies towards "external integration" at the expense of "internal integration", in the sense of a denser set of links between consumer, intermediate and capital goods industries (Wade, 2003a). This is the case, in particular, when a high import content of exports, including those associated with the activities of TNCs, misleadingly suggests successful industrialization and technological upgrading of domestic production, when, in reality, the domestic value added of these activities is small. Consequently, developing-country policymakers need a pragmatic and strategic perspective on how FDI can fit into their wider development agenda in ways that bring about structural and technological change.

(b) *Embedding investment promotion in a wider industrialization strategy*

The above arguments indicate that developing countries may be well advised to adopt – in the context of a private-sector-led, market-based economy – a broader industrial strategy, which combines temporary protection with public support that nurtures the innovative capabilities of domestic private enterprises and increases their rate of investment and technological upgrading. Indeed, the fourth argument in favour of proactive national economic policies relates to the pattern of support; it stresses the importance of combining industrial policy with a strategy that takes into account the relationship between trade and growth.

As mentioned earlier, one linkage between exports and growth is through market size. Exporting enlarges the market for domestic production, and thus offers scale economies at the firm level made possible by mass production techniques. It also provides a range of externalities at the industry level, including economies of specialization and agglomeration. Moreover, the nexus between the availability of foreign exchange earnings from expanded exports and the need for foreign exchange to finance imports of capital goods and intermediate inputs – required to build up industrial capacity and competitive strength – reduces technological constraints that would otherwise impede the development process.

> It is important to combine industrial policy with a strategy that takes into account the relationship between trade and growth.

But these linkages between trade and growth do not necessarily imply the rapid opening up of markets. While the experience of successfully industrializing economies points to the importance of strong export performance (*TDR 2003*), cross-country regressions attempting to establish a causal link between import liberalization and growth have failed to deliver robust findings (Rodriguez and Rodrik, 2000). This is partly due to processes of cumulative causation (i.e. the fact that the levels of past and present activities in a sector are a determinant of current patterns of comparative advantage). As argued by Burgess and Venables (2004: 118), in these instances, broad-based "liberalization actually impedes growth by inhibiting infant industries and local accumulation of knowledge."

The difficulty in establishing a robust empirical causal relationship between openness to trade and higher growth is also due to the fact that successfully integrating developing countries have adopted a wide variety of trade policy approaches. These range from partial liberalization through the establishment of export processing zones (as in China and Mauritius) and opening up different sectors at different speeds (as in India), or ambitious broad-based unilateral trade liberalization (as in Chile), to a combination of unilateral trade reforms and an aggressive pursuit of regional and bilateral trade deals (as in Mexico). Moreover, these different trade policies have been combined with various complementary policies. As a result, econometric studies encounter severe methodological problems related to measurement, reverse causation and omitted variable bias.

While recognizing that there may be several different means of trade integration that can successfully support economic growth, in most historical patterns of successful industrialization, industrial policy has been part of a wider strategy in which the structure of imports and exports progresses through a number of stages. During the earliest stages of economic development, production and exports consist largely of primary commodities, while imports comprise mainly manufactures. Subsequent stages of industrialization generally involve, first, increased production (and reduced imports) of manufactured producer goods, accompanied by increased imports of machinery and equipment. This is followed by a stage of net exports of consumer goods and a reduction in imports of capital goods. Finally, a stage of mature industrialization is reached in which most capital goods are produced at home and basic consumer goods are imported (Kaldor, 1966; Akyüz, 2005). From this perspective, acquiring the ability to competitively produce goods that were previously imported is inherent in rapid economic change, and implementing some temporary protection does not imply adopting an "anti-trade" strategy, because import replacement needs to go hand in hand with policy-supported export development.

While this process follows a clear trajectory of progress towards the efficient production of more technology- and knowledge-intensive products, it does not converge to a predefined point. Rather, choice is involved across a whole range of industries and products in each stage of development, influenced by geography, size, relative factor endowments, the decision of entrepreneurs and policy. The trade policies used to animate this complex process can be characterized as "strategic trade integration" – a more measured approach to liberalization combined with proactive industrial policies and outward orientation (*TDR 1996*).

The precise policy mix will depend on the stage of industrial development and the particular requirements of different manufacturing industries. Thus the specific product category candidates for public support policies in a country will depend on many factors, and are likely to change during the course of economic development as their skill and technology content gradually increase. During the initial phase of industrial expansion that emphasizes resource-based and labour-intensive manufactures, price signals resulting from traditional comparative advantage and reflecting an economy's relative abundance of natural resource and low-skilled labour endowments can provide strong investment incentives for entrepreneurs. Since these sectors tend not to be very demanding in terms of technological mastery, the start-up costs of investment designed to discover their cost structure in the domestic economy are likely to be small. As a result, support measures can be of relatively small size, and can be phased out after a short period of learning and expansion in world markets.

> Public support policies have to shift to other product categories in the course of economic development as their skill and technology content gradually increase.

As these basic industrial sectors mature and become internationally competitive, they are likely, over time, to encounter difficulties in competing on international markets as domestic wages rise, low-cost competitors emerge, and sector-specific limits of learning and productivity growth approach. Hence, more dynamic and skill- and technology-intensive industries need to be promoted, and any existing protection and support to the traditional industries need to be phased out. Industries in the medium-technology-intensive range typically include electrical machinery, basic chemicals, automobiles, consumer electronics and semiconductors – sectors that, historically, have played a key role in successful late-industrializing countries. Further industrial upgrading will allow some industrializing economies to develop production and export activities in high-technology-intensive manufactures, such as aerospace industries and biotechnology.

In all successful industrialization experiences of the twentieth century the gradual process of technological upgrading has followed this general pattern. But it is clear that the sequential devel-

Figure 5.1

**STYLIZED REPRESENTATION OF SUPPORT POLICIES
FOR DIFFERENT CATEGORIES OF MANUFACTURES**

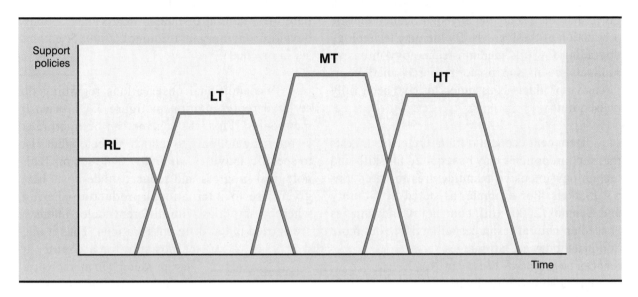

Source: Adapted from Akyüz, 2005: 22.
   Note: This is a stylized representation and should not be viewed as a precise mapping of relative levels of support measures
      required for specific product categories in individual countries. For the allocation of individual products to the four
      categories, see *TDR 2002*, annex to chapter III.
      RL: Resource-based and labour-intensive manufactures.
      LT: Low-technology-intensive manufactures.
      MT: Medium-technology-intensive manufactures.
      HT: High technology-intensive manufactures.

opment of individual industrial sectors will differ across countries, depending on initial conditions, such as geography, economic size and relative factor abundance, as well as on policy choices.

These considerations suggest a structure of support policies as described in a stylized manner in figure 5.1. In this schema, policy support for a specific product category is introduced once the technological barriers to entry are no longer out of reach for domestic manufacturers. It is withdrawn once domestic manufacturers have attained technological mastery, once the increase in domestic wages makes production no longer profitable at an internationally competitive level, and when benefits from economies of scale and learning by doing approach exhaustion. Thus the key feature of the stylized representation in figure 5.1 is that support policies follow a non-linear path; that is, any specific product category is a candidate for public support policies only for a limited period of time.

It is difficult to establish meaningful benchmarks for the size of support policies; these will depend on product-specific and, in particular, country-specific characteristics. Thus the exact positions and slopes of the lines in figure 5.1 should be seen merely as a schematic illustration of a general pattern. In this stylized representation, the relative strength of support policies for each product category depends on the incremental increase in skill and technology content as production moves from one product category to the next, and on a country's cumulative manufacturing experience. Previous manufacturing experience will have allowed a country to benefit from dynamic external economies (e.g. through the creation of technological capacities) and to establish a network of auxiliary manufacturing activities. As a result, it is likely that the level of support required to move from medium- to high-technology-intensive products will be lower than that required to move from traditional industries to medium-technology-intensive products. Moreover, during the earlier stages of industrialization, which concentrate on resource- and labour-intensive products, there would be no protection against imports of other manufactures[13] since they will be an important source for satisfying domestic demand, given that there is not yet any significant domestic production of these goods. By the time technology upgrading towards medium-technology-intensive products sets in, support for resource- and labour-intensive products is assumed to have been fully phased out.

The recent economic literature also suggests that support policies may be required for skill- and technology-intensive manufactures to enter global markets. For example, as stated by Gomory and Baumol (2000: xiii), comparative advantages "based on natural resources still exist ... but more dominant today are advantages that can be *acquired*. These can be advantages conferred by being established in an industry and gaining thereby either specialized knowledge or economies of scale or scope" (emphasis in original). Acquired, as opposed to natural, comparative advantage plays a key role in medium- and high-technology-intensive manufactures for which economies of scale or scope and high start-up costs are a key characteristic. To quote again Gomory and Baumol (2000: 6), "much of modern technology requires activities to be carried out on a very large scale in order to be economical and competitive. Consequently entry into one of these industries, against an entrenched competitor, is slow, expensive, and very much an uphill battle if left to free-market forces."

Thus, while the process of industrial upgrading and strategic trade integration implies outward orientation, it is not a process that is driven by unfettered market forces. Rather, beyond the earliest stages of industrialization, the provision of temporary support to promote increasingly higher skill- and technology-intensive industries helps the economy to progress through a series of overlapping industries, as well as to continuously increase productivity and acquire technological mastery over a wider range of products. Thus, policy choices are crucial to countries' trading patterns,

because international trade does not lead to one, uniquely determined, best economic outcome based on natural national advantages. On the contrary, "there are *many possible outcomes* that depend on what countries actually choose to do, what capabilities, natural or human-made, they actually develop" (Gomory and Baumol, 2000: 5, emphasis in original).

Two additional observations regarding the stylized representation in figure 5.1 are worth mentioning. First, the scheme can be interpreted as referring not only to industrial sectors but also to specific activities within the same sector. Technological progress and reduced trade costs have given rise to international production-sharing, whereby activities with different factor intensity are carried out at different locations. Thus it may be possible for a country to start producing in an industrial sector by carrying out labour-intensive functions and undertaking gradual technological upgrading, leading eventually to its being able to carry out the most technologically intensive activities in that particular sector. Second, one reason to combine temporary protection and temporary subsidies is that the maintenance of dynamic scale economies requires both successive innovative investments and learning processes. Temporary subsidies facilitate innovative investments, while temporary protection allows learning processes to unfold. But the potential for learning in each specific activity diminishes with growing experience in that activity, so that learning and innovative investment depend on each other: new innovative investment opens new possibilities for further learning, which in turn provides the basis for the productive use of a new round of innovative investments, and so on (Mayer, 1996).

The question often arises as to whether developing-country governments have the administrative and institutional capability to design and implement well-conceived support policies. For example, Pack and Saggi (2006: 28) point to the alleged severe information constraints of industrial policy: "The range and depth of knowledge that policy makers would have to master to im-

> Industrial upgrading implies outward orientation, but it is not a process driven by unfettered market forces.

plement a successful policy is extraordinary. They would have to understand the relevance of, and be accurately informed about, a huge range of complex questions and have the ability to accurately evaluate very subtle differences." However, the same governments are expected to carry out other complex tasks, such as implementing trade and financial liberalization and privatization. Indeed, many of them are supported in these efforts through capacity-building assistance, for example, for the implementation of WTO agreements.

These implementation-related arguments are based on the view that industrial policy tends to rely on excessively complex methods and targets for a wide range of industrial sectors at the same time. Indeed, import substitution strategies in some countries in Latin America and South Asia relied on a wide-ranging and often overlapping use of import quotas, exchange controls and domestic content rules in addition to industrial tariffs. This often made it difficult to determine how much support an administrative regulation actually provided, which government institution was ultimately responsible for that support, and who benefited, how much and from which measure.

However, as shown by Amsden (1989, 2001) and Wade (1990), compared to the broad-based support in much of Latin America during the 1960s and 1970s, the scope of sectoral support policies and programmes in the post-Second World War cases of successful economic catch-up was rather modest, yet, in aggregate, much more effective. Implementing these kinds of support policies does not require sophisticated calculations, and the associated information requirements do not go beyond those needed for routine decision-making by managers in TNCs, such as estimating demand elasticities and the technology requirements for internationally competitive domestic production of particular goods. Most importantly, a key objective of the institutional mechanisms that are intimately linked with

> The maintenance of dynamic scale economies requires both successive innovative investments and learning processes. ...

> ... Temporary subsidies facilitate innovative investments, while temporary protection allows learning processes to unfold.

these kinds of support policies is to promote information exchange between the private sector and the government with the aim of identifying the most serious obstacles to diversification and structural change, and determining the kinds of policies most likely to remove these obstacles.

Another argument against proactive trade and industrial policies, which also addresses implementation issues, is that it risks giving rise to rent-seeking; that is, State intervention creates additional "wastes" that may more than offset the benefits it produces, because private agents divert resources to unproductive activities in order to capture rents generated by government intervention. But as in the case of information constraints, institutional mechanisms exist that can substantially reduce the risk of rent-seeking.

Thus, while it is correct to say that successful sectoral support policies require a certain implementation capability on the part of governments, there are various institutional arrangements to address implementation issues, and, more generally, to generate, distribute and revoke economic rents and coordinate investment in a way that meets wider development goals. These institutional arrangements are discussed in chapter VI below. What is important at this point is to recognize that the acceleration of industrial development and technological catch-up is not just a question of policy reform; it also requires the strengthening of administrative capacity and institutions.

In sum, the adoption of proactive trade and industrial policies can be anchored firmly in economic theory if the recent revival of arguments supporting the creative functions of markets, which played a key role in the theoretical debate among early development economists (Meade, 1955; and the authors discussed in Toner, 1999, and Ros, 2000), and the more recent theoretical contributions regarding the creation of new areas of comparative advantages (Gomory and Baumol, 2000; Puga and Venables, 1996, 1999) are taken into account. From this perspective, proactive trade and industrial policies can enhance the information and coordination mechanisms of markets and help economies achieve technological mastery and international competitiveness in a range of increasingly technologically sophisticated products. The following section addresses key issues relating to how the rationale for proactive trade and industrial policies can be made operational and translated into concrete national economic policies.

2. Principles and types of policies for stimulating the dynamic forces of markets

The formulation of any prescription for development policy must recognize the large differences between developing countries and the need to respect their unique characteristics. Nevertheless, there are some common features that permit consideration of general policy principles for developing countries as a whole, while bearing in mind that such principles need to be translated into specific types of policies adjusted to the particular circumstances of individual countries.

For the implementation of proactive trade and industrial policies there is a range of choices regarding general principles and specific types of policies. General principles refer to the characteristics of economic policy, for example, the balance between private initiative and public policy support, or the extent to which policies apply horizontally across multiple sectors, or selectively at the sectoral or even subsectoral level.[14] Specific types of policies refer to specific measures that operationalize such general principles.

(a) General policy principles

One general principle concerns the balance between private initiatives and public policy support. Latin America's import-substitution strategy of the 1960s and 1970s has sometimes been char-

acterized as "State-led industrialization" as opposed to the so-called "market-led industrialization" strategy pursued in East Asia since the 1960s (World Bank, 1993). However, it has become generally accepted that this characterization is a misinterpretation of the historical facts (see, for example, World Bank, 2005). The main difference between the strategies pursued in these developing regions is that industrial policy has not been as concerted and coherent in Latin America as in East Asia. For example, Bruton (1998: 912) notes that industrial policies under import-substitution regimes often levied tariffs on an ad hoc basis, with the consequence that "a great hodgepodge of rates appeared, with virtually no evidence of any consideration of costs or efficiency." Moreover, the impact of specific trade and industrial policy measures cannot be expected to be proportional to their intensity. The intensity of intervention in Latin America was higher than in East Asia. However, whereas support policies in East Asia were strategically designed and implemented, in Latin America, governments often adopted unsystematic and overlapping measures, making it difficult to establish a clear link between policy measures and targets.

Modern support policies give the lead role to private enterprises, supporting their innovative investments as well as their efforts to get imported technologies to work well under local conditions. This support is complemented by trade policy support designed to achieve international competitiveness in increasingly more technologically sophisticated products.

A second general principle of proactive trade and industrial policies that aim at strengthening the creative forces of markets is that in order to foster diversification and technological upgrading subsidies should be given only to investment that is undertaken to discover the cost function of new goods or new modes of production in the respective economy.[15] This implies that such policies should not be employed as defence mechanisms to support industries where production and employment are threatened the most by foreign competitors that have successfully upgraded their production. For example, this general principle does not support selective trade protection or other selective support measures that many developed countries are still applying in agriculture or in labour-intensive manufacturing sectors such as the clothing industry.

Neither does this general principle support a large number of contemporary industrial policy measures which focus on attracting FDI and related export-oriented activities.[16] Rodrik (2004: 28) emphasizes the current importance of such measures, stating that "industrial policies [privileging exports and foreign investment] have run rampant during the last two decades." This widespread support is based on the expectation that FDI inflows will facilitate industrialization and development in host countries by enabling them to benefit from foreign investors' production technology, organizational and managerial skills, and marketing know-how, as well as by entering their marketing networks. Moreover, host countries expect to benefit from knowledge spillovers and other favourable externalities of FDI. However, as already mentioned, empirical studies have found very little systematic evidence of technological and other externalities obtained in this manner. Perhaps most importantly, FDI inflows and export promotion may reinforce host countries' existing comparative advantage based on the relative abundance of natural resources or cheap labour, ignoring the importance of productivity gains and structural transformation that is at the heart of the rationale for proactive trade and industrial policies.

A third general principle is that policy support should not be open-ended. Instead, it should be given only on the basis of clearly established operational and achievable goals, observable criteria for monitoring it and specific time horizons. Regarding the latter, a key question is how one can ensure that the policy support lasts long enough to motivate entrepreneurs to invest, but short enough to force investors to keep improving productivity. Historical experience shows that where supporting policies were of a blanket and virtually permanent character, they failed to curb inertia and rent-seeking. In East Asia, by contrast, attaining the policy objectives has been achieved by the establishment of strict performance criteria related to productivity, as verified through performance in international markets.[17]

The rapid growth of exports provides the key demand stimulus to ignite a cumulative process of high investment, high profits, high savings and high growth. Moreover, export performance provides a clear, neutral standard to evaluate the performance of firms receiving public policy support. Export data have the additional advantage that they cannot be faked, and that they provide a relatively clean measure of the relative competitiveness of domestic producers. The establishment of clearly defined and quantifiable performance criteria also makes it easier to identify failures and withdraw any associated support. Finally, by imposing performance standards on investors, the government subjects itself to evaluation by objective criteria. Indeed, the aim of performance requirements is not for the government to pick winners, but to know when there is a loser.

A fourth general principle is to base the determination of policy measures on an intense dialogue between ministries, industry associations and research institutions; that is, on a deliberation process, rather than on autonomous decisions of government entities. The aim of this process is to exchange information on the government's vision regarding structural change and development strategies, on the views of industry associations regarding business opportunities and investment constraints, and on research institutions' assessments of national and international technology developments. The leadership and decision-making power of the individuals who participate in the deliberation process play a fundamental role in its success. Participants from business associations need to be representative, with sufficient economic and political weight. As for government officials, Wade (2006) points out that the authority for carrying out support policies must

> The lead role of private enterprises needs to be complemented by policy support to achieve competitiveness in technologically increasingly sophisticated products.

> Policy support should not be open-ended.

vest in agencies with demonstrated competence, while the implementing agencies must be monitored closely by and be accountable to a principal with a clear stake in the outcomes and with political authority at the highest level, and they must maintain the capacity to reinvent and refashion themselves as economic conditions change. Institutional issues are addressed in more detail in chapter VI below.

In sum, modern public policies combine private initiatives with public support. This should be embedded in processes that rely on reciprocal control mechanisms and on information and coordination commitments from both sides. An important objective of such processes is knowledge generation. While these processes are inevitably characterized by trial and error, it is important to minimize the economic costs of mistakes. Yet, attempting to prevent any mistakes risks leading to no innovative investment at all.

The aim is not to pick winners, but to know when there is a loser.

(b) Specific types of policies

As already mentioned, how these general principles are translated into specific types of policies depends on a country's particular initial conditions and stage of economic development. Also, they should be the outcome of a deliberation process to determine which public support policies are likely to have the greatest impact. Nonetheless, a brief discussion of a number of possible types of policies may be useful for illustrative purposes.[18]

Fiscal incentives, direct public credit and subsidies are measures that lower the cost of innovative investment. They can thus reduce uncertainty among potential investors as to the profitability of innovative investment that can be easily emulated. Fiscal incentives may take the form of tax deductions and tax credits for particular types of innovative activities or the acquisition of national or imported, embodied or disembodied, technology related to innovation. Direct public credit may take the form of loans by development banks for innovative investment and the acquisi-

tion of technology, and be granted with preferential interest rates and favourable repayment schedules. Subsidies may be allocated to entrepreneurs by competition according to their projects' potential to bring about diversification and technological upgrading as well as knowledge spillovers or the creation of forward and backward linkages.

Venture capital organizations can play an important role in providing risk capital, since obtaining loan finance is particularly difficult for innovative investment, given that the profitability of the innovation and its potential market are not yet known. But in addition to uncertainties and asymmetric information regarding the profitability of a project and the potential opportunistic behaviour of entrepreneurs, venture capital organizations themselves often face financing constraints. The resulting desire for zero default may lead to underfunding. In these circumstances, development banks and other public actors that are motivated by social returns and externalities, rather than private profit, can play a crucial role. In particular, when domestic sources of investment finance are constrained, credits from development banks can also be an alternative to FDI for financing investment.

Undertaking research and development (R&D) activities in public research institutes constitutes a third specific type of public policy. A major problem, however, is that the resources devoted by the government to R&D may be substantial in fiscal terms, because of the proportion of the budget they absorb, yet insufficient to cover a broad science and technology infrastructure and to provide a meaningful level of subsidies for R&D. These budgetary constraints are exacerbated where the provision of funds is more horizontal and less targeted. One solution could be to deploy a scheme allowing for the partial recovery of public R&D outlays through royalty payments by the private users of public research output commensurate with their profits. Another possibility could be to introduce a system of allocating subsidies for R&D through competitions designed in conformity with the general innovation promotion strategy. Given the current income boom from natural-resource exports in many developing countries, a further possibility could be to earmark income from State companies, and royalties or tax income for R&D in research institutions designed to generate innovations either for product diversification, research into new technologies, or capacity building among suppliers.

Technology development can also be supported by the creation of science and technology parks that provide incentives (for example, in the form of tax breaks, subsidized credits, or permission to exceed normal debt-equity ratios) for the establishment of firms that identify, transfer, diffuse and absorb foreign industrial technologies and subsequently undertake innovation. Such incentives may be complemented by offering attractive salaries in order, for example, to encourage the return migration of skilled nationals. Developing-country governments could also consider paying or subsidizing royalty payments, and support the application of technology by negotiating on behalf of domestic firms that are able to apply the technology.

In addition to the use of these traditional instruments, the potential of strategic standard setting for technology development has recently gained attention. In the economics of technological change, formal standardization closely interacts with international property rights protection (UNIDO, 2005). The timing and scope of technical standard setting plays an important role in the diffusion of patents and the related new products and technologies. Thus it contributes to channelling collective efforts towards technological progress. On the other hand, standard setting can be a mode of selection for the use of product and process innovations that are protected by intellectual property rights and thus favour one set of innovative firms over another. Consequently, strategic setting of compatibility standards can be a means of stimulating domestic technology research efforts and the creation of non-proprietary technology. Successful pursuance of these goals can increase the ability to exercise leverage in negotiations with overseas patent holders and, as a long-term objective, help to develop domestic proprietary technology. These issues apply mostly to high-technology-related product markets, such as, recently, in the information and communications technology industries, which have seen a rapid succession of patented new technologies in an environment of multiple standards.[19]

The vast majority of developing-country markets are likely to be too small, with too little purchasing power to impose technology standards that favour the production of domestic firms. This is because foreign firms producing in conformity with existing internationally applied technology standards serve much larger user bases and can realize economies of scale and learning effects. Inappropriate standard setting by developing countries may therefore stifle technology transfer to their economies. However, standards are often shaped by market needs and users' preferences, rather than simply by technology requirements. If a developing country, or a group of developing countries, can provide a large enough user base with promising market potential, it may rival an existing technology that enjoys property rights protection. Given its large domestic market, its large pool of educated researchers and experienced returnees from overseas, and its substantial expenditure in high-tech research, China (either on its own or in concert with other Asian economies) appears to have acquired such a position (Ernst, 2004; Linden, 2004), but this is an unusual case among developing countries.

Governments need to have a clear vision for their economy's future technology development if they are to benefit from the support to technology upgrading and the development of proprietary knowledge that strategic standard setting can provide. Only when promising new technologies are identified at their very early stages can standardization influence basic research activities and subsequent pilot production. Moreover, standard setting should specify the performance of components, rather than their design, in order to avoid conflicts with patents protecting those components. Governments should also offer attractive licensing schemes to provide incentives for innovative, R&D-intensive companies to participate in standardization processes (UNIDO, 2005).

Specific policy measures related to strategic integration include selective liberalization through differentiated intervention, granting duty drawbacks and establishing temporary admission regimes for selected imports (e.g. capital equipment and intermediate inputs), and the creation of export processing zones that offer preferential tax and customs treatment. Such measures have been successfully employed for industrial development in a wide range of developing countries, and have often been complemented by selective treatment of FDI inflows through, for example, restrictions on FDI entry, ownership ceilings, barriers to hostile takeovers, or the imposition of performance requirements.

As already mentioned, the above discussion of specific policy measures is intended to illustrate some of the options available to developing-country policymakers; it is not intended to provide an exhaustive list. In addition, it is doubtful whether any of these policy instruments can be used successfully in isolation. Rather, policymakers will need to have a vision for the economic development of their country in order to tailor these instruments to local conditions and link them with other policies in support of development.

C. Restrictions imposed by international agreements on policy autonomy: an inventory

Unlike monetary and financial multilateral arrangements, discussed in chapter IV, the multilateral trading regime is organized around a set of negotiated, binding and enforceable rules and commitments. Negotiated under the aegis of the GATT/WTO, these rules provide the basis for regulating international trade. The core principles of this regime are reciprocity and non-discrimination, as reflected in the most-favoured nation (MFN) rule and the commitment to national treatment (i.e. equal treatment of domestic and foreign goods and enterprises in domestic markets). Leaving aside a number of general exceptions,[20] as well as exemptions that specifically apply to developing countries (see below), the multilateral trading regime is thus intended to provide what is often called a "level playing field", by extending the same legal rights and obligations to all member States of the WTO.

Since the mid-1980s, rapid and broad-based trade liberalization has been a central condition attached to loans from multilateral lending organizations, as well as to aid flows and debt relief from major developed-country donors. But the current wide scope of multilateral governance in the area of trade is associated with the Uruguay Round Agreements (URAs) and the establishment of the WTO in 1995. The Uruguay Round (UR) brought about industrial tariff reductions, negotiated on a request-and-offer basis, rather than through the use of a formula approach based on a percentage reduction in average tariffs, as well as through "zero-for-zero" reductions for some product groups, including under the Information Technology Agreement.[21] Moreover, the UR resulted in a new set of agreements on trade in goods – an extension of the General Agreement on Tariffs and Trade (GATT) which the WTO absorbed – as well as additional agreements on so-called "trade-related" activities. These include the Agreement on Trade-related Aspects of Intellectual Property Rights (TRIPS), the General Agreement on Trade in Services (GATS) and the Agreement on Trade-related Investment Measures (TRIMs), as well as the Agreement on Subsidies and Countervailing Measures (SCM). It also established a unified and binding dispute settlement mechanism. The Agreements were adopted as a so-called "single undertaking" – countries had to accept the package of

Agreements in its entirety. The resulting expansion of the scope of the multilateral trading regime means that key aspects of countries' regulatory regimes that affect how national economies operate have become subject to multilateral disciplines.

The multilateral trade regime has accorded exemptions to developing countries. In negotiations, they are allowed to grant less-than-full reciprocity under Article XXVIII bis of the GATT, adopted in 1958. Moreover, the so-called "enabling clause", adopted in 1979 and generally known as special and differential treatment (SDT), accords developing countries exemptions to the MFN rule, by allowing them to benefit from more favourable market access conditions. However, the UR brought a change in perspective on SDT. Prior to the Round, exemptions from the MFN rule and the principle of reciprocity were seen as a recognition by the international community that in order to provide some kind of parity between developed and developing countries, developed countries needed to give developing countries access to their markets without requiring them to open up their own markets on a reciprocal basis. These exemptions also gave developing countries some possibilities to pursue legally their own nationally determined development policies. Following the UR, SDT has basically come to mean that developing countries, and especially the least developed among them, are accorded longer transition periods for full implementation of all rules and commitments in the WTO.

Especially since the early 1990s, many developing countries have increasingly complemented multilateral trade negotiations in the WTO with regional or bilateral agreements, including with developed countries and regions, in particular the United States and the EU. Regional or bilateral agreements with large developed countries offer substantial benefits to developing-country members as they usu-

> The rules and commitments of the international trading regime restrict the *de jure* ability of developing nations to adopt national development policy.

> Rules and commitments, which in *legal* terms are equally binding for all countries, in *economic* terms might impose more binding constraints on developing countries.

ally provide greater market access than multilateral agreements, and often include a wider range of products than traditional trade preference schemes such as the Generalized System of Preferences (GSP). Moreover, their adoption is generally expected to lead to additional FDI. On the other hand, greater integration often involves additional steps towards regulatory disciplines, and thus further constrains the *de jure* ability of developing countries to adopt appropriate national regulatory and development policies, particularly with regard to FDI and intellectual property rights.

The constellation of these rules and commitments, as well as the associated exceptions and exemptions, constitute a complex legal structure that offers scope for different interpretations and practices. Against this background, this section concentrates on the often voiced concern that, since the rules and commitments of the international trading regime restrict the *de jure* ability of developing nations to adopt national development policy, they limit the possibilities for governments to deploy policies in support of further productive and technological development. More specifically, there is concern that these rules and commitments could deny the use of the very policy measures that were instrumental in the development of today's mature and late industrializers. To the extent that this is the case they thus reduce the flexibility of national governments to pursue their development objectives. Another concern is that these rules and commitments, which in *legal* terms are equally binding for all countries, in *economic* terms might impose more binding constraints on developing, compared to developed, countries because of the differences in their respective structural features and levels of industrial development. The discussion in this section concentrates on rules and commitments associated with the TRIMs, SCM and TRIPS Agreements and tariff regulations.

1. *The Agreement on Trade-related Investment Measures (TRIMs)*

One important area that the URAs have brought under multilateral jurisdiction involves a range of investment measures that have been used by many developing and some developed countries as part of broad strategies aimed at nurturing domestic industry and achieving technology transfer. The TRIMs Agreement is designed to clarify the relationship between a country's investment policy and the core rules of the multilateral trading regime by identifying measures considered incompatible with national treatment and forbidding the application of quantitative restrictions that link imports to export performance (e.g. trade or foreign exchange restrictions) or export restrictions based on domestic sales.[22]

The Agreement does not define "trade-related investment measures", nor does it provide objective criteria for identifying them. The appendix to the Agreement gives guidance to governments to decide which of their measures violate the Agreement by providing an "illustrative list" of prohibited regulations. Countries are required to notify the WTO of such measures and eliminate them following the termination of transition periods.[23]

The imposition of performance requirements on foreign investors is a key regulatory measure that has been affected by the TRIMs Agreement. Many governments, in developing and developed countries alike, have used performance requirements, which generally aim to increase the linkages between foreign investors and local manufacturers. One commonly employed performance requirement concerns local content regulations, which are intended to increase domestic value added, thereby generating additional national income and employment, as well as encouraging the transfer of technology. Other frequently used performance requirements relate to export performance or trade balancing, which require firms to match their use of imported inputs in their export products with an equal share of domestically

produced inputs in order to integrate the affiliates in the host countries into their global/regional production networks. Foreign exchange balancing rules, which require foreign investors to meet foreign exchange needs for imports through exports, rather than by converting local earnings into foreign exchange, have also often been used.

Chang (2002), for example, shows that today's developed countries extensively employed performance requirements to maximize domestic value added. A number of developed countries continued the use of performance requirements in the early post-Second World War period (WTO and UNCTAD, 2002). Local content requirements were also a widely used instrument that strengthened backward integration and increased domestic value added, in particular in the automobile industry.

> TRIMs have affected the imposition of performance requirements on foreign investors.

Developed countries have increasingly replaced explicit performance requirements with trade policy measures that achieve essentially the same objectives as performance requirements but are consistent with WTO rules (Kumar, 2005: 185). One example is screwdriver regulations (i.e. regulations governing imports by trading partners of parts and components), which have been used by the EU (Safarian, 2003).

While developed countries extensively employed performance requirements in one form or another at earlier stages of their industrial development, developing countries have only recently started to use these policy tools to foster their industrialization and technological upgrading. This is closely related to the increasing importance of international production networks, where developing-country exports often include a high import content of technology-intensive parts and components, while domestic value added mostly consists of wages paid for simple assembly activities. In this context, domestic content requirements have been used to increase technology transfer to developing-country producers and to foster the use of domestically produced parts and components. Empirical evidence on the effectiveness of such measures suggests that well-conceived performance requirements "that have clear objectives and are effectively enforced are not only able to meet their objectives, but may also bring significant favourable externalities to the host countries" (Kumar, 2005: 193). However, developed countries have brought a number of cases against developing countries before the WTO dispute settlement mechanism, especially in the automotive sector, invoking the rules and commitments of the TRIMs Agreement.[24]

The TRIMs Agreement does not restrict the provision of incentives to attract FDI, even though the economic effect of such incentives may be similar to the provision of subsidies, and even though such incentives may affect international investment and trade flows as much as domestic content requirements. This is the case, in particular, for activities in international production networks where TNCs are known to practice trade-restricting policies with respect to their foreign affiliates (Kumar, 2005: 194).

Regional and bilateral investment agreements can be considerably more restrictive than TRIMs because they address all measures regulating FDI, and not only those that are considered "trade related". Moreover, many such agreements allow firms, rather than just governments, to bring cases to arbitration. Thus they go much further towards regulatory harmonization. By contrast, developing countries' bilateral and regional trade agreements with developed countries play a peculiar role in the area of TRIMs, as they weaken rather than reinforce multilateral commitments. This is because, through the rules of origin, local content requirements have also, by definition, been included in preferential trade agreements between developing countries and large importing countries/regions, such as the United States and the EU. Given that developed-country parties to such trade agreements can tailor local content requirements to their needs, these measures have not been brought before the dispute settlement mechanism of the WTO. Di Caprio and Amsden (2004: 23) therefore argue that preferential trade agreements present developing-country WTO "members with an escape hatch from limitations on that particular aspect of TRIMs."

It also needs to be recognized that FDI-regulating measures that do not violate national treatment or impose quantitative restrictions con-tinue to be consistent with WTO rules. For example, governments can impose technology transfer requirements which specify that a foreign company conduct a certain proportion or type of its research and development activities locally and transfer or license a specified technology to domestic firms. Or a licence could be granted for the establishment of an assembly plant only if the foreign investor simultaneously establishes a plant that produces required intermediate inputs. Governments can also require that domestic investors retain a proportion of a firm's equity or that a specific percentage of their technology personnel be recruited domestically (Shadlen, 2005a: 759).[25] In reality, however, only countries with substantial leverage over foreign investors are able to use such measures.

2. The Agreement on Subsidies and Countervailing Measures (SCM)

The SCM represents another outcome of the UR that impinges directly on national rule-making authority. It addresses multilateral disciplines for regulating the provision of subsidies, as well as the use of countervailing measures to offset injury to an industry in the importing country caused by imports that are subsidized in the country of origin. The SCM covers mainly the industrial sector; special rules apply to agriculture, and the General Agreement on Trade in Services (GATS) has no rules on subsidies (although the current WTO-negotiations are addressing this issue).

The SCM defines a subsidy as a financial contribution made by a government or any public body within the territory of a WTO member that confers a benefit. Such benefits can result from direct payments, foregone revenues and rights, government guarantees and equity participation, the provision of goods and services below market value, or from differential application of certain rules to different sectors and activities, such as bank credits directed to specific sectors and activities with preferential conditions.

The Agreement represents a significant tightening of disciplines compared with the pre-UR regime, which did not include comprehensive rules and regulations on the use of subsidies, and allowed developing countries greater leeway to use subsidies for export promotion and import substitution. It broadens the scope of regulations relating to subsidies as it binds WTO members[26] (except for the poorest among them, as discussed below) and extends to measures of subnational governments, State-owned enterprises and private entities that carry out functions that would normally be vested in the government.

> The SCM Agreement affects the selective function of policy.

As the Agreement only applies to specific subsidies, that is, those targeted at an enterprise, industry, or group of enterprises or industries, it affects the selective function of policy. Non-specific subsidies are not affected because they are presumed not to distort the allocation of domestic resources; these include subsidies for the provision of physical and social infrastructure, or subsidies resulting from low energy taxes that benefit all enterprises, as well as subsidies earmarked for specific enterprises according to their size or similar criteria. The Agreement prohibits subsidies that are conditional on export performance or on the use of domestically produced goods (but countries with a per capita income below $1,000 are exempted from this prohibition) and makes specific subsidies "actionable", which means that they are subject to challenge through multilateral dispute settlement or countervailing action. While this distinction between specific and non-specific subsidies is straightforward in legal terms, in practice it is not always easy to differentiate (Anderson, 2002). This may leave some room for developing countries to design subsidies that help import-competing or exporting firms without contravening WTO disciplines.

> Subsidies impose a cost on public budgets, which developed countries can afford more easily than developing countries.

Article 8 of the original SCM provision defined certain specific subsides as non-actionable. Subsidies extended to research fell in this category, as did subsidies in the pursuit of regional or environmental objectives.[27] The permitted subsidies for R&D included the financing of venture capital funds and the provision to the private sector of technologies and innovations developed in government research laboratories. Also included in this category was public procurement policy in support of the proliferation of domestically defined standards for particular technologies. Moreover, in order to support a shift in economic activity to new products or the use of new technologies, activities could be subsidized as long as they were in the pre-competitive phase (i.e. before they resulted in the production of goods that were exported or subject to significant import competition).

It is, however, important to note that the provision that classified these subsidies as non-actionable came up for review in 2000, when no agreement over its extension could be reached. Thus these subsidies have now become actionable.

The Doha Declaration revisited this issue along with the proposal of some countries to allow certain subsidies for development. More specifically, it stated that the Ministerial Conference "takes note of the proposal to treat measures implemented by developing countries with a view to achieving legitimate development goals, such as regional growth, technology research and development funding, production diversification and development and implementation of environmentally sound methods of production as non-actionable subsidies, and agrees that this issue be addressed ... [as an outstanding implementation issue]. During the course of the negotiations, Members are urged to exercise due restraint with respect to challenging such measures" (WTO, 2001: 6). Meanwhile, however, the issue of Article 8 subsidies seems to have been eclipsed by negotiations on other issues.

According to Aguayo Ayala and Gallagher (2005), this call for restraint has been respected, and developed and developing countries alike continue to use such subsidies under a tacit agreement not to challenge them under the dispute settlement mechanism. To the extent that this is the case, the SCM agreement is a good illustration of how WTO rules and commitments that are equally binding, legally, impose more binding constraints on developing countries economically. Firstly, subsidies impose a cost on public budgets, which developed countries can afford more easily than developing countries. For example, Aguayo Ayala and Gallagher (2005: 19) estimate that in 2003 the EU-15 spent a total of about 50 billion euros on Article-8-type subsidies, mainly consisting of State aid and Structural Fund payments. This corresponds to about 25 per cent of developing countries' total annual gross domestic expenditure on R&D (UNESCO, 2005).

Secondly, Article-8-type subsidies are of concern primarily to developed countries in their quest to develop high-tech capabilities and technological innovations. They differ from subsidies conditional on export performance or on the use of domestically produced goods, which were frequently used by the late industrializers to foster industrialization and technological catch-up. Indeed, Article-8-type subsidies can be a key device for developed countries in their shift away from the provision of basic funding for scientific R&D towards a strategic approach that establishes and targets research priorities in frontier sectors such as information and communications technology, biotechnology and nanotechnology, alongside new challenges arising in more traditional sectors, such as health care, national defence and the environment. These are areas that many developed-country policymakers have come to consider as crucial for economic growth and national prosperity (see section D below).

Probably the most serious drawback of the SCM Agreement for development is that it prohibits making subsidies conditional on export performance. This has been an important instrument in East Asia's reciprocal control mechanisms, which have often been identified as key to the greater success of industrial policy in that region compared to Latin America (Evans, 1995). Thus the SCM Agreement withdraws a major monitoring standard that outward-oriented sectoral strategies in East Asia used successfully to ensure that support was given only to those enterprises that were able to compete in international markets. It

is possible to establish other performance standards under a reciprocal control mechanism (such as the percentage of technology personnel employed, the percentage of sales contributed by new products and the allocation of retained earnings). But none of these alternatives enable a performance-based incentive policy that ensures international competitiveness and minimizes the risk of abuse and rent-seeking.

These effective asymmetries cast some doubt on arguments, such as made by Amsden (1999), that the bark of WTO law is worse than its bite. According to this argument the SCM Agreement formally leaves open the possibility of supporting industrial upgrading, as developing countries maintain the ability to provide "boundless" subsidies for science and technology and the development of human capital. The main problem, the argument goes, is that developing countries have failed to take advantage of the major types of non-actionable subsidies. It is probably true that subsidies is an area where, in principle, the main challenge for many developing countries is to use the existing flexibilities of the multilateral regulations through innovative policy measures. However, in practice, budgetary constraints may prevent some developing countries from using subsidies as part of their industrial policies.

3. The Agreement on Trade-related Aspects of Intellectual Property Rights (TRIPS)

The TRIPS agreement establishes global mandatory minimum standards for the granting and protection of intellectual property rights in several areas, particularly copyrights and patents.[28] It also provides a dispute resolution and enforcement mechanism. Countries are free to decide how to implement these provisions in accordance with their own legal and institutional systems. Application of TRIPS in developing countries (except the LDCs[29]) has been mandatory since 2000. According to Article 7, protection and enforcement of these rights must contribute to the promotion of technological innovation and the transfer and diffusion of technological knowledge in order to improve social and economic welfare. They must also ensure a balance between the rights and obligations of the parties.

Many believe TRIPS to be the most controversial of URAs because of its potential to restrict access of developing countries to technology, knowledge and medicines. The importance of the Agreement for industrial development lies in the fact that the procurement of proprietary knowledge has been among the key determinants of both early and late industrialization. The history of intellectual property rights protection shows that countries with low levels of technological capacity have generally used weak standards until they reached a level of development at which their industries could benefit from intellectual property rights protection. Chang (2002) points out that many of the now developed countries did not adopt intellectual property rights legislation or strict intellectual property rights standards when they were in the process of economic catch-up.

Prior to their implementation of the TRIPS agreement, developing countries' patent regimes typically included instruments to restrict the private rights of (largely foreign) patent holders (Amsden, 2001). Such instruments aimed to create more opportunities for local firms to access foreign innovations, thereby encouraging learning and technological progress via imitation. This enabled these countries to move beyond a critical threshold level for domestic technological skills and promote national firms that were eventually able to engage in export activities. Knowledge procurement occurred in different ways, but reverse engineering from imported goods played an important role. This was facilitated by relatively weak enforcement of intellectual property protection, particularly of patents.

The TRIPS Agreement severely restricts reverse engineering and other forms of imitative innovation since it upholds the private rights of pat-

> TRIPS implies an asymmetry that favours the producers and holders of protected intellectual property, mainly in developed countries ...

> ... at the expense of those trying to gain access to protected intellectual content, mainly in developing countries.

ent holders. As a result, it tends to limit access of developing countries to proprietary knowledge. More precisely, TRIPS has introduced a number of limitations on developing countries in designing their patent regimes. It broadens the scope of patents by requiring countries to extend patent protection to all fields of technology, while previously, countries could deny patents to certain types of goods or inventions in order to encourage reverse engineering; it extends the duration of patent protection uniformly to 20 years, while previously, countries could offer patents of short duration; it reduces the scope of exceptions, which are limited to very specific cases; and it limits governments' ability to regulate patent holders, while previously, countries could make the granting of patents that provided monopoly benefits conditional upon local production or licensing and on the transfer of technology to local users (Shadlen, 2005a).[30]

The kinds of limitations introduced by TRIPS implies an asymmetry that favours the producers and holders of protected intellectual property – mainly in developed countries – at the expense of those trying to gain access to protected intellectual content, mainly in developing countries. Moreover, the Agreement requires developing countries to expand and enhance their intellectual property regimes, while providing very little to effectively facilitate and promote their access to technology. Indeed, the provisions in the Agreement are specific, binding and actionable with regard to the protection of intellectual property, and non-compliance with these provisions can be challenged under the WTO's dispute settlement mechanism. By contrast, provisions regarding technology transfer and technical cooperation, which are of importance mainly for developing countries are of a "best endeavour" nature and vaguely worded, making them difficult to enforce. As a result, non-compliance with these provisions is difficult to prove and, on a practical level, subject to no penalty.

Another expression of this asymmetry of favouring incentives for the creation of patentable knowledge at the expense of the dissemination and use of such knowledge is the implied additional cost – in the form of royalties – to developing countries of acquiring useful technology. The potential economic costs of the TRIPS Agreement for developing countries to acquire patentable knowledge may be illustrated by the fact that in 2001 only five developed countries (France, Germany, Japan, the United Kingdom and the United States) accounted for 83.6 per cent of the total patent applications filed in the EU, Japan and the United States. And 82 per cent of scientific articles worldwide were published in the OECD area, nearly two thirds of which were from G-7 countries (OECD, 2005: 9 and 40). The surplus in the OECD-countries' technology balance increased from $9.6 billion in 1993 to $30.4 billion in 2003 (OECD, 2005: 203). Moreover, technology transfer is increasingly taking place within multinational firms, which reduces the importance of contractual and non-equity modes of technology transfer and makes it increasingly difficult for developing countries to obtain useful technology on a commercial basis as envisaged by TRIPS.

> Regional and bilateral trade agreements with developed countries often foreclose part of the autonomy left open to developing countries by TRIPS.

While acknowledging that TRIPS would cause a significant revenue transfer from developing to developed countries, it has sometimes been argued that its application would bring about higher returns to knowledge generation, which in turn will spur knowledge diffusion to developing countries, including through increased flows of FDI. However, there is no persuasive evidence for this (Correa, 2000). A further economic handicap is that patentable research is increasingly carried out in private entities, with the result that most research activities are driven by their expected economic pay-off. Given the limited financial resources of most developing-country firms, there is a bias in the research agenda against those areas that are primarily of importance to developing countries.

Even though TRIPS has placed significant constraints on countries' autonomy in intellectual property matters, it has left room for variation across countries. For example, developing countries can impose stringent rules on patent disclosure (i.e. disclosure of the intervention that is sufficiently clear and comprehensive for a skilled person in the related activity to reproduce the inventive step), and subsequently grant narrow patents, i.e. patents that protect a very limited range of variations and thus offer no – or little – protection for variations that are not explicitly claimed. Or they can liberally grant improvement patents to local actors and protect their "minor" innovations, which often refer to incremental innovations that build on more fundamental discoveries and are thus crucial for tailoring imported technologies to local conditions. Such flexibilities allow local actors to "invent around" patents without governments risking litigation for infringement. Kumar (2003) argues that the patent regime in place in Japan after the Second World War until the 1980s provided for the granting of narrow patents, and that this regime served as a model for the late industrializers in Asia. Another example is flexible use of compulsory licences that allow a government to authorize itself or third parties to use a patent without the permission of the patent holder. Compulsory licences historically have been an important component of countries' patent regimes, and they are granted in a wide range of situations (UNCTAD and ICTSD, 2005). The TRIPS Agreement continues to leave countries with a significant degree of autonomy in this regard, as it grants countries "considerable leeway to impose non-voluntary licensing of patented interventions for any legitimate purpose and without undue constraints" (Reichman and Hasenzahl, 2003: 2).

However, many developing countries have engaged in regional and bilateral trade agreements with developed countries that often foreclose part of the autonomy left open to developing countries by TRIPS. For example, the United States – and to some extent the EU (Shadlen, 2005b) – uses regional arrangements to introduce legislation and practices that go beyond the levels of intellectual property protection under TRIPS (USTR, 2004).[31]

One of the greater obligations imposed by many regional and bilateral trade agreements concerns the reduced ability of governments to use compulsory licensing as a policy instrument (see, for example, Maskus, 1997). In general, regional and bilateral trade agreements do not allow developing governments to issue compulsory licences except during declared states of national emergency, and even then they require increased levels of prior negotiations with the patent holder; moreover, where such licences are granted, the agreements substantially restrict the rights of the licensee (Shadlen, 2005a).[32]

International harmonization of substantive and enforcement rules on intellectual property rights has been further pursued at the World Intellectual Property Organization (WIPO), especially in the ongoing negotiations on a Substantive Patent Law Treaty (SPLT). Discussions on the work programme of the SPLT so far have not led to an agreement as to whether aspects such as prior art, grace period, novelty and inventive step should be included, as suggested by developed countries. Developing countries fear that adoption of the developed countries' proposal would eventually result in the further harmonization of national patent laws in areas of patent law that have so far been left to the discretion of national legislation. This would risk further reducing developing countries' flexibilities to decide on the stringency of requirements for disclosure and the standards for granting patents, because it would eliminate countries' ability to determine what an invention is and how the patentability standards are set (see, for example, Correa, 2005).

4. Industrial tariffs

The use of industrial tariffs is in many respects not the best tool to promote diversification and technological upgrading. For a number of developing countries, domestic markets are too small to sustain the scale needed for production to be internationally competitive. Hence, tariffs may end up protecting infant industries that are unable to come anywhere near world market price and quality combinations. Industrial production needs to have an export component to reach an efficient scale, and protection alone may well discourage efforts to export. Also, as noted earlier, protection can easily be abused, in the sense of being unrelated to efforts to improve productivity: once granted, firms will lobby vigorously to maintain the protection. Therefore, industrial tariffs need to be used with great caution.

In spite of the numerous drawbacks of tariff use, developing-country policymakers may be hesitant to abandon industrial tariffs, mainly for three reasons. First, tariffs remain an important source of fiscal revenue for many developing countries. According to Kowalski (2005), should tariffs be completely abolished, many low-income countries would need to replace, on average, around 18 per cent (and in some cases over 50 per cent) of their tax revenues with sources other than import duty (see also Laird, Vanzetti and Fernandez de Cordoba, 2006: 7). While the importance of trade taxes in total revenue collection generally declines with economic development, in upper-middle-income countries import duties accounted, on average, for about 12 per cent of total revenue in the late 1990s. Improved tax collection and broadening of the tax base can reduce the revenue shortfall resulting from declining taxes. However, many developing countries have already substantially lowered the share of import duties in their total revenues over the past two decades,[33] while low-income countries in particular have been unable to recover the revenues lost from trade liberalization (Baunsgaard and Keen, 2005). As a result, they are likely to experience difficulty in finding supplementary sources of revenue that further tariff reductions would necessitate. Moreover, the decline in government revenue resulting from a reduction in import duties may lead to an increase in public deficits or a decline in public investment. But public investment has a crucial impact on economic development because it seeks to improve education, health and other social indicators. And public investment is often complementary to private investment, so that a decline in public investment below a critical level can seriously compromise an economy's development prospects (*TDR 2003*). On the other hand, tariff cuts could lead to a substantial increase in imports, with lower tariff rates levied on a higher volume of imports; in principle, this could maintain the value of import levies, but this is unlikely to occur because of balance-of-payments constraints.

Second, the provision of subsidies, rather than broad-based protection, could provide the incentives required for innovative investment, as discussed above. However, as already mentioned, the SCM Agreement has highly circumscribed the use of subsidies in areas where, formerly, both the mature and late industrializers of today actively used them during their economic catch-up. Moreover, as mentioned earlier, tight budgetary constraints limit developing countries' ability to use subsidies.

Third, and perhaps most importantly, the economic impact of changes in industrial tariffs is often assessed in terms of welfare gains or losses resulting from the reallocation of existing resources. From this perspective, a trade policy aimed at low and uniform tariffs across industrial sectors with full binding coverage will maximize a country's welfare benefits.[34] But such an assessment pays little attention to the implications of tariff cuts and harmonization for capital accumulation, technological change and productivity growth that underlie industrialization and economic development.

It may be useful to recall that industrial tariffs were the main element of protection that today's developed countries used during their industrial development. As illustrated in table 5.1 and analysed in some detail by Bairoch (1993), the United States maintained average industrial tariffs at around 40 per cent, and never below 25 per cent except for short periods, throughout most of the period between 1820 and 1945. Regarding the United Kingdom, Bairoch (1993: 46) notes that prior to its substantial move towards free trade with the repeal of the Corn Laws in 1846, Britain had achieved its technological lead "behind high and long-lasting tariff barriers". He also notes that the country had actively used infant industry protection, export subsidies, import tariff rebates on inputs used in manufacturing for export, and export quality control. Table 5.1 also shows that at the beginning of economic catch-up in West European countries

> A flexible tariff policy consists of maintaining bound tariffs at a higher level and ...

> ... modulating applied tariffs on particular industrial sectors around a lower average level.

following the Second World War, the level of tariffs on manufactured products was also fairly high (see also, Chang, 2002).

Comparing tariff levels at similar levels of per capita income (measured at purchasing power parity) shows that average tariffs in today's developed countries were much higher when they had similar per capita income levels as today's developing countries (see also Akyüz, 2005). In this sense, tariff policy in today's developing countries appears to be relatively liberal. Towards the end of the nineteenth century, when the United States had a per capita income similar to today's weighted average level in developing countries (i.e. about $3,700 in 1990 dollars measured in purchasing power parity), the level of its weighted average applied tariffs on manufactured goods was close to 50 per cent, compared to 6.5 per cent in developing countries today (tables 5.1 and 5.2). In 1950, when the United States had evolved as the world's technological leader with a per capita income more than double the average level in today's developing countries, the level of its weighted applied tariffs on manufactured products still exceeded the current level in today's developing countries. When the United States had the same level of per capita income as the Republic of Korea today, its weighted applied tariffs were higher (7.0 per cent compared to 4.5 per cent), and when it had the same per capita income level as Brazil, China or India today, its tariffs were several times higher. This is also true, to varying degrees, for the European countries in table 5.1 (i.e. Germany, France and the United Kingdom).

These comparisons of the relative levels of tariff protection between the developed countries during their catch-up phases and today's developing countries do not tell the whole story. Developed countries also benefited from the additional protection of natural trade barriers in the form of transportation and information costs, which were higher in the past than they are today. More importantly, the productivity gap between

Table 5.1

TARIFFS ON MANUFACTURED PRODUCTS AND PER CAPITA INCOME IN SELECTED DEVELOPED COUNTRIES, 1820–1980

Country	1820[a]	1875[b]	1913	1950	1980
	Tariffs, weighted averages				
	(Per cent)				
United States	35–45	40–50	44.0	14.0	7.0
United Kingdom	45–55	0	0.0	23.0	8.3
Germany	8–12[c]	4–6	13.0	26.0	8.3
France	.. [d]	12–15	20.0	18.0	8.3
	Per capita income				
	(1990 international dollars)				
United States	1 257	2 445	5 301	9 561	18 577
United Kingdom	1 707	3 191	4 921	6 907	12 928
Germany	1 058	1 821	3 648	3 881	14 113
France	1 230	1 876	3 485	5 270	15 103

Source: Tariff data from Bairoch, 1993: 40; income data from Maddison, 2001: 264, 276–279.
   a Very approximate rates. Range of averages, not extremes.
   b Per capita income data for 1870.
   c Prussia.
   d Numerous and large restrictions on imports of manufactured products render calculations of average tariff rates insignificant.

developed and catching up countries, which is the main justification for tariff protection in catch-up periods, is much greater now than it was in the past. Thus in order to obtain the same degree of actual protection, today's developing countries would need to impose relatively higher tariffs than those that were used by the now developed countries during their catch-up periods (Chang, 2002: 67).

Chang (2002) shows that the great importance of tariffs in promoting economic development until the 1920s was associated with the underdevelopment of other instruments of public policy. Governments' limited abilities to raise tax revenues circumscribed their use of subsidies. Moreover, non-tariff measures such as quotas, voluntary export restraints and anti-dumping were developed only after the Second World War, before evolving into standard instruments in support of industrial development. Therefore, in a sense, the limited

range of trade policy instruments available to developed countries until the 1920s resembles the situation faced by developing countries today, given that WTO rules and commitments curtail the use for economic catch-up of instruments such as export-related subsidies, performance requirements for foreign investors, and reverse engineering and imitating of foreign technology.

As proposed by Akyüz (2005), in such circumstances, it would be important for developing countries to be able to modulate applied industrial tariffs in order to pursue a pattern of public support policies such as that illustrated in figure 5.1 above. That is, the variation of applied tariffs levied on particular product categories, in accordance with their path of technological upgrading, could be a key instrument of sectoral policy. To be sure, this kind of tariff policy does not imply either the imposition of high applied tariffs for all sectors at any one time or the imposition of high average applied tariffs. On the contrary, it is likely to result in lower average applied tariffs than would be the case if tariff policy were looked at from a tariff line by tariff line perspective.

This kind of flexible tariff policy would be best accommodated by a strategy of maintaining bound tariffs at a relatively higher level (or maintaining a large part of industrial tariffs unbound) and modulating applied tariffs on particular industrial sectors around a relatively lower average level. This would be possible if industrial tariff reduction obligations from international agreements extended only to average tariffs, and not to individual tariff lines,[35] which has indeed been the case in all multilateral trade agreements concluded so far.

Apart from supporting diversification and technological upgrading, this tariff policy pattern provides several additional advantages (see also Akyüz, 2005: 26). First, it would balance multilateral disciplines with national policy flexibility, because it would encourage countries to choose applied levels of their industrial tariff lines within the overall limit of an average bound tariff, rather than seeking revenue maximization or accommodation of wide-ranging demands from lobby groups. Second, it would encourage policymakers to view tariff protection for specific industries at the lower rung of the technology ladder as a temporary measure, to be phased out and replaced by tariff protection for industries at higher rungs of the ladder until they are able to compete in world markets. Third, as a consequence, it would encourage policymakers to take a longer-term view of their economy's technological development and multilateral commitments.

> The current multilateral negotiations on NAMA are set to reduce the flexibility in setting and binding tariffs.

> Since the Uruguay Round reduced the freedom to use other policy instruments, the relative importance of industrial tariffs has increased.

A number of developing countries have maintained a tariff regime that allows them to modulate applied tariffs on manufactured goods. Table 5.2 shows that for developing countries as a group and for all individual developing countries in the table, except China, bound tariffs on manufactures significantly exceed applied tariffs,[36] thus leaving room to adjust tariffs in support of domestic producers. Moreover, many developing countries have less than full binding coverage or deploy significantly different levels of both bound and effectively applied tariffs across manufactured goods, as shown by relatively high values of the coefficient of variation that reflects intersectoral dispersion. Among the countries in the table, India maintained the greatest degrees of freedom, as its tariff regime combined relatively high levels of bound and applied tariffs, as well as sizeable intersectoral dispersion and a relatively low binding coverage.[37] This tariff profile left India significant space for tariff modulation. By contrast, Chile has a relatively low level of tariffs, very little intersectoral dispersion and full binding coverage. China and Mexico have also conserved relatively little flexibility in their tariff profile. The other countries in the table occupy intermediate positions as they either conserve relatively high tariff levels but little intersectoral dispersion and (close to) full binding coverage (Argentina, Brazil and Egypt), or relatively low tariff levels but with some intersectoral dispersion and less than full binding coverage (the Republic of Korea).

The current multilateral negotiations on non-agricultural market access (NAMA) are set to reduce this flexibility in tariff setting and binding that developing countries have maintained. The framework adopted for modalities of industrial tariff reductions, as contained in Annex B of the so-called July Package (WTO, 2004) stipulates a reduction in tariffs according to a non-linear Swiss formula, and an increase in binding coverage. While at the time of writing (June 2006) the definition of full modalities remained to be negotiated, the overall objective of the adopted approach is to bind and reduce all industrial tariffs with a view to harmo-

Table 5.2

TARIFFS ON MANUFACTURED PRODUCTS AND PER CAPITA INCOME IN SELECTED DEVELOPING COUNTRIES AND COUNTRY GROUPS, 1985–2005

		Applied tariffs			Bound tariffs				
		Simple average		Weighted average	Simple average		Weighted average	Binding coverage	Memo item:
Country	Year	(Per cent)	Coefficient of variation	(Per cent)	(Per cent)	Coefficient of variation	(Per cent)	(Per cent)	Per capita income[a]
Argentina	1985	28.3	..	26.2	..	..	..	..	10 008
	1990[b]	14.8	0.5	13.6	31.7	0.2	32.5	100.0	10 755
	1995 *	13.1	0.6	9.0	31.6	0.2	32.0	100.0	11 254
	2000	15.3	0.5	11.2	31.6	0.2	32.2	100.0	12 174
	2005	10.9	0.7	9.4	31.6	0.2	32.7	100.0	12 222[c]
Brazil	1985	60.7	..	53.5	..	..	..	..	6 640
	1990	34.4	0.5	28.1	30.7	0.2	28.7	100.0	6 497
	1995	13.7	0.6	12.7	30.7	0.2	30.0	100.0	6 940
	2000	17.0	0.4	14.8	30.6	0.3	29.6	100.0	7 301
	2005	12.6	0.6	9.1	30.6	0.3	28.6	100.0	7 531[c]
Chile	1985	19.8	..	18.5	..	..	..	..	4 969
	1990[b]	11.0	0.1	10.9	25.0	0.0	25.0	100.0	6 764
	1995	10.7	0.2	10.6	25.0	0.0	24.9	100.0	7 999
	2000	9.0	0.0	9.0	25.0	0.0	25.0	100.0	9 115
	2005	5.0	0.5	4.4	25.0	0.0	25.0	100.0	9 993[c]
Mexico	1985	12.1	..	11.1	..	..	..	..	7 870
	1990[d]	14.4	0.3	13.0	35.0	0.1	34.9	100.0	7 758
	1995	12.5	0.5	7.7	35.0	0.1	34.8	100.0	7 619
	2000	18.0	0.4	14.6	35.0	0.1	65.4	100.0	9 046
	2005	8.5	1.0	2.8	35.0	0.1	35.5	100.0	9 010[c]
China[e]	1985	41.9	..	33.2	..	..	..	..	1 181
	1990[b]	40.0	0.8	35.6	9.5	0.7	8.9	100.0	1 944
	1995[f]	21.3	0.7	18.2	9.5	0.7	7.9	100.0	2 971
	2000	15.8	0.6	13.5	9.5	0.7	6.0	100.0	3 928
	2005[c]	9.5	0.7	5.8	9.5	0.7	5.3	100.0	5 419
India	1985	101.9	..	99.4	..	..	..	..	1 385
	1990	79.9	0.5	70.8	35.5	0.5	29.3	71.5	1 701
	1995[g]	28.9	0.3	21.1	35.4	0.5	31.2	71.3	2 154
	2000[h]	30.7	0.3	28.3	35.4	0.5	30.0	71.3	2 480
	2005	17.7	0.4	12.6	35.5	0.5	28.0	71.5	2 885[c]
Rep. of Korea	1985	23.4	..	22.5	..	..	..	..	6 649
	1990	12.8	0.2	11.4	11.0	2.1	7.3	95.4	9 792
	1995	7.8	0.2	7.3	11.2	2.2	7.2	95.4	13 597
	2000[i]	8.0	0.3	6.2	11.3	1.8	6.1	94.8	15 143
	2005[c]	7.2	2.1	4.5	11.3	1.7	6.4	94.8	18 840
Egypt	1985	37.5	..	30.8	..	..	..	..	2 845
	1990	..	..	..	..	..	..	..	2 896
	1995	24.0	0.9	22.2	28.5	0.7	26.4	99.3	3 025
	2000[j]	19.2	0.7	17.5	28.5	0.7	25.1	99.3	3 326
	2005[k]	19.0	0.9	16.9	28.4	0.7	24.9	99.2	3 729

/...

Table 5.2 (concluded)

TARIFFS ON MANUFACTURED PRODUCTS AND PER CAPITA INCOME IN SELECTED DEVELOPING COUNTRIES AND COUNTRY GROUPS, 1985–2005

Country	Year	Applied tariffs			Bound tariffs				Memo item:
		Simple average (Per cent)	Coefficient of variation	Weighted average (Per cent)	Simple average (Per cent)	Coefficient of variation	Weighted average (Per cent)	Binding coverage (Per cent)	Per capita income[a]
Memo item:									
Developing countries									
	1985	..	..	..	..	..	..	..	2 946
	1990	26.1	0.9	20.5	26.7	0.7	17.7	68.6	2 875
	1995	14.8	0.9	9.5	32.6	0.5	19.8	73.2	3 225
	2000	14.0	0.8	11.3	36.5	0.5	19.1	70.7	3 612
	2005[c]	10.5	1.1	6.5	30.2	0.5	15.6	67.9	3 915

Source: Tariff data for 1985 from UNCTAD, 1994. All other tariff data from UNCTAD, *TRAINS* Database at WITS. Income data from World Bank, *World Development Indicators* (*WDI*) Database.

Note: The data in the table refer to manufactures, and thus exclude tariffs applied in a number of sectors (such as extractive industries) that are included in industrial tariff data (i.e. the subject of NAMA negotiations). Data for developing countries are only indicative, because averages are based on less than full country coverage for some years.

a PPP (constant 2000 international dollars), data for developing countries as a group refer to the median.

b 1992.   c 2004.   d 1991.

e Data for applied tariffs are based on a more recent list, that includes a larger number of tariff lines than the list used for data on bound tariffs. Thus, prior to China's accession to the WTO in 2001, the numbers in the table for applied tariffs can exceed those for bound tariffs, even with full binding coverage.

f 1996.   g 1997.   h 2001.

i 1999.   j 1998.   k 2002.

nizing them, both across countries and across individual tariff lines.

In sum, a developing country's tariff policy needs to be part of a long-term industrialization strategy. Selective trade liberalization should be in line with a country's ability to achieve technological upgrading. In addition, temporary protection should be combined with export promotion associated with quantitative targets that are easy to monitor and allow governments to withdraw support from firms that do not achieve upgrading targets. Given the numerous drawbacks and risks associated with their use, tariffs need to be implemented with considerable caution. But since the URAs reduced the degrees of freedom for developing countries to use other policy instruments designed to support diversification and technological upgrading, the relative importance of industrial tariffs has increased.

D. Industrial dynamism and national policies: recent experiences

The objective of this section is, first, to provide empirical evidence of industrialization and technological upgrading in developed and developing countries over the past 25 years and, second, to present a few selected case studies on the associated trade and industrial policies. It attempts to set the general context in which countries have undertaken trade and industrial policies and examines whether, how and to what extent multilateral trade rules and commitments have affected countries' autonomy in policy-making and implementation.

1. Industrial dynamism: recent empirical evidence

The degree of expansion of their manufactured exports and improvement of their share in world trade, particularly in high-tech products, is often taken as a measure of the pace of industrialization and technological upgrading in developing countries. However, the higher import content of domestic production brought about by trade liberalization, together with the greater participation of developing countries in import-dependent, labour-intensive, low-value-added processes in international production networks, implies that increases in their manufactured exports may often have taken place without commensurate increases in income and value added, as discussed in *TDR 2002*.

Table 5.3 presents data on the shares of developed and developing economies in world manufacturing trade and production over the past 25 years. Comprehensive data on manufacturing value added (MVA) are available only up to 2003, so that they do not reflect the more recent impact of trade and industrial policies. The data show that success in exporting manufactures is not an appropriate indicator of a country's industrial development. They reveal a pattern comprising the following features:

- The shares of developing economies both in world manufactured exports and world MVA showed a sharp increase during the period 1980–2003, but growth in exports was much stronger than in value added. This contrasts with the experience of developed countries, whose share in world manufacturing exports fell between 1980 and 2003, while their share in world MVA rose significantly.

- There has been wide variation in industrial performance across developing regions, leading to a rise in the concentration of industrial activities. South and East Asia are the most industrialized in the developing world; their combined share in total world MVA has increased the most, more than doubling since 1990 to exceed 17 per cent in 2003. The Latin America and Caribbean region has experienced the strongest decline in its share of world MVA, the sharpest fall being in the 1980s and early 2000s.

- China succeeded in more than tripling its share in both world MVA and world manufactured exports between 1990 and 2003. Its experience closely resembles that of the Re-

Table 5.3

SHARE OF SELECTED DEVELOPING ECONOMIES AND REGIONAL GROUPS IN WORLD MANUFACTURING VALUE ADDED AND MANUFACTURED EXPORTS, 1980–2003

(Percentage share)

Region/economy	Share in world manufacturing value added				Share in world exports of manufactures[a]			
	1980	1990	2000	2003	1980	1990	2000	2003
Developed countries[b]	64.5	74.1	74.9	73.3	74.1	77.9	67.3	65.4
Developing countries	16.6	17.0	22.8	23.7	18.9	18.3	28.9	29.7
Latin America and the Caribbean	7.1	5.6	5.4	4.4	4.3	2.4	4.7	4.1
Argentina	0.9	0.8	0.8	0.5	0.2	0.3	0.3	0.3
Brazil	2.9	2.2	1.1	0.9	0.8	0.8	0.8	0.8
Chile	0.2	0.1	0.2	0.2	0.2	0.2	0.2	0.2
Mexico	1.9	1.1	2.0	1.7	0.8	0.5	2.7	2.2
South and East Asia	7.4	8.7	15.2	17.2	7.6	13.6	21.7	22.7
China, Taiwan Province of	0.6	1.1	1.3	1.1	1.3	2.3	2.7	2.3
Republic of Korea	0.7	1.4	2.2	2.3	1.1	2.2	3.1	3.0
ASEAN-4	1.2	1.5	2.4	2.8	1.0	2.0	4.2	3.7
Indonesia	0.4	0.5	0.9	1.1	0.2	0.4	0.8	0.6
Malaysia	0.2	0.2	0.5	0.5	0.4	0.7	1.6	1.5
Philippines	0.3	0.2	0.3	0.3	0.2	0.2	0.7	0.5
Thailand	0.3	0.5	0.7	0.8	0.2	0.6	1.1	1.1
China	3.3	2.6	6.6	8.5	1.0	1.7	4.3	6.5
India	1.1	1.1	1.2	1.4	0.3	0.5	0.7	0.9
Africa	0.9	0.9	0.8	0.8	5.4	2.6	1.8	2.0

Source: UNCTAD secretariat calculations, based on UNIDO, *Handbook of Industrial Statistics 1996*; UNIDO, *International Yearbook of Industrial Statistics, 2006*; World Bank, *World Development Indicators* online; Taiwan Province of China, *Monthly Bulletin of Statistics* online; UN COMTRADE and UNCTAD estimates.

Note: Calculations in current dollars.

a To ensure data comparability, the definition of this product category follows industrial statistics. It therefore includes processed primary products in addition to manufactures, as defined in trade statistics. For further discussion of this statistical issue, see Wood and Mayer, 1998. Using the definition of manufactures in trade statistics (i.e. SITC 5 through 8 less 68) has a negligible effect on the shares of the individual countries listed in the table. By contrast, it results in a number of sizeable changes for country groups. Most of these changes are confined to 1980 when, based on the definition of manufactures in trade statistics, the share in world exports of manufactures was 15.5 per cent for developing countries and 78.1 per cent for developed countries (using the UNIDO country classification). The remaining discrepancy with respect to *TDR 2002*, table 3.5 for 1980 trade data is due to data (re-)estimation, in particular for China.

b To ensure data comparability, the definition of this group is that used by UNIDO prior to 2006. Hence, contrary to the current standard definition of the United Nations, it does not include the Czech Republic, Estonia, Hungary, Latvia, Lithuania, Poland and Slovakia.

public of Korea between 1980 and 2000, which (together with the Taiwan Province of China) is often portrayed as exemplifying successful economic catch-up among the late industrializers.[38] This outcome strongly con-

trasts with that of Mexico, whose share in world manufactured exports increased more than fivefold during the 1990s, while its share in world MVA only about doubled during the same period. Moreover, both these shares de-

Figure 5.2

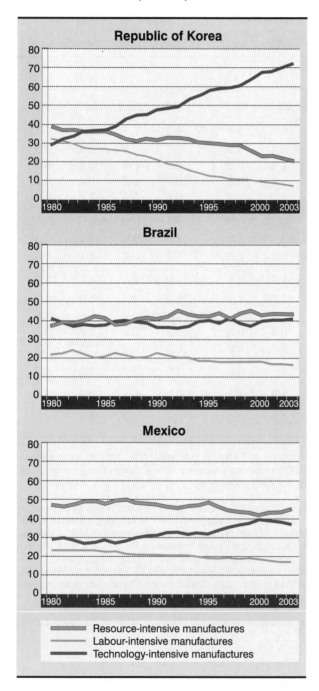

**SHARE IN TOTAL MANUFACTURING VALUE ADDED
OF MAJOR PRODUCT CATEGORIES IN THE
REPUBLIC OF KOREA, BRAZIL AND
MEXICO, 1980–2003**

(Per cent)

Source: UNCTAD secretariat calculations, based on data for
Mexico and the Republic of Korea from OECD, *Structural Analysis* (STAN) Database; and on data for Brazil from ECLAC, *Program for the Analysis of Industrial
Dynamics* (PADI) Database.

Note: The shares are based on values in 1985 dollars. For
a detailed explanation of the product categorization,
see the notes to this chapter.

clined during the early 2000s. Brazil also
shows an interesting development, with its
share in world manufactured exports remaining largely unchanged over the past 25 years
and its share in world MVA falling significantly, during the 1980s, and even more so
during the 1990s.

These different experiences in industrial development across individual developing countries
are closely related to changes in the composition
of the respective countries' industrial activities,
as shown in figure 5.2. The figure concentrates
on Brazil, Mexico and the Republic of Korea, because comprehensive data for China are not available. The Republic of Korea shows the classic
picture of successful industrial structural change
and technological upgrading. While the shares of
resource-intensive and labour-intensive products
in that country's total industrial activities fell during the period 1980–2003, the share of technology-
intensive products grew continuously, to reach
72 per cent in 2003.

Brazil and Mexico show an entirely different picture. Mexico experienced a slight increase
in the share of technology-intensive products in
its total industrial activities between 1995 and
2000, which is likely to have been associated with
the growing activities in the automobile sector
following the entry into force of the North American Free Trade Agreement (NAFTA) in 1994. Nevertheless, resource-intensive manufactures have
maintained the highest share in the country's industrial activities. Brazil experienced little change
in the relative importance of the three categories
of industrial production over the period 1980–2003.

2. National policies for industrial development: some recent experience

(a) Latin America

Most countries in Latin America adopted
comprehensive economic reform programmes
during the 1980s and early 1990s, which emphasized more stringent monetary and fiscal policies,
liberalization, privatization and deregulation (as
noted in chapter II). These were accompanied by

the discontinuation of inward-oriented industrialization strategies and, in most cases, the dismantling of institutional structures, such as development banks, that had been of major importance to those strategies. However, in the mid-1990s, there was a growing belief that, even though the reforms had been successful in bringing about macroeconomic financial stability, they were not achieving the promised results in terms of economic growth and sustainable improvement in the countries' balance of payments. Moreover, the industrial restructuring process that accompanied economic reform had led to the undesired outcome of premature deindustrialization (i.e. a decline in the share of industry in aggregate output and employment accompanied by the growing importance of the primary sector, rather than by that of the services sector as has generally been the case in the benign process of deindustrialization in developed countries). As discussed, for example, in *TDR 2003* and Cimoli et al. (2006), the pattern of industrial production and trade, which had resulted from policies that relied on unfettered market forces, was shifting the composition of output and exports towards natural-resource-based products at the expense of those sectors that have the greatest potential for productivity growth and technological upgrading (i.e. manufactures, and particularly the high-technology-intensive ones).

In the mid-1990s, a significant number of countries in Latin America – in particular Brazil, Colombia and Mexico – adopted medium- or long-term plans for the (re-) development of their industrial sector, and a number of other countries began to implement policies with the same objective, though through a less formalized strategy. The general approach of these plans and strategies has been to: (i) maintain their macroeconomic orientation, emphasizing financial stability and broad-based trade liberalization, often accompanied by financial liberalization, with a view to achieving an efficient allocation of resources in response to signals from world market prices; and (ii) complement this macroeconomic policy with microeconomic policies designed to make their domestic enterprises internationally competitive and facilitate their international integration. These microeconomic policies have often been embedded in national competitiveness strategies,[39] sometimes specifically targeted at small- and medium-sized enterprises (SMEs), with the general aim of fostering labour productivity and technological innovation in existing industries. Such business promotion policies have been combined with measures designed to attract FDI through improvements in the host countries' locational advantages.[40] FDI has also been sought with the objective of developing production, particularly for export activities in new industrial sectors for the respective host country (Melo, 2001; Peres, 2006).[41]

The specific policy measures employed to achieve the central objective of enabling domestic enterprises to gain a competitive edge over their foreign competitors have differed across the countries of the region. In general, they have been aimed at promoting exports, output growth and investment, and higher productivity and competitiveness. Tax and credit incentives have been the most important types of policy instruments for the promotion of exports, particularly of non-traditional exports. Such fiscal incentives have been characterized by a reduced use of subsidies and an emphasis on tax refunds on domestic inputs or duties paid on imported inputs, and the creation of export processing zones.

The main objective of credit policies to promote exports has been to provide access to working capital or initial investment financing for new export activities. These loans are generally offered at domestic market rates, which are usually higher than those of international financial markets. Brazil's programme for the financing of exports (PROEX) is a major excep-

> In the mid-1990s, a significant number of countries in Latin America adopted plans for the (re-) development of their industrial sector ...

> ... attempting to enable domestic enterprises to gain a competitive edge over their foreign competitors.

tion, as it allows Brazilian exporters of certain goods and services, or their foreign importers, to obtain trade finance on international market conditions (i.e. granting mainly interest equalization payments).[42] Embraer, the Brazilian manufacturer of regional aeroplanes, has been one of the firms to use this programme. However, in 1996–1999, Canada, home to Embraer's main competitor, Bombardier, challenged the compatibility of PROEX with WTO rules and commitments. The WTO dispute settlement panel ruled that the subsidies granted under PROEX were inconsistent with the SCM Agreement's provision prohibiting the use of subsidies contingent upon export performance. While Brazil appealed against this ruling,[43] it also changed the provisions of PROEX. Subsequently, ruling on a further challenge from Canada, the WTO panel report of July 2001 established that the revised PROEX falls under the exceptions provided in Annex I of the SCM Agreement, and thus is not against WTO rules and commitments.[44] While this illustrates that WTO rules and commitments can reduce the degrees of freedom of national policy-making, it also highlights the fact that (i) the WTO provides a transparent legal structure to deal with disputes, and thus minimizes the risk of "trade wars", (ii) while much leeway in policy-making may have been lost under multilateral rules, countries can nevertheless retain a degree of flexibility through creative policy-making, and (iii) significant administrative and negotiating capacities are required to fully benefit from the WTO regime.

Policies to promote output growth and investment have also emphasized credit and tax incentives. Generally, these incentives have been provided to all economic sectors, but some have a sector-specific dimension. Contrary to much of the policies adopted in connection with the inward-oriented industrialization strategies of the past, which focused on support to manufacturing activities, recent fiscal incentives and loans by development banks have emphasized extraction industries (such

> Incentives have been provided to all economic sectors, but some have a sector-specific dimension ...

> ... emphasizing extraction industries, tourism, or services.

as the oil, mineral or forestry sectors), tourism, or a variety of services sectors (ranging from infrastructure to the film industry). In some countries (e.g. Brazil and Mexico), a variety of sectors benefit from credit and tax incentives, but most countries have focused support on a narrow range of sectors (Melo, 2001: table 3).[45] However, Mexico's recent plan (contained in the National Plan for Development, 2001–2006) to adopt sector-specific policies to stimulate investment with a view to generating greater domestic value added and strengthening the linkages among local production chains has been hampered by insufficient budgetary funds and by long delays in implementation (Moreno-Brid, Rivas Valdivia and Santamaria, 2005: 14).

The promotion of scientific and technological upgrading has been an important element in policies designed to improve enterprise productivity and international competitiveness. As with export promotion and support to output growth and investment, the provision of credit and fiscal incentives have been the main types of policy instruments used to promote technological upgrading. Other instruments include government funding of R&D projects and strengthening cooperation between public research institutions and private enterprises. However only limited budgetary resources seem to have been made available for technology development and innovation. For example, in Brazil, public funding covered only 10 per cent of private sector R&D activities during the period 1998–2000; much of the rest was sourced from company profits, given that the high domestic interest rate provided little incentives for financing such activities through loans (De Negri, 2006). Another type of policy used to promote scientific and technological development has been support to SMEs, which are often considered highly important in innovation. Particularly in countries of the Andean Community (Bolivia, Colombia, Ecuador, Peru, and Venezuela) or in Central America (Peres, 2006), this has taken the form of support to SME clusters (i.e. an agglomeration of SMEs in the same or related lines of business located in a given geographical area).[46]

While the bulk of policy support mentioned so far has been applied to all economic sectors, many countries in Latin America have also used sector-specific measures. For example, credit and fiscal incentives have been directed mainly to attract FDI in high-technology-intensive sectors, such as the information and communications technology sector, and in the automotive industry. However, the shift away from relatively centralized tax policies supportive of economic development and their increasing devolution to regional and local governments has often led to "fiscal wars", whereby different regions and municipalities offer increasingly generous incentive packages to attract new TNCs or trigger their relocation away from existing TNC production sites within the same country. In Brazil, for example, in order to make the automotive sector more attractive to FDI, individual incentive packages amounted to as much as $300,000 per job, leading some observers to conclude that subsidies of this size are likely to exceed the gains from reallocating plants within Brazil (Christiansen, Oman and Charlton, 2003).

Such incentives were offered to TNCs in the hope that they would provide technological and knowledge spillovers to domestic producers, as well as facilitate the integration of such producers into international markets, such as through their participation in TNC-managed international production networks (Lugones, 2006). Mexico, among the countries in Latin America, has gone furthest in this regard. In December 1993 (i.e. just before NAFTA took effect), Mexico enacted a new law on FDI that simplified administrative procedures and eliminated virtually all restrictions on FDI in manufacturing. The law also provided for the progressive removal of all performance requirements on FDI in the automotive sector. Moreover, imported inputs for re-exportation were allowed to enter the country tax-free. As a result

of such tax benefits "manufacturing firms that rely on foreign inputs entering as temporary imports pay approximately 30% lower input costs than similar firms which use locally produced inputs" (Moreno-Brid, Rivas Valdivia and Santamaria, 2005: 22). This is probably why, during the period 1990–2000, producers of auto parts that enjoyed such tax benefits through the *maquiladora* regime increased output and employment much more than those that did not benefit from such a regime, even though the latter experienced more rapid productivity growth (Mortimore and Barron, 2005: 20). Indeed, it is doubtful whether the provision of such benefits has supported the entry of domestic enterprises into international production networks and contributed to domestic industrial development. Rather, it may ultimately have benefited mainly the automobile manufacturers in the United States by increasing their competitiveness vis-à-vis their Asian competitors in the United States market (Mortimore and Barron, 2005).

Partly in reaction to this, in the early 2000s, the Mexican Government attempted to transform the export platforms, which had mainly carried out assembly activities of imported production inputs for re-export to the United States. It sought to convert them into manufacturing centres that would produce auto parts in addition to assembling them into vehicles, and aimed at other large markets for automobiles in addition to the United States, such as the EU and Japan. Free trade agreements were used as a major instrument to that effect, because it was expected that the rules of origin associated with these agreements would bring about increased levels of local content. However, according to Mortimore and Barron (2005: 25–26), this strategy has largely failed, mainly because very few enterprises located in Mexico were able to provide parts and components that would meet international price and quality standards. This demonstrates the difficulties of the Mexican automotive industry in re-establishing local production linkages and furthering technological upgrading, which may have been due to the adverse effects of previously overgenerous treatment of FDI.

> A major shortcoming of industrialization strategies in Latin America has been the lack of coherence between the measures taken at the micro level and the macroeconomic environment.

If comprehensive tax incentive packages to attract FDI had not been offered, there may have been sufficient additional budgetary revenues to significantly increase the Government's ability to provide greater funding support to R&D and innovative activities.

In sum, the microeconomic policies that governments in many Latin American countries have adopted since the mid-1990s may have been successful in supporting the international integration of domestic enterprises and in attracting more FDI to the region. On the other hand, these policies do not appear to have significantly moved production and export patterns towards products of higher technology intensity. According to Peres (2006), it is not easy to assess the success of the microeconomic policies in these terms because in many cases they have been adopted in the absence of quantitative criteria that would have enabled an objective assessment of their effects.

Nevertheless, a significant shortcoming of the current industrialization strategies in many Latin American countries relates to the lack of coherence between the adopted microeconomic measures and the prevailing macroeconomic environment. The orthodox macroeconomic policy stance of most countries in the region helped to bring inflation under control and establish a reasonable degree of monetary and fiscal discipline. However, partly due to a loss of macroeconomic policy autonomy resulting from rapid liberalization and closer integration into the global economy, financial stabilization has often been accompanied by significant instability in key prices, such as real wages, exchange rates, interest rates and assets, that exert a strong influence on resource allocation and investment decisions. High interest and exchange rates have exacerbated this situation and impeded investment and technological change (see, *TDR 2003,* chap. VI). Thus the macroeconomic framework has not been conducive to the creation and expansion of productive capacity and the improvement of productivity and international competitiveness, which were the main objectives that the microeconomic measures sought to achieve.

In addition, the emphasis on export promotion through measures that apply to all economic sectors has tended to boost international competitiveness of domestic enterprises within a production and export pattern based on existing comparative advantage related to the abundant endowment in most countries of the region of natural resources and/or low-skilled labour. However, these sectors are generally not capable of generating sizeable growth in productivity and value added. This policy stance has been reinforced by the fact that tight budgetary constraints of many Latin American countries have prevented them from allocating sufficient financial resources to support R&D and innovation activities and the further development of technological capabilities. Innovation policies have been too broad-based, which, although substantial in overall fiscal terms,[47] has meant that they have been insufficient for making a meaningful contribution to R&D and innovation activities in individual sectors. Moreover, budgetary constraints were exacerbated by the generous tax incentives to FDI. More recently, the current commodity price boom and the associated higher budgetary revenues have given many Latin American governments greater flexibility in this respect. It is also worth noting that technological and knowledge spillovers from FDI have fallen short of expectations, and have been insufficient to improve domestic technology and productivity to create a competitive domestic export sector in high-value-added manufactures. The disappointing impact of FDI on industrial development may have been partly due to the overly generous incentive packages offered in competing for that FDI. In some instances, this shortcoming may also have been related to the fact that rules and commitments in international trade agreements prohibit the use of performance criteria for FDI of the kind applied in the East Asian NIEs during their economic catch-up.

(b) China

The structural transformation of China's economy is of particular interest for several reasons. First, it has been accompanied by very rapid economic growth, which led China to become the fourth largest economy in the world by 2005. Second, China's economic development over the past 30 years has been based on various development strategies, including central planning, inward-oriented import-substituting industrialization along with a strong export orientation, and an open-door policy regarding FDI. These strategies were used at different times, but in some cases also simultaneously in different parts of the economy. Third, the various types of proactive economic policies and wide range of instruments that have shaped China's economic development have continuously been adapted to changes in the underlying development strategy, as well as to changing circumstances in the domestic and international environment. This has been the case, in particular, in the run-up to, and in the aftermath of, China's accession to the WTO. Thus the process of China's economic transformation over the past 30 years may be characterized as "experimental gradualism", with the use of heterodox policies in a creative and often innovative manner.

Distinct from economic transformation in most other developing countries, China's process of industrialization and structural change has been part of a general economic transition from a centrally planned economy towards a market economy. Thus, much policy support has consisted of a gradual and selective adoption of regulations that have governed the pace and pattern of the transition towards a market economy. Key elements in this transition have been the reduction of the role of State-owned enterprises (SOEs), and the gradual and selective introduction of market incentives through the regulatory reform of price systems and of the regimes governing domestic labour mobility, external trade and FDI. On the other hand, government policy has played an important role in directing both domestic and foreign investment towards specific sectors.

Investment promotion has mainly taken the form of sizeable public investment in physical infrastructure, direct government financing, the provision of credit at preferential interest rates, and tax rebates. In the absence of an efficient domestic securities market, bank loans were the major source of corporate finance. Fixed investment expanded faster between the late 1980s and the late 1990s, directed at targeted industries and sectors that benefited from preferential credit,

> In China, much policy support has consisted of a gradual and selective adoption of regulations regarding the pace and pattern of the transition towards a market economy.

mainly from State-owned banks. Moreover, manufacturing industries and industries based on non-agricultural raw materials enjoyed tax rates up to 80 per cent lower than those imposed on other industries (Lu, 2001: 342 and 348).

FDI has played a pivotal role in China's changing industrial structure. It was attracted through the creation in 1980 of four Special Economic Zones, where imported inputs and exports were exempted from duties and new enterprises were offered extended periods of tax exemption. Since 1992, inward FDI has increased, as firms in Taiwan Province of China and Hong Kong (China), under increasing pressure from rising wages in their labour-intensive industries, were driven to find new low-wage production locations elsewhere to maintain their international competitiveness. This contributed to accelerating industrial restructuring in China from heavy to light industry. Later, in the 1990s, a growing number of international production networks, in which TNCs organize several suppliers in different locations, supported industrial restructuring from light industry to capital- and technology-intensive industries. Chinese locations have come to play a central part in such networks, in particular in electronics. Since 1999, on average, about 15 per cent of total FDI flows to China have been invested in the electronics industry (MOFCOM, 2006a).

In addition to the provision of fiscal incentives, the government has influenced the sectoral distribution of FDI by screening potential FDI inflows. Guidelines and regulations were issued explicitly identifying "prohibited", "permitted", or "encouraged" types of FDI. The latter offered incentives to FDI in high-tech industries through extensive preferential treatment such as tax rebates and/or exemptions, duty free imports of capital equipment and better access to public infrastructure and utilities such as gas and electricity (MOFCOM, 2006a). In order to attract FDI incorporating more sophisticated technologies for export-oriented industrial production, the Government streamlined administrative procedures and offered incentive packages in "free trade and high-technology development zones", including the provision of heavily subsidized land and energy.

China's foreign trade policy has been an integral part of its strategy for industrial development. It was very industry-selective, with extensive import restrictions before China's accession to WTO. Until then, foreign trade had supported industrial restructuring in two ways. First, gradual and phased trade liberalization enabled imports of technology which China would not otherwise have access to, and which were essential for structural changes in Chinese industry (see *TDR 2002*). Second, foreign trade allowed the export of surplus production, without which these structural changes, based on a combination of a large surplus of labour and rapidly increasing investment – both domestic and foreign – would not have been sustainable given the narrowness of China's domestic market, in particular before 1990.

Exporting firms benefited from various pricing, tax and loan privileges, as well as support for technological upgrading, to maintain and increase their exports. With the deepening of China's economic reforms and, in particular, the decentralization of foreign trade, which led to a massive entrance of private enterprises, many of the incentives have been phased out, non-tariff barriers gradually dismantled and tariff barriers lowered significantly. Indirect instruments such as tax rebates have become increasingly important to boost trade in the Government's "encouraged" industrial sectors.

Over time, technological upgrading has become one of the greatest challenges in Chinese economic development. China's exports continue to have a relatively high import content, particularly of technology-intensive parts and components, as indicated by the fact that in 2005, 55 per cent of the exports fell into the category of processing trade, and in the same year 88 per cent of Chinese high-tech exports came from foreign-funded enterprises (FFEs) and 66 per cent from wholly foreign-owned enterprises (MOFCOM, 2006b). As recognized in China's five-year plan for 2006-2010, making scientific and technological advancement and domestic innovation a driving force for structural change and social development is of particular policy relevance at China's current stage of industrialization. So far, only a small number of firms have been reinvesting a significant share of their profits in R&D. The reliance on FDI for technological upgrading appears to have weakened domestic innovation and application of knowledge: since the 1990s, FFEs in China filed by far the largest proportion of patent applications, with local firms filing less than 20 per cent (Cao, 2004: 8). This may further inhibit technological progress in Chinese industry. Another problem lies in the application of patents: only 10 per cent of the domestically owned patents were applied in production annually between 1985 and 2003, in stark contrast to an annual average of 60 to 80 per cent in developed countries.[48] The lack of initiative on the part of domestic enterprises to innovate and upgrade technology may also be due to the wide technology gap between Chinese firms and competitors in advanced countries, which makes catching up very costly and highly risky for individual enterprises. Moreover, within international production chains Chinese firms have tended to be locked into labour-intensive activities, a tendency that has been reinforced by China's tax rebate system. The system was successful inasmuch as it contributed significantly to China's trade expansion, but it has done so by encouraging processing and assembling activities.

> Technological upgrading has become one of the greatest challenges in Chinese economic development.

As a result, advanced technology in China's export industry is still highly concentrated in affiliates of TNCs. This is evidenced by the high and growing share of FFEs in China's high-tech exports compared to their share in the country's total exports. In 2005, the share of FFEs in high-tech exports was 88 per cent, compared to 45 per cent in 1995, while the share of FFEs in China's total exports rose from 31 per cent to 58 per cent in the same period (MOFCOM, 2006b). At the beginning of China's opening up, policies towards FDI included measures aimed at coercing technology transfer and enhancing backward linkages. The FDI approval process frequently included explicit provisions for technology transfer in the form of local content requirements and production export quotas. In addition, joint venture projects served to obtain technology through collaboration in production, research or training. With China's accession to the WTO, in particular its commitment to abide by the TRIMs Agreement, these practices had to be abandoned. Besides, as China's FDI regime has been liberalized and administrative power increasingly decentralized, there has been growing competition among local governments to attract FDI. As a result, incentives to foreign investors have tended to become more generous, so that they frequently benefit from better than national treatment with little pressure for technology transfer, and there is risk of a race to the bottom in bidding for FDI. Although TNCs in China appear to have considerably increased their investment in R&D, this has been driven mainly by the abundant human resources available there, and their aim to create R&D centres close to the potentially rapidly growing Chinese market in order to adapt advanced technology to specific demands of local consumers (UNCTAD, 2005: 110–111). Overall, however, the level of diffusion of competitive technology of TNCs in China is still low.

With the end of the WTO transition period, most of the elements of China's earlier industrial policy have been phased out, in particular infant industry trade protection measures, preferential interest and tax rates, as well as some forms of direct financial assistance to industries. This has brought new challenges for the design and implementation of industrial policy. For instance, when the clauses covering technology requirement and export content in the Law of Wholly Foreign Owned Enterprises were repealed upon China's accession to the WTO, many FFEs separated from their local joint-venture partners to become wholly-owned foreign enterprises, making technological and other spillovers from FDI more difficult to obtain. Moreover, the possibilities for the Government to support domestic industries have diminished considerably. Recently, Canada, the EU and the United States requested consultations with China concerning its regulating of imports of automotive parts and components in order to support the development of the Chinese automobile industry, which they considered to be inconsistent with some WTO/GATT agreements.

Although direct intervention favouring domestic industries has declined with the growing importance of the private sector and China's accession to the WTO, the Government is still retaining a guiding role via indirect instruments such as taxation, the provision of guidelines for science and technology development[49] and certain forms of public financial support for related expenditures. At present, a reform of the system of value-added tax rebates is under discussion.[50] In the past, these rebates, which favoured raw materials and parts and components used as inputs for manufactured exports, had a significant impact on the structure of China's trade and industrial development in favour of processing trade. Now, increasingly it is believed that relying too much on the comparative advantage of labour-intensive products may discourage the upgrading of China's position to higher value-added production in the international supply chain. Another ongoing debate is about the possible elimination of the dual corporate tax system applied to foreign investors and domestic companies.[51] So far, foreign investors benefit from lower tax rates of between 15 and 24 per cent compared to domestic companies that have to pay 33 per cent. In addition, foreign investors are entitled to tax holidays if they invest in "encouraged sectors" or poor regions in China. Changes in these government policies are bound to have an impact on China's future industrial structure.

(c) Recent industrial policy in France

France has often been characterized as the European representative of State-led developmentalism. Particularly prior to economic liberalization in the 1980s, France pursued a developmentalist industrial policy supported by subsidies, credit controls, indicative planning, and direct intervention in State-owned enterprises. While liberalization eliminated government control over the allocation of credit by banks and other financial institutions, which previously had been the principal tool of industrial policy, subsidies survived, although they were used to a lesser extent. The importance of indicative planning was also drastically reduced, and, in any case, had already become less development orientated, given that in the aftermath of the economic slowdown of the

1970s industrial policy was directed more at avoiding bankruptcies and unemployment rather than at espousing an enlightened vision of economic development.

French industrial policy has traditionally focused on the development of sectors designated as being of national interest, such as steel and computer technology in the 1960s, nuclear power and telecommunications in the 1970s, electronics in the 1980s, and high-technology sectors more recently. The institutional structure in which industrial policy is embedded and the instruments used have been evolving over time in response to changes in the world economy, in particular the change in the international monetary system after 1973.[52] There was also concern that the strategy of nurturing national champions might cause industrial policy to be "captured" by the economic sectors it was designed to serve and develop, with the result that the instruments used would serve to create sectoral rents rather than accelerating national economic modernization.

France's recent industrial policy reforms mark a further evolution in the choice of institutional framework and policy instruments. Reflecting the general trend towards decentralization in that country, the new approach gives substantially more weight to local and regional government entities, even though the central Government retains a strong role. The new initiative also marks a shift away from a State-led approach based on the nurturing of a few large national enterprises to a private-sector-led approach. It relies on partnerships between firms (both large enterprises and SMEs, most of which collaborate with foreign, particularly German, enterprises), educational centres and research institutions in which the State mainly plays a merely facilitating role.

France's new industrial policy started, in 2002, a process aimed at defining a strategy for the promotion of clusters of competitiveness (*"pôles de compétitivité"*).[53] This resulted in the identification of 74 such clusters in 2005[54] and the launch of six clusters in March 2006. This new industrial policy is based on the observation that

> France's new industrial policy promotes clusters of competitiveness ...

having successfully narrowed the technology gap with the world leader, the United States, during the 1950s, 1960s and 1970s, in the past few years France's industrial development has not kept pace with technological progress and economic growth in some other developed countries, particularly the United States. This is reflected in (i) a decline in the contribution of manufacturing to total value added relative to that in other developed countries (in addition to the common trend in developed countries towards a growing services sector); (ii) a specialization pattern biased in favour of traditional, relatively low-technology-intensive sectors (such as agro-industry and transport equipment) at the expense of dynamic high-tech sectors; and (iii) growing international competition from developing countries and Central European economies in France's traditional industrial sectors, which has been accompanied by the relocation of some activities in these sectors from France to relatively low-wage countries, as well as by an erosion of the international competitiveness of France's existing high-tech sectors (Beffa, 2005).

Some observers have identified insufficient research and innovation activities as the root cause of the concentration of France's industrial specialization in relatively low-technology-intensive sectors and of its difficulties in developing high-tech sectors (Beffa, 2005; Jacquet and Darmon, 2005). Thus the main objective of France's new industrial policy is to promote research and innovation and improve industrial efficiency. It is expected that this will help increase the country's growth potential and social cohesion, change its pattern of industrial specialization by according greater importance to high-tech sectors, and enable the achievement of the highest level of technological competencies (Jacquet and Darmon, 2005: 72).

The clusters of competitiveness bring together enterprises, educational centres and private and public research institutions to work in partnership on common projects with a view to attaining a critical mass of economic activity within a geographical area. They aim to achieve technological innovation that will improve the competitiveness of French enterprises on international markets of substantial size or growth potential. There are two types of clusters: (i) a relatively small number of clusters, the research activities of which are organized around a specific area of technology with innovative activities aimed at applications at the technological frontiers (e.g. in biotechnology, nanotechnology and space industries); and (ii) a larger number of clusters that conduct more applied research closely targeting existing industrial sectors and markets with a significant growth potential at the global level (CIADT, 2004; Jacquet and Darmon, 2005: 63–74). Both types of clusters emphasize active partnerships for innovation.

The clusters were selected on the basis of a competitive process with the objective of identifying projects capable of making a significant contribution to the development of enterprises for which innovation is central to their competitiveness. Under the general oversight of the Inter-ministerial Committee for Regional Planning and Development (CIADT), which was chaired by the Prime Minister and which also had the final decision-making authority, the selection process was conducted by independent experts from the business, research and educational sectors, as well as by government experts at both local and ministerial levels. The assessment criteria included the cluster's potential for creating value added through innovation, for playing a leading role on international markets, for its reliance on a partnership with different actors, and the coherence of its economic development strategy with that of the geographical region in which it is located (CIADT, 2004).

... with the main objective to step up research and innovation and improve industrial efficiency.

The State's financial contribution to the clusters amounts to 1.7 billion euros for the period 2005-2007. The direct financial benefits take the form of subsidies, tax exemptions and reduced social contributions, as well as specific financial support and guarantees. These are supplemented by priority treatment in terms of the provision of IT-equipment and speedy administrative procedures, staffing of public research institutions, appraisal and exchange of technological knowledge, and a range of other measures (Jacquet and Darmon, 2005: 70–71 and 83; OECD, 2006: 77).

The funds are granted on the condition that the supported activities are not relocated (Jacquet and Darmon, 2005: 70).

While increasing the local ownership of projects, the decentralization, combined with the high fragmentation of local and regional State entities into multiple levels, has increased the administrative complexities of decision-making and poses an additional challenge to maintaining coherence in government actions. In addition, the selection process includes a sizeable element of subjectivity, as no strictly defined quantitative criteria are used. Moreover, it is not clear how the clusters' performance will be evaluated. Perhaps, most importantly, the call for project submission vastly exceeded expectations, resulting in the creation of more than four times the initially expected number of recognized clusters, while the funds allocated for their support were only doubled. This raises the question as to whether the allocated funds are sufficient to obtain the objective of reaching a critical mass (OECD, 2006: 16).

The new industrial policy in France has been designed under the general umbrella of the so-called "Lisbon Strategy". This Strategy, adopted at the European Council Summit in 2000[55] and updated in 2005, aims at increasing R&D intensity in the EU. The action plan of 2005, which reformulated the Strategy's priorities, provides an integrated approach to improving the conditions for business investment in R&D and innovation in order to meet the goal of increasing overall investment in research in the EU from 1.9 per cent of GDP to 3 per cent by 2010 (Commission of the European Communities, 2005).[56]

Within this EU-wide framework, the French approach is distinguished by its greater emphasis on a required increase in the contribution of public funds to industrial research. Beffa (2005), for example, notes that in the United States this share is between 12 per cent and 21 per cent, depending on the industrial sector, while in France, it is only 12 per cent on average for all industrial sectors. Moreover, France allocates much fewer of these funds than the United States to non-defence-related research in industrial frontier technologies. The funding provided to the competitiveness clusters attempts to narrow both these gaps.

This policy of broad-based sponsorship of partnerships between government, business, and educational and research institutions to advance industrial R&D and innovation has been a general tendency in developed countries over the past few years. It reflects a move away from public support to the development of productive capacity towards fostering innovation for the development of knowledge-based industries. Within this new strategy, support measures appear to be mainly of a general nature, but in practice they imply according priority to particular industrial sectors that have been identified, in one way or another, as offering considerable potential for innovation. As noted by Weiss (2005: 732), developed-country governments have implemented an extensive range of programmes to promote high-tech firms. These include support for pre-competitive R&D, facilitating access to venture capital, and the expansion and upgrading of a sophisticated infrastructure for the promotion and protection of intellectual property, information and telecommunications, and the appraisal and exchange of technological knowledge via pubic-private collaborative projects.

> Developed countries have the budgetary capacity to provide massive public support.

One reason for this shift towards the promotion of R&D and innovation activities has been the perception that outsourcing activities or the relocation of entire production units to cheaper locations no longer involves only labour-intensive assembly stages; it is also increasingly affecting more skilled activities. This has caused concern because it is generally believed that, contrary to the outsourcing of labour-intensive activities to lower-wage regions, a process that actually may improve an outsourcing firm's international competitiveness, outsourcing of high-tech activities deprives an economy of part of its dynamic development potential. Anxiety over the outsourcing of IT-based services to India has perhaps been the most vivid expression of this concern.

Multilateral trading rules provide sufficient latitude for developed countries to implement this strategy. As discussed in the previous section, the provision in Article 8 of the SCM Agreement allows subsidies for R&D and regional and environmental development activities, although they are now actionable. The fact that the developed countries have the budgetary capacity to provide massive public support to such activities highlights the asymmetry involved in the use of Article-8-type subsidies.

E. Conclusions: options for policy innovation

Experience with reforms over the past 15 years, as well as recent developments in economic theory concerning the creation of new areas of comparative advantage, provide a strong rationale for the adoption of proactive trade and industrial policies.

However, specific policy measures that successful countries have adopted cannot easily be emulated by other countries. Nevertheless, there are some common general principles underlying their success, and governments, through creative policy-making, could choose specific types of public support policies adapted to their country's particular local conditions, including its stage of economic and institutional development.

An assessment of the extent to which various international trade arrangements have restricted the degrees of freedom of developing countries to pursue proactive trade and industrial policies gives a mixed picture. On the one hand, WTO rules and commitments have made it far more difficult for developing countries to combine outward orientation with the unorthodox policy instruments that the mature and late industrializers employed to promote economic diversification and technological upgrading. The rules and commitments limit policy space in three areas. First, they severely restrict the use of subsidies to develop local production of new products or new modes of production; probably the greatest obstacle to sensible industrial policies in this context is the pro-

International trade arrangements have limited policy space in several areas.

hibition under the SCM Agreement to provide subsidies contingent on export performance.[57] Second, they prohibit the imposition on foreign investors of performance requirements that favour technology transfer and the use of domestically produced components. And third, they make it difficult or costly for domestic producers to undertake reverse engineering and imitation through access to technology that is covered by patent or copyright protection. Given these constraints, the URAs, by implication, lead to an increase in the relative importance of temporary protection in the form of industrial tariffs. Developing countries thus may find that tariffs are one of the few policy options left, and in this respect it may be of interest to modulate applied tariffs on particular industrial sectors around a stable average level of industrial tariffs, in line with a country's pace and pattern of technological upgrading. However, even this option is likely to be limited by the current WTO negotiations, as well as by RTAs.

On the other hand, under the current set-up of multilateral trade rules, countries still have the possibility to pursue policies that will be able to help generate new productive capacity and new areas of comparative advantage. Such types of policies largely concern the provision of public funds in support of R&D and innovation activities. Countries in a position to use the WTO rules and commitments to this effect can continue to support their own industries, target national champions, and generally promote national efforts towards technological advancement.

The case studies in section D of this chapter, which attempt to shed some light on the kinds of policies that have been used to support industrial development and technological upgrading over the past few years, indicate that:

- Coherence between macro- and microeconomic policies is crucial. A macroeconomic policy stance that leads to high domestic interest rates and an overvalued exchange rate is not conducive to investment that can bring about productivity growth and improve the international competitiveness of domestic enterprises, even when microeconomic and structural policies provide incentives for such investment.

- A coherent policy strategy that supports industrial development and technological upgrading also requires a pragmatic and strategic approach aimed at making FDI fit into the development agenda in a way that would help bring about not only faster and more sustained growth, but also structural and technological change. However, in the current international economic environment, where many countries compete with each other for FDI, only countries with a skilled labour force and a large enough domestic market and purchasing power potential are likely to have sufficient leverage over TNCs to secure technology transfer and productivity spillovers. On the other hand, even those countries will find it difficult to exert such leverage if there is intensive domestic competition for increased FDI through generous incentive packages at the provincial or municipal levels – a lesson learned from the experiences of some Latin American countries and China, as noted above.

- The shift in emphasis from trade and industrial policies based on protectionist measures for a limited number of industrial activities towards the provision of public funds to support all economic sectors has a significant fiscal impact. Subsidies imply a cost to public budgets, in the form of a loss of fiscal revenues (e.g. through tax exemptions) or an increase in fiscal expenditure (e.g. through the provision of subsidies), while protectionist measures in the form of tariffs provide fiscal revenues. Thus, as emphasized by Wade (2006), by pursuing public support policies solely on the basis of the provision of public funds, developing countries risk encountering serious budgetary and financial constraints, which will allow substantially lower levels of support compared to those provided in the past and those that developed countries continue to be able to provide.

- It also needs to be borne in mind that WTO rules and commitments carry the *threat* of sanctions, but the eventual imposition by trading partners of retaliatory tariffs or other measures depends on the actual damage.[58] Consequently, as long as the damage caused by a trading partner's infringement of rules is small, a WTO member State is unlikely to invoke the dispute settlement mechanism and initiate the imposition of sanctions. It would appear that this confers additional degrees of freedom on countries whose importance in world trade is relatively small.[59]

Thus, developing-country governments may wish to take advantage of the degrees of freedom in national policy-making that have remained untouched by the URAs. Indeed, the observation that multilateral rules still allow countries a certain degree of freedom to adopt open-economy industrial policies and that infringements are liable to challenge only when the dispute settlement mechanism is invoked, has led to the hypothesis that "[w]hat constrains sensible industrial policy today is largely the willingness to adopt it, not the ability to do so" (Rodrik, 2004: 32).

However, the asymmetries in the URAs should not be underestimated. They result from the fact that while the negotiated agreements extend to all WTO members in the same way in terms of *legal* obligations, they are much more burdensome for developing countries in *economic* terms. This implies that it is crucially important to look at the "level playing field" metaphor not in terms of *legal* constraints, but in terms of *economic* constraints, considering countries' different structural features and levels of industrial development.

Moreover, what is left of the degree of freedom for developing-country policymakers after the URAs has been reduced through regional and bilateral free trade agreements with developed countries. These agreements typically extend the range of disciplines beyond those found in the URAs regarding investment regulation and intellectual property rights protection.

Current trade negotiations threaten to further curtail the degree of freedom for developing country-policymakers. At the multilateral level, the threats are probably greatest in the intellectual property rights negotiations being conducted under the aegis of WIPO – where developed countries are pushing for further harmonization of national patent regulations – and in the current multilateral trade negotiations on industrial tariffs.[60] Concerning the negotiations on industrial tariffs, employing a harmonizing formula (across products and/or countries), cutting tariffs line-by-line rather than just on average, would reduce the degree of freedom for developing countries to protect some industrial sectors while liberalizing others. Most importantly, it will reduce the flexibility to increase tariffs that had previously been cut, as shown by Laird, Vanzetti and Fernández de Córdoba (2006).[61] Maintaining existing degrees of freedom for national policy-making would imply extending the notion of flexibility to the right to exempt some sectors from tariff-binding and tariff-cutting commitments, and to the right to maintain the *average* level of tariffs at negotiated levels while being able to flexibly raise and lower tariffs in specific sectors, as deemed necessary for industrial upgrading and development.

It needs to be recognized that developing-country policymakers willingly signed on to many of the commitments in international trade agreements, which implied a reduction in their *de jure* policy autonomy. This was motivated by the expectation that the resulting benefits would far outweigh the costs of such commitments. Another possible reason for doing

> Developing countries may find that tariffs are one of the few policy options left.

> Some degrees of freedom in national policy-making remained untouched by the URAs, but the asymmetries in the URAs should not be underestimated.

so may have been the fear of adverse reactions by multilateral lending agencies, international financial markets and foreign investors. As Finger and Nogues (2002) note, at the end of the UR, developing countries were faced with the choice of accepting what was proposed or risk being marginalized in the international trade regime.[62] Regarding bilateral trade agreements, it appears that the emphasis on export promotion as a development strategy led many developing countries to believe that securing and increasing access to developed-country markets by signing free trade agreements is almost an end in itself.

More recently, however, developing countries have been making concerted efforts to prevent a further reduction of their policy autonomy and to recover some of their lost autonomy (Gallagher, 2005: 12). This implies that, in light of their experience with adherence to the existing multilateral rules and disciplines, many governments today believe that too much policy autonomy was conceded during the UR, without gaining much in return. According to this view, some of the concessions developing countries made in the URAs, such as in TRIPS and TRIMs, were on the understanding that these were in exchange for developed countries' providing improved market access. However, as discussed in chapter III above, developed countries have largely failed to follow through on their side of the deal.

The Doha Work Programme has yet to deliver on the development promise of the Doha Declaration. The eventual outcome may well further reduce flexibility in policy-making by developing countries, particularly in the area of industrial tariffs. On the other hand, a failure of the ongoing multilateral negotiations could result in greater importance being given to regional or bilateral free trade arrangements as the legal mechanisms that define rules and disciplines in international trade. While these arrangements may improve developing countries' access to developed-country markets, they may entail a reduction in the degree of freedom in national policy-making that could be greater than that emerging from a Doha Round Agreement.

This could make it even more difficult to develop the supply capacity needed to take advantage of improved export opportunities. ■

Notes

1   As discussed in *TDR 2005*, India's reliance on the services sector is the major exception to this pattern but to what extent India can sustain rapid economic growth without rapidly expanding its manufacturing sector is an open question.

2   There is no generally accepted definition of industrial policy. Chang (1996: 60) defines it "as a policy aimed at *particular industries* (and firms as their components) to achieve the outcomes that are *perceived by the state* to be *efficient* for *the economy as a whole*" (emphasis in original). In a similar vein, Pack and Saggi (2006: 2) argue that "industrial policy is basically any type of selective intervention or government policy that attempts to alter the sectoral structure of production toward sectors that are expected to offer better prospects for economic growth than would occur in the absence of such intervention, i.e., in the market equilibrium". In this sense, the desired outcome of industrial policy can be considered to be the creation of new production capacity and new comparative advantage, enabling an economy to progress upwards in the international division of labour. By contrast, Rodrik (2004: 3) stresses that "the analysis of industrial policy needs to focus not on the policy *outcomes* – which are inherently unknown ex ante – but on getting the policy *process* right" (emphasis in original).

3   It has also been questioned whether developing-country governments have the administrative and institutional capability to design and implement active trade and industrial policies. This issue is addressed in chapter VI.

4   A further argument, associated with the literature on "strategic trade theory" initiated by Brander and Spencer (1985), relates to international rent shifting on the basis of strategic interdependence among a small number of firms. However, the policy outcome of this argument is very sensitive to even small changes in the underlying model assumptions. Moreover, the model is often based on the interdependence of a duopolist structure (i.e. a market structure that is most relevant for high-tech enterprises in developed countries). Thus, apart from isolated cases, such as that relating to the aircraft firms Embraer and Bombardier, there appears to be little in strategic trade theory of relevance for developing countries.

5   These arguments stem largely from the concept of circular and cumulative causation that posits a circular relationship between growth in productivity and growth in total output. The main proponents of this concept – including Young, Rosenstein-Rodan, Hirschman, Myrdal, Kaldor and, more recently, Cornwall, McCombie and Thirlwall – employ similar or related analytical tools as those of recent empirical studies of late industrialization (e.g. Amsden, 1989, 2001; Wade, 1990, 2003a; *TDR 1996, 2003*). They argue that there are pervasive and significant increasing returns and externalities; complementarities in investment, production and consumption; endogenous technical change and factor creation; imperfect information, and a dependence of the capital-labour ratio on the size of the market, which, taken together, contradict the conditions for general equilibrium (see Toner, 1999, and Ros, 2000, for detailed accounts).

6   This also largely depends on the extent to which productivity growth translates into an increase in aggregate demand (i.e. issues related to income distribution).

7   With international trade in intermediate goods, domestic producers may import their production inputs. However, such imports are likely to pose problems of technology adaptation similar to those related to the purchase of foreign machinery and equipment.

8   To be sure, innovation in developing countries does not generally mean pushing out the technology frontier. Rather, it means developing products or processes at home that are new for the specific economy but that may already be well established in world markets.

9   Technical evaluations may provide some indication of the cost structure, but undertaking such an evaluation itself represents an initial investment.

10   Noland and Pack (2005: 4) argue that the existing technological barriers will cause the entry of imitators to be slow, so that the innovative enterprise will have a considerable time period during which it will not face much competition from local firms. However, if the speed of imitative entry depends on the degree of technological innovation, it is likely that the size of the start-up investment will also depend on the size of existing technological barriers, thereby extending the time period required to recover the start-up investment.

11   In the discussion on the volatility of different types of capital inflows (*TDR 2003*), it has been noted that in the evolving international environment, where finance has assumed a more prominent role in shaping international economic relations, liberalization of financial flows and related innovations in financial market instruments allow for hedging of FDI flows. This tends to blur the distinction between FDI and other types of capital flows by making FDI much more footloose and less stable than the kind often proposed in the argumentation in support of FDI as the key driver of industrialization in developing countries.

12   In new economic geography models, the structure of production in individual countries is determined, as in traditional trade theory, by the interaction between country characteristics and industry characteristics. But while traditional trade theory focuses on relative factor endowments of countries and factor intensities of goods, the mechanisms of new economic geography models also take into account market size and countries' geographical distance from the markets of the main developed countries, as well as the transport intensity of the industrial sectors, including the level of transport costs and the dependence on intermediate inputs. Mayer (2004) examines the relevance of these models for developing countries.

13   In the past, many countries maintained restrictions on imports of luxury consumer goods, but this was motivated not so much by industrial policy as by foreign-exchange management considerations.

14   Moreover, as a fundamental rule, it is clear that, to be successful, any kind of trade and industrial policy requires a stable macroeconomic environment conducive to investment.

15   Policy support for product or process innovation will be more successful if it can be directed at those activities with the highest potential to crowd in complementary investment and create technological spillovers. But the creation of linkages and interfirm spillovers very much depends on, among other things, the prevailing industry structure (i.e. whether all activities in an industrial sector are combined in large firms, such as in the *chaebols* of the Republic of Korea, or whether there is a dense network of smaller firms with forward and backward linkages). It is probably easier for large enterprises to exploit scale economies before potential imitative competitors enter the market, as well as to benefit from spillovers. On the other hand, this reduces the case for supportive policies designed to reduce the cost of innovative investment. An alternative may be to combine more horizontal support, targeted at new activities and processes more generally, with more selective measures aimed at fostering diversification and structural change.

16   Lall (2004), for example, builds a classification of different types of industrial policy around the attitude towards FDI based on a "competitiveness strategy", which seeks to identify the kind of public support required to attract FDI while laying the ground for knowledge spillovers.

17   Experience suggests that performance criteria should be related to productivity growth and structural change, rather than to a multiplicity of objectives such as rent transfer to particular groups on an ethnic, family, gender or interest group basis.

18   In addition to using formal policy tools, governments can also seek to exercise influence through informal administrative guidance, coercing recalcitrant firms if necessary. Wade (2003a: xxi–xxii), for example, describes how "nudging" foreign firms to switch supplies from imports to domestic producers, or nudging established industries quickly to provide markets for firms in innovative industries, was used in Taiwan Province of China. This kind of persuasion involved a mix of methods, such as promises of goodwill for future ventures, or delaying the granting of permission to import (that had earlier been approved quickly and automatically).

19   Examples include the incompatibility of standards between IBM personal computers and Apple Macintosh, computer chips made by Intel and other firms, or competing standards for third-generation telephone handsets, optical disk storage or high-definition televisions. By contrast, open source software is an example of global compatibility because it makes the source code of an application available via the Internet.

20   Departing from the MFN rule, there are provisions that allow free trade agreements and customs unions among WTO members under certain conditions. Moreover, the so-called "escape clause" allows a WTO member to suspend its obligations as a tem-

porary emergency measure, accompanied by the adoption of adjustment policies.

21   The agreements also included liberalization commitments relating to non-tariff barriers, as well as commitments in the areas of agriculture and services, but these are not considered here.

22   Investment-related disciplines of the multilateral trading regime are also contained in the General Agreement on Trade in Services (GATS) as part of mode 3 (i.e. supply through commercial presence). For a detailed discussion of this area, see Wade, 2003b; and Cho and Dubash, 2005.

23   These transition periods were five years for developing countries (i.e. until the end of 2000), and seven years for the least developed countries (LDCs), with some further extensions granted to countries experiencing implementation difficulties for development, finance or trade reasons.

24   This concerns disputes Nos. 51, 52, 65 and 81 against Brazil; Nos. 146 and 175 against India; Nos. 54, 55, 59 and 64 against Indonesia; No. 195 against the Philippines, and Nos. 339, 340 and 342 against China. For details, see www.wto.org/english/tratop_e/dispu_e/dispu_status_e.htm.

25   Since TRIMs applies only to trade in goods, governments can impose local procurement requirements with respect to services such as banking, insurance and transport, as long as such measures remain possible under GATS disciplines.

26   This is in contrast to the Subsidies Code of the Tokyo Round, which was voluntary and extended only to national governments.

27   Subsidies for research had to be for activities conducted by firms or by higher education or research establishments on a contract basis with firms, on the condition that the assistance covered not more than 75 per cent of the cost of industrial research or 50 per cent of the cost of pre-competitive development activity. Eligible regions were defined as those whose per capita income did not exceed 85 per cent of the country's average or those whose unemployment quota had been at least 110 per cent of the country's average over a three-year period. Regarding environmental objectives, subsidies were permitted for the "promotion of adapting existing facilities to new environmental regulations".

28   The Agreement refers to seven areas of intellectual property: copyrights, trademarks, geographical indications, utility models, patents, integrated circuits and undisclosed information.

29   The LDCs have been granted a general transition period until 1 July 2013, and an additional extension until 1 January 2016 with regard to patents and undisclosed information relating to pharmaceutical products.

30   While the focus of this discussion is on the impact of the TRIPS Agreement on industrial development, it should be noted that access to medicines in developing countries has gained considerable attention. This has mainly a humanitarian dimension, but it can also be of considerable importance for pharmaceutical industries in developing countries. The Doha Declaration clarified the need to interpret TRIPS from a public health perspective, and thus improved the Agreement's developmental aspects in terms of access to medicines. It explicitly recognizes the flexibility within TRIPS to grant compulsory licences and the right of countries to determine the grounds on which these are granted. The WTO decision of 30 August 2003 waives the limitation on exports of generic products if they go to countries having insufficient manufacturing capacity.

31   For specific examples, see Morin, 2003; and Shadlen, 2005b.

32   The advent of the avian influenza made compulsory licensing a global issue because of the widespread perception that patent protection of the apparently only efficient drug in this area is a barrier to preparations for combating a potential pandemic. For a detailed discussion of the impact of developing countries' bilateral free trade agreements with the EU and the United States on intellectual property rights that affect access to medicines, see Correa, 2006.

33   Kowalski (2005: 11) points out that in upper-middle-income countries, the share of import duties in total government revenue fell from about 20 per cent in the late 1980s to about 7 per cent in the early 2000s; the respective shares for lower-middle-income countries were 25 per cent and 16 per cent, and for low-income countries 27 per cent and 19 per cent respectively.

34   Full binding coverage and uniform tariffs also contribute to greater predictability of trade policy and market access, and thus foster the stability of the international trading system (Francois and Martin, 2002). But this is true only if the resulting loss of flexibility in tariff policy is not replaced by a greater application of non-tariff measures, which are generally less transparent than tariffs. Moreover, it is exchange-rate instability that often constitutes the most serious threat to the predictability and stability of international trade flows and the international trading system (*TDR 2004*).

35   Moreover, developing countries would need to be able to raise tariffs in particular industrial sectors without much cost. GATT Article XVIII: A and XVIII: C allows countries to remove tariff concessions or use quotas for infant industry protection, but in order to do so they have to "negotiate" and "compensate". While these obligations maintain transparency and help to avoid abuse, this procedure can be cumbersome and involve costly compensation. The so-called "escape clause" under Article XIX allows a WTO member State to suspend

its obligations under certain conditions in order to safeguard its industry. However, these safeguards can be invoked only as temporary emergency measures and must be accompanied by adjustment; thus they do not provide an instrument for promoting competitive industrial production.

36 This discrepancy between bound and applied tariffs is partly due to unilateral trade liberalization that many developing countries have undertaken either voluntarily or as a result of conditionalities imposed by multilateral lending institutions.

37 This statement relates to a comparison of India with the other countries in the table, but, as noted above, not with respect to the now developed countries when they were at India's current level of per capita income.

38 However, industrial upgrading in the Republic of Korea has largely relied on national enterprises, while it appears that much of the high-value-added industrial activity in China occurs in wholly foreign-owned enterprises, as discussed below.

39 This emphasis on international competitiveness is well illustrated by the fact that one of the main policy actions included in Brazil's Multi-Annual Plan for the period 1996–1999 was a reduction of the so-called "Brazil-cost", that is, "the extra labor and fiscal costs producers (both foreign and domestic) have to bear when producing in Brazil as opposed to producing in foreign countries" (Melo, 2001: 10).

40 Peres (2006) also notes that in bilateral or multilateral free trade negotiations, representatives from Latin American countries sometimes attempt to improve export opportunities for new industrial activities in order to promote industrial development.

41 This has been the case, in particular, for countries closely linked to the United States markets, either through geographical proximity or formal trade arrangements, such as Mexico and the smaller Central American and Caribbean countries.

42 For details on PROEX, see www.bb.com.br/appbb/portal/gov/ep/srv/fed/AdmRecPROEX.jsp. In a sense, it could be argued that, in terms of export finance, PROEX simply seeks to bring Brazilian exporters on an equal footing with their competitors in countries that have sustained macroeconomic stability and strong financial markets.

43 Moreover, in 2001–2003, Brazil challenged the compatibility with WTO rules and commitments of the low-interest financing provided by the Canadian Government to a foreign importer of Bombardier aircraft. In February 2002, the WTO dispute settlement panel ruled that this aid constituted an illegal subsidy.

44 As pointed out by Goldstein (2002: 112), to prevent abuse of the programme, financing must be at market rates plus a risk premium; loans must be for no longer than 10 years, and they must cover no

more than 85 per cent of the purchase in question. For a legal assessment of the WTO dispute settlement panel ruling, see Doh, 2003: 14–15.

45 For details on the criteria used for the selection of specific sectors, see Peres, 2006.

46 Employment creation and regional development have been additional objectives of support to SME clusters.

47 Gross domestic expenditure on R&D accounts, on average, for only 0.6 per cent of GDP in Latin America and the Caribbean, compared to 1.2 per cent in China, 1.8 per cent in the EU and 2.8 per cent in the United States (UNESCO, 2005).

48 See *China Daily,* Speed application of high-tech advance, 14 February 2006.

49 National Guideline on Medium and Long-term Programme for Science and Technology Development (2006–2020).

50 See *China Daily,* China to adjust export tax rebates, 6 June 2006 (http://en.ce.cn/Business/Macroeconomic/200606/15/t20060615_7365602.shtml).

51 See *Shanghai Securities Daily*, Merger of the dual tax system has reached the Ministry of Finance, 6 June 2006 (www.china.org.cn/chinese/zhuanti/2006ssgclt/1231761.htm).

52 Loriaux (2003: 108–109) argues that the move from fixed to flexible exchange rates in 1973 rendered a policy of State-controlled bank credit very costly because it led to an "overdraft economy" in which interest rate hikes had little or no impact on the demand for credit by businesses.

53 Jacquet and Darmon (2005: 86) point out that the creation of clusters of competitiveness is the "offensive" part of France's industrial policy, which has been complemented by a "defensive" part consisting of tax credits and other fiscal benefits for industrial sectors and geographical regions facing economic difficulties. For detailed information on clusters of competitiveness, see www.competitivite.gouv.fr/.

54 Some of the 67 initially chosen projects were merged, while the projects for an additional nine clusters were approved in December 2005 (Ministère de l'Economie, des Finances et de l'Industrie, 2006).

55 The European Council meeting in Lisbon in March 2000 set the objective of making Europe the most competitive and dynamic knowledge-based economy in the world by the year 2010 by, *inter alia*, creating a knowledge-based economy and enhancing competitiveness and innovation.

56 Apart from promoting the use of public procurement to stimulate research and innovation, the new initiatives in the action plan include: a revised State aid policy, which aims to reduce State aid gradually while refocusing it on activities that are likely to have the most sustainable impact on competitiveness, jobs and growth, and that promote cross-

border cooperation in research; tax incentives for firms to invest more in innovative areas; efforts towards the creation of an attractive single market within the EU for researchers, structural cohesion and regional funding focused more on research and innovation; and financial instruments to support research within SMEs (Commission of the European Communities, 2005).

57 Contrary to the broad-based and virtually unconditional protectionist measures that often accompanied inward-looking, import-substituting industrialization strategies, export targets were the main performance standard imposed by East Asian governments on business as a reciprocal control mechanism for public policy support. They were designed to help the supported production activities achieve international competitiveness and to minimize the risk of rent-seeking and other abuse of public policy support.

58 However, in some instances, the mere threat of sanctions from other countries may have an impact on a country's policy-making.

59 The generally long time lapse between the adoption of a certain policy measure that potentially infringes rules and the ruling of a dispute settlement panel may allow countries with strong administrative capabilities to achieve the intended goal and discontinue the policy measure before such a ruling and the potentially associated sanctions are adopted.

60 Another area is the negotiations on a multilateral investment agreement, now dormant, that aimed at removing virtually all restrictions on FDI.

61 It may also induce an even greater use of anti-dumping measures and countervailing duties, which are inherently discriminatory and costly to implement.

62 According to Finger and Nogues (2002: 334), influential developed countries had announced that they would withdraw from the GATT as soon as the WTO came into existence. This implied that a country that did not accept the "grand bargain" of the URAs would not have enjoyed protection from discriminatory treatment, either from the new WTO or the old GATT rules and regulations.

Notes for figure 5.2:
The product categories are based on the International Standard Industrial Classification (ISIC) Rev. 3 for Mexico and the Republic of Korea; and on ISIC Rev. 2 for Brazil. Resource-intensive manufactures include: 15, 16, 20, 21, 23, 26, 27 and 28 in Rev. 3, and 311, 313, 314, 331, 341, 353, 354, 362, 369, 371, 372 and 381 in Rev. 2. Labour-intensive manufactures include: 17, 18, 19, 22, 25, 36 and 37 in Rev. 3, and 321, 322, 323, 324, 332, 342, 355, 356, 361 and 390 in Rev. 2. Technology-intensive manufactures include: 24, 29, 30, 31, 32, 33, 34 and 35 in Rev. 3, and 351, 352, 382, 383, 384 and 385 in Rev. 2. This classification is based on the categories used in *TDR 2002*, chap. III.

References

Aguayo Ayala F and Gallagher KP (2005). *Preserving Policy Space for Sustainable Development: The Subsidies Agreement at the WTO*. Winnipeg, International Institute for Sustainable Development.

Akyüz Y (2005). The WTO negotiations on industrial tariffs: What is at stake for developing countries? Geneva, Third World Network.

Amsden AH (1989). *Asia's Next Giant: South Korea and Late Industrialization*. Oxford, Oxford University Press.

Amsden AH (1999). Industrialization under new WTO law. Paper prepared for the UNCTAD High-level Round Table on Trade and Development: Directions for the Twenty-first Century. TD(X)/RT.1/7. Geneva. 1 December 1999.

Amsden AH (2001). *The Rise of "the Rest": Challenges to the West from Late-Industrializing Economies*. New York, Oxford University Press.

Anderson K (2002). Economywide dimensions of trade policy and reform. In: Hoekman B, Mattoo A and English P, eds., *Development, Trade and the WTO. A Handbook*. Washington, DC, World Bank.

Bairoch P (1993). *Economics and World History. Myths and Paradoxes*. Chicago, University of Chicago Press.

Baldwin R (1969). The case against infant industry protection. *Journal of Political Economy*, 77: 295–305.

Baunsgaard T and Keen M (2005). Tax revenue and (or?) trade liberalization. Working Paper no. WP/05/12, International Monetary Fund, Washington, DC.

Beffa JL (2005). *Pour une nouvelle politique industrielle*. Paris, La documentation française.

Bora B, Lloyd PJ and Pangestu M (2000). Industrial policy and the WTO. *World Economy*, 23 (4): 543–559.

Brander J and Spencer B (1985). Export subsidies and international market share rivalry. *Journal of International Economics*, 18: 83–100.

Bruton H (1998). A reconsideration of import substitution. *Journal of Economic Literature*, 26: 903–936.

Burgess R and Venables AJ (2004). Toward a microeconomics of growth. In: Bourguignon F and Pleskovic B, eds., *Accelerating Development. Proceedings of the Annual World Bank Conference on Development Economics*. New York, World Bank and Oxford University Press.

Cao C (2004). Challenges for technological development in china's industry: Foreign investors are the main providers of technology. *China Perspectives,* no. 54 July/August. Paris, French Centre for Research on Contemporary China. Available at: www.cefc. com.hk/uk/pc/articles/art_ligne.php?num_art_ ligne=5401.

Chang HJ (1996). *The Political Economy of Industrial Policy*. Houndsmill and London, Macmillan.

Chang HJ (2002). *Kicking Away the Ladder: Development Strategy in Historical Perspective*. London, Anthem.

Chang HJ (2005). Kicking away the ladder: "good policies" and "good institutions" in historical perspective. In: Gallagher KP, ed., *Putting Development First. The Importance of Policy Space in the WTO and International Financial Institutions*. London and New York, Zed Books.

Chang HJ (2006). Policy space in historical perspective with special reference to trade and industrial policies. *Economic and Political Weekly*, 41: 627–633, 18 February.

Cho AH and Dubash NK (2005). Will investment rules shrink policy space for sustainable development? Evidence from the electricity sector. In: Gallagher KP, ed., *Putting Development First. The Importance of Policy Space in the WTO and International Financial Institutions*. London and New York, Zed Books.

Christiansen H, Oman C and Charlton A (2003). Incentives-based competition for foreign direct investment: the case of Brazil. Working Paper on International Investment no. 2003/1. Paris, OECD Directorate for Financial, Fiscal and Enterprise Affairs.

CIADT (Comité Interministériel d'Aménagement et de Développement du Territoire) (2004). Appel à projet: pôles de compétitivité. Paris. Available at:

www.competitivite.gouv.fr/IMG/pdf/Appel_a_
projets_poles_de_competitivite_VF.pdf.

Cimoli M et al. (2006). Growth, structural change and
technological capabilities: Latin America in a comparative perspective. Working Paper no. 2006/11.
Pisa. Laboratory of Economics and Management
(LEM), University of Pisa.

Commission of the European Communities (2005). More
research and innovation – investing for growth and
employment: a common approach. Document COM
(2005) 488 final. Brussels.

Correa CM (2000). *International Property Rights, the
WTO and Developing Countries. The TRIPS Agree-
ment and Policy Options*. London and Kuala
Lumpur, Zed Books and Third World Network.

Correa CM (2005). An agenda for patent reform and harmonization for developing countries. Paper prepared
for the Bellagio Dialogue on Intellectual Property
and Sustainable Development: Revising the Agenda
in a New Context, 24–28 September. International
Centre for Trade and Sustainable Development
(ICTSD).

Correa CM (2006). Implications of bilateral free trade
agreements on access to medicines. *Bulletin of the
World Health Organization*, 84 (5): 399–404.

Das BL (2003). *The WTO and the Multilateral Trading
System: Past, Present and Future*. London, New York
and Penang, Zed Books and Third World Network.

De Negri J (2006). Innovation, technology and performance of Brazilian industrial companies: major research findings. UNCTAD seminar presentation.
Mimeo. Brasilia, Institute for Applied Economic
Research (IPEA).

Di Caprio A and Amsden AH (2004). Does the new international trade regime leave room for industrialization
policies in the middle-income countries? Working
Paper no. 22 for the World Commission on the Social
Dimension of Globalization. Geneva, Policy Integration Department, International Labour Office.

Doh JP (2003). The Bombardier-Embraer dispute and its
implications for Western Hemisphere integration.
Policy Papers on the Americas, XIV (12). Washington, DC, Center for Strategic and International
Studies.

Ernst D (2004). Internationalisation of innovation: Why
is chip design moving to Asia? Working Paper 64,
East-West Center, Honolulu, HI, March.

Evans P (1995). *Embedded Autonomy: States and Industrial Transformation*. Princeton, NJ, Princeton University Press.

Finger JM and Nogues JJ (2002). The unbalanced Uruguay Round outcome: the new areas in future WTO
negotiations. *World Economy*, 25 (3): 321–340.

Francois JF and Martin W (2002). Binding tariffs: why
do it? In: Hoekman B, Mattoo A and English P, eds.,
Development, Trade and the WTO: A Handbook.
Washington, DC, the World Bank.

Gallagher KP (2005). Globalization and the nation-state:
reasserting policy autonomy for development. In:
Gallagher KP, ed., *Putting Development First: The
Importance of Policy Space in the WTO and Inter-
national Financial Institutions*. London and New
York, Zed Books.

Goldstein A (2002). EMBRAER: from national champion
to global player. *CEPAL Review*, 77: 97–115.

Gomory RE and Baumol WJ (2000). *Global Trade and
Conflicting National Interests*. Cambridge, MA, and
London, MIT Press.

Hausmann R and Rodrik D (2003). Economic development as self-discovery. *Journal of Development
Economics*, 72 (2): 603–633.

Imbs J and Wacziarg R (2003). Stages of diversification.
American Economic Review, 93 (1): 63–86.

Jacquet N and Darmon D (2005). *Les Pôles de Compétitivité*.
Paris, La documentation française.

Kaldor N (1966). *Causes of the Slow Rate of Economic
Growth of the United Kingdom*. Cambridge, Cambridge University Press.

Kowalski P (2005). Impact of changes in tariffs on developing countries' government revenue. Trade Policy
Working Paper no. 18. Paris, Organisation for Economic Co-operation and Development (OECD).

Krueger AO (1990). Government failures in development.
Journal of Economic Perspectives, 4: 9–23.

Kumar N (2003). Intellectual property rights, technology
and economic development: experiences of Asian
countries. *Economic and Political Weekly*, 23: 209–
225, 18 January.

Kumar N (2005). Performance requirements as tools of
development policy: lessons from developed and
developing countries. In: Gallagher KP, ed., *Putting
Development First: The Importance of Policy Space
in the WTO and International Financial Institutions*.
London and New York, Zed Books.

Laird S, Vanzetti D and Fernandez de Cordoba S (2006).
Smoke and mirrors: making sense of the WTO industrial tariff negotiations. UNCTAD Policy Issues
in International Trade and Commodities Study Series no. 30. United Nations publication, sales no.
E.05.II.D.16, New York and Geneva.

Lall S (2004). Reinventing industrial strategy. The role
of government policy in building industrial competitiveness. G-24 Discussion Paper no. 28. United
Nations document no. UNCTAD/GDS/MDPB/G24/
2004/4, New York and Geneva.

Landes DS (1998). *The Wealth and Poverty of Nations.
Why Some are so Rich and Some are so Poor*. New
York and London, WW Norton.

Levine R and Renelt D (1992). A sensitivity analysis of
cross-country growth regressions. *American Economic Review*, 82: 942–963.

Linden G (2004). China standard time: a study in strategic industrial policy. *Business and Politics*, 6 (3),
article 4. www.bepress.com/bap/vol6/iss3/art4.

Loriaux M (2003). France: a new 'capitalism of voice'? In: Weiss L, ed., *States in the Global Economy: Bringing Domestic Institutions Back In*. Cambridge and New York, Cambridge University Press.

Lu D (2001). Industrial policy and resource allocation: Implications on China's participation in globalization. *China Economic Review*, 11 (4): 342–360.

Lugones G (2006). Recent policy experiences of structural change in Latin America: selected case studies. Mimeo. Geneva, UNCTAD.

Maddison A (2001). *The World Economy: A Millennial Perspective*. Paris, Organisation for Economic Co-operation and Development (OECD).

Maskus KE (1997). Implications of regional and multilateral agreements for intellectual property rights. *World Economy*, 20: 681–694.

Mayer J (1996). Learning sequences and structural diversification in developing countries. *Journal of Development Studies*, 33 (2): 210–229.

Mayer J (2004). Industrialization in developing countries: some evidence from a new economic geography perspective. UNCTAD Discussion Paper no. 174. Geneva.

Meade JE (1955). *Trade and Welfare: The Theory of International Economic Policy,* Vol. 2. London, New York and Toronto, Oxford University Press.

Melo A (2001). Industrial policy in Latin America and the Caribbean at the turn of the century. Working Paper no. 459, Inter-American Development Bank, Washington, DC.

Ministère de l'Economie, des Finances et de l'Industrie (2006). *Tableau de Bord de l'Innovation. 14e édition*. Paris. Available at: www.industrie.gouv.fr/observat/innov/pdf/tbi14.pdf.

MOFCOM (2006a). FDI Statistics by Ministry of Commerce (China). Available at: http://kjs.mofcom.gov.cn/aarticle/bn/bs/200601/20060101437606.html.

MOFCOM (2006b). *FDI Statistics and Analysis of High-tech Imports and Exports of 2005*. Department of Science and Technology of the Ministry of Commerce (China), January. Available at: www.mofcom.gov.cn, accessed 29 Jan. 2006.

Moreno-Brid JC, Rivas Valdivia JC and Santamaria J (2005). Mexico: economic growth, exports and industrial performance after NAFTA. *Serie Estudios y Perspectivas*, ECLAC, Santiago.

Morin JF (2003). Le droit international des brevets : entre le multilatéralisme et le bilatéralisme américain. *Etudes Internacionales*, 34 (4): 537–562.

Mortimore M and Barron F (2005). Informe sobre la industria automotriz mexicana. *Serie Desarrollo Productivo* no. 162, ECLAC, Santiago.

Noland M and Pack H (2005). The East Asian industrial policy experience: implications for the Middle East. Working Paper 05–14, Institute for International Economics, Washington, DC.

OECD (2005). *Science, Technology and Industry Scoreboard 2005*. Paris. Organisation for Economic Co-operation and Development.

OECD (2006). *Examens Territoriaux de l'OCDE : France*. Paris, Organisation for Economic Co-operation and Development.

Pack, H (2000). Industrial policy: growth elixir or poison? *World Bank Research Observer*, 15: 47–67.

Pack H and Saggi K (2006). The case for industrial policy: a critical survey. Working Paper 3839, the World Bank, Washington, DC.

Peres W (2006). El (lento) retorno de las políticas industriales en América Latina y el Caribe. *Serie Desarrollo Productivo* no. 166, ECLAC, Santiago.

Puga D and Venables AJ (1996). The spread of industry: spatial agglomeration in economic development. Discussion Paper 1354, Centre for Economic Policy Research, London.

Puga, D and Venables AJ (1999). Agglomeration and economic development: import substitution versus trade liberalization. *Economic Journal*, 109: 292–311.

Reichman JH and Hasenzahl C (2003). Non-voluntary licensing of patented inventions: Historical perspective, legal framework under TRIPS, and an overview of the practice in Canada and the USA. Issue Paper no. 5, UNCTAD-ICTSD Project on IPRs and Sustainable Development. Geneva, UNCTAD and ITCSD.

Rodriguez F and Rodrik D (2000). Trade policy and economic growth: a skeptic's guide to the cross-national evidence. In: Bernanke B and Rogoff KS, eds., *Macroeconomics Annual 2000*. Cambridge, MIT Press.

Rodrik D (2004). Industrial policy for the twenty-first century. Discussion Paper no. 4767, Centre for Economic Policy Research, London. November.

Rodrik D (2006). Goodbye Washington Consensus, Hello Washington Confusion? Mimeo. January. Available at: http://ksghome.harvard.edu/~drodrik/Lessons%20of%20the%201990s%20review%20_JEL_.pdf.

Ros J (2000). *Development Theory and the Economics of Growth*. Ann Arbor, MI, University of Michigan Press.

Safarian AE (2003). The use and impact of performance requirements in developed countries. In: *UNCTAD, The Development Dimension of FDI: Policy and Rule-Making Perspectives*. Proceedings of the Expert Meeting held in Geneva from 6–8 November 2002. Document no. UNCATD/ITE/IIA/2003/4, United Nations publication, sales no. E.03.II.D.22, United Nations, New York and Geneva.

Sala-i-Martin X, Doppelhofer G and Miller RI (2004). Determinants of long-term growth: a Bayesian averaging of classical estimates (BACE) approach. *American Economic Review*, 94: 813–835.

Scitovsky T (1954). Two concepts of external economies. *Journal of Political Economy*, 62 (2): 143–151.

Shadlen K (2005a). Exchanging development for market access? Deep integration and industrial policy under multilateral and regional-bilateral trade agreements. *Review of International Political Economy*, 12: 750–775.

Shadlen K (2005b). Policy space for development in the WTO and beyond: the case of intellectual property rights. Working Paper no. 05–06, Global Development and Environment Institute, Tufts University, Medford.

Singh A (2005). Special and differential treatment: the multilateral trading system and economic development in the twenty-first century. In: Gallagher KP, ed., *Putting Development First: The Importance of Policy Space in the WTO and International Financial Institutions*. London and New York, Zed Books.

Stiglitz JE (2005). Development policies in a world of globalization. In: Gallagher KP, ed., *Putting Development First: The Importance of Policy Space in the WTO and International Financial Institutions*. London and New York, Zed Books.

Toner P (1999). *Main Currents in Cumulative Causation: The Dynamics of Growth and Development*. Houndsmill and London, Macmillan.

Tsangarides CG (2005). Growth empirics under model uncertainty: Is Africa different? Working Paper no. 05/18, International Monetary Fund. Washington, DC. January.

UNCTAD (1994). *Directory of Import Regimes. Part I: Monitoring Import Regimes*. UNCTAD/DMS/2/ Rev.1 (PART I). United Nations publication, sales no. E.94.II.D.6, New York.

UNCTAD (2000). *World Investment Report 2000: Cross-border Mergers and Acquisitions and Development*. United Nations publication, sales no. E.00.II.D.20, New York and Geneva.

UNCTAD (2005). Globalization of R&D and developing countries. UNCTAD/ITE/IIA/2005/6, Geneva.

UNCTAD and ICTSD (2005). *Resource Handbook on TRIPS and Development*. Cambridge, Cambridge University Press.

UNCTAD (various issues). *Trade and Development Report*, United Nations publication, New York and Geneva.

UNESCO (2005). *Science Report 2005*. Paris, UNESCO.

UNIDO (2005). *Industrial Development Report 2005. Capability Building for Catching-up. Historical, empirical and policy dimensions*. United Nations publication, sales no. E.05.II.B.25, Vienna. United Nations Industrial Development Organization.

United States Trade Representative (USTR) (2004). The Work of USTR – Intellectual Property. Washington, DC. Available at: www.ustr.gov.

Wade RH (1990). *Governing the Market*. Princeton, Princeton University Press.

Wade RH (2003a). Creating capitalisms. Introduction to the 2003 edition of *Governing the Market*. Princeton, Princeton University Press.

Wade RH (2003b). What strategies are viable for developing countries today? The World Trade Organization and the shrinking of 'development space'. *Review of International Political Economy*, 10 (4): 621–644.

Wade RH (2006). Bringing industrial policies back in: Breaking the policy monopoly. Mimeo. Background paper prepared for UNCTAD's *Trade and Development Report 2006*.

Weiss L (2005). Global governance, national strategies: how industrialized states make room to move under the WTO. *Review of International Political Economy*, 12 (5): 723–749.

Wood A and Mayer J (1998). Africa's export structure in a comparative perspective. African Development in a Comparative Perspective, Study no. 4, UNCTAD, Geneva.

World Bank (1993). *The East Asian Miracle: Economic Growth and Public Policy*. New York and Oxford, Oxford University Press for the World Bank.

World Bank (2005). *Economic Growth in the 1990s. Learning from a Decade of Reform*. Washington, DC, World Bank.

WTO (2001). Implementation-Related Issues and Concerns. Decision of 14 November 2001. Document WT/MIN(01)/17, World Trade Organization, Geneva.

WTO (2004). The July 2004 Package. Available at: www. wto.org/english/tratop_e/dda_e/dda_package_ july04_e.htm

WTO and UNCTAD (2002). Joint Study on Trade-Related Investment Measures and Other Performance Requirements. WTO document G/C/W/307/Add.1, Geneva.

Zeira J (1997). Investment as a process of search. *Journal of Political Economy*, 95: 204–210.

Chapter VI

INSTITUTIONAL AND GOVERNANCE ARRANGEMENTS SUPPORTIVE OF ECONOMIC DEVELOPMENT

A. Introduction

In the preceding chapter it has been argued that economic policies in support of industrialization and technological upgrading need to aim not just at efficiency gains, but also, primarily, at strengthening the creative forces of markets to induce capital accumulation and promote innovation and productivity. The present chapter examines institutional and governance structures at both the national and international levels that are best suited to complement these policies.

There is an increasing consensus among economists and policymakers that national institutions are a critical determinant of the pace of per capita income growth. But there is much less agreement as to what their role should be in helping to achieve sustained economic growth and development and, by implication, what types of institutional arrangements are appropriate to achieve these objectives.

Conventional wisdom envisages the main role of institutions as being one of reducing transaction costs so as to create missing markets and make existing markets function more efficiently.

According to this view, the main objective of economic policies is to ensure an efficient allocation of resources in the context of competitive equilibrium, supported by universally applicable forms of institutions, particularly for granting and protecting property rights. This goal is to be achieved by identifying "global best practices" derived from the current institutional set-up in developed countries and transplanting them to developing countries.

Another view, which emphasizes the need for developing countries to achieve economic catch-up through industrialization and structural change, envisages an additional role for institutions, which supports and accelerates the dynamic transformation of developing economies. From this perspective, their crucial role is to provide mechanisms for the effective implementation of policies designed to achieve high rates of investment and encourage the adoption of new technologies. Moreover, the dynamic evolution of economies is determined much less by efficiency criteria than is assumed by the conventional view. Thus, the guiding principle of institutional change should not be to use institutions to reduce departures from the competitive equilibrium ideal of neoclassical economics, but instead to address the information and coordination failures that undermine decision-making and improve checks and balances on the use of government discretion. While such institutional arrangements have to fulfil similar functions in different countries, the form of institutions will vary from country to country, as well as within the same country over time.

> Coherence between policies and institutional arrangements is of crucial importance for successful economic development.

The need for proactive trade and industrial policies to support and accelerate capital accumulation and structural change has long been recognized in development economics, as discussed in the previous chapter, and a large number of developing countries pursued such policies until the beginning of the 1980s. However, at the time, it was not well recognized that the successful implementation of such strategies requires a complementary set of institutional and administrative capabilities.[1] It was only when the successful experiences of the late industrializers, particularly in East Asia, had been properly assessed that the importance of

supportive institutional arrangements came to be more widely acknowledged (see, for example, Amsden, 1989, 2001; Wade, 1990; *TDR 1994, 1996*; Evans, 1995; Chang, 1996).[2] A key finding of these studies is that coherence between policies and institutional arrangements is of crucial importance for successful economic development.

Section B of this chapter addresses these issues in relation to national institutions, and section C discusses institutional and governance arrangements at the international level. Polanyi (1944) was among the first to highlight the governance problems that arise when the regulatory reach of a country's economic, political and administrative institutions is confined to its national borders, while forces unleashed by globalization and growing integration into world markets increasingly constrain countries in enabling their citizens to realize their goals. Section C substantiates the argument that only well-structured and appropriately functioning multilateral governance arrangements can resolve this problem.

B. National institutional and governance structures in support of sustained economic growth

1. Institutions and governance

Conceptually, no clear distinction can be made between institutions and governance. Governance refers to the exercise of political, economic and administrative authority in managing a country's affairs at all levels. It comprises a complex set of mechanisms, processes, relationships and institutions through which citizens and groups articulate their interests, exercise their rights and obligations and mediate their differences.[3] Thus institutions are one part of governance structures, but they have a wider reach than governance structures. They encompass both formal and informal social structures and mechanisms, including rules and regulations that affect the behaviour of individuals and the functions of the State.

Institutions have often been defined as the rules of the game, or a set of humanly devised formal and informal constraints on political, economic and social interactions (North, 1990). This definition, which has been a hallmark of "new institutional economics", sees human actors as making rational choices in market transactions that, under given and unchanging preferences, maximize their utility. The function of institutions is to give individuals the opportunities and incentives to engage in profitable market activity by transmitting information, enforcing property rights and contracts, and managing the degree of competition.

By contrast, the approach of what is sometimes called "old institutional economics" advocates a broader view of institutions (Hodgson, 2004). It argues that a country's historical and cultural context is, through its impact on habits, a crucial determinant of the country's institutions and of the activities and behaviour of its citizens, an important aspect of which includes non-selfish values (Hodgson, 1998). From this perspective, institutions not only *constrain* the behaviour of individuals, they also *enable* the achievement of goals requiring supra-individual coordination, and are *constitutive* in shaping the ways that groups and individuals use to define their preferences (Chang and Evans, 2005: 100).

The differing views on what shapes preferences and behaviour, and what should be the role of institutions in this connection, also imply diverging opinions about the role of the State and the scope for discretionary, as opposed to rules-based, policies. Much of neoclassical economics, which is complemented by the new institutional economics, views economic policies as being adopted and implemented by self-seeking politicians and bureaucrats who have limited ability to collect information and implement policies and who are subject to pressure from interest groups. This, the argument goes, often results in government failure in the form of regulatory capture, rent-seeking, and corruption, which distort the supposed rationality of the market system. According to this view, the functions of the State need to be restricted through deregulation and privatisation, and the scope for policy discretion needs to be reduced by strengthening rules of conduct or setting up politically independent agencies involved in policy-making (e.g. independent central banks) bound by strict rules.

By contrast, from the perspective of old institutional economics, it is erroneous to assume that individuals have preconceived and unchanging selfish preferences. Rather, there is an interrelationship between institutions and the preferences and behaviour of individuals (Hodgson, 2005). This interrelationship means, first, that institutions can be seen as the cumulative outcome of past behaviour of individuals and past policy actions. In this sense, institutions are the path-dependent outcome of a society's preferences, behavioural patterns and policies. As emphasized by Rodrik, Subramanian and Trebbi (2004), the legitimacy and desirability of institutional arrangements have a large element of context specificity, stemming from differences in countries' cultural and historical trajectories, other initial conditions, and the political economy of decision-making processes.

Second, as argued by Chang and Evans (2005), who emphasize the constitutive role of institutions, this interrelationship implies that both formal rules and informal norms influence human preferences, as well as individuals' views on legitimate targets of policy and legitimate actions needed to achieve those targets. To the extent that institutions emphasize non-selfish values, individuals can internalize many such values. In this sense, policy-making is a process whereby individuals with different views on the legitimacy and contestability of existing targets and instruments compete with each other. Thus appropriate institutions can ensure that interest groups attempting to alter the "rational" order of markets according to their own specific interests do not dominate the policy-making process.

Third, the interrelationship between institutions and the preferences and behaviour of individuals also implies that desirable outcomes of

> Institutions influence the preferences of individuals and their views on legitimate policy targets and actions.

> The *functions* that institutions have to fulfil must be distinguished from the *forms* of institutions that serve those functions best.

institutional arrangements can be achieved by a variety of context-specific designs. Thus, for example, Chang (1998) and Rodrik (2005) emphasize the need to distinguish the *functions* that institutions have to fulfil in order to promote economic development from the *forms* of institutions that serve those functions best. For instance, the function of institutional arrangements to secure property rights – much emphasized by institutional reform agendas – can be achieved through different forms of legislation and different degrees of independence of the judiciary system and contract enforcement arrangements. A frequently cited example in this context refers to the fact that in a country with no formal definition of property rights (such as China), those rights may in reality be more secure[4] than in some of the countries where property rights are formally defined and protected and where a formally independent judiciary system exists (see, for example, Rodrik, Subramanian and Trebbi, 2004). Another example relates to the vast differences between Japan, the United States and Europe (as well as within Europe) in institutional set-ups to protect property rights, regulate markets and address social protection. Both these examples indicate that institutional outcomes are more directly related to the effectiveness with which institutions perform their functions, and only indirectly to the forms that such institutions take.

As emphasized by Rodrik, Subramanian and Trebbi (2004), recognizing the difference between institutional functions and their forms means that economic policy targets (such as the protection of property rights, macroeconomic stability, or industrial restructuring) can be achieved through a variety of institutional forms. It does not imply that economic principles work differently in different places, but rather that transferring specific forms of institutions from developed to developing economies is not a sufficient condition for good economic performance.

2. Institutions and market efficiency

Much of the current debate on the role of institutions in economic development emphasizes their function in reducing uncertainty and promoting market efficiency. Some see their role as being to ensure that markets function as closely as possible to the ideal of neoclassical economics, which is that competitive markets result in the efficient allocation of resources (see, for example, World Bank, 2001). According to this view, implementation of economic policies associated with the "Washington Consensus" has failed to bring about good economic results because of the absence of supporting institutions in most developing countries. As a result, multilateral lending institutions and many donor governments have increasingly attached governance-related conditionality – often referred to as second-generation reforms – to their loans and grants.

From this perspective, transaction costs are considered the main reason why the functioning of actual markets deviates from its theoretical ideal.[5] Transaction costs arise from contested or unclear property rights, incomplete or asymmetric information and related external effects, as well as inefficient and costly contract enforcement and dispute resolution. Corruption may further increase transaction costs, and can even disrupt contract enforcement and property rights protection. It is therefore suggested that transaction costs can be minimized by restricting the activities of the State to the creation and enforcement of property rights and the rule of law, the provision of public goods (such as physical infrastructure, education and health) and regulation in favour of creating missing markets and enhancing the efficiency of existing ones. Under these conditions, private investors pursuing their individual profit maximization objective would drive economic development and maximize the economic welfare of the economy as a whole.

Proponents of this approach point to empirical evidence from cross-country regressions, in which the level or the growth rate of per capita income is regressed on specific institution-related measures. These analyses typically find a positive correlation between the quality of institutions and economic growth to argue that an improvement in market-enhancing institutional conditions (such as the protection of property rights, the rule of law and anti-corruption policies) will promote growth and accelerate convergence with advanced countries.

The methodology of these econometric studies has been criticized for three main reasons. First, these studies generally use institution-related indicators that are highly subjective. The complex nature of institutional structures makes it difficult to find quantifiable objective indicators of the quality of these structures. As a result, the studies employ institution-related indicators based on interpretation by researchers of data from risk- or credit-rating agencies or by respondents to local survey questionnaires. According to Kaufmann, Kraay and Mastruzzi (2005), the major advantage of employing such subjective measures is that they encompass all the formal as well as informal elements of institutions. However, a major problem of any subjective institution-related measure is that the perceived quality of a country's institutions is strongly influenced by its current economic performance.

> **Good institutions and good economic performance are interrelated.**

Moreover, this approach does not enable any conclusions to be made about operational policy. An analysis based on the perceived impact of a country's institutional arrangements on its economic performance cannot determine which specific forms of arrangements lead to the perceived outcome. Any institutional outcome, such as secure property rights, may be induced by alternative institutional forms. Thus, assessing "how well the rules of the game with regard to property rights are perceived to operate, and not what those rules are" (Rodrik, 2004: 12) does not give any practical indication as to the institutional design required to obtain such an outcome.

Second, virtually all empirical studies have found that developed countries generally rank higher in measures of institutional quality than developing economies, no matter what measure is used (see also fig. 6.1). But it is less clear whether

Figure 6.1

CORRELATION BETWEEN INSTITUTIONAL QUALITY AND PER CAPITA INCOME, 2004

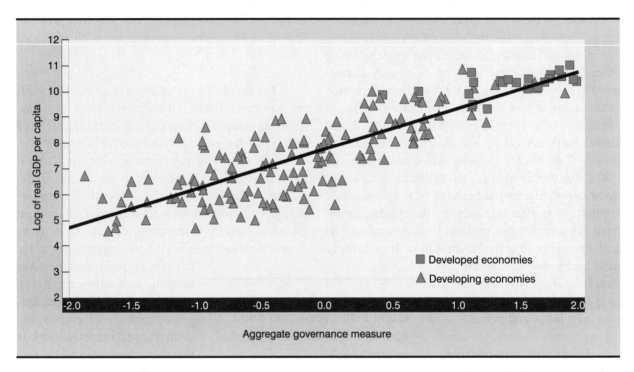

Source: UNCTAD secretariat calculations, based on data from Kaufmann, Kraay and Mastruzzi, 2005; and UNCTAD *Handbook of Statistics*, various issues.
Note: The aggregate governance measure is the unweighted average of the six measures provided by Kaufmann, Kraay and Mastruzzi, 2005.

this can be taken to imply a causal effect of institutional quality on economic performance. This is because these cross-country regression analyses are subject to serious econometric identification problems, in particular those related to omitted variable bias and reverse causality. Institutions and economic performance will differ among countries for a variety of reasons. However, given that the quality of institutions is a complex phenomenon that is not directly observable, and that it is therefore impossible to take account of all these differences in econometric estimations, the effects of omitted variables may be ascribed to institutional differences, thereby greatly exaggerating the effects of institutions on economic performance. The problem with reverse causality is that in this context good institutions and good economic performance are likely to influence each other, and are thus interrelated. For example, the impact of good economic performance on good institutions may

be due to the fact that economically well performing countries have the fiscal resources to construct and effectively implement an institutional structure that can ensure low transaction costs for all market participants.[6]

As proposed by Khan (2004), the test required to establish a causal relationship between an improvement in institutional quality in terms of the above measures and income convergence with developed countries is to see if developing countries that rank higher in such measures at the beginning of a period of time actually experience income convergence during that period. Such a test provides only weak support to the hypothesis that an improvement in institutions designed to create missing markets and make existing markets more efficient will promote growth and accelerate convergence with developed countries, as illustrated in table 6.1 and figure 6.2.

Table 6.1

GOVERNANCE INDICATORS AND PER CAPITA INCOME GROWTH, 1995–2005

	Developed countries	*Converging developing countries*	*Diverging developing countries*	***Memo item:*** *Countries of Central and Eastern Europe*
Number of countries	27	45	88	26
Median of aggregate governance measure	1.62	-0.19	-0.26	-0.27
Range of aggregate governance measure	0.64–1.93	-2.12–1.82	-2.08–1.33	-1.75–0.89
Median rate of real per capita income growth	2.48	3.90	0.95	5.19

Source: See figure 6.1.

Note: Data refer to 1995 for the aggregate governance measure, and to 1995–2005 averages for real per capita income growth in dollars.

The 186 economies for which the commonly used institutional and governance data provided by Kaufmann, Kraay and Mastruzzi (2005)[7] are available may be grouped as follows: 27 developed countries, 26 Central and Eastern European countries,[8] and 133 developing economies, which can be separated into 88 diverging and 45 converging developing economies depending on whether or not their average rate of real per capita growth during the period 1995–2005 exceeded the median rate of growth in developed countries during that period.

Table 6.1 shows that the median of the quality of governance index for converging developing economies is only moderately better than that for diverging developing economies. It also shows a large overlap in the range of variation of this measure for these two groups of economies. This raises some doubts as to whether an improvement in institutional quality as measured by this index actually causes income convergence of developing economies with developed countries.

Figure 6.2 shows that for the pool of developed and developing countries there is a very weak positive relationship between the score on the quality of governance index in 1995 and real per capita income growth during the period 1995–2005, as indicated by the trendline. It also shows that this positive relationship is largely due to the

fact that developed countries score high in terms of both institutional quality and per capita income growth, and that the vast majority of developing economies score low on both these measures. However, as discussed above, the subjective nature of the governance measure makes it likely that scores on the basis of that measure may well increase with a country's good economic performance, making it difficult to determine the direction of causality. The location in the figure of the group of converging developing economies is critical for establishing the direction of causality. However, as already indicated in table 6.1, these economies do not generally have better governance scores than the diverging developing economies.

In sum, this evidence indicates that diverging as well as converging developing economies score relatively low in terms of the quality of the governance measure. This suggests that aiming at large-scale institutional reform in the short run is seldom necessary to accelerate growth. While achieving sustained economic convergence will eventually require constructing those institutions that are similar to those in today's developed countries, the initial move of developing countries onto a path of income convergence can be achieved with minimal changes in that direction. In order to explain institution-related differences between developing countries in terms of their growth performance, an examination of other dimensions of

Figure 6.2

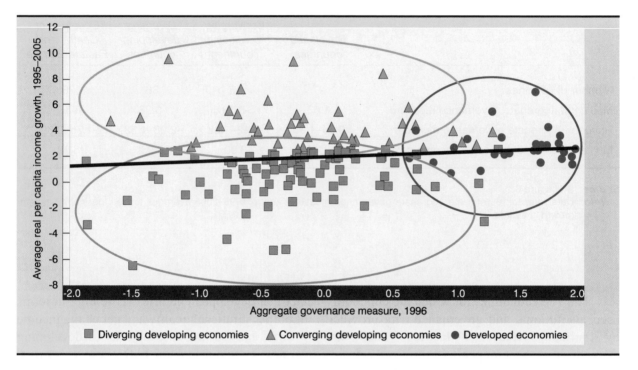

**GOVERNANCE AND PER CAPITA INCOME GROWTH,
SELECTED GROUPS OF ECONOMIES, 1995–2005**

■ Diverging developing economies   △ Converging developing economies   ● Developed economies

Source: See figure 6.1.
  Note: See figure 6.1.

institutional capabilities is required (see section 3 below).

Third, while so called "instrumental variable estimations" can be used to clarify the identification problems mentioned above, the resulting findings do not provide useful conclusions for policy-making. Indeed, finding suitable instrumental variables (i.e. indicators that are exogenous determinants of institutional quality) has proven to be a formidable task. Those studies that have used such exogenous instruments have often given rise to disagreement about the role and relative importance of institutions, on the one hand, and the instrumental variables themselves, on the other. In particular, there has been a debate as to whether geography has an impact on economic development beyond its effects on institutions.

For example, Hall and Jones (1999) use a country's distance from the equator and the pro-

portion of its population that speaks English as instruments to measure the quality of institutions (which they call "social infrastructure"). They argue that these variables proxy for the adoption of institutions that protect property rights and, more generally, for the strength of the supposedly "good British influence" on a country's institutions. Acemoglu, Johnson and Robinson (2001) argue that the mortality rates among early European settlers in a colony determined whether those settlers would stay in the more hospitable places and build European-style institutions, including those protecting property rights, or simply install resource-extractive or resource-plundering institutions.

Others (e.g. Gallup, Sachs and Mellinger,1999; Sachs, 2003) argue that geographical and ecological variables (such as climate zone, disease ecology and distance from the coast) have a significant direct impact on economic performance. They suggest that institutional choices in the past were influenced by the direct effects of geography on production systems, human health and environmental sustainability.[9] Engerman and Sokoloff (2002) point out that climate and factor-endowment conditions in the Caribbean and Brazil were well suited to growing crops like sugar, which at the time were of high value on the world market, and gave rise to significantly different institutions from those that were established later in the temperate zones of North America. Rodrik, Subramanian and Trebbi (2004) emphasize that the mortality rates of European settlers in the study by Acemoglu, Johnson and Robinson (2001) may be a useful instrument for the immediate statistical purpose of avoiding identification problems, but that it is nonetheless doubtful whether this approach captures the major historical forces that shaped institutional arrangements in former colonies and whether it explains economic divergence.[10] Indeed, income divergence in the past two or three centuries of countries that were never colonized (Afghanistan, Ethiopia, Japan, Thailand and Turkey) has been as great as among formerly colonized countries (Rodrik, Subramanian and Trebbi, 2004).[11]

The institutions discussed so far mainly concern the establishment of secure and stable property rights as an important element in incentives for entrepreneurs to invest and innovate. The presence of a stable and investment-friendly macroeconomic environment is another crucial determinant of such incentive. The inherent instability of financial markets, in particular, can have adverse effects on investment. Institutional solutions to this problem have concentrated on the implementation of procedural devices and regulatory frameworks. These attempts have focused on the role of institutions in facilitating individual decision-making by increasing the predictability of what other market participants will do in a particular context.

In the policy area, attempts to increase the certainty of individual decision-making have often addressed the question of political factors, such as election campaigns, to influence fiscal and

> **Large-scale institutional reform in the short run is seldom necessary to accelerate growth.**

monetary policy. With regard to monetary policy, a widely employed institutional solution to this problem has been the delegation of monetary authority to an independent central bank that follows a clearly determined and pre-announced monetary policy rule,[12] and/or, according to Rogoff (1985), the appointment of a conservative central banker.[13] Particularly in situations of hyperinflation, some countries have used a fixed nominal exchange rate or a currency board as an anchor for monetary policy. Institutional measures such as an exchange-rate anchor may be necessary in the initial stages of a price stabilization strategy. However, in practice, such strategies often lack a credible exit option. As a result, their prolonged use has contributed to substantial capital inflows, which in turn have initially led to an overvaluation of the real exchange rate that has eventually been corrected through a reversal of capital inflows. The resulting gyrations in the real exchange rate have made it difficult for entrepreneurs to make long-term plans and impaired investment.[14]

3. Institutions and structural transformation

To the extent that economic restructuring, technological upgrading and productivity growth depend on better resource allocation, improving market efficiency is clearly desirable. But the preceding chapter has argued that economic catch-up largely depends on industrialization and technological upgrading, and that to this end proactive trade and industrial policies need to reinforce the creative functions of markets that drive the dynamic transformation of developing economies. An important element of this policy strategy is the creation of "rents" that boost corporate profits above their free-market levels. Thus institutional arrangements that successfully manage economic rents must complement proactive support policies.

As with the discussion of principles and types of policies in the preceding chapter, it is possible to identify a number of generally desirable functions of institutions that must complement proactive trade and industrial policies. As already mentioned, the specific institutional forms of these functions are largely context specific. Each country needs to discover which specific form will provide the appropriate incentives to achieve the desired institutional outcome, based on its particular circumstances.

One such function concerns strategic collaboration between the government, business organizations and institutions of learning and innovation. Such collaboration aims at: (i) coordinating investment activities with scale economies, where the interdependence of individual investment decisions makes the investments and profits of one entrepreneur partly dependent on the investment decisions of others,[15] and (ii) exchanging information on the government's vision of development strategies, the entrepreneurs' views on business opportunities and investment constraints, particularly those related to the production of new products and the use of new modes of production, and on research institutions' assessments of national and international technology developments. Such arrangements help the government to design, implement and coordinate policy measures, because they allow the gathering of information on investment ideas and an assessment of the technology requirements needed to make such investments profitable. In addition, they allow identification of areas that require better coordination among State agencies and where changes in legislation and regulation could eliminate unnecessary transaction costs or other impediments to investment. This would also help to assign responsibilities for solving identified impediments and, more generally, to indicate which individual/agency should be approached to find a solution to a specific problem. Furthermore, such institutionalized forms of government-business collaboration allow the soliciting of subsidies and financial backing for new activities when needed, encourage cooperation among private firms, and between them and research institutes, and enable a bundling of all the different elements of support to new investment.

Another function is the imposition and enforcement of performance criteria on the recipients of the rents, in particular by using the disciplines of the international market in order to prevent rents from becoming permanent. The absence of such criteria, or failure to enforce them, would run the risk of causing unproductive rent-seeking, which would eventually weaken entrepreneurship and hamper productivity growth. Linking support to performance requirements ensures that the initial rents are essentially part of a nurturing exercise and that the rents will eventually be withdrawn as the supported activity matures. Moreover, such a link lends transparency and accountability to policy support, because it forces decision-makers to clarify and justify their actions. It also provides a yardstick for the evaluation of outcomes.

Thus, clear quantitative criteria for success or failure need to be formulated. Given the objective to support and accelerate productivity growth, success criteria should be related to productivity. Moreover, they should include a sunset clause to prevent open-ended support. This institutional function of identifying and disciplining under-performing firms ("losers") is often overlooked in conventional assessments of industrial policies, which tend to equate industrial policy with "picking winners". In a sense, it represents the "stick" that is a necessary complement to the "carrot" provided by the creation of temporary rents from subsidies or protection.[16]

> Institutional arrangements to manage economic rents must complement proactive support policies.

A third function of institutional arrangements is the provision of institutions that facilitate the incorporation of increasingly more advanced technology into production processes. The protection of clearly defined property rights is an important incentive to generate and absorb new technologies. However, as already mentioned, this protection can take many forms. Detailed codification of private ownership rights is not the only institutional form for providing innovative entrepreneurs with the possibility to appropriate at least a substantial part of the innovation rent. What matters more is that property rights are acknowledged de facto, as the experience of China between 1979 and 1993 indicates (see, for example, Qian, 2003).

Given that the availability of a well-skilled labour force is a key element of an economy's ability to innovate, adapt existing technologies and achieve learning-by-doing externalities in the production process, the existence of appropriate educational institutions (particularly for science and technology as well as vocational training) is clearly important for an economy's technological development. The same is true for the promotion of domestic knowledge generation in research institutes and universities. But the effectiveness of the output of these institutions depends largely on their links with corporate research and on the institutional structure of the corporate sector itself. Chang (1998), for example, points out that large enterprises may have the organizational structure and financial ability to conduct their own R&D, while an industry structure with a large proportion of small firms will require more government involvement in R&D.

The institutional structure of the financial system influences the scope of domestic investment financing beyond retained corporate profits. Compared to a capital-market-based system, a bank-based financial system may be better equipped to overcome the information and coordination problems in capital markets that pose a major obstacle to rapid investment and innovation. It facilitates the financing of productive investment from money and credit creation rather than from a pool of savings, and can thereby provide decisive stimuli for capital accumulation and growth. It also facilitates the allocation of credit from private sector financial institutions under government guidance, and from State-owned banks to finance investment in innovative activities (*TDR 1996*: 129). Moreover, bank-based financial systems are usually considered to be better at creating a corporate governance culture that emphasizes long-term development goals rather than short-term profits.

Fourth, the design and successful implementation of support policies require a strong and competent meritocratic civil service[17] that is not unduly burdened with immediate political concerns. The relationship between the State bureaucracy and the private sector should be one of "embedded autonomy" (Evans, 1995). The State bureaucracy should be closely connected to the business community through the State-business links discussed above. This fosters its responsiveness to required changes in policy design and implementation, and reduces the risk of its becoming a power unto itself and pursuing its own objectives. But the State bureaucracy should nonetheless retain a degree of autonomy that is essential for long-term policy-making, rather than being unduly subject to day-to-day politics and risk becoming overburdened with multiple objectives, many of which may be short-term in nature.

Civil service activities will be more effective if they provide support to economic activities that are national priorities and are supported at the highest political levels. Moreover, the strength of the civil service also depends on the coherence of support policies. Thus, State agencies that design and implement policies need to have coherent goals. Relatively greater homogeneity in values, preferences and political objectives across a country's political landscape will make it easier to formulate and implement a coherent policy strategy. It will also make it easier to enforce performance requirements as non-performing beneficiaries of policy support will not be able to play different political factions off against each other.

Finally, institutional arrangements must address distributional conflicts and promote social coherence.[18] This function of institutions is an important complement to proactive support policies, in particular because the creation of rents is not a harmonious process. Rather, it can give rise to distributional conflicts that can quickly cause deviation from a sustainable growth path and undermine the perceived legitimacy of the policy strategy adopted to spur development. While rela-

> Linking support to performance requirements ensures that the initial rents are part of a nurturing exercise ...

> ... and that the rents will be withdrawn as the supported activity matures.

tively equitable income distribution fosters social cohesion, taking into account the preferences of large segments of the population for the formation of new institutions and the reform of existing ones also plays a role in this context.

As emphasized by Evans (2005), wide participation by a country's citizenry in the setting of policy priorities along with institutional change will allow the country to discover what institutional forms are best suited to its specific circumstances. Although there is considerable scope to learn from experience elsewhere, eliciting and aggregating local knowledge provides better ideas of how to build effective organizations and institutions, particularly administrative norms, legal rules and other governance mechanisms, rather than technocratically imposing institutional blueprints. Participatory processes are also likely to better define the most appropriate legitimate goals of development. Moreover, they will increase the sentiment among citizens of ownership of the government's policy strategy.

4. Conclusions

Institutional arrangements are an important determinant of the effectiveness of domestic policy instruments in influencing national target variables. The presence of institutions to support the efficiency of existing markets and the creation of missing ones appears to be necessary, particularly in advanced stages of economic catch-up. However, the statistical correlation between per capita income levels and indicators of "good governance" does not point to the need to adopt the long list of institutional and governance reforms prescribed by the conventional reform agenda as a necessary condition for the initiation of a successful catch-up process.

By contrast, putting in place institutional arrangements that successfully manage economic rents associated with proactive trade and industrial policies in support of structural transformation is of particular importance in initiating and supporting a process of sustained growth and structural change. Once an economy is on a path of sustained catch-up growth, the government's capacity to sup-

port the creation of high-quality institutions through increasing public expenditure will also rise. Improved economic performance and strengthened public sector support for institution-building will enhance the process of institutional transformation, which will feed back into the growth process by enhancing the effectiveness of public policies.

Yet the widespread scepticism about the capacity of the State to create and manage growth-promoting rents cannot be ignored. Part of this scepticism is clearly justified, given the poorly performing institutional set-ups in a large number of developing countries. The restoration of peace and basic social order is a prerequisite for any institutional reform and economic development in countries that have experienced long years of civil strife and external conflicts. Indeed, there can be little doubt that some States will be more effective than others in implementing the institutional arrangements that have a major impact on the effectiveness of proactive trade and industrial policies for achieving their objectives.

Much of this effectiveness depends on the professionalism of the bureaucracy and the efficiency of information exchange between the public and private sectors. But it also depends on the extent to which nationwide State entities wield authority in policy-making and their access to budgetary resources that can be directed to those goals, including through the creation and withdrawal of rents.

In terms of "good governance", the East Asian States often performed rather poorly, but they had a different set of governance capabilities that were growth enhancing. Formal and informal arrangements for collaboration between the government, business organization and institutions for learning and innovation played an important role, as did the existence of reciprocal control mechanisms and the presence of a strong and competent meritocratic civil service.

The precise form of institutional arrangements depends on the specific mechanisms through which the State attempts to accelerate investment and technological upgrading. The diversity of the experience of successful catching up in East Asia indicates the importance of the compatibility of the governance capabilities that States have and the growth-enhancement strategies they are attempting to implement.[19] Country-specific conditions have clearly helped the development of these institutional arrangements in East Asia. This has sometimes been interpreted as implying that the kind of economic catch-up experienced in East Asia cannot be replicated elsewhere. However, as emphasized by Akyüz, Chang and Kozul-Wright (1998), the important point is not whether these economies' particular set of initial economic and cultural conditions equipped their societies for economic development better than others. All country-specific conditions contain elements which may either hold back or support future development, and the challenge is to explore whether and how pro-development elements can best be promoted.

Moreover, it should not be presumed that institutional arrangements required to successfully manage more orthodox policies are less demanding than those needed to accompany proactive support policies. As emphasized by Chang (2003: 310), "the fact that many developing countries have tried during the last half-a-century to build institutions that are needed to have a well-functioning market economy, often with little success, is testimony to the difficulties involved in constructing the institutions required for a well-functioning market economy."

Developing countries may wish initially to pursue a limited number of proactive policies that do not require the management of significant amounts of rents, but can contribute to the accumulation of capabilities and know-how that will prove useful in conducting more sophisticated support policies later. Designing policies to maximize the gains from hosting TNCs in selected areas may provide a particularly important area for policymakers in early phases of institutionally managed proactive policies. A gradual strategy of this kind would allow a government and its bureaucracy to learn their country's specificities regarding the types of incentives that are effective and for what purpose, and to identify any possible loopholes that might exist in otherwise well-designed policies.

> Institutional arrangements determine the effectiveness of domestic policy instruments in influencing national policy targets.

C. Multilateral institutions and global economic governance

1. Introduction

The considerable, and still growing, degree of global interdependence in contemporary world economic relations provides a strong rationale for a well-structured system of global economic governance.[20] Such a system would ensure the provision of global public goods such as international economic and financial stability. It would be represented by coherent multilateral institutional arrangements, created by inter-governmental agreements to voluntarily reduce sovereignty on a reciprocal basis. The guiding principle of these arrangements would be to manage the interface between different national systems, rather than reducing national difference and establishing one omnipotent economic and legal structure. These arrangements would design, implement and enforce multilateral rules and disciplines. Such a system of global collective action would make a key contribution to minimizing adverse international spillovers and other negative externalities created by national economic policies that focus on maximizing national benefits.

Self-centred national economic policies can generate adverse negative spillover effects beyond a country's borders. The spread of financial crises through contagion, even to countries with sound policies and good fundamentals, is one example. Moreover, global economic interdependence provides an opportunity for policymakers in influential economies to deliberately use beggar-thy-neighbour types of policies. They may be tempted to employ commercial, macroeconomic, financial or exchange-rate policies in pursuit of certain national economic objectives – such as attaining mercantilist goals or postponing the adjustment of internal or external imbalances – which may harm the economic performance of other countries. In the absence of multilateral disciplines and cooperation, retaliatory action by adversely affected countries could lead to instability and disruptions in international economic relations that might leave all countries worse off.

For global collective action to be acceptable to all parties, it must result from a consultative process based on full, equal and voluntary participation of all the parties concerned. However, there is a natural inclination, particularly by internationally powerful countries, to shape multilateral rules and commitments in a way that gives them the maximum degrees of freedom to pursue their own national economic goals, while restricting the degrees of freedom for others in areas where national interests conflict. Countries that feel disadvantaged by the way multilateral rules and commitments are formulated and implemented can, in principle, stay out of or leave the multilateral arrangements in question and conduct international relations on a bilateral basis. But countries with little power internationally (i.e. the vast majority of developing countries) will rarely follow this route, because coercive action is likely to be even stronger in bilateral relationships with major economic and political powers.

How to determine the right balance between maintaining sovereignty in national economic policy-making and constraining it through multilateral disciplines and collective governance remains a contentious issue. Chang (2006) makes the general argument that a liberal economist who values autonomy and choice for individuals should not try to restrict national autonomy of developing countries, including their right to be wrong.

> There is no *quantifiable* single balance between multilateral disciplines and national policy autonomy that suits all countries.

More directly related to the multilateral trade regime, Kleen and Page (2005: 48–49) argue that flexibilities in disciplines should aim to give developing countries what they want, not what developed countries, or researchers, think is "good for them". This could be understood as advocating an "everything goes" approach whereby governments would be allowed to implement any policies they think maximize their country's interests. But these authors clearly recognize that the absence of multilateral disciplines can disrupt international economic relations and/or bias them in favour of those countries that wield substantial economic or political power. Perhaps more importantly, as discussed earlier in this chapter and in the preceding two chapters, economic theory, borne out by history, suggests that there are a number of general principles underlying development-enhancing policies and institutions which can guide policymakers in their development strategies.

On the other hand, the extension of legally binding external constraints on national economic policies, as well as a generally less permissive attitude to the granting of waivers, may be viewed as subscribing to a "one-size-fits-all" approach. However, when there are information asymmetries and unequal capacities among countries to participate in the processes leading to an agreement on multilateral rules and disciplines, or when these rules and disciplines are perceived as unduly impinging on legitimate national development aspirations, they could be called into question and result in a repudiation of the institutions overseeing those disciplines. Hence, determining the right balance between national sovereignty and multilateral disciplines is very much a question of finding the right compromise between a "one-size-fits-all" and an "everything-goes" approach.

Any perception that multilateral disciplines extend too far and constrain the attainment of legitimate national development goals greatly depends on an individual economy's structural characteristics and its level of development. There is no *quantifiable* single balance between multilateral disciplines and national policy autonomy that suits all countries or applies across all spheres of economic activity. The degree of national policy autonomy needed to promote national economic development differs across countries. For example, the maturity of a country's institutional development and its pattern of domestic production will influence the depth of its integration into international financial markets and its FDI policies. Economic size and natural resource endowments will influence the depth of a country's trade integration, while the pattern of domestic support policies will vary with a country's level of industrial development, as discussed in chapter V. By the same token, at any level of economic development, the optimal degree of openness for benefiting a country is likely to differ across different spheres such as trade, investment, finance, labour and technology. For example, countries would be well-advised to postpone capital market integration until they have successfully integrated into other areas, notably trade *(TDR 2004*, chap. IV). Such differences in the optimal degree of openness may extend beyond narrow economic areas to involve equity considerations or the preservation of national culture and national institutions.

In the Sao Paulo Consensus (paragraph 8) reached at UNCTAD XI in 2004, the international community recognized that "it is particularly important for developing countries, bearing in mind development goals and objectives, that all countries take into account the need for appropriate balance between national policy space and international disciplines and commitments." However, multilateral arrangements do not appear to move in that direction.

The current system of global economic governance does not seem to be entirely satisfactory, largely because of the existence of two overlapping asymmetries. First, contrary to the existing institutional structure in international trade, current international monetary and financial arrangements are not organized around a multilateral rules-based system that applies a specific set of core principles to all participants. This asymmetry has particularly strong adverse effects on developing countries because self-centred national monetary and financial policies can have much more damaging effects than those caused by trade and trade-related policies. Despite increased international financial instability, and recurrent financial crises in emerging markets – along with their attendant adverse effects for both the economic prospects of many developing countries and the healthy expansion of international trade flows – there has been no attempt to fill the vacuum created by the breakdown of the Bretton Woods arrangements. This asymmetry is a major reason behind the lack of coherence in international policy-making *(TDR 2004)*.

Second, the multilateral rules and commitments governing international economic relations are, in legal terms, equally binding for all participants,[21] but in economic terms they are biased towards an accommodation of the requirements of the national development strategies of developed countries. As discussed in chapter V, the measures prohibited under WTO rules and regulations are of diminishing importance at relatively advanced levels of development, where much of economic advance depends on pushing out the technology frontier. At the same time, they reduce the degree of freedom for national economic policies designed to promote productive capacity at earlier stages of industrialization. By contrast, the measures permitted – or at least not explicitly prohibited – are those that allow developed countries to sponsor technology- and knowledge-intensive industries.

Taken together, these two asymmetries result in multilateral rules and practices that seek to deepen economic integration in a number of areas crucial to the interests and priorities of developed countries, and reduce the degrees of freedom for national economic policies in areas crucial for

> The scope of multilateral disciplines may be too narrow in international monetary and financial relations, but it may well be too large in the area of international trade.

industrialization and economic catch-up. Thus, in *qualitative* terms, and from the perspective of development, the scope of multilateral disciplines in the current pattern of global economic governance would appear to be too narrow in the area of international monetary and financial relations, but may well be too large in the area of international trade. The quality of a global' partnership for development can be expressed not only in terms of the existence or absence of multilateral rules and disciplines but also in terms of the context of these rules and the degree to which this context reflects the interests and needs of the different parties in a balanced and equitable manner.

2. *International monetary and financial rules and disciplines*[22]

The rapid pace of globalisation in monetary and financial relations has not been accompanied by an equally rapid change in multilateral monetary and financial rules and disciplines. The Bretton Woods institutions have progressively assumed different mandates and have extended their functions to areas far from those that they had been given originally (such as structural reforms covering a wide range of economic and social matters in developing countries and in economies in transition). Yet they appear to exercise little control over key international financial problems like exchange-rate volatility, huge and prolonged balance-of-payments imbalances, the dominance of short-term financial flows over long-term ones, and recurrent financial crises. Nor do they seem to possess the appropriate instruments for responding to these problems.

Above all, the existing global economic governance system lacks institutional arrangements that could exercise multilateral discipline on exchange rates. Until the early 1970s, the power of markets to generate unexpected and erratic movements in exchange rates was limited in part by the low value of financial market transactions relative both to trade transactions and to the amount of foreign exchange reserves. The power of markets was also constrained by capital controls and the obligation, under the Bretton Woods system, of central banks to intervene in foreign-exchange

markets in order to maintain exchange-rate stability. The system restricted the kind of short-term capital flows that were motivated by interest arbitrage and that had proven so damaging in the interwar period. By defining narrow exchange-rate bands, the Bretton Woods system also limited the ability of governments to manipulate the exchange rates of their currencies. This was intended to prevent beggar-thy-neighbour policies based on competitive depreciation, the lack of such prevention having been among the most damaging policy failures of the interwar period.

These institutional arrangements allowed the Bretton Woods system to ensure a balance between national policy autonomy on the one hand and multilateral disciplines on the other. Sacrificing formal monetary autonomy was rewarded by stability in the financial markets and better foresight in international trade and in related decisions concerning investment in fixed capital.

However, the Articles of Agreement in the IMF provided for changes in par values "to correct, or prevent the emergence of, a fundamental disequilibrium" (Article IV and Schedule C of the IMF Articles of Agreement). In many cases this adjustment was supported by the provision of financing from IMF resources to enable countries "to correct maladjustments in their balance of payments without resorting to measures destructive of national or international prosperity" (Article I of the IMF Articles of Agreement). At the same time, the conditionalities associated with this financing entailed macroeconomic adjustments in borrowing countries to support the reduction of external imbalances, with the aim of protecting both the financial integrity of the Fund and the revolving nature of its resources.

The balance between financing and adjustment in crisis situations has gradually been lost since the termination of the Bretton Woods exchange-rate system. Instead of providing adequate liquidity to allow countries to weather payments difficulties, the IMF started to impose extensive adjustments in macroeconomic and even in structural policies. Indeed, the Fund sought to impose the kind of policies that the architects of the post-World War II international monetary system had wanted to avoid on countries facing payments difficulties – that is, adjustment through austerity –

irrespective of the causes of the payments difficulties. These difficulties might result from domestic factors such as a loss of the overall competitiveness of the economy, excessive domestic spending or distortions in the price structure; or from external disturbances such as terms-of-trade shocks, hikes in international interest rates, trade and exchange-rate measures introduced by another country, or the volatility of capital flows and international speculation.[23]

Today the IMF may intervene in a country's exchange-rate policy only if that country asks for financial support from the Fund and thus becomes subject to IMF conditionality. Hence the IMF has no grip on possible exchange-rate misalignments in an economy that runs a balance-of-payments surplus, or in deficit countries that still have access to borrowing in international financial markets or issue a currency that other market participants are willing to continue holding in their portfolios, as in the case of the United States. Therefore, negotiations on exchange rates among the most important currencies, when they occur, are held outside the IMF, mainly at the G-7 meetings or in bilateral talks among the most important players.

This highlights a basic asymmetry and shortcoming in the current international financial system: the institution that is in charge of promoting exchange-rate stability and of avoiding excessive and prolonged payments disequilibria is unable to impose meaningful disciplines on the policies of those economies that run the most significant external imbalances and whose exchange-rate volatility has the most significant negative impact on the international economy. The Fund's policy oversight is confined primarily to its poorest members, who need to draw on its resources because of their lack of access to private sources of finance and, occasionally, to emerging-market economies experiencing currency and financial crises. As a result, the bulk of the adjustment burden in case of external imbalances is concentrated in a group of developing and transition economies despite the fact that the source of such imbalances may be found in the developed world.

> The existing global economic governance system lacks institutional arrangements that exercise multilateral discipline on exchange rates.

In fact, in a financially highly-integrated world the Fund is unable to tackle one of the main sources of current-account imbalances in developing countries, namely, exchange-rate misalignments that are due mainly to volatile, and often speculative, short-term capital flows. As UNCTAD has repeatedly shown (e.g. *TDR 2004*, chap. IV, section C), exchange-rate gyrations are not always driven by policy errors in the receiving countries. Even countries following orthodox monetary policies of price stabilization can be subject to strong overshooting of their exchange rates, leading first to over- and then to undervaluation. Capital flows, which have come to have a much stronger impact on nominal exchange rates than trade flows, are closely related to short-term financial conditions. For example, speculation that aims at exploiting short-term interest rate differentials for arbitrage profit can eventually lead to pressure on the exchange rate and become destabilising even if the countries involved have only slightly diverging inflation rates.

This behaviour is often at the origin of the boom-and-bust cycles in emerging markets. A more balanced and effective international financial system, one that also takes into account the specific needs of developing countries, should be designed to protect countries against overshooting and undershooting of the exchange rate by discouraging this kind of arbitrage through a truly international exchange-rate management system and/or by controls. In the absence of such a system, due to the unwillingness of the major developed countries to make the necessary multilateral commitments, developing countries must be allowed to manage exchange rates and capital flows at the national or regional levels, as discussed in chapter IV of this *Report*.

The globalized economy requires a new multilateral approach to managing the most important international price, the exchange rate. New or reformed institutions promoting a system of stable exchange rates to ensure a predictable trading environment would need to represent better the interests of countries at different stages of development and become more symmetrical in the treatment of the different member States. The main objective of institution building in this context would be the prevention of systemic crises in emerging markets, prevention based on the close monitoring of trade imbalances and global exchange-rate misalignments. Separating surveillance from lending decisions taken by the international financial institutions and assigning such surveillance to an independent authority could improve its quality, legitimacy and impact.

3. Rules and commitments in the multilateral trade regime

The GATT/WTO provides negotiated, binding and enforceable rules and commitments that constitute the multilateral trade regime. The resultant certainty and predictability of international trade are arguably key benefits of this regime. Moreover, the core principle of non-discrimination, as embodied in the most-favoured nation (MFN) rule, provides that trade concessions given by one member to any other member will be extended to the entire membership. This kind of reciprocity is an essential component of any system of global collective action. The WTO dispute settlement process is intended to protect members from unilaterally imposed restrictive trade policy measures, which is of particular importance for weak countries that otherwise could face undue pressure from economically or politically more powerful countries. To the extent that this regulatory system functions effectively, it is an important tool for development because it minimizes the risk of disruptive changes in trade flows. Moreover, the GATT/WTO rules have granted developing countries important exceptions regarding both the MFN rule, by allowing them to enjoy preferential and more favourable market access, and the reciprocity principle, by allowing them to grant developed countries less than full reciprocity in multilateral trade negotiations.

Thus the multilateral trade regime, in principle, provides a framework for an orderly, rules-based system of international trade, with appropriate checks and balances, arbitration of inter-State disputes and determination of the sanctions to be applied. However, de facto this regime has been under increasing pressure to expand the number of areas regulated by multilateral disciplines and to move towards the establishment of a homogeneous regulatory framework. However, such a move would not adequately take into account asymmetries existing among the different actors in the world economy.

A variety of factors have contributed to this development. First, many developing countries perceive that the so-called "trade-related" agreements of the Uruguay Round, which were discussed in chapter V, commit them to renouncing the policy autonomy that both the mature and late industrializers had enjoyed during their periods of economic catch-up. They believe such autonomy to be indispensable for maintaining an appropriate degree of flexibility in multilateral commitments that would give them the option to adopt national support policies which other countries have used to accelerate industrial development and technological catch-up, even if they may not currently have the intention or the budgetary and institutional resources to use that option.

Second, developing countries accepted new commitments stemming from these "trade-related" agreements (notably TRIPS) as part of the grand bargain of the Uruguay Round in exchange for improved access to developed-country markets of interest to developing-country exporters, particularly agricultural goods and textiles and clothing. But, as discussed in chapter III, progress in this area (particularly in agriculture) has fallen short of expectations, while new forms of selective protectionism have gained in importance. Imbalances in the outcome of the Uruguay Round Agreements are reflected, *inter alia*, in numerous implementation-related issues and concerns (Finger and Schuler, 2000). From this perspective, the global partnership for development between developed and developing countries has not materialized, and developing countries have expressed concerns about the failure of the Uruguay Round to deliver fully the benefits that had been estimated by various international organizations (OECD, 1993; World Bank and OECD, 1993) before the end of the Round.

Third, the perception of continuing asymmetries biased against developing countries has been reinforced by the reinterpretation of the principle of "special and differential treatment" (SDT). Prior to the Uruguay Round Agreements, the case for SDT was couched in developmental terms, notably that it would be undesirable for developing countries to pursue policies and subject themselves to disciplines that may be sensible for developed countries owing to differences in their economic structure and levels of development. By contrast, the main concern of SDT since the conclusion of the Uruguay Round appears to have been that of assisting developing countries in implementing the WTO disciplines (Whalley, 1999). Thus developing countries are offered extra time and technical assistance to enhance capacity in order to facilitate their adjustment. As noted by Hoekman (2005: 406), it is now recognized that these provisions are inadequate "as these are arbitrary and are not accompanied by or based on an objective assessment of whether (and when) implementation of a specific set of (proposed) rules will be beneficial to a country."

Fourth, WTO negotiation procedures have often given the impression of less than full transparency and participation, so that some countries appear to have stronger influence than others. Decisions taken in so-called "green room" meetings or in other gatherings of a limited number of members are often presented to the entire membership as fait accompli. These procedures may have resulted from well-intentioned attempts to preserve practicality and efficiency in complex decision-making. However, they have prompted concerns about unequal influence and unequal representation of national priorities in processes the results of which affect all participants. As such, the increasing difficulty in reaching decisions on the basis of equal participation of all members is intimately linked to the growing number of WTO members.

Indeed, the increasing participation of developing countries in the multilateral trade regime, which dates back to the Uruguay Round, has given universality to multilateral rules and regulations in the area of international trade. It has brought together countries that may not necessarily be

> The increasing participation of developing countries in the multilateral trade regime brings together countries that may not be "like-minded".

"like-minded", as was the case when the GATT was founded. As noted by Kleen and Page (2005: 48) "if the WTO members now accept that the organisation should aim for universal membership, in order to ensure that the benefits of certainty and predictability apply to all trade by its members, then both the possibility that some countries are permanently 'different' and the certainty that some will not share the same approach to all rules imply that the WTO must either limit its rules to those that can benefit and be accepted by all members or allow permanent derogations for countries with different economies or different approaches to economic policy." The Task Force on Trade (United Nations Millennium Project, 2005: 185) notes that designing generic rules is particularly difficult when it comes to behind-the-border policies, and suggests that agreements in this area should be flexible and encourage experimentation, learning and competition (similar to the flexibilities envisaged in the GATS architecture).

Hence an inclusive multilateral trade regime must build in flexibility in order to avoid a deadlock in multilateral negotiations with attendant adverse effects on the substantial gains that multilateral disciplines in the area of international trade have achieved. Failure to provide flexibility might lead to increased doubts by influential segments of civil society as to the legitimacy of the multilateral trading rules and disciplines at large.

So how can the multilateral trade regime move forward? Further discussions and negotiations at the multilateral level will need to explore a range of options. As noted, for example, by Rodrik (2001), if the multilateral trade regime is to maximize the development potential of developing countries, the criterion by which rules and commitments governing global trade are judged should be whether they appropriately fit a trade dimension to the development needs and goals of developing countries, rather than whether they maximize market access and international trade per se.[24]

It is likely that this exploration of options will aim at creating a new framework or new guidelines for SDT in the WTO, as noted, for example, by Kleen and Page (2005), Hoekman (2005) and Singh (2005).[25] The Doha Ministerial Declaration (paragraph 44), reaffirming the importance of SDT by stating that "provisions for special and differential treatment are an integral part of the WTO agreements" also called for a review of SDT provisions with the objective of "strengthening them and making them more precise, effective and operational". Establishing a new framework would probably need to start from the recognition that SDT for developing countries means redressing structural imbalances, rather than giving concessions.

An inclusive multilateral trade regime needs flexibility to avoid a deadlock in negotiations.

From this perspective, developed countries would need to agree to move to a new framework or new guidelines for SDT without receiving any concessions in return. This could also be considered one of the tasks for developed countries to undertake within the global partnership for development.

There are, in principle, two options to reflect differences among countries in their structural characteristics or approaches to economic policy (see, for example, Kleen and Page, 2005; and Hoekman, 2005). The first option is to adopt a country-specific approach that would allow member countries to selectively opt out of specific rules and commitments, depending on their specific national priorities. Different variants of this option have been proposed, *inter alia*, by Rodrik (2001) and Singh (2005). The basic principle of this option would be to provide flexibility for developing countries to seek some latitude in the application of multilateral disciplines consistent with the pursuit of national development goals. Singh (2005), for example, argues that prior to the single undertaking adopted for the Uruguay Round Agreements, SDT allowed countries to follow different paths towards development as there was no requirement for each country to follow all the rules. He suggests a re-conceptualization of SDT which would allow developing countries to subscribe to certain portions of multilateral agreements as they develop, without the obligation to commit to all portions at once.[26]

This option would ensure that each developing country has the flexibility to determine independently the scope of multilateral disciplines which it wishes to implement, and thus avoid threats of retaliation for non-compliance with disciplines that it sees as constraining its development strategy. It would also leave intact the current practice of leaving individual countries to determine whether they should invoke SDT. However, its major drawback is that it would effectively result in a multi-track multilateral trade regime, thus conflicting with the basic rule of non-discrimination and complicating adherence to the consensus-based norm of the multilateral trade regime. Moreover, it runs the risk of leading to a proliferation of specific agreements, with disciplines that may well go beyond the desired scope of developing countries for many years to come. Thus countries that opt out will not enjoy the benefits of existing multilateral disciplines, and might not be able to renegotiate them once they decide to sign on to a specific agreement.

The second option is to adopt an agreement-specific approach that would set specific criteria for individual agreements to determine whether members could opt out of the application of negotiated disciplines for a limited period of time. A major difficulty of this approach is to determine whether the exemptions from the specific agreements should be defined before discussing which countries would be entitled to them, or the other way round. Regarding country selection, the criteria used could include a variety of economic indicators relating to countries' levels of development. As with the first option, following this second option would also lead to differentiation between developing countries. However, contrary to self-selection, as in the first option, in this case differentiation would be based on objective criteria. As noted by Kleen and Page (2005), determination of the kinds of criteria used and the specific levels chosen would need to be the outcome of negotiations, which would have to strike a balance between a country's needs and the potential damage inflicted on other members by relaxing an agreed rule.

According to Das (2003), the provisions on SDT need to become an integral part of the WTO rules and disciplines, rather than being treated as exceptions as at present. Das (2003: 186–187) argues that the main goal of the GATT/WTO system is to ensure a fair sharing of the benefits from liberalization of trade in goods of services. Therefore, the protection of intellectual property rights (and, thus, the TRIPS agreement) should be taken out of the WTO system and placed in either the World Intellectual Property Organisation (WIPO) or a separate organisation of its own.[27] Moreover, in order to enhance the impact of developing countries' trade integration on the development of their domestic productive capacity, Das (2003: 190–191) argues that developing countries should be allowed to impose domestic-content requirements on firms, which are now prohibited under the national-treatment principle of the TRIMS agreement and to subsidize selected economic sectors.

With regard to the Agreement on Subsidies and Countervailing Measures, this proposal implies that member States could consider setting aggregate limits to subsidies that WTO member governments can use while allowing them flexibility in the allocation of subsidies to firms and economic sectors, as proposed by Akyüz (2006). Multilateral trade negotiations could determine the aggregate limit on subsidies, as well as its reduction over time, while maintaining allocative flexibility. Such a scheme would be similar to the provisions on Aggregate Measures of Support (AMS) for agriculture, under which WTO members have set targets for percentage reductions while leaving considerable flexibility to member governments in the allocation of reductions across different agricultural products. It would also allow governments to modulate the sectoral pattern of domestic support policies outlined in figure 5.1 above.

The options suggested here are intended simply to sketch out some possible ways forward. There may well be other options. Moreover, what will eventually be adopted will need to result from multilateral discussions and negotiations. What is important at this point is to recognize that the wide disparity in structural characteristics and approaches to economic policies among the membership of a universal WTO requires greater flexibility. ∎

Notes

1   While such a complementary set of institutions was not spelt out, early development economists (e.g. Hirschman, 1981), nevertheless, clearly recognized the fundamental difference between the rules and institutions governing developed countries and those existing in developing economies.

2   Wade (2005), for example, argues that the difficult task is not defining and adopting proactive trade and industrial policies, but designing a bureaucracy with sufficient motivation, legitimacy and creativeness to be able to choose the right instruments for achieving the intended objectives of those policies.

3   This definition of governance has been proposed by the United Nations Development Programme (UNDP), which sees "good" governance as characterized by participation, transparency, accountability, rule of law, effectiveness and equity (see http://mdg-guide.undp.org/?page=glossary_3).

4   According to Qian (2003), local communities (townships or villages), rather than individuals or the central government, held the formal ownership rights in township and village enterprises between 1979 and 1993. The efficiency loss stemming from the absence of private property rights was compensated

by an implicit ownership guarantee from local governments that for fiscal reasons had a strong interest in the prosperity of these enterprises.

5 This argumentation is closely related to the so-called "Coase theorem", according to which the neoclassicial ideal of efficient competitive markets is obtained when market transactions are cost-free.

6 Kaufmann and Kraay (2002) and Keefer (2004) find a weak but negative reverse causality, suggesting the absence of a virtuous circle between better governance and better economic outcomes. But Dixit (2006: 7) notes that even negative reverse causality can create an econometric problem requiring instrumental variables. The use of instrumental variables to address the problem of reverse causality is discussed later in this chapter.

7 These data aggregate a large number of indices available from other data sources into six broad governance indicators: voice and accountability (measuring political, civil and human rights), political instability and violence (measuring the likelihood of violent threats to or changes in government, including terrorism), government effectiveness (measuring the competence of the bureaucracy and the quality of public service delivery), regulatory burden (measuring the incidence of market-unfriendly policies), rules of law (measuring the quality of contract enforcement, the police and the courts, as well as the likelihood of crime and violence), and control of corruption (measuring the exercise of public power for private gain, including both petty and grand corruption and State capture).

8 These categories follow those used by the United Nations up to 2004 (i.e. the Czech Republic, Estonia, Hungary, Latvia, Lithuania, Poland, Slovakia and Slovenia are classified in the category of countries in Central and Eastern Europe, rather than as developed countries).

9 By contrast, Acemoglu, Johnson and Robinson (2002) point to some "geographically handicapped" countries that are now relatively poor but were relatively rich some 500 years ago (e.g. the Aztec and Inca empires) or in early colonial times (e.g. Barbados, Cuba and Haiti), arguing that these "reversals of fortunes" were more related to colonial history, extractive policies and institution-building than to geography.

10 Bockstette, Chanda and Putterman (2002) show that a long history of a territory-wide polity and experience with large-scale administration may make for more effective government and more rapid economic growth. Many colonized countries suffer a relative lack of State antiquity, which stems in part from colonization itself and in part from the artificial regrouping of territories by colonial rulers, who often caused post-colonial States to be incongruent with pre-colonial political structures and boundaries.

11 Moreover, as argued by Dixit (2006: 4), "[t]aken literally, these findings constitute a message of pessimistic determinism: if your country lacks the right prior or starting conditions, its economic future is bleak." On a humorous note, Dixit (2006: 6) argues that these studies recommend a developing country "to use plate tectonics to move itself to a more favourable location, or to turn the clock back and invite British colonizers, of course cleaning up the local disease environment and getting rid of mineral resources beforehand."

12 For a critical assessment of this proposition see, for example, Bibow, 2004, and Forder, 2001.

13 Another kind of solution has emphasized reputation-related mechanisms (Barro and Gordon, 1983).

14 See *TDR 2003*, chap. VI, for a detailed discussion of these issues in the context of economic reforms in Latin America.

15 Regarding specific forms of institutional functions, one attempt to address the problem of investment coordination has been the establishment of large industrial conglomerates, such as the *chaebols* in the Republic of Korea. Unifying decision-making on interrelated investment and production processes into one management structure significantly reduces uncertainty in investment decisions about the availability of auxiliary activities that in part determines profits. Another attempt, which has relied on a more decentralized and differentiated market structure with relatively smaller enterprises, has been the creation of institutional coordination mechanisms, such as the deliberation councils in Taiwan Province of China.

16 The East Asian late industrializers successfully used such reciprocal control mechanisms to make the privileges of local entrepreneurs conditional on technological upgrading and international competitiveness, as often measured by export success, rather than allowing such privileges to be taken for granted, as pointed out by Amsden (1989), Wade (1990), and Evans (1995).

17 Rauch and Evans (2000) show that the key ingredients of effective state bureaucracies include competitive salaries, internal promotion and career stability, and recruitment based on merit.

18 Rodrik (1999), for example, emphasizes the need for strong domestic institutions of conflict management to deal with the consequences of external shocks, such as terms-of-trade declines or reversals in capital flows.

19 For detailed accounts of how institutional arrangements complemented proactive trade and industrial policies in East Asia's late industrialization, see, for example, *TDR 1994* and *1996*; Evans, 1995; Akyüz, Chang and Kozul-Wright, 1998; and Chang, 1998.

20 The following paragraphs in this section partly draw on Akyüz (2006).

21   However, SDT is often expressed in terms of best endeavour.

22   This section partly draws on Akyüz (2006).

23   The only multilateral discipline left in the IMF is "avoidance of restrictions on current payments and discriminatory currency practices". According to Article VIII of the Articles of Agreement members are obliged to avoid such restrictions and must obtain the approval of the Fund to impose "restrictions on the making of payments and transfers for current account transactions". This article provides the possibility for countries to impose exchange controls on current transactions in situations where the Fund has formally declared a currency to be "scarce" because the demand for a currency threatens the ability of the Fund to supply that currency (Article VII). In principle, this scarce-currency clause may help put pressure on surplus countries, but it has never been implemented.

24   This will imply a major departure by trade negotiators from their past practices which seemed to be based on following mercantilist rules, "in which an increase in exports ... is a victory, and an increase in imports ... is a defeat" (Krugman, 1997: 114).

25   For an account of recent negotiations in the area of SDT, see Kleen and Page (2005: 37–43). In what follows, only SDT related to regulatory matters is discussed. For discussions on SDT relating to preferential market access and the provision of technical and financial assistance to help developing countries implement multilateral rules, see, for example, Kleen and Page, 2005, and UN Millennium Project, 2005.

26   As noted by Hoekman (2005: 418), plurilateral agreements lead to a similar outcome, with the difference that they do not entail the presumption that a country will eventually join and thus be subject to all the rules and commitments.

27   The Task Force on Trade (UN Millennium Development Project, 2005: 215) also concludes that, from an economic point of view, intellectual property rights should probably not have been included in the WTO because they "require a very delicate balance of market forces and public action—a balance unlikely to be the same for countries with wide differences in terms of income and technology, all the more because obligations of the TRIPS Agreement also tend to be 'one size fits all', taking no account of levels of development and varying interests and priorities."

References

Acemoglu D, Johnson S and JA Robinson (2001). The colonial origins of comparative development: an empirical investigation. *American Economic Review*, 91 (5): 1369–1401.

Acemoglu D, Johnson S and JA Robinson (2002). Reversal of fortune: geography and institutions in the making of the modern world income distribution. *Quarterly Journal of Economics*, 117 (4): 1231–1294.

Akyüz Y (2006). Multilateral discipline and the question of policy space. Background paper for *TDR 2006*.

Akyüz Y, Chang HJ and Kozul-Wright R (1998). New perspectives on East Asian development. *Journal of Development Studies*, 34 (6): 4–36.

Amsden AH (1989). *Asia's Next Giant: South Korea and Late Industrialization*. Oxford, Oxford University Press.

Amsden AH (2001). *The Rise of "the Rest": Challenges to the West from Late-Industrializing Economies*. New York, Oxford University Press.

Barro R and Gordon D (1983). Rules, discretion and reputation in a model of monetary policy. *Journal of Monetary Economics*, 12 (1): 101–120.

Bibow, J (2004). Reflections on the current fashion for central bank independence. *Cambridge Journal of Economics*, 28 (4): 549–576.

Bockstette V, Chanda A and Putterman L (2002). States and markets: the advantages of an early start. *Journal of Economic Growth*, 7 (4): 347–69.

Chang HJ (1996). *The Political Economy of Industrial Policy*. Basingstoke and London, Macmillan.

Chang HJ (1998). The role of institutions in Asian development. *Asian Development Review*, 16 (2): 64–95.

Chang HJ (2003). *Globalisation, Economic Development and the Role of the State*. London and New York, Zed Books and Penang, Third World Network.

Chang HJ (2006). Policy space in historical perspective with special reference to trade and industrial policies. *Economic and Political Weekly*, 41 (7): 627–633, 18 February.

Chang HJ and P Evans (2005). The role of institutions in economic change. In: De Paula S and Dymski GA, eds., *Reimagining Growth: Towards a Renewal of Development Theory*. London and New York, Zed Books: 99–140.

Das BL (2003). *The WTO and the Multilateral Trading System: Past, Present and Future*. London and New York, Zed Books and Penang, Third World Network.

Dixit A (2006). Evaluating recipes for development success. *Working Paper* no. 3859. Washington, DC, World Bank, March.

Engerman SL and Sokoloff KL (2002). Factor endowments, inequality, and paths of development among new world economies. *Economia*, 3 (1): 41–109.

Evans P (1995). *Embedded Autonomy: States and Industrial Transformation*. Princeton, NJ, Princeton University Press.

Evans P (2005). The Challenges of the 'Institutional Turn': New Interdisciplinary Opportunities in Development Theory. In: Nee V and Sweberg R, eds., *The Economic Sociology of Capitalist Institutions*. Princeton, Princeton University Press: 90–116.

Finger JM and P Schuler (2000). Implementation of Uruguay Round commitments: the development challenge. *The World Economy*, 23 (4): 511–525.

Forder J (2001). The theory of credibility and the reputation-bias in policy. *Review of Political Economy*, 13 (1): 5–25.

Gallup JL, Sachs JD and Mellinger AD (1999). Geography and economic development. In: Pleskovic B and Stiglitz J, eds., *Annual World Bank Conference on Development Economics 1998*. Washington, DC, World Bank.

Hall RE and Jones CI (1999). Why do some countries produce so much more output per worker than others? *Quarterly Journal of Economics*, 114 (1): 83–116.

Hirschman A (1981). The rise and decline of development economics. In: Hirschman A, ed., *Essays in Trespassing*. Cambridge, Cambridge University Press.

Hodgson GM (1998). The approach of institutional economics. *Journal of Economic Literature*, 36 (1): 166–192.

Hodgson GM (2004). *The Evolution of Institutional Economics. Agency, Structure and Darwinism in American Institutionalism*. London and New York, Routledge.

Hodgson GM (2005). Institutions and Economic Development: Constraining, Enabling and Reconstituting. In: De Paula S and Dymski GA, eds., *Reimagining Growth: Towards a Renewal of Development Theory*. London and New York, Zed Books: 85–98.

Hoekman B (2005). Operationalizing the concept of policy space in the WTO: beyond special and differential treatment. *Journal of International Economic Law*, 8 (2): 405–424.

Kaufmann D and Kraay A (2002). Growth without governance. *Economia*, 3 (1): 169–215.

Kaufmann D, Kraay A and Mastruzzi M (2005). Measuring governance using cross-country perceptions data. Mimeo. Washington, DC, World Bank. Available at: www.worldbank.org/wbi/governance/pdf/ MeasuringGovernancewithPerceptionsData.pdf.

Keefer P (2004). A review of the political economy of governance: from property rights to voice. Working Paper no. 3315. Washington, DC, World Bank.

Khan MH (2004). State failure in developing countries and institutional reform strategies. In: Tungodden B, Stern N and Kolstad I, eds., *Toward Pro-Poor Policies. Aid, Institutions, and Globalization*. Proceedings of the Annual World Bank Conference on Development Economics – Europe 2003. New York, World Bank and Oxford University Press: 165–195.

Kleen P and Page S (2005). Special and differential treatment of developing countries in the World Trade Organization. Global Development Studies no. 2. Stockholm, Swedish Ministry of Foreign Affairs, Overseas Development Institute.

Krugman P (1997). What should trade negotiators negotiate about? *Journal of Economic Literature*, 35 (1): 113–120.

North DC (1990). *Institutions, Institutional Change and Economic Performance*. New York, Cambridge University Press.

OECD (1993). *Assessing the Effects of the Uruguay Round*. Trade Policy Issues no. 2. Paris, Organisation for Economic Co-operation and Development.

Polanyi K (1944). *The Great Transformation: The Political and Economic Origins of Our Time*. Boston, Bacon Press.

Qian Y (2003). How reform worked in China. In: Rodrik D, ed., *In Search of Prosperity: Analytical Narratives on Economic Growth*. Princeton and Oxford, Princeton University Press: 297–333.

Rauch JE and Evans PB (2000). Bureaucratic structure and bureaucratic performance in less developed countries. *Journal of Public Economics*. 75 (1): 49–71.

Rodrik D (1999). Where did all the growth go? External shocks, social conflict, and growth collapses. *Journal of Economic Growth*, 4 (4): 385–412.

Rodrik D (2001). *The Global Governance of Trade: As if Development Really Mattered*. New York, United Nations Development Programme (UNDP).

Rodrik D (2004). Getting institutions right. *CESifo DICE Report*, 2/2004: 10–15. Munich, IFO Institute.

Rodrik D (2005). Growth strategies. In: Aghion P and Durlauf SN eds., *Handbook of Economic Growth*. Amsterdam, Elsevier: 967–1014.

Rodrik D, Subramanian A and Trebbi F (2004). Institutions rule: the primacy of institutions over geography and integration in economic development. *Journal of Economic Growth*, 9 (2): 131–165.

Rogoff K (1985). The optimal degree of commitment to an intermediate monetary target. *Quarterly Journal of Economics*, 100 (4): 1169–1190.

Sachs JD (2003). Institutions don't rule: direct effects of geography on per capita income. Working Paper no. 9490. National Bureau of Economic Research (NBER). February.

Singh A (2005). Special and differential treatment: the multilateral trading system and economic development in the twenty-first century. In: Gallagher KP, ed., *Putting Development First: The Importance of Policy Space in the WTO and International Financial Institutions*. London and New York, Zed Books: 233–263.

UNCTAD (various issues). *Trade and Development Report*. United Nations publication, New York and Geneva.

United Nations Millennium Project Task Force on Trade (2005). *Trade for Development*. London and Sterling, VA, Earthscan.

Wade RH (1990). *Governing the Market*. Princeton, Princeton University Press.

Wade RH (2005). Escaping the squeeze: lessons from East Asia on how middle-income countries can grow faster. In: B Laperche, ed., *John Kenneth Galbraith and the Future of Economics*. Basingstoke, Palgrave Macmillan

Whalley J (1999). Special and differential treatment in the Millennium Round. Working Paper no. 30/99. Warwick (United Kingdom), Centre for the Study of Globalisation and Regionalisation (CSGR), University of Warwick.

World Bank (2001). *Building Institutions for Markets. World Development Report 2002*. Washington, DC, Oxford University Press and World Bank.

World Bank and OECD (1993). *Trade Liberalization: Global Economic Implications*. Paris, OECD Development Centre and World Bank.

UNITED NATIONS CONFERENCE ON TRADE AND DEVELOPMENT

Palais des Nations
CH-1211 GENEVA 10
Switzerland
(www.unctad.org)

Selected UNCTAD Publications

Trade and Development Report, 2005
United Nations publication, sales no. E.05.II.D.13
ISBN 92-1-112673-8

Chapter   I   Current Issues in the World Economy

Chapter   II   Income Growth and Shifting Trade Patterns in Asia

Chapter   III   Evolution in the Terms of Trade and its Impact on Developing Countries

        Annex   Distribution of Oil and Mining Rent: Some Evidence from Latin America, 1999–2004

Chapter   IV   Towards a New Form of Global Interdependence

Trade and Development Report, 2004
United Nations publication, sales no. E.04.II.D.29
ISBN 92-1-112635-5

Part One   Global Trends and Prospects

    I   The World Economy: Performance and Prospects

    II   International Trade and Finance

Part Two   Policy Coherence, Development Strategies and Integration into the World Economy

    Introduction

    III   Openness, Integration and National Policy Space

    IV   Fostering Coherence Between the International Trading, Monetary and Financial Systems

        Annex 1   The Concept of Competitiveness

        Annex 2   The Set-up of Econometric Estimates of the Impact of Exchange Rate Changes on Trade Performance

    Conclusions and Policy Challenges

Trade and Development Report, 2003   United Nations publication, sales no. E.03.II.D.7
ISBN 92-1-112579-0

Part One   Global Trends and Prospects

    I   The World Economy: Performance and Prospects

   II   Financial Flows to Developing Countries and Transition Economies

  III   Trade Flows and Balances

        Annex: Commodity prices

Part Two   Capital Accumulation, Economic Growth and Structural Change

   IV   Economic Growth and Capital Accumulation

    V   Industrialization, Trade and Structural Change

   VI   Policy Reforms and Economic Performance: The Latin American Experience

Trade and Development Report, 2002   United Nations publication, sales no. E.02.II.D.2
ISBN 92-1-112549-9

Part One   Global Trends and Prospects

    I   The World Economy: Performance and Prospects

   II   The Multilateral Trading System After Doha

Part Two   Developing Countries in World Trade

  III   Export Dynamism and Industrialization in Developing Countries

        Annex 1:   Growth and classification of world merchandise exports
        Annex 2:   United States trade prices and dynamic products
        Annex 3:   International production networks and industrialization in developing countries

   IV   Competition and the Fallacy of Composition

    V   China's Accession to WTO: Managing Integration and Industrialization

Trade and Development Report, 2001   United Nations publication, sales no. E.01.II.D.10
ISBN 92-1-112520-0

Part One   Global Trends and Prospects

    I   The World Economy: Performance and Prospects

   II   International Trade and Finance

Part Two   Reform of the International Financial Architecture

  III   Towards Reform of the International Financial Architecture: Which Way Forward?

   IV   Standards and Regulation

    V   Exchange Rate Regimes and the Scope for Regional Cooperation

   VI   Crisis Management and Burden Sharing

Trade and Development Report, 2000   United Nations publication, sales no. E.00.II.D.19
                                                          ISBN 92-1-112489-1

Chapter   I   The Current Global Recovery and Imbalances in a Longer-term Perspective

Chapter   II   The World Economy: Performance and Prospects

Chapter III   International Markets

Chapter IV   Crisis and Recovery in East Asia

******

China in a Globalizing World   United Nations publication, sales no. E.05.II.D.23
                                                          ISBN 92-1-112683-5

China's Spectacular Growth since the Mid-1990s – Macroeconomic Conditions and Economic Policy Changes
Heiner Flassbeck, in collaboration with Sebastian Dullien and Michael Geiger

Globalization and the Integration of China into the World Economy
Yuanjiang Sun

China and its Neighbours: Partners or Competitors for Trade and Investment?
John Weiss

Why is China the World's Number One Anti-Dumping Target?
Yuefen Li

China's New Concept for Development
Jiyao Bi

FDI in China: Trends and Macroeconomic Challenges
Sebastian Dullien

Market Opening, Enterprise Learning and Industry Transformation – A Case Study of China's Car Industry
Hong Song, Chai Yu

******

These publications may be obtained from bookstores and distributors throughout the world. Consult your bookstore or write to United Nations Publications/Sales and Marketing Section, Bureau E-4, Palais des Nations, CH-1211 Geneva 10, Switzerland (Fax: +41-22-917.0027; Tel.: +41-22-917-2614/2615/2600; E-mail: unpubli@unog.ch; Internet: https://unp.un.org); or United Nations Publications, Two UN Plaza, Room DC2-853, New York, NY 10017, USA (Tel.: +1-212-963.8302 or +1-800-253.9646; Fax: +1-212-963.3489; E-mail: publications@un.org).

G-24 Discussion Paper Series
Research papers for the Intergovernmental Group of Twenty-Four
on International Monetary Affairs and Development

No. 40	May 2006	Lucio SIMPSON	The Role of the IMF in Debt Restructurings: Lending Into Arrears, Moral Hazard and Sustainability Concerns
No. 39	February 2006	Ricardo GOTTSCHALK and Daniela PRATES	East Asia's Growing Demand for Primary Commodities – Macroeconomic Challenges for Latin America
No. 38	November 2005	Yilmaz AKYÜZ	Reforming the IMF: Back to the Drawing Board
No. 37	April 2005	Colin I. BRADFORD, Jr.	Prioritizing Economic Growth: Enhancing Macroeconomic Policy Choice
No. 36	March 2005	JOMO K.S.	Malaysia's September 1998 Controls: Background, Context, Impacts, Comparisons, Implications, Lessons
No. 35	January 2005	Omotunde E.G. JOHNSON	Country Ownership of Reform Programmes and the Implications for Conditionality
No. 34	January 2005	Randall DODD and Shari SPIEGEL	Up From Sin: A Portfolio Approach to Financial Salvation
No. 33	November 2004	Ilene GRABEL	Trip Wires and Speed Bumps: Managing Financial Risks and Reducing the Potential for Financial Crises in Developing Economies
No. 32	October 2004	Jan KREGEL	External Financing for Development and International Financial Instability
No. 31	October 2004	Tim KESSLER and Nancy ALEXANDER	Assessing the Risks in the Private Provision of Essential Services
No. 30	June 2004	Andrew CORNFORD	Enron and Internationally Agreed Principles for Corporate Governance and the Financial Sector
No. 29	April 2004	Devesh KAPUR	Remittances: The New Development Mantra?
No. 28	April 2004	Sanjaya LALL	Reinventing Industrial Strategy: The Role of Government Policy in Building Industrial Competitiveness
No. 27	March 2004	Gerald EPSTEIN, Ilene GRABEL and JOMO K.S.	Capital Management Techniques in Developing Countries: An Assessment of Experiences from the 1990s and Lessons for the Future
No. 26	March 2004	Claudio M. LOSER	External Debt Sustainability: Guidelines for Low- and Middle-income Countries
No. 25	January 2004	Irfan ul HAQUE	Commodities under Neoliberalism: The Case of Cocoa
No. 24	December 2003	Aziz Ali MOHAMMED	Burden Sharing at the IMF
No. 23	November 2003	Mari PANGESTU	The Indonesian Bank Crisis and Restructuring: Lessons and Implications for other Developing Countries
No. 22	August 2003	Ariel BUIRA	An Analysis of IMF Conditionality
No. 21	April 2003	Jim LEVINSOHN	The World Bank's Poverty Reduction Strategy Paper Approach: Good Marketing or Good Policy?
No. 20	February 2003	Devesh KAPUR	Do As I Say Not As I Do: A Critique of G-7 Proposals on Reforming the Multilateral Development Banks
No. 19	December 2002	Ravi KANBUR	International Financial Institutions and International Public Goods: Operational Implications for the World Bank

/...

G-24 Discussion Paper Series

Research papers for the Intergovernmental Group of Twenty-Four
on International Monetary Affairs and Development

No. 18	September 2002	Ajit SINGH	Competition and Competition Policy in Emerging Markets: International and Developmental Dimensions
No. 17	April 2002	F. LÓPEZ-DE-SILANES	The Politics of Legal Reform
No. 16	January 2002	Gerardo ESQUIVEL and Felipe LARRAÍN B.	The Impact of G-3 Exchange Rate Volatility on Developing Countries
No. 15	December 2001	Peter EVANS and Martha FINNEMORE	Organizational Reform and the Expansion of the South's Voice at the Fund
No. 14	September 2001	Charles WYPLOSZ	How Risky is Financial Liberalization in the Developing Countries?
No. 13	July 2001	José Antonio OCAMPO	Recasting the International Financial Agenda
No. 12	July 2001	Yung Chul PARK and Yunjong WANG	Reform of the International Financial System and Institutions in Light of the Asian Financial Crisis
No. 11	April 2001	Aziz Ali MOHAMMED	The Future Role of the International Monetary Fund
No. 10	March 2001	JOMO K.S.	Growth After the Asian Crisis: What Remains of the East Asian Model?
No. 9	February 2001	Gordon H. HANSON	Should Countries Promote Foreign Direct Investment?
No. 8	January 2001	Ilan GOLDFAJN and Gino OLIVARES	Can Flexible Exchange Rates Still "Work" in Financially Open Economies?
No. 7	December 2000	Andrew CORNFORD	Commentary on the Financial Stability Forum's Report of the Working Group on Capital Flows
No. 6	August 2000	Devesh KAPUR and Richard WEBB	Governance-related Conditionalities of the International Financial Institutions
No. 5	June 2000	Andrés VELASCO	Exchange-rate Policies for Developing Countries: What Have We Learned? What Do We Still Not Know?
No. 4	June 2000	Katharina PISTOR	The Standardization of Law and Its Effect on Developing Economies
No. 3	May 2000	Andrew CORNFORD	The Basle Committee's Proposals for Revised Capital Standards: Rationale, Design and Possible Incidence
No. 2	May 2000	T. Ademola OYEJIDE	Interests and Options of Developing and Least-developed Countries in a New Round of Multilateral Trade Negotiations
No. 1	March 2000	Arvind PANAGARIYA	The Millennium Round and Developing Countries: Negotiating Strategies and Areas of Benefits

******

G-24 Discussion Paper Series are available on the website at: www.unctad.org. Copies of *G-24 Discussion Paper Series* may be obtained from the Publications Assistant, Macroeconomic and Development Policies Branch, Division on Globalization and Development Strategies, United Nations Conference on Trade and Development (UNCTAD), Palais des Nations, CH-1211 Geneva 10, Switzerland (Fax: +41-22-917.0274).

UNCTAD Discussion Papers

No. 180	Oct. 2005	Jörg MAYER and Pilar FAJARNES	Tripling Africa's Primary Exports: What? How? Where?
No. 179	April 2005	S.M. SHAFAEDDIN	Trade Liberalization and Economic Reform in Developing Countries: Structural Change or De-Industrialization
No. 178	April 2005	Andrew CORNFORD	Basel II: the revised framework of June 2004
No. 177	April 2005	Benu SCHNEIDER	Do global standards and codes prevent financial crises? Some proposals on modifying the standards-based approach
No. 176	Dec. 2004	Jörg MAYER	Not totally naked: textiles and clothing trade in a quota free environment
No. 175	Aug. 2004	S.M. SHAFAEDDIN	Who is the master? Who is the servant? Market or Government?
No. 174	Aug. 2004	Jörg MAYER	Industrialization in developing countries: some evidence from a new economic geography perspective
No. 173	June 2004	Irfan ul HAQUE	Globalization, neoliberalism and labour
No. 172	June 2004	Andrew CORNFORD	The WTO negotiations on financial services: current issues and future directions
No. 171	May 2004	Andrew CORNFORD	Variable geometry for the WTO: concepts and precedents
No. 170	May 2004	Robert ROWTHORN and Ken COUTTS	De-industrialization and the balance of payments in advanced economies
No. 169	April 2004	Shigehisa KASAHARA	The flying geese paradigm: a critical study of its application to East Asian regional development
No. 168	Feb. 2004	Alberto GABRIELE	Policy alternatives in reforming power utilities in developing countries: a critical survey
No. 167	Jan. 2004	R. KOZUL-WRIGHT and P. RAYMENT	Globalization reloaded: an UNCTAD perspective
No. 166	Feb. 2003	Jörg MAYER	The fallacy of composition: a review of the literature
No. 165	Nov. 2002	Yuefen LI	China's accession to WTO: exaggerated fears?
No. 164	Nov. 2002	Lucas ASSUNCAO and ZhongXiang ZHANG	Domestic climate change policies and the WTO
No. 163	Nov. 2002	A.S. BHALLA and S. QIU	China's WTO accession. Its impact on Chinese employment
No. 162	July 2002	P. NOLAN and J. ZHANG	The challenge of globalization for large Chinese firms
No. 161	June 2002	Zheng ZHIHAI and Zhao YUMIN	China's terms of trade in manufactures, 1993–2000
No. 160	June 2002	S.M. SHAFAEDDIN	The impact of China's accession to WTO on exports of developing countries
No. 159	May 2002	J. MAYER, A. BUTKEVICIUS and A. KADRI	Dynamic products in world exports

/...

UNCTAD Discussion Papers

No. 158	April 2002	Yilmaz AKYÜZ and Korkut BORATAV	The making of the Turkish financial crisis
No. 157	Nov. 2001	Heiner FLASSBECK	The exchange rate: Economic policy tool or market price?
No. 156	Aug. 2001	Andrew CORNFORD	The Basel Committee's proposals for revised capital standards: Mark 2 and the state of play
No. 155	Aug. 2001	Alberto GABRIELE	Science and technology policies, industrial reform and technical progress in China: Can socialist property rights be compatible with technological catching up?
No. 154	June 2001	Jörg MAYER	Technology diffusion, human capital and economic growth in developing countries
No. 153	Dec. 2000	Mehdi SHAFAEDDIN	Free trade or fair trade? Fallacies surrounding the theories of trade liberalization and protection and contradictions in international trade rules
No. 152	Dec. 2000	Dilip K. DAS	Asian crisis: Distilling critical lessons
No. 151	Oct. 2000	Bernard SHULL	Financial modernization legislation in the United States – Background and implications
No. 150	Aug. 2000	Jörg MAYER	Globalization, technology transfer and skill accumulation in low-income countries
No. 149	July 2000	Mehdi SHAFAEDDIN	What did Frederick List actually say? Some clarifications on the infant industry argument
No. 148	April 2000	Yilmaz AKYÜZ	The debate on the international financial architecture: Reforming the reformers
No. 147	April 2000	Martin KHOR	Globalization and the South: Some critical issues
No. 146	Feb. 2000	Manuel R. AGOSIN and Ricardo MAYER	Foreign investment in developing countries: Does it crowd in domestic investment?
No. 145	Jan. 2000	B. ANDERSEN, Z. KOZUL-WRIGHT and R. KOZUL-WRIGHT	Copyrights, competition and development: The case of the music industry

******

UNCTAD Discussion Papers are available on the website at: www.unctad.org. Copies *of UNCTAD Discussion Papers* may be obtained from the Publications Assistant, Macroeconomic and Development Policies Branch, Division on Globalization and Development Strategies, United Nations Conference on Trade and Development (UNCTAD), Palais des Nations, CH-1211 Geneva 10, Switzerland (Fax: (+41-22- 917.0274).

QUESTIONNAIRE

Trade and Development Report, 2006

In order to improve the quality and relevance of the Trade and Development Report, the UNCTAD secretariat would greatly appreciate your views on this publication. Please complete the following questionnaire and return it to:

Readership Survey
Division on Globalization and Development Strategies
UNCTAD
Palais des Nations, Room E.10009
CH-1211 Geneva 10, Switzerland
Fax: (+41) (0)22 917 0274
E-mail: tdr@unctad.org

> The questionnaire can also
> be completed on-line at:
> www.unctad.org/tdr/questionnaire

Thank you very much for your kind cooperation.

1. What is your assessment of this publication?

	Excellent	*Good*	*Adequate*	*Poor*
Overall	☐	☐	☐	☐
Relevance of issues	☐	☐	☐	☐
Analytical quality	☐	☐	☐	☐
Policy conclusions	☐	☐	☐	☐
Presentation	☐	☐	☐	☐

2. What do you consider the strong points of this publication?

_____
_____
_____

3. What do you consider the weak points of this publication?

_____
_____
_____

4. For what main purposes do you use this publication?

Analysis and research	☐	Education and training	☐
Policy formulation and management	☐	Other (*specify*) _____	

5. Which of the following best describes your area of work?

Government	☐	Public enterprise	☐
Non-governmental organization	☐	Academic or research	☐
International organization	☐	Media	☐
Private enterprise institution	☐	Other (*specify*) _____	

6. Name and address of respondent (*optional*):

_____
_____
_____

7. Do you have any further comments?

_____
_____
_____